LONELY PLANET'S

GLOBAL DISTILLERY TOUR

CONTENTS

INTRODUCTION

The verdict is in: now is an exciting time to be a spirit drinker. Not so long ago, being a fan of liquor meant your go-to drink was a G&T, a rum and coke or a whisky on the rocks, rather than a beer or glass of wine. But times they are a-changing. The explosion of craft distilleries in the past five years has transformed the global spirits (and cocktails) landscape.

This is in no small part thanks to a gin revival, kick-started by a change to UK spirits licensing laws in 2009. But craft distilling has caught on all over the world, and with it drinkers' desire to see the places where the spirits are made and learn about the craft-masters who make them. Renewed interest in spirits has also led us to rediscover drinks that a few years ago had all but disappeared from our cocktail cabinets. Touring a centuries-old monastic distillery in rural France, for example, is just as fascinating as that hip little tasting bar in a disused warehouse in New York.

WHAT ARE CRAFT SPIRITS?

The American Craft Spirits Association stresses that what we think of as 'craft' is ultimately 'in the eye of the beholder', but broadly defines craft spirits as those made in distilleries that are independently owned and operated, produce fewer than 750,000 gallons a year, and are transparent about their ingredients, distillery location and ageing process.

Not every distillery featured in this book is a craft producer, and not all craft spirit makers offer tours and tastings at their distilleries, but it is the (predominantly small) distilleries that are open to the public that Lonely Planet has chosen to focus on in this book: the tasting rooms where gin botanicals grow outside the front door, whisky grain is tractored in from a neighbouring farm, or ingredients such as wildflower honey are gathered from local bee hives to make rum.

In fact, the entries in this book show that one of the greatest defining characteristics of craft distilleries around

the world is this desire to make use of what grows on their doorstep: be that apples in Canada, indigenous fynbos plants in South Africa, or green ants (!) in Australia.

The global gin craze, in particular, has been boosted by a heightened interest in fresh, local ingredients: many gin makers are focusing on the botanical element of the distilling process to create genuinely local products with flavour profiles that reflect the place where the spirit was made. In the UK – gin's historic heartland – the number of distilleries more than doubled to 315 between 2013 and 2018, largely down to the so-called 'ginaissance'. Yet the entries in this book show the craft gin trend is truly global.

And it's not just gin that is benefiting from an artisan touch. Distillers – particularly in the USA and Australia – are concocting all manner of boozy victuals, from coffee rums to sheep whey vodka, and interesting liqueurs flavoured with spiced honey, maple or chocolate. The indulgences of a new school of mad scientists? Perhaps, but that's all part of the fun.

WHY GO DISTILLERY TOURING?

There can be no greater transparency for drinkers than touring the distilleries themselves, handling the ingredients and tasting the spirits before labels have even been slapped on the bottles. For many craft producers, distillery tours and tastings have become a key way of raising their profile and creating a community following. Tour a distillery and you could well get unparalleled access to the master distillers, who take no greater pleasure than bending your

ear to tell you how the spirits are made, what to mix them with and when to drink them – information that could never be gleaned from the back of a bottle in a shop. Stories, too, are part of the charm of touring distilleries: why a Ukrainian nuclear engineer ended up making vodka and whisky in New Zealand, or how a film and TV producer got the chance to grow his gin botanicals in an English castle.

It's also likely that tasting at the source will get you a few shot-glasses worth of tipples that will never make it into the stores, as many craft distillers are dabbling with limited-edition spirits. Gin, for example, takes just a matter of hours to produce, meaning the possibilities for unique small batches are endless. You can be the distillery guinea pigs: all you have to do is book a tour.

HOW TO USE THIS BOOK

Within each of the 33 countries in this book, we've organised the distilleries alphabetically by region. In the entry for each distillery, we've suggested the must-try drink or tasting experience and also recommended local sights, so distillery tourers can explore the local area in between tasting sessions.

Among the distillery entries, we've also included a small number of bars that are best-in-class for their selection of one particular drink, such as arak in Lebanon or tuak in Malaysia, and for which distilleries are hard to find. And at the back of the book, you'll find a section dedicated to cocktails: our take on the best mixology magic in the world, and the bars that serve them. Bottoms up!

1. FERMENTATION

All spirits begin as a liquid with a lower alcoholic volume (ABV). These are made by milling, pressing and mashing fruits, plants or grains. Yeast is added, which consumes naturally occurring sugars and creates CO_2 and alcohol as by-products.

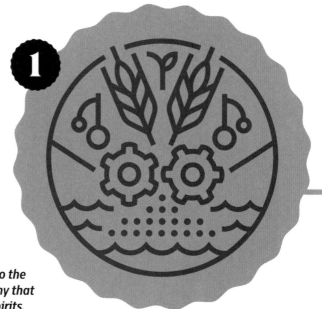

Distillation is what takes alcohol to the next boozy level. Here's the alchemy that goes into making your favourite spirits, from brandy to baijiu.

THE DISTILLAT

4. FLAVOURING AND AGEING

Flavours can be added after distillation, or spirits can be blended together (as with whisky). Botanical flavours can also be added through re-distillation (as with gin). Meanwhile, some spirits are rested to soften and mature their flavour, which is also how they gain a darker colour.

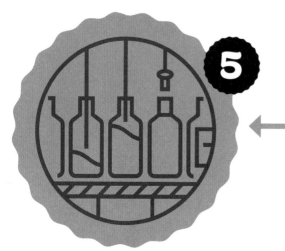

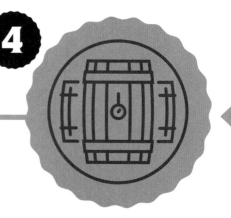

5. BOTTLING

Spirits are cut with water to bring them to strength (typically around 40% ABV) before bottling. Many craft distilleries bottle, label and seal by hand, with a batch number added to each.

2

2. EVAPORATION

A copper pot still or a column still is filled with the fermented alcoholic liquid and slowly heated. When it reaches a temperature of 78.37°C, the liquid boils and the alcohol evaporates. It moves up the still as vapour, separating it from water.

ION PROCESS

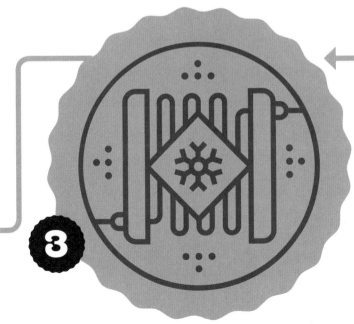

3

3. CONDENSATION

This steam hits a condenser, where it cools and turns to a liquid – a more concentrated alcohol with an altered flavour profile. The early run-off known as the 'heads' is volatile and intense; the 'heart' comes next and is smooth and balanced; the 'tails' at the end contains funkier notes. Typically, only the 'heart' from each batch is captured.

AFRI
THE MIDD

CA&
LE EAST

CAPE TOWN

Ever the innovator in food and drink, South Africa's most progressive city is leading the country's craft gin revolution, with local distillers infusing spirits with floral botanicals including indigenous fynbos and tea leaves. The Woodstock enclave is a hotspot for imaginative tastings and tours.

BEIRUT

Alcohol isn't widely consumed in the Middle East, but the capital of Lebanon is a hedonistic exception. Traditionally, the tipple of choice is arak – a clear spirit made from distilled wine and aniseed by many a home producer, then brought to the big city by bars such as Anise.

LEBANON

How to ask for an arak? Please baddi arak baladeh (Beiruti dialect includes a mix of Arabic, English and French!)

Signature spirit? Arak, mixed with water, ice, and sometimes a sprig of fresh mint

What to order with your arak? It's likely you'll get a dish of salted peanuts and/or a tumbler of carrots in salted lemon juice. If you are hungrier than that, order hummus and tabbouleh

Do: seek out arak flavoured with a drizzle of sharab al-toot, a syrup made from the mulberry crop every spring. Its sweetness tempers the burn of the spirit, which can reach 80 to 120 proof

Beirut is renowned as a hedonistic city, and you won't find much here to disprove this reputation. But to get a real sense of Lebanon's drinking culture, start your initiation over the mountains in the Bekaa Valley.

Unless you're very unlucky, the day you visit the Bekaa will be gloriously bright. The Romans were the first to celebrate the Bekaa's climate; the megalithic ruins of the ancient solar cult of Heliopolis (Sun City) still stand in the centre of the modern-day town of Baalbek. These days, however, there are certainly more grapes basking in the Bekaa sun than holiday-making UV devotionalists: the region is practically administered by militant group and Shia political party Hezbollah, which discourages immodest dress and, for that matter, drinking.

But within the vine-covered confines of the Valley's wineries and distilleries, visitors quaff drink and guzzle food with an abandon that might make Epicurus blush. The wineries draw day-trippers from Beirut at weekends, who spend hours sampling Lebanese mezze (small plates) from heaving tables, and take full advantage of near-universal policies of open wine and arak.

In the early evening, revellers pile into cars to travel back to Beirut (make sure yours is a taxi), where the party continues in the bar districts of Mar Mikhaël and Hamra. Rounds of drinks are punctuated by doudou shots: vodka, a squeeze of lemon, a few shakes of Tabasco sauce, and an olive. Fair warning: like the Beiruti lifestyle, doudou shots are addictive.

The English word 'alcohol' is derived from the Arabic word *al-kohl*, meaning elixir or cure. Before leaving Beirut, raise a glass to those early Arab alchemists who first burned wine.

■ BAR
ANISE

Mar Mikhaël, Beirut www.facebook.com/
AniseCorridorBar; +961 7097 7926

◆ Food ◆ Transport
◆ Bar

THINGS TO DO NEARBY

Orient 499
A treasure trove of exotic oriental handicrafts, with ornate mirrors, bewitching silver sculptures, sepia photos and vintage Arabic movie posters and streets signs. *www.orient499.com*

Tenbelian Spices
Hidden away in Beirut's Armenian souk, Tenbelian stocks hundreds of different spices, nuts, dried fruits, rose petals, honey and its speciality grape walnut sausage.

Tawlet
A unique restaurant where female chefs travel from across Lebanon, preparing daily lunch buffets of regional dishes such as spicy raw beef, spinach man'oush flatbreads and minced-lamb croquettes. *www.tawlet.com*

Beirut Art Residency
The latest arrival on Beirut's dynamic cultural scene, this alternative space by the port runs residence programmes for emerging local and international artists, plus an exhibition space. *www. beirutartresidency.com*

In the middle of Beirut's frenetic nightlife scene sits this cool cocktail bar resembling a James Bond movie, with suave white-jacketed barmen serving Hemingway Martinis. But Anise is also dedicated to Lebanon's national drink, arak – a clear alcohol made from distilled wine and green aniseed, which is aged in stone amphoras and, when served, turns milky white as water is added.

It may look like pastis or raki, but this spirit is very different. Although there are some industrial producers, arak is essentially a home-brew tradition, and Anise owner Hisham Al Housein scours the mountains and valleys of Lebanon buying up small-batch gallon jars, made from village farmers who grow their own grapes, distilling with handmade copper contraptions modelled on medieval alembics.

There are always six hand-crafted araks on Anise's drinks list, identified by the name of the village, while the producer and indigenous grape variety is kept secret. Don't expect to see arak-based cocktails, as Hisham explains: 'We only serve arak neat, the real way to appreciate it, as it has always been drunk by our elders.' Arak is the perfect accompaniment to Lebanese mezze, so order the *bulgur kibbeh* (croquettes), stuffed with labneh and pine nuts.

DOMAINE DES TOURELLES

Jdita-Chtoura Rd, Bekaa Valley;
www.domainedestourelles.com; +961 8540 114

◆ Distillery　◆ Shop
◆ Tours

There's a unique drama to drinking arak. By itself, the thirsty might mistake it for water. Combined with water, the mixture turns cloudy – a pure, cool white that results from the microemulsification of water with the essential oil of anise. The effect is similar in all anise-flavoured spirits in the Mediterranean, but according to Christiane Issa Nahas of Domaine des Tourelles in Lebanon's Bekaa Valley, a winery that produces Arak Brun, arak from these vines is the *ne plus ultra*. 'It's the land here, the terroir of the Bekaa,' she says. 'The grapes feel very comfortable.'

Given that white grapes and anise (the latter introduced in the third distillation) are arak's only two ingredients, they have to be the best. Domaine des Tourelles imports its anise from the Syrian town of Hina, behind the Jebel Sheikh, known since antiquity for its anise.

Arak Brun's reputation was built during the Lebanese civil war (1975-1990) when money became tight and the wealthy reluctantly accepted Brun – because it was a superior, branded arak – as a substitute for wine.

The priggish may sniff, but arak is one spirit that should be drunk alongside food. For one thing, Lebanese folk tradition has it that anise aids digestion. The high alcohol content also sterilises any unwashed vegetables lurking in the tabbouleh. 'Our ancestors invented arak for Lebanese mezze!' says Issa proudly. Pick up a bottle or three to drink with dinner.

THINGS TO DO NEARBY

Baalbek ruins
Gawp slack-jawed at the soaring Temple of Bacchus in the ancient city of Heliopolis, one of the best-preserved Roman ruins in the world.

Taanayel Ecolodge
A mud-brick ecolodge and restaurant, surrounded by famed dairy producers. Proceeds go toward the Lebanese charity Arc en Ciel. *www.arcenciel.org/activities/ecolodge-de-taanayel/*

Anjar ruins
The Umayyads repurposed Greek and Roman structures to build this 8th-century city. Some columns still bear Greek inscriptions.

Zahle restaurants
The strip of restaurants along the Berdawni River in the town of Zahle serve Lebanese mezze as birds chirp in the trees above. Sip your arak and nibble *kibbeh nayyeh* (Lebanon's answer to steak tartare).

SOUTH AFRICA

How to ask for a spirit without mixers? 'Straight' –
English is widely used in South Africa
Signature spirit? Brandy
What to order with your spirits? Coke
Do: Beware South Africa's 'shooter' culture, in which
nights are punctuated by potent shots, including
tequila, Jägermeister and Springbokkies
(Amarula Cream and peppermint liqueur, reflecting
the green-and-gold Springboks rugby top)

Spirits have been produced at the southern tip
of Africa for as long as colonials have sat on the
veranda extolling the virtues of G&T's quinine
for combating malaria. Africa's oldest distillery, the James
Sedgwick Distillery, traces its whisky-making history back to
the 19th century, when the eponymous British sea captain
arrived in Cape Town by clipper.

Today, as with many aspects of South African life, the
Rainbow Nation's various racial and cultural groups have
different liquor traditions and preferences. For Afrikaners, the
descendants of the Boers who fought two wars against the
gin-swigging Brits, only brandywyn (brandy) and coke will do.
The classic homegrown brandy brand to enjoy with your braai
(barbecue) is Klipdrift, aka 'Klippie', and for dessert there's
Amarula Cream, a bushveld Baileys made with marula fruit.

Dedicated liquor lovers can also seek out the Boer
moonshine known as mampoer, a potent peach brandy

that's popular in northern farming towns; containing 50%
to 80% alcohol, the drink is one of the strongest worldwide.
It was named after the pugnacious 19th-century Pedi
chief Mampuru by small-holders, who gained their land
as a result of his conflicts with the colonial authorities.
The Cape's equivalent poison, clear brandy distilled
from grapes, is known as witblits ('white lightning'), but
we recommend concentrating instead on the region's
burgeoning craft gin scene. Developing the traditional,
juniper-dominant gins introduced by the Dutch and British,
canny distillers are creating botanical infusions using the
indigenous fynbos vegetation, part of the Unesco-protected
Cape Floral Kingdom stretching roughly from Table
Mountain to the Garden Route. Watering holes dedicated to
'mother's ruin' abound in the Mother City, while Bascule Bar
at the luxurious Cape Grace Hotel has one of the southern
hemisphere's largest whisky collections.

TIME ANCHOR DISTILLERY

7 Sivewright Ave, New Doornfontein, Johannesburg,
Guateng; www.timeanchor.co.za; +27 72 495 1983

◆ Distillery ◆ Bar
◆ Shop ◆ Transport

Johannesburg's first craft gin distillery is housed in a small warehouse on the edge of Maboneng, a vibrant, regenerated area of the city's gritty downtown. Rather than tours, Time Anchor specialises in structured tasting events (check the website for dates). The main event is sampling the distillery's colourful 'Mirari Trio' of gins, crafted from all-natural ingredients and handpicked botanicals. The Blue includes grains of paradise, from a peppery tasting plant native to West Africa, and cubeb pepper, native to Indonesia. Amber uses Boekenhout raw honey, the much-revered rooibos, and fynbos. The Pink gin, with damask rose, green cardamom and an infusion of natural rose water, is perfect in the Blackberry G&T, using Fentimans pink grapefruit tonic and blackberry G&T jam.

THINGS TO DO NEARBY

Main Street Walks
Explore Maboneng – 'place of light' in Sotho – on an interactive tour with an in-the-know local, including a visit to the oldest traditional healers' market in the city. *www.mainstreetwalks.co.za*

Market on Main
This buzzy Sunday food market has grown out of Maboneng's first creative hub, Arts on Main, and is the go-to place for pan-African produce, as well as local design. *www.marketonmain.co.za*

■ **BAR**

WILD ABOUT WHISKY

506 Naledi Drive, Dullstroom, Mpumalanga;
www.wildaboutwhisky.com; +27 13 254 0066

◆ Shop
◆ Bar

Dullstroom is not what you expect to find in sunny South Africa: this is trout-fishing country, as well as one of the country's coldest towns, thanks to its location above 2000m on the Highveld plateau. Inspired by this bracing setting, Wild About Whisky offers the southern hemisphere's largest whisky menu, featuring well over 1000 whiskies, 45 tutored tastings and a shop with 300 bottles.

Whisky-worshipping staff, who tour the Scottish distilleries annually, guide you through tastings with themes such as Islay malts, American bourbons, 18-year-olds and 'to peat or not to peat'. The tastings of six half-tots (15ml servings) also cover other spirits from craft gins to tequilas. Don't miss educating your palate with tastings themed around the latest distilling trends, such as Scotch single malts without age statements.

THINGS TO DO NEARBY

Blyde River Canyon Nature Reserve
Rock formations and waterfalls punctuate a drive through the world's third-largest canyon, where the Drakensberg Escarpment meets the Lowveld. *www.mtpa.co.za*

Dullstroom Bird of Prey & Rehabilitation Centre
Learn about raptor species and the dangers facing them, with flying displays involving peregrine falcons, kestrels, buzzards and black eagles. *www.birdsofprey.co.za*

HOPE ON HOPKINS

7 Hopkins St, Salt River, Cape Town
www.hopeonhopkins.co.za; +27 21 447 1950

◆ Tours ◆ Transport ◆ Food
◆ Shop ◆ Distillery ◆ Bar

Pioneers of the South African gin revolution, Leigh Lisk and Lucy Beard opened Cape Town's first artisan gin distillery with three stainless steel pot stills that enthusiasts can observe on Hope on Hopkins' popular Saturday tour. In the small modern tasting room, Leigh and Lucy make suggestions on pairings and then let guests pick and mix their own gin, tonics and garnishes. Tasty snacks such as local charcuterie and spicy olives are also included.

The duo's gins are made with local malted barley and Table Mountain water. While they produce whimsical limited editions, such as pomegranate gin for summer, and a winter gin using sour figs and oranges; the bottle to take home is the Salt River Gin, made with wild rosemary, South African fynbos and the indigenous medicinal herbs buchu and kapokbos.

THINGS TO DO NEARBY

Neighbourgoods Market
Every Saturday, hundreds of fashion, food and wine stalls open around Woodstock's Old Biscuit Mill – a paradise for eating, drinking and shopping.
www.neighbourgoods market.co.za

Township Art Tour
Local artist Juma Mkwela takes small groups into sprawling Gugulethu township for a unique art tour visiting painters, vegetable gardens and a street-food canteen. *www. townshiparttours.co.za*

PIENAAR & SON

1 Roeland Terrace, City Bowl, Cape Town
www.pienaarandson.co.za; +27 21 461 4993

◆ Tours ◆ Transport ◆ Bar
◆ Shop ◆ Distillery

Schalk Pienaar designed his own stills and had them made locally, using skills he honed during four decades working as a manufacturer of distilling equipment. His son Andre is the young gun master distiller, using the custom-designed kit to produce two gins and a vodka, made with local maize and sold in sleek Italian bottles.

Their small urban distillery has exposed brick walls and beams overlooking the shiny stills popping with pipes and valves, which can host tour-goers and also drop-in visitors wishing to sample. The dry English-style Empire Gin has refreshing hints of citrus, cucumber and pine; the Orient Gin is a must-try, with notes of vanilla, mandarin and ginger that pay homage to the maritime spice trade that influenced Cape Town in the 17th and 18th centuries.

THINGS TO DO NEARBY

The Book Lounge
A short stumble from Pienaar & Son is the city's best independent bookshop, with a winning combo of knowledgeable staff, African novels and non-fiction, and regular events.
www.booklounge.co.za

District Six Museum
The museum shows how this area, which used to be a multicultural neighbourhood, was razed under apartheid and its inhabitants forcibly relocated out of town.
www.districtsix.co.za

WOODSTOCK GIN COMPANY

399 Albert Rd, Woodstock, Cape Town
www.woodstockginco.co.za; +27 21 821 8208

◆ Food   ◆ Tours   ◆ Bar
◆ Distillery   ◆ Shop   ◆ Transport

THINGS TO DO NEARBY

Zeitz MOCAA

This revolutionary museum, dedicated to contemporary African art, is located in a stunning, immense 1920s concrete grain silo right on Cape Town's harbour waterfront.
www.zeitzmocaa.museum

Biesmiellah

Order a spicy feast of Cape Malay dishes at this Bo-Kaap canteen. You'll get to savour dishes such as bobotie and kingklip curry, which are influencing chefs all over the city.
www.biesmiellah.co.za

Woodstock Grill and Tap

The city's best beer pub offers tours of its brewery, eight artisan ales, juicy steaks and healthy salads. Its latest innovation is craft gin and tonic on tap.
www.woodstockgrill.co.za

Street Art

Graffiti artists have transformed Woodstock's backstreets with murals. Wander between Albert and Victory, Barron and Essex streets to witness giant elephants, giraffes and gorillas.

This micro-distillery in bohemian Woodstock produces arguably the most innovative range in South Africa. Master distiller Simon Von Witt uses Cape Town's lush mountain vegetation – rose geranium, honeybush, wild sage and South Africa's emblematic fynbos flower – to impart intriguing floral aromas. But what also singles out Woodstock's signature Inception Gin is that it has two different labels – and flavours – depending on the base alcohol used to make it. The first (white label) uses a blend of local chenin and sauvignon grapes; the second (yellow label) uses a craft Weissbier base for a punchier, more caramelised spirit.

Woodstock's most original creation is High Tea Gin, which features South Africa's distinctive rooibos leaf, more well-known for making tea. Von Witt conducts tastings at tables facing a glass wall with the distillery's pot stills and vats on the other side (also open to walk-in drinkers). His method is to lead tasters through all his gins neat, then get them to sample again using craft tonic waters with creative garnishes such as gooseberry and rosemary, cinnamon bark or orange peel.

Courtesy of Woodstock Gin

CAPE TOWN GIN & SPIRITS COMPANY

Cape Town Gin Hidden Door, Heritage Sq, cnr
Shortmarket & Bree Sts; www.capetowngincompany.com
◆ Shop ◆ Transport
◆ Bar

This gin distillery takes its inspiration from the city at the foot of Table Mountain, and has a tasting room at Heritage Square – central Cape Town's elegant complex of bars and restaurants, housed in Cape Dutch, Georgian and Victorian buildings. It has three handcrafted, small-batch spirits to taste: the Cape Town Classic Dry Gin remembers the Dutch and British colonials who brought gin to the Cape two centuries ago, when juniper berries were the predominant flavour; while the Cape Town Rooibos Red Gin, another winner at the 2017 World Drinks Awards, is infused with South Africa's indigenous rooibos tea grown in the nearby Cederberg range. Don't miss the equally colourful Cape Town Pink Lady Gin, a hibiscus- and rose-petal-infused tribute to the city's very grand (and very pink) Mount Nelson Hotel.

THINGS TO DO NEARBY

Bree Street
You'll find artisanal everything on this foodie thoroughfare, where hip establishments sell goodies from tapas to cocktails. *www.capetown. travel/visitors/eat-drink/ bree-street*

Mount Nelson Hotel
Liked the pink gin? Visit the pink lady herself, aka 'the Nellie', for a sumptuous high tea to remember, in leafy grounds that have hosted the likes of Queen Elizabeth. *www.belmond.com*

DEEP SOUTH DISTILLERY

53 Heron Park, Wildevoelvlei Rd, Kommetjie, Western
Cape; www.deepsouthdistillery.co.za; +27 21 783 0129
◆ Distillery ◆ Shop
◆ Tours ◆ Bar

Opened in 2017, this recent entrant to Cape Town's craft-distillery scene is located in the southern section of the mountainous peninsula leading to Cape Point, Africa's southwesternmost tip. City dwellers call this creative and alternative area 'the lentil curtain'.

Deep South's small-batch gins use floral and herbal botanicals from the surrounding Cape Floral Region. Hidden away on an industrial park in the surf town of Kommetjie, the distillery's main product is Cape Dry Gin, infused with juniper, honeybush and buchu; the latter two botanicals are types of endemic local fynbos vegetation, more commonly found in tea and brandy respectively. Call ahead to arrange a distillery tour and don't miss tasting Deep South's second flagship tipple, Ruby Gin, with its ruby-red colour and floral flavours.

THINGS TO DO NEARBY

Chapman's Peak Drive
Drive, cycle or walk the 5km-long 'Chappies', one of the world's most beautiful coastal roads, with views over Hout Bay on the Cape Peninsula's Atlantic side. *www.chapmanspeak drive.co.za*

Boulders Penguin Colony
Across the Cape Peninsula on False Bay, boardwalks lead to the beaches and boulders frequented by a colony of some 3000 delightful waddling African penguins. *www.tmnp.co.za*

INVERROCHE

Old Riversdale Rd, Still Bay, Western Cape;
www.inverroche.com; +27 28 754 2442

◆ Distillery   ◆ Shop
◆ Tours   ◆ Bar

This pioneer of South Africa's craft gin scene was established in 2011 in a rugged coastal setting at the western end of the Garden Route by Lorna Scott and her son Rohan, who had tinkered for a few years on a copper pot-still known as 'Mini Meg' before graduating to the 1000-litre 'Magnaminous Meg'. Their three gins reflect Inverroche's location in the Cape Floral Kingdom, using a handful of the 9000-plus types of indigenous fynbos that exist in this Unesco-inscribed botanical region. The environment is high on this distillery's agenda: by working with local botanists to find new ways of using the local flora in their spirits, the Scotts hope they will help protect the habitat by further stimulating a conservation economy in the broader community.

The Inverroche Gin Classic is infused with fynbos harvested from limestone-rich lowland soils, giving it grassy juniper notes upfront, then assertive florals leading to a dry and spicy finish. The distillation process involves

THINGS TO DO NEARBY

Mossel Bay
In this relatively undeveloped Garden Route hub, hit the beach, spot whales from land or water and learn about the 15th-century Portuguese explorers who passed by. *www.visitmosselbay.co.za*

Swellendam
South Africa's fourth-oldest settlement, established in 1743, sleepy Swellendam has several thatched Cape Dutch properties and a jail to explore. *www.visitswellendam.co.za*

Point of Human Origins
Long before they started making gin, humans were living at Pinnacle Point, as this Middle Stone Age archaeological cave site shows. Guided tours explore the coastal cave. *www.humanorigin.co.za*

De Hoop Nature Reserve
This stunning fynbos-clad coastal reserve is good for hiking and mountain biking. Its five-day Whale Trail offers sightings of ostriches, Cape mountain zebras and, of course, whales. *www.dehoopcollection.com*

layering the fynbos in steam baskets within the wood-fired still, allowing the gently heated spirit vapour to extract the aromatic oils from the botanicals. The Inverroche Gin Verdant and Inverroche Gin Amber, infused with mountain and coastal fynbos respectively, gain their golden tints by undergoing this process twice. Don't miss a tasting, distillery tour or the monthly Gin Sensorium and School, in which you make your own gin.

JAMES SEDGWICK DISTILLERY

79 Stokery Rd, Wellington, Western Cape;
www.threeshipswhisky.co.za; +27 72 415 3440

◆ Distillery   ◆ Shop
◆ Tours

Africa's oldest distillery, established in the Cape Winelands town of Wellington in 1886, unusually produces both malt and grain whiskies on the same site. Most are under the Three Ships banner, but Bain's Cape Mountain Whisky (the world's only 100% South African maize whisky) was named World's Best Grain Whisky at the World Whiskies Awards 2018.

Tours of the distillery cover the whisky-making process from milling the raw ingredients through to maturation and blending, followed by a tasting that pairs apple crisps, smoked beef, chocolate mousse and more with the house single malts and blends. The tasting room is a knockout, overlooked by a few of the site's 150,000 whisky casks. Creating your own 50ml blend in the micro-distillery is a highlight.

THINGS TO DO NEARBY

Bainskloof Pass
Andrew Geddes Bain, the 19th-century engineer and namesake of Sedgwick's single-grain whisky, built this epic mountain pass, which you can ascend from Wellington on Route 301.
http://bainskloof.com

Wellington wineries
Wellington has a wine route of more than a dozen farms, where you can taste, dine and sleep. Try, for example, a gourmet pie and wine pairing at Imbuko.
www.wellington.co.za/ wellington-wine-farms

THE
AMER

ICAS

KENTUCKY

Visitors to this USA state will get a rip-roaring romp through the country's best bourbon distilleries. Producers here run the gamut from international brands operating out of 19th-century heritage sites to progressive all-female teams and boutique start-ups, all with a dash of Southern charm.

BRITISH COLUMBIA

The past five years has been boom time for craft Canadian distilleries, nowhere more so than in British Columbia, where micro-distillery bars have been forged out of old warehouses and garages. Local produce is being used in all manner of seasonal spirits, such as amaro, whisky and honey-based vodka.

OAXACA

Tequila may be a byword for Mexican spirits, but mezcal in Oaxaca offers some of the most interesting distillery touring opportunities. This colourful state is where rural palenques harvest spiky agave plants, roast their hearts in pits and distil the smoky spirit traditionally, often in clay pots.

BOLIVIA

How to ask for a spirit without mixers? Un singani puro por favor

Signature spirit? Singani

What to order with your spirits? With singani, order ginger ale or lemonade and lime

Don't: Drink cocoroco. This sugar-cane moonshine is around 96% ABV and could drive you loco

One of Bolivia's best-kept secrets is its one-of-a-kind national tipple singani, an unaged spirit distilled from white Muscat of Alexandria grapes. The Spanish colonists planted high-altitude vines in Tarija, close to the Argentine border, as far back as the 16th century. But just as Bolivia's wines are unknown outside the country, an international audience is only just discovering singani – and from an unlikely source. Hollywood director Steven Soderbergh was so smitten by this aromatic spirit while filming the blockbuster movie *Che* (2008), he began to import his own label, Singani 1963, to the US; now he's taking it global.

Traditionally drunk with ginger ale and lime in a Chuflay cocktail, it wasn't until Gustu – part gourmet restaurant, part philanthropic project – opened in La Paz in 2012 that it began to be mixed, muddled and macerated into creative cocktails.

Now more unique spirits are popping up. Master Blends' Gin La República – choose from Andina or Amazónica – is distilled at high altitude with a bespoke blend of Andean and Amazonian botanicals. The company is also working on tonic water for a truly Bolivian G&T, as well as a new-recipe Cocalero (not to be confused with cocoroco) – a liqueur flavoured with Bolivia's coca leaf. The country's first premium vodka, 1825, is triple-distilled using pure

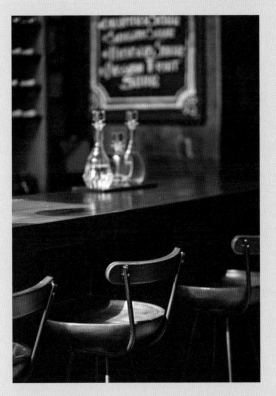

Andean mountain water and high-grown Amazonian wheat, and has already won medals at major international spirit competitions, while Andean Culture Distillery is on a mission to create Bolivia's first whisky.

The locals – apart from students – tend to save their drinking for the weekends, but there's a burgeoning bar scene in cities like La Paz and Santa Cruz. Family get-togethers start with a *cocktelito* (singani and orange juice) and move on to Chuflay, while the indigenous Aymara's tipple of choice is beer.

■ BAR
GUSTU BAR

Ave Costanera 10, La Paz
www.gustu.bo; +591 2 211 7491

◆ Food   ◆ Bar
◆ Shop   ◆ Transport

THINGS TO DO NEARBY

Restaurant Gustu

Gustu's restaurant is known for innovative tasting menus using only native produce, from eight to around 18 courses that can be paired with local wine, beer and cocktails. *www.gustu.bo*

Urban Rush

If you're looking for adrenaline-inducing adventure, try rap jumping – face-first abseiling – down a 50-metre building in central La Paz. *www.urbanrush bolivia.com*

MUSEF

Housed in an 18th-century palace, the National Museum of Ethnography and Folklore is a colourful and contemporary overview of Bolivia's diverse cultures. *www.musef.org.bo*

Calle Jaén

Stroll down colourful Calle Jaén, where the restored colonial buildings are filled with boutiques, cafés and five small museums, covering art, history and gold, that you can visit on a single ticket.

Gustu's groundbreaking bar in the Bolivian capital of La Paz is dedicated solely to Bolivian booze and was the first to put the national tipple, singani, centre stage. The Danish restaurant manager and head sommelier Bertil Levin Tøttenborg – one of Gustu's few imports – and bar manager Wei Chin Chau stock singani from four small wineries producing top-notch spirits without chemicals or pesticides. Like wine, singani's flavour changes with the terroir. It's often very floral, but the higher the altitude the more herbal it becomes, and Gustu also serves the more intensely flavoured, oak-aged versions that the larger distilleries, such as Casa Real, Rujero and Casa Grande, are releasing.

Gustu Bar's interior celebrates the country as much as its drinks list, with recycled colonial window frames and vibrant weavings from Potosí. You can pair your booze with mini versions of Paceño street-food favourites, including the pork-stuffed sandwich de chola. Menu highlights include Gustu's reinvention of the classic Chuflay – singani mixed with their own second-fermented ginger kombucha and a few drops of fresh ginger juice – and Atatau, a drink for spice lovers that translates as 'more pain' in Quechua, where singani infused with fiery locoto pepper has been muddled with huacatay, an Andean mint-like herb, to create one hot cocktail.

1825 VODKA

Avenida Punato 136, Parcopata, El Alto;
www.1825vodka.com; +591 69 82 94 47

◆ Distillery   ◆ Shop
◆ Tours

Bolivia's only homegrown vodka pays homage to its roots, from the name – the year of independence – to the design of the bottle, symbolising both the Andes and the Amazon. Aside from the country's singani distilleries, Innobe, which was set up by three young Bolivian entrepreneurs, is the only company that makes its own alcohol from scratch. It grinds Amazonian wheat from Santa Cruz and collects pure mountain water from the nearby Cordillera Real de los Andes before triple distilling it in state-of-the-art machinery. To date, it's won two international awards.

The small-batch distillery is in the ever-growing city of El Alto, perched on a breathtakingly high plateau, more than 4000 metres above sea level. It's a one-hour drive from central La Paz and you can arrange transport with the tour.

THINGS TO DO NEARBY

Feria 16 de Julio
Ride Mi Teleférico's red cable-car line up to El Alto's colossal Sunday morning market above La Paz. Said to be Latin America's largest, if you can't find it here it probably doesn't exist.

Wrestling cholitas
Sunday afternoon at the Multifuncional de la Ceja de El Alto means a blur of pigtails and petticoats, as the wrestling cholitas bounce off the ropes in high-octane bouts.*www.redcapwalkingtours.com*

CASA REAL

Santa Ana, Tarija;
www.vendimiacasareal.com; +591 67 37 08 68

◆ Distillery   ◆ Shop
◆ Tours

Casa Real is one of the powerhouse producers of Bolivia's singular spirit singani, set in the year-round, springlike climate of the Santa Ana Valley at the heart of Tarija's Ruta del Vino in Bolivia's deep south.

Director of production and oenologist Jorge Furió is at pains to point out that there's nothing like singani anywhere else in the world. The spirit's distinctive floral nose is down to a combination of terroir and production method and, unlike Peruvian pisco, it's made from one grape, aromatic Muscat of Alexandria, grown at about 2000 metres above sea level.

Inside the distillery you'll see Cognac-style alembic stills where Don Lucho and director Steven Soderbergh's Singani 63 are made. Finish off by trying the double-distilled black-label Gran Singani with lime and ginger ale in a Chuflay cocktail.

THINGS TO DO NEARBY

Campos de Solana
Try Bolivia's surprisingly good wines at Casa Real's sister label Campos de Solano, also in Tarija – the Riesling 2016 and red Trivarietal 2014 are particular standouts. *www.camposdesolana.com*

Valle de los Condores
This pioneering nonprofit runs one- to four-day high-altitude treks through the subtropical forest around Tarija, where magnificent condors glide and circle. *www.valledelos condores.com*

CANADA

How to ask for a spirit without mixers? Neat, please
Signature spirit? Whisky
What to order with your spirits? Fresh oysters on the coasts; poutine (fried potatoes slathered with gravy and topped with cheese curds) in Quebec; ketchup chips (ketchup-flavoured potato crisps) everywhere else
Do: Try a Caesar – a distinctively Canadian version of a Bloody Mary, blending vodka, Worcestershire sauce, hot sauce and Clamato (tomato-clam) juice

When a country borders three oceans and spans six time zones across 10 provinces and three territories, its drinking options are bound to be varied – whether you're downing a beer with your mates in a St John's pub, sipping a glass of wine during *cinq-à-sept* (the 5-to-7pm happy hour) in Montreal, or exploring the craft cocktail scene on a mild Vancouver evening.

In Canada, which stretches 5500km from east to west, the first distillery opened in Quebec City in 1769. The country's early distillers produced rum and then whisky; by the 1800s, Toronto whisky-maker Gooderham & Worts had become the largest distillery in the world. Unbeknown to many, Canada remains among the top whisky-producing nations, selling roughly 75% of its commercial output to the US.

Yet Canada's modern craft distilling movement is relatively new, with many provinces changing their laws only in the past several years to enable micro-distilleries to set up shop. By Canadian federal law, spirits must age in wood for a minimum of three years to be called whisky, so even if a micro-distillery's goal is to produce whisky, most begin by making unaged vodka and gin.

But that's where the similarities end. Across Canada, you'll find craft distilleries producing spirits from all different bases – from locally grown wheat, rye or corn to apples and even honey – and flavouring them with spruce tips, berries and many other regional products. And in this big, diverse country, that means lots of unique – and delicious – drinks behind the bar.

PARK DISTILLERY

219 Banff Ave, Banff, Alberta;
www.parkdistillery.com; +1-403-762-5114

◆ Food   ◆ Tours   ◆ Bar
◆ Distillery   ◆ Shop   ◆ Transport

THINGS TO DO NEARBY

Banff National Park

Hike 1600km of mountain
trails, canoe glacier-fed
lakes, explore rocky
canyons or cycle scenic
byways in Canada's first
— and most visited —
national park.
*www.pc.gc.ca/en/pn-np/
ab/banff*

**Mount Norquay
Via Ferrata**

Challenge yourself on this
guided climbing route
that takes you across
suspension bridges, up
ladders and along rock
faces with amazing views
over the mountains.
www.banffnorquay.com

The Banff Centre

See what's happening at
this art-focused campus
above town, which hosts
lectures, music, theatre
and other events
throughout the year.
www.banffcentre.ca

Banff Upper Hot Springs

Soak away your adventure-
(or alcohol-) induced aches
and pains in this outdoor
pool, fed by natural hot
springs and surrounded
by mountain peaks.
www.hotsprings.ca

Canada's only distillery located in a national park opened in 2015 in the Rocky Mountain town of Banff. Its facility on Banff's main street is part distillery and part lively restaurant-pub, with timber-hewn walls, light fixtures made of antlers, and local trout, chicken and steaks cooked over open fires. There's even a campfire-inspired dessert, the 'smoking s'more bar,' made from dark chocolate ganache and torched marshmallow on a graham cracker crust – a makeover of a Canadian classic. This split personality has made it a convivial hub for both locals and the floods of visitors who travel to Banff National Park for year-round outdoor pursuits.

Park Distillery's team describes its distilling process as 'glacier to glass', drawing water from six glaciers high in the Rockies and using grains grown on Alberta family farms. Free 30-minute tours run every afternoon (book ahead), where visitors can learn more about the spirits-making process and sample the products. Among its signature spirits are a classic vodka and an Alpine Dry Gin, flavoured with spruce tips and other botanicals. An espresso vodka made with locally roasted coffee beans and a traditional rye whisky are also made here, but top billing goes to the quintessentially Canadian Maple Rye, a sweet-and-spicy whisky produced from Alberta grain and Quebec maple syrup.

LONG TABLE DISTILLERY

1451 Hornby St, Vancouver, British Columbia;
www.longtabledistillery.com; +1-604-266-0177

◆ Food   ◆ Shop   ◆ Transport
◆ Distillery   ◆ Bar

When Charles Tremewen and his wife Rita opened Vancouver's first micro-distillery in 2013, Charles hand-finished the 14ft-long redwood slab that serves as the tasting bar and gave the distillery its name. Behind it, the distillery produces several varieties of gin and vodka, using Canadian-grown grains, in its 300-litre copper-pot still. Cucumber gin and small batches of seasonal spirits, such as aquavit infused with caraway, anise and Seville orange, or herbal amaro, are among its distinctive products.

Stop in for a three-sample tasting and staff will explain what happens in the distilling room, which you can see through a wall of windows. Weekends are the best time to linger, though, as a limited snack menu is offered and regular events are hosted, such as Gin & Tonic Fridays.

THINGS TO DO NEARBY

False Creek Seawall
Walk down the hill to False Creek, the scenic waterway that wends through downtown Vancouver, where you can follow the paved seawall path alongside several beaches.
www.vancouver.ca

Granville Island
Catch a ferry across False Creek to this popular waterside Vancouver destination to explore the art studios and graze through the lively Public Market.
www.granvilleisland.com

ODD SOCIETY SPIRITS

1725 Powell St, Vancouver, British Columbia;
www.oddsocietyspirits.com; +1-604-559-6745

◆ Distillery ◆ Shop ◆ Transport
◆ Tours ◆ Bar

THINGS TO DO NEARBY

Powell Brewery
One of several eastside craft breweries, Powell has a cosy tasting room furnished with light woods. It's known for its Old Jalopy Pale Ale and its changing seasonal brews. *www.powellbeer.com*

Doan's Craft
Inside a converted house, this family-run brewery has a tiny tasting room where an elaborate black-and-white mural by local artist Ola Volo decorates the walls. *www.doanscraftbrewing.com*

The Pie Shoppe
Two sisters craft sweet and savoury pies, available whole or by the slice, at this cheerful bakery. Try nectarine or blueberry in summer, and chocolate pecan year-round. *www.thepieshoppe.ca*

Vancouver East Cultural Centre
At its two eastside venues, The Cultch programmes an eclectic mix of music, theatre and dance events, featuring local and international performers. *www.thecultch.com*

In the East Vancouver neighbourhood that's now home to numerous craft breweries, Odd Society Spirits lives up to its name by going against the grain. Founder and chief distiller Gordon Glanz left a career in technical writing and translating to study distilling in Scotland before returning to launch his own with his wife, Miriam Karp.

Despite the education in Scotland, Gordon's signature spirit is actually a vodka rather than a whisky. East Van Vodka is produced in a former motorcycle garage, along with Wallflower Gin and Mongrel, a rye-based moonshine whisky, using German-made copper pot stills and a 15ft distilling column. In the front room, an old-style cocktail lounge with a long bar and marble-topped tables is a great spot to linger.

Check out the massive ghostly painting by local artist Shwa Keirstead, which hangs over the bar. You can also keep an eye on what's happening in the distilling room through the floor-to-ceiling windows, or call ahead to book a full distillery tour.

As well as the signature spirits, try Odd Society's less-common tipples: a smooth, dessert-friendly crème de cassis, made from British Columbia blackcurrants, and an unusual (and especially delicious) bittersweet vermouth.

VICTORIA DISTILLERS

9891 Seaport Place, Sidney, British Columbia;
www.victoriadistillers.com; +1-250-544-8217

◆ Food   ◆ Tours   ◆ Bar
◆ Distillery   ◆ Shop   ◆ Transport

Launched in a cottage among the evergreens on Vancouver Island, Victoria Distillers – one of Canada's first craft spirits makers – made its reputation on gin. It grew out of its original base and relocated north of the British Columbia capital of Victoria, where it now resides in a waterfront warehouse with an airy lounge and bar.

The distillery uses organic botanicals and cask-ages its distinctive Oaken Gin to give it a herbal, caramel finish. Equally unusual is its Left Coast Hemp Vodka, distilled from organically grown Canadian hemp seeds.

Ask to try its special edition Empress 1908 Gin – a vivid indigo spirit, blended with tea, that turns lavender when you add tonic or citrus thanks to the inclusion of butterfly pea blossoms as an ingredient. Have your camera ready.

THINGS TO DO NEARBY

Shaw Centre for the Salish Sea
Learn about the coastal ecosystem at this hands-on aquarium, where jellyfish, salmon and other colourful Pacific sea creatures swim in the tanks.
www.salishseacentre.org

Gulf Islands National Park Reserve
Catch the summertime ferry from the town of Sidney to Sidney Island to sunbathe at the beach, hike island trails, or camp by the shore. **www.pc.gc.ca/en/ pn-np/bc/gulf**

WAYWARD DISTILLATION HOUSE

2931 Moray Ave, Courtenay, British Columbia;
www.waywarddistillationhouse.com; +1-250-871-0424

◆ Distillery ◆ Shop ◆ Transport
◆ Tours ◆ Bar

Wayward co-owner Dave Brimacombe was a home-based fermenter, making beer, wine and mead (honey wine), before he turned his experimentation to distillation. It was only when he tried distilling his mead that the idea for a sweet-toothed distillery was hatched. And so it was that Brimacombe and his wife Andrea launched Wayward Distillation House in 2014, which became the first distillery in Canada to use honey as the base for all its spirits.

In a Comox Valley warehouse on Vancouver Island's east coast, the distillery team blends unpasteurised British Columbia clover honey with yeast and water to produce mead, then distils that mead into honey-based vodkas and gins. It also crafts its Drunken Hive Rum from molasses made from caramelised honey, instead of a traditional sugar-based

THINGS TO DO NEARBY

Forbidden Brewing Co
Hidden below a Courtenay hotel, this teeny nano-brewery usually has eight beers on tap. Look for the black IPA, organic pilsner or organic pale ale. *www.forbiddenbrewing.com*

40 Knots Vineyard and Estate Winery
Visit for a complimentary tasting at the Comox Valley's largest wine maker, known for whites such as pinot gris, ortega and 'Ziggy', made from siegerrebe grapes. *www.40knotswinery.com*

I-Hos Gallery
This gallery and shop, operated by the K'ómoks First Nation, displays carvings, jewellery, textiles, masks and other works by indigenous artists. *www.ihosgallery.com*

Atlas Café
A long-standing downtown Courtenay favourite, this colourful cafe cooks up hearty breakfasts and a world-wandering menu that journeys from enchiladas to noodle bowls to local seafood. *www.atlascafe.ca*

product. Wayward also produces a custom honey gin for the Fairmont Waterfront Hotel in Vancouver, which raises bees and makes honey on its rooftop, working in partnership with Hives for Humanity — an organisation that trains local disadvantaged communities to work with bees.

When you stop in for a complimentary tasting, be sure to sample the smooth and flavourful Krupnik — a spiced honey liqueur that's modelled on a Polish spirit of the same name.

IRONWORKS DISTILLERY

2 Kempt St, Lunenburg, Nova Scotia;
www.ironworksdistillery.com, +1-902-640-2424

◆ Distillery   ◆ Shop
◆ Tours   ◆ Transport

THINGS TO DO NEARBY

**Half Shell Oysters &
Seafood**
The slick production line
of oyster-shucking is a joy
to behold at this open-
air summer dining spot
with knockout harbour
views from its deck.
***www.facebook.com/
thehalfshelllunenburg***

Peggy's Cove
Photo fodder for
thousands of happy-
snappers, this teeny
South Shore fishing
settlement is home to less
than 40 residents and
has an ends-of-the-earth
feel that makes
it a delight to wander.

Lunenburg Walking Tours
Jelly bean-coloured
architecture, seafaring
folklore and a tapestry of
European immigration are
brought to life on this tour
of Lunenburg, whose old
town is a Unesco site.
***www.lunenburg
walkingtours.com***

**Fisheries Museum
of the Atlantic**
Nosedive into the fishing
heritage of Atlantic Canada
at this harbourfront
museum, which looks back
as far as the days of the First
Nations Mi'kmaq people.
***https://fisheriesmuseum.
novascotia.ca***

On Nova Scotia's historic south shore in the colourful seaside town of Lunenburg, this small-batch distillery draws inspiration from the 1893 mariners' blacksmiths shop within which it operates.

The charred mouth of the blacksmith's old brick furnace and a sepia image of the clapboard workshop in its heyday greet visitors stepping into the barnlike interior. This space would have once been a sweltering hive of industry stoked by ironworks fires used to supply local shipbuilders; now you'll find it warmed by the simmer of the German-made still used to cook up Ironworks' gins, vodkas and fruit liquors. Mind the oak barrels, which are proliferating so fast the owners can no longer confine them to the cosy basement barrel room where you'll get to do tastings during your tour.

Ironworks' liquors are fermented slowly for a fuller flavour and the owners are hell bent on making hyper-local products. That means gin using local juniper berries, balsam fir bud brandy and foraged rosehips from down the road, and vodka made with Nova Scotian apples – everything comes from within a 150-mile radius. Try the pear 'eau de vie' brandy, containing a fully grown pear harvested in the bottle at a local farm.

KINSIP HOUSE OF FINE SPIRITS

66 Gilead Rd, Bloomfield, Ontario;
www.kinsip.ca; +1-613-393-1890

◆ Distillery   ◆ Shop
◆ Tours

 On the shores of Lake Ontario, within weekending distance of Toronto, Prince Edward County is one of Canada's fast-growing wine-producing regions, with more than 40 wineries and an increasing number of craft breweries. Kinsip House of Fine Spirits produces not wines or suds, though; it's the county's first small-batch spirits maker.

In a grand 1874 brick manor that was once home to a well-to-do hops grower, set in the farmland outside the town of Bloomfield, Kinsip crafts gin, vodka from Canadian whole wheat, and several whiskies, including Crimson Rye and bourbon-style Wild Oat. More unusually, the distillery also produces a Japanese spirit called shochu, distilled from a blend of barley and rice, as well as a slightly smoky, oak barrel-aged shochu variety.

Drop into the Victorian-style tasting room for samples, or book a 30-minute guided tasting, where you'll learn about the distillery and its production process while you taste three different spirits. Still want to learn more? Reserve a one-hour tour and tasting, which adds a guided walk through the distilling facilities. If you'd prefer something to pair with your pancakes, rather than your pâté, try Kinsip's maple syrup aged in whisky barrels.

THINGS TO DO NEARBY

Oeno Gallery and Sculpture Garden
Taste wine, then check out the art at this high-end gallery in the grounds of Huff Estates, one of Ontario's largest wineries. *www.oenogallery.com*

Sandbanks Provincial Park
Lounge on the Lake Ontario sands and hike over the expansive dunes at this popular park, where its namesake beach extends for nearly 11km. *www.ontarioparks.com/park/sandbanks*

From the Farm Cooking School
Chef and food writer Cynthia Peters offers cooking classes in her farmhouse kitchen, where you'll learn about local ingredients as you prepare a meal. *www.fromthefarm.ca*

Arts Trail, Taste Trail
Follow these self-guided routes to explore the county's art studios and galleries, or its wineries, breweries, bakeries and restaurants; download a map or brochure online. *www.artstastetrail.com*

JUNCTION 56 DISTILLERY

45 Cambria St, Stratford, Ontario;
www.junction56.ca; +1-519-305-5535

◆ Distillery   ◆ Shop
◆ Tours   ◆ Transport

Junction 56 lies in the unlikely locale of Stratford, a small town two hours from Toronto that would be a blip on the map were it not for its giant annual theatre festival. Housed in a former lumberyard, the distillery produces gin, vodka and an unaged 'moonshine' whisky brewed from corn grown on the owner's cousin's nearby farm.

Junction 56 takes its name from a tidbit of railroad history: Stratford was at the junction of two rail lines when trains first arrived in the region back in 1856. Take a one-hour tour through the production room to learn about Junction 56's distilling process, then sample its range. The Fireshine cinnamon liqueur – moonshine steeped in a cinnamon tea blend created by a local tea sommelier – is especially delicious.

THINGS TO DO NEARBY

Stratford Festival
North America's largest classical repertory theatre fest runs from April to October. Book a behind-the-scenes tour if you want to peek backstage.
www.stratfordfestival.ca

Stratford Chef School
Students at this culinary institute host an annual dinner series with international visiting chefs. To up your own cooking game, take a class yourself.
www.stratfordchef.com

NICKEL 9 DISTILLERY

90 Cawthra Avenue, Unit 100, Toronto, Ontario;
www.nickel9distillery.com; +1-647-341-5959

◆ Distillery   ◆ Shop
◆ Tours   ◆ Transport

The province of Ontario is one of Canada's major apple-growing regions, so when buddies Chris Jacks and Harris Hadjicostis from Toronto decided to open a distillery, they looked for a way to capitalise on this abundant local crop. Undeterred by the fact that neither of them had any distilling experience, they launched Nickel 9 in 2017 with Northern Temple vodka made from apples.

You can sample it at the tasting bar, crafted from reclaimed wood, at their micro-distillery in Toronto's cool Junction neighbourhood, where the duo are now working on expanding their range with drinks such as a calvados-style apple brandy. Start by trying the vodka straight, to appreciate its clear, crisp, not-too-sweet taste with a hint of fruit, before moving on to in-house cocktail creations.

THINGS TO DO NEARBY

Museum of Contemporary Art
Housed inside a renovated 1919 aluminum foundry, MOCA features cutting-edge art by Canadian and international creators.
www.museumof contemporaryart.ca

Halo Brewery
Sample eclectic changing brews poured by self-proclaimed 'beer geeks' at this petite microbrewery, including the Shapeshifter sour IPA and Tokyo Rose, a rosehips-scented saison.
www.halobrewery.com

CIRKA DISTILLERIES

2075 Cabot, Montreal, Quebec;
www.cirka.ca; +1-514-370-2075

- Distillery
- Shop
- Tours
- Transport

Montreal's first 'grain to bottle' distillery to open to the public is Cirka. It occupies an industrial brick-walled space near the historic Lachine Canal, south of the city centre. Co-founders Paul Cirka, John Frare and JoAnne Gaudreau launched the distillery in 2014 and now make both their Vodka Terroir (distilled in a 24ft vodka column) and Gin Sauvage from Quebec-grown non-GMO corn, infusing the latter spirit with a forest-inspired blend of more than 30 botanicals.

Cirka offers tours and tastings by appointment, and the distillery also runs periodic cocktail mixology classes. The must-try spirit is Gin375, released in 2017 to mark Montreal's 375th anniversary, which is sweetened with honey and infused with cranberry, sour cherry and wild rose petals.

THINGS TO DO NEARBY

Lachine Canal

Stroll or cycle along the linear park that follows this 13.5km waterway – now a national historic site – between Montreal's Old Port and Lake Saint-Louis. *www.pc.gc.ca/en/lhn-nhs/qc/canallachine*

Atwater Market

Stock up on cheeses, charcuterie, chocolates and more in this 1933 brick market building; good for snacks or a picnic by the Lachine Canal. *www.marchespublics-mtl.com*

©Marie-Alexandre Talbot/Courtesy of |Cirka Distillers (2)

RUM 101

Rum was first distilled in the Caribbean during the 17th century when imperial European powers were eagerly planting their flags on the volcanic ridges and drifting sandbars of the far-flung archipelago. Sugar cane plantations quickly blanketed the tropics, and it was discovered soon thereafter that a viable alcoholic beverage could be made from the molasses runoff, and other by-products, of the sugar-refining process. The liquor — rum — was instantly fashionable among the colonies throughout the New World, and quickly became as lucrative an endeavour as the slave and sugar trades. In fact, rum was so important in the American colonies that it encouraged the creation of Britain's Sugar Act — an unfounded hike in taxation, and one of the mechanisms that ultimately spawned the advent of the American Revolution.

Dozens of Caribbean colonies produced their own versions of the liquor for their respective crowns, and today rum can be sorted into three general categories: British, French and Spanish. There are, of course, complexities and exceptions to the rule, but British- and Spanish-style rums are, by and large, produced from molasses, while French-style rums come from cane juice. When creating molasses-based rums, the most important element to tweak and perfect is the distillation process itself, but with French rums the approach is treated more like wine. The drink earns its flavours from the terroir, with environmental factors affecting flavour profiles.

While most spirit definitions come with a long list of rules and exceptions, rum is an umbrella term for the alcoholic drink derived from cane-related ingredients whose fermentation is encouraged by adding yeast and water, distilled (mostly) in a column still, and barrel aged for at least

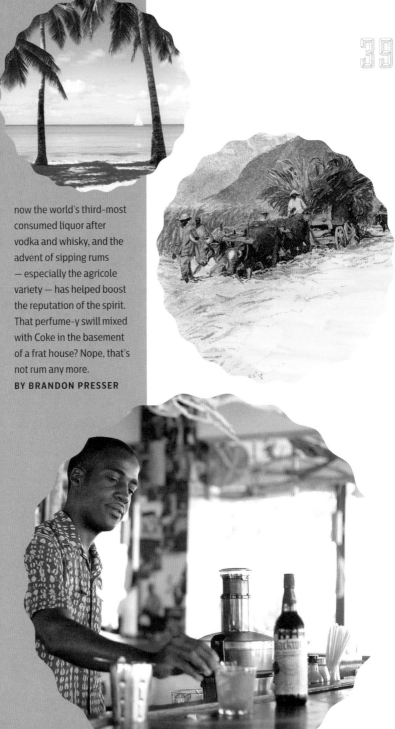

39

one year (in everything from old bourbon barrels to steel drums). Recipes and regulations depend on the nation; Spanish-style rums — añejo rums — are smooth in taste, while English-style rums are generally darker and have a more pronounced molasses sensibility. When you're drinking something from the top-shelf at your favourite Tiki bar somewhere else in the world, you're likely drinking the añejo variety. Cachaça in Brazil falls into the rum family, too.

French products, on the other hand, are so different that they've been given an AOC (appellation d'origine contrôlée), similar to how the French region of Champagne is the only place that can produce real-deal champagne, while the rest of the world has to call it sparkling wine. On Martinique it is called rhum agricole, and the island's distilleries harvest cane from different corners of their islands, each one producing its own version of the coveted, terroir-rich spirit.

Rum, as it turns out, is now the world's third-most consumed liquor after vodka and whisky, and the advent of sipping rums — especially the agricole variety — has helped boost the reputation of the spirit. That perfume-y swill mixed with Coke in the basement of a frat house? Nope, that's not rum any more.

BY BRANDON PRESSER

Clockwise from left: ©GANNA MARTYSHEVA/Shutterstock, ©Matteo Colombo/Getty Images, North Wind Picture Archives Alamy Stock Photo; Daniel Di Paolo

CARIBBEAN

How to ask for a drink? Many islanders speak English; in French territories such as Martinique and St Barth, say 'Un ti' punch s'il te plaît'

Signature spirit? Rum

What to order with your spirits? Accras, or fish fritter appetisers

Don't: Drink Piña coladas before dinner; this is a rookie mistake and will fill you up on the heavy cream. Go for a Planter's Punch – or planteur – which has the same amount of sweetness without the froth

It's been so long since Columbus sailed through, naming all the islands after saints, that the New World is starting to look pretty old. And one of the Caribbean's biggest legacies is its rum, with compelling variations as you hop from island to island.

In many ways, the alcohol refined from sugar cane molasses is one of the best ways to understand what makes each of these tropical crags tick. The French islands covet their rum like wine; testament to their strong culture of food and drink, which rules the way both locals and visitors consume the islands' bounty – evening quaffs and perhaps a midday supplement are the norm. On the British and Spanish isles, the Anglo Saxon penchant for beer has played a significant role in diversifying the bar culture beyond rum, whether it's at weekend barbecues or beachside haunts.

Like the drinking culture, the distillery experience in the Caribbean can be sharply divided into two categories. One caters to mainstream tourists embracing a 'fun and sun' approach to their island vacay, and the other is geared towards a more discerning traveller interested in using spirits to decode the region's history.

A distillery's target audience is usually informed by the methods used to refine their alcohol – but how can you tell before signing up for a visit? In general, big brands such as Bacardi subscribe to the first type of visit, while boutique establishments take more care when creating small-batch brews, but not all rum houses are created equal. The best way to do your sleuthing work is to enquire about the tasting experience provided. If the rum offered is being mixed with juices then be prepared to down your holiday's cocktail quota; distilleries that treat rum like a spirit to be sipped or swigged are the ones that will better illuminate the processes and history involved.

CALLWOOD RUM DISTILLERY

Cane Garden Bay, Tortola, British Virgin Islands;
www.facebook.com/callwoodrumdistillery; +1-284-495-9383

◆ Distillery ◆ Shop
◆ Tours

For generations the Callwood family has been making rum in an ancient stone building that's now practically subsumed by the jungle. Dating back more than 300 years, it's one of the Caribbean's oldest distilleries and although badly hit by Hurricane Irma in 2017, life here has slowly returned to normal. A tour of the atmospheric grounds reveals stacks of sugar cane, the press mill that crushes the cane into juice, copper pots that boil the juice, wooden barrels where it ferments, and the coil-laden stills that fire it into alcohol.

THINGS TO DO NEARBY

Cane Garden Bay Beach
This gently sloping crescent of sand hosts rocking bars and water-sports vendors, though many are still getting back up to speed after 2017's Hurricane Irma.

Smuggler's Cove
This gorgeous beach is lightly trod compared with its neighbours, as access is via a crazy-narrow road. Nigel's Boom Boom Bar and Grill stokes the party in the cove.

D' Coalpot
Spicy jerk meats, curries, rotis, grilled fish and other West Indian staples emerge from the kitchen in heaping portions at this local hotspot.
www.dcoalpotbvi.com

Sugar Mill Restaurant
Lobster ravioli and other modern Caribbean dishes hit the candlelit tables shimmering in the stone boiling house of a bygone rum distillery.
www.sugarmillhotel.com

The process is much the same as it has been for centuries, except these days diesel engines power the machinery instead of donkeys. And the Callwoods stick to a technique most other producers have brushed aside: they distil their rum from pure cane juice, not molasses, which they say renders it hangover-proof. Four types of rum emerge, all bottled under the Arundel label: a white rum, four-year-old rum, 10-year-old rum and blended rum called the Panty Dropper. While there's no cocktail room, staff pour shots of each at a makeshift bar surrounded by a hodgepodge of casks, bottles and lanterns.

MUSEO DEL RON HAVANA CLUB

Ave del Puerto 262, cnr Sol, Habana Vieja, Havana;
www.havanaclubmuseum.com; +53 7 861 8051

◆ Tours ◆ Bar

◆ Shop ◆ Transport

Although the name Havana Club is a trademark that dates to the 1930s, the rum business was established by José Arechabala in 1878. It was nationalised by the state under Fidel Castro, and has been Cuba's national rum muse ever since. This entertaining museum in an 18th-century mansion tells its story.

The museum hosts a detailed scale model of a distillery and visits include a guided tour through the history and production of Cuban rum, which is made with local sugar cane – an important factor in the final flavours of the spirit.

Havana Club produces several rum varieties, including a light rum popular with Cuban cocktail mixologists, and several *añejos* (aged rums) designed for sipping; you'll taste the seven-year-old version at the end of your tour.

THINGS TO DO NEARBY

Malecón
Havana's iconic seawall is the locals' favourite promenade, excellent for people watching, jogging or dancing to the beat of traditional music played live on the street.

Plaza Vieja
One of the five plazas that make up a *tour de rigueur* of Havana's oldest quarter. Come here for a glimpse of Cuba's baroque architecture and a drink in the square.

APPLETON ESTATE

Nassau Valley, St Elizabeth, Jamaica;
www.appletonestate.com; +1 876 963 9215, 9216 or 9217

◆ Food ◆ Tours ◆ Bar
◆ Distillery ◆ Shop

'Jamaican rum-making is like our driving,' says Joy Spence. 'Passionate, bold, and determined.' Having become the world's first female master blender in 1997, Joy remains at the helm of this historic yet pioneering rum brand, and Appleton's new visitor centre – the Joy Spence Appleton Estate Rum Experience – is named in her honour.

At 265 years old, Appleton is the oldest continuously run sugar estate and distillery in Jamaica, set amid the sprawling cane fields, lush steep-sided hollows and distinctive conical hills of Cockpit Country. Retaining complete control of the rum-making process from cane to cocktail, all ingredients are cultivated or sourced on the estate, including limestone-filtered water from its own spring. A combination of column and pot-still distillation adds vanilla, coffee and Appleton's signature orange-peel note to Jamaica's typically bold style.

Sampling during the tour is generous. As well as tutored tastings of Appleton's core to long-aged range, it includes

THINGS TO DO NEARBY

Little Ochie
If Kingstonians are willing to drive the two-plus hours to dine at this rustic beach-side seafood emporium in Alligator Pond, you know it's got to be something special. Order lobster or grilled conch.

YS Falls
Decidedly less hectic than Jamaica's perennially busy Dunn's River Falls, and just a 30-minute drive from the distillery, cool down in these vivid blue waters before a distillery tour.
www.ysfalls.com

Floyd's Pelican Bar
Sip rum punch and play dominoes with the locals, a mile out to sea. Initially built as a hangout for fishermen, this driftwood-constructed bar can be reached by boat from Treasure Beach or Black River.

Black River
Spot crocodiles among the reeds, sail through ancient mangroves and dine at crab shack Sister Lou's on a tour up-river from this settlement a 40-minute drive from Appleton.

a welcome cocktail named Stormy Valley (which mixes Signature Blend with lime, ginger beer and Angostura bitters), a classic rum punch to take on outdoor parts of the tour, and a miniature of Signature Blend to take home. Try your hand at cane-juicing and sugar boiling, visit the barrel house, and try fresh cane juice. The on-site jerk-focused restaurant is a must, if you can bear to hold off from the various roadside stalls on the drive up.

From left: ©Mark Read/Lonely Planet (3); Daniel Di Paolo

RHUM CLÉMENT

Domaine de l'Acajou, Le François; Martinique; www.rhum-clement.com; +596-596-54-62-07

◆ Tours
◆ Shop

The vast estate at Habitation Clément dates to 1887 and was the birthplace of the world's first and most distinguished brand of *rhum agricole*. Today the distillation of Clément's products has moved off-site, but the hallowed grounds of this estate still offer the best opportunity to explore Martinique's elaborate rum history.

The main mansion, Domaine de l'Acajou, sits regally at the site's highest elevation and has a sea-facing veranda. Lush gardens lined with fig trees and coconut palms lead the way to the original distillery complex, now frozen in time with caption banners taking tourists through the elaborate rum-making process. At the end of your visit, take a tasting experience and don't leave without a bottle of the cinnamon-y 10-year Grand Reserve.

THINGS TO DO NEARBY

Fort-de-France
Weathered by the intense humidity of the tropics, Martinique's walkable capital is stately but crumbling, much like the romantic streets of Havana in Cuba.

Îlet Oscar
A castaway's delight, this teeny islet off the windward side of the island has a small inn with four rooms, a rasta-ramshackle restaurant and bar.
www.iletoscar.com

SAINT JAMES

St-James Plaine de l'Union, Sainte-Marie; Martinique; www.saintjames-rum.com; +596-596-69-30-02

◆ Food   ◆ Tours
◆ Distillery ◆ Shop

Saint James' main museum and tasting room are located in a gabled plantation manse that looks like a set piece from *Gone With the Wind*. The working distillery is still on site, and is a charming amalgam of old and new equipment and techniques. Tours take travellers from plantation to bottle filling and can either be conducted on foot or by antique steam train – a vestige from the height of the sugar industry when ambitious colonists sought to crisscross the island with a network of locomotive tracks.

Tastings are generous, taking enthusiasts through Saint James' award-winning line of sipping rums – go for the *rhum agricole* aged six to 10 years, which garnered prizes at the 2016 International Rum Conference in Madrid.

THINGS TO DO NEARBY

Depaz Distillery
Sample the spirits at Depaz's on-site restaurant to taste-test the palpable differences between the sugar cane grown on the leeward and windward sides of the island.
www.depaz.fr

Cap Est
Martinique's most refined place to stay is this Relais & Châteaux property, which pairs its local *agricole* rums with a menu of refined French favourites from the sea.
www.capest.com

HOUSE OF ANGOSTURA

Cnr Eastern Main Rd & Trinity Ave, Laventille, Trinidad;
www.angostura.com/tours; +1 868-623-1841 Ext 255

◆ Distillery ◆ Shop
◆ Tours ◆ Transport

Courtesy of House of Angostura

Look inside any Trini's kitchen pantry and you'll find the distinctive yellow cap and oversize label of Angostura bitters. Created as a stomach settler in 1824 by a German surgeon who later fled here from war-torn Venezuela, the aromatic bitters seem woven into the very DNA of Trinidad.

More recently though, House of Angostura has turned its time-honed talents to the production of rum. It may be Trinidad's only remaining distillery, but Angostura boasts the most-awarded rum range in the world. There's White Oak, 5 Year Old, 7 Year Old, 1919, and top-of-the-range 1824. What typifies its style? 'We're clean but not too clean, dirty but not too dirty. There are fruity notes without the oily notes, we don't get as funky as the Jamaicans, but we're packed with flavour,' says master distiller John Georges.

THINGS TO DO NEARBY

Ariapita Avenue
'Liming' means to hang out, and there's no better place to see and be seen than the nightlife and restaurant district of Trinidad's capital, Port of Spain.

Richard's Bake & Shark, Maracas Beach
Head to Richard's for a Trini speciality: deep-fried shark fillet in a deep-fried dough ball. Throw on fresh mango chutney and hot pepper sauce, as the basslines boom across this lively beach.

Lady Young Lookout
Sample corn soup, Yardie's legendary jerk, or be brave and try a sour tamarind ball at the food stalls that overlook Port of Spain, where calypso players also ply their wares.

Sri Dattatreya Temple
Marvel at this temple's 26m-tall statue of the Hindu god Hanuman Murti, located in the village of Carapichaima, before heading a short drive away to the nearby Waterloo Temple, known as the Temple in the Sea.

A visit to the House of Angostura includes rum sampling, a tour of the barrel-filled warehouses, the stills, and the locked door behind which the secret recipe for the bitters is stored. There's also ample memorabilia from the cocktail boom of the 1910s to 1920s, when Angostura bitters became known around the world. Perhaps most uniquely, there's also an 8000-strong collection of rare butterflies, collected by local lepidopterist Malcolm Barcant.

MEXICO

How to ask for a spirit without mixers? Me gustaria una copita de mezcal por favor

Signature spirit? Depending on the region, either mezcal or tequila

What to order with your spirits? Botanas (snacks) – like spicy and salty peanuts, and crisp tortillas with soft fresh cheese – will commonly be given along with your drink.

Do: Tip in bars, although it's not a formal necessity; in general a 10% tip is a nice gesture and indicates that you've enjoyed the service

Mexico's spirits industry mostly revolves around one special natural inhabitant: the agave plant. This spiky succulent, similar in appearance to aloe, thrives in the country's multi-coloured clay soil and grows in arid, desert-like areas. Although almost every state in Mexico produces an agave spirit, the two major regions are Jalisco for tequila – an area full of regional delicacies, open-air markets, and sprawling landscapes – and Oaxaca for mezcal – a state that also draws visitors for its world-renowned cuisine, mix of indigenous cultures, and yearly festivals like the Guelaguetza dance and Dia de los Muertos.

Historically, mezcal was defined as any agave spirit made in Mexico, including tequila, and it's only in recent years that the two spirits have become distinct. The first name for tequila, which dates to the 17th century, was Vino De Mezcal De Tequila. The tequila region became so well known for its particularly delicious variety of mezcal that marketing efforts – and a hefty dose of good luck – helped the tequila brand take off and become its own spirit category.

Mexico also produces spirits made from sugar cane and other fruits, but in this country tequila and mezcal rule. Both spirits can be found in virtually every bar and they are drunk at social engagements, after work in sawdust-floor bars, and at weddings, birthdays and funerals. Mezcal is usually taken neat, while tequila is more commonly found in cocktails – unless, that is, you're sipping the family reserves.

Today, tequila is distinguished by using only one variety of agave, the Blue Weber Agave, while the broader mezcal category uses around 30 different varieties. The production process is also distinct: in tequila production, the agave hearts are essentially steamed, while for mezcal they are roasted in underground pits, imparting a slightly smoky flavour. Another key difference is the tradition of ageing in wood. Tequila follows in the footsteps of whisky, where a longer aged tequila is regarded as more premium. In the mezcal world, most spirits are kept out of wood to preserve the flavour of the plant, and ageing in wood doesn't affect the prestige of the product.

From top left: © Sergio Lubezky/500px. Courtesy of © elena marini silvestri / La Perla del Mezcal

"The main challenge with the growth in demand of agave spirits is making sure culture and tradition are not distorted or misrepresented, while keeping an open mind to innovation"

— **GERMÁN GUTIÉRREZ GAMBOA, MEZCAL PRODUCER, LAGRIMAS DE DOLORES**

The origins of distillation in Mexico are controversial, with scholars and scientists still pondering evidence for distillation before the arrival of Europeans. What we do know is that the ancient Mesoamericans enjoyed pulque. This low-alcohol beverage is completely distinct from agave spirits as it's made from the fermented sap of the plant, rather than the hearts. Pulque is still very much part of Mexico's modern drinking culture, and is considered a delicious treat that must be consumed fresh. You'll see it in local markets and find pulqueria bars dedicated to it, particularly in Mexico City where they've had a recent resurgence.

Indeed, all over Mexico the scene is shifting from casual drinking toward appreciation of craft spirits and education. With the explosion of international interest, locals increasingly want to create an experience that pays homage to traditions while being open to experimentation. In all cases you'll find that these spirits are deeply integrated into the communities – most people who taste them will develop a lifelong love affair with them and the cultures they represent.

TOP 5 SPIRITS

- **Reposado Tequila** Siete Leguas, Jalisco
- **Blanco Tequila** ArteNom, Jalisco
- **Cenizo Mezcal** Lagrimas de Dolores, Durango
- **Pulquero Mezcal** La Locura, Oaxaca
- **San Luis Potosi Mezcal** Alma Mezcalera, San Luis Potosi

■ BAR
MEZCALOTECA

Reforma 506, Centro, Oaxaca; www.mezcaloteca.org;
+52 951 514 0082 / +52 951 316 0448

◆ Tours   ◆ Tours   ◆ Bar
◆ Shop   ◆ Shop   ◆ Transport

Without visiting a *palenque* (rural distillery), this is the best place in mezcal's heartland to try traditionally prepared agave distillates. The knowledgeable team at Mezcaloteca works with more than 40 *maestro mezcaleros* across Mexico to encourage conservation efforts and help them market and export their spirits, which feature at its downtown tasting room in Oaxaca City.

With a long wooden bar and stools for just 20 drinkers, staff can customise tastings for mezcal virgins and agave aficionados alike (book ahead). Blended and single-variety distillates are on offer, as well as those made with wild-crafted and rare agave species, and prepared in vessels from glass to copper, and clay to leather. Some are just-bottled; try to get a sample that's been aged for up to 20 years.

THINGS TO DO NEARBY

Ethnobotanical Garden at Santo Domingo Church
This curated collection of native Oaxacan vegetation explores the state's biodiversity, and the significance of local flora within indigenous cultures.
www.jardinoaxaca.mx

Rufino Tamayo Prehispanic Art Museum
Oaxaca artist Rufino Tamayo was profoundly influenced by indigenous art and culture, and bequeathed more than 1000 prehispanic artifacts to this museum.
www.rufinotamayo.org.mx

GRACIAS A DIOS

Santiago Matatlán, Oaxaca;
www.thankgad.com; +52 1 442 256 3105

- ◆ Food
- ◆ Tours
- ◆ Bar
- ◆ Distillery
- ◆ Shop
- ◆ Transport

Sprawling fields of agave surround Gracias a Dios; the family has propagated and planted at least 30,000 maguey 'babies' since opening – three plants for every bottle sold – to combat the dwindling populations of wild plant varieties used to make mezcal.

Oscar Hernández Santiago, the fourth-generation *maestro mezcalero* behind Gracias a Dios, uses a traditional distillation process that involves stone grinding, pit cooking, natural yeast fermentation and wood-fired copper stills. It takes about 30 days to complete. Visitors can also book to spend a night in the family's well-equipped casita.

Along with four *silvestre* (wild agave) mezcals, and six other espadin products, Gracias a Dios produces a unique agave gin using 32 botanicals representing the 32 Mexican states.

THINGS TO DO NEARBY

Tlacolula Tianguis
The small town of Tlacolula transforms on Sundays as this weekly market takes over the streets. Come for the fresh mountain veggies, colourful crafts and sweet pulque.

Yagul
This archaeological site and natural monument in the Tlacolula Valley dates back to at least 3000 BC and has views in all directions. Don't miss the massive petroglyphs at the entrance.

REAL MINERO

Santa Catarina Minas, Oaxaca;
www.realminero.com.mx; +52 951 520 6139

- ◆ Food
- ◆ Tours
- ◆ Distillery
- ◆ Shop

According to Graciela Angeles, mezcal is more than just a drink. 'You not only taste the essence of the plant, but the history and culture of the land it comes from,' she says. Graciela's family are true *mezcaleros* and have been distilling mezcal for at least four generations in the dusty town of Santa Catarina Minas.

A tour of their distillery includes a visit to the nursery, where fields are filled with different varieties of sculptural-looking agave, before an explanation of the hands-on production process at the *palenque* – here mezcal is made in the age-old way, roasting the agave hearts in stone-lined pits and distilling it in clay pots. Afterwards, you'll taste four mezcals, including their Espadin and Tobala. Try it with some nibbles (order ahead) and taste it neat to appreciate the smoky flavour.

THINGS TO DO NEARBY

Casa Oaxaca El Restaurante
Alejandro Ruiz – the godfather of new-Oaxacan cuisine – serves sophisticated takes on regional delicacies at his award-winning restaurant. *www.casaoaxacael restaurante.com*

State Museum of Popular Art
Oaxaca is famed for its rich tradition of folk art, and this fascinating, modern museum in San Bartolo Coyotepec is dedicated to all its forms.

CASA CORTES PALENQUE

Camino a la Presa, Santiago Matatlán, Oaxaca;
www.casacortes.mx; +52 951 514 2734

◆ Tours
◆ Distillery

THINGS TO DO NEARBY

La Biznaga
Back in central Oaxaca City, an hour from Santiago Matatlán, this restaurant is one of the few places to score fresh pulque, delivered daily. It also specialises in homemade traditional Oaxaca cuisine.
García Vigil 512, Oaxaca

Monte Albán
This Unesco World Heritage Site is home to a large number of pre-Columbian ruins. Tours are easily booked from Matatlán city centre, including transport and the entry tickets.

Fondita Lupita
Located in the city-centre market Sánchez Pascuas, this food stand churns out authentic mole, hot chocolate, and other traditional Oaxacan foods including spicy homemade salsas.
www.oaxaca-mio.com

Comedor Jessy
Conveniently situated along Carretera Cristobal Colon, the main highway in Matatlán, this roadside eatery is as authentic as it gets. Locals enjoy daily specials for breakfast and lunch.

Matatlán is the mezcal capital of the world, with a highway lined with road-facing distilleries offering tastings, tours and bottles for sale. Tucked away along this road, a 25-minute drive outside of the city centre, is the Casa Cortes *palenque* (distillery). It's a small operation that mixes rustic and modern, with handmade wooden furniture and a few horses to frame the view, juxtaposed with a minimalist, impeccably clean distillation area.

The in-ground pit they use for roasting agave hearts is right in front of the distillery area, and visitors who are lucky enough to arrive on a roast day can see the men loading the pit and even offer to help. The palenque is on family-owned land and while the distillery works with other distillers to produce its three lines of mezcal, what it distils here goes into each of its brands: Casa Cortes, Nuestra Soledad, and El Jolgorio.

Tours are casual yet deeply informative, allowing visitors to get up close and personal with each step of the process. Don't leave without tasting all the mezcal on offer; while the line-up on any given day varies, the family is known for superior spirits and generosity.

Courtesy of ©Max Kelly Photography/Casa Cortes (2)

MEZCAL DON AGAVE

Teotitlán del Valle, Oaxaca; www.mezcaldonagave.com;
+52 951 204 7286

◆ Food   ◆ Tours   ◆ Bar
◆ Distillery ◆ Shop   ◆ Transport

The small weaving village of Teotitlán del Valle 30km east of Oaxaca City is where Mexico's Ruta de Mezcal begins. Three mezcal producers are based in the vicinity of this scenic backwater, but the largest is Don Agave, with airy outdoor covered seating.

During a tour, your guide will introduce you to various species of agave in the gardens, explaining the process of growing them or 'hunting' them in the wild. You will be able to taste spirits of both young and aged espadin – the agave species with the shortest maturation time, and the only one easily cultivated as a crop. You can also try up to 10 varieties

THINGS TO DO NEARBY

Dainzú
Inhabited for 1000 years and abandoned by 300 CE, this archaeological farming village is almost always completely empty. Stay for a picnic – bring bug spray. *www.inah.gob.mx/es/zonas/86-zona-arqueologica-dainzu*

Tree of Tule
By width, this tree is one of the largest in the world. It is a 1400-year-old Montezuma cypress at the heart of the town of Santa María del Tule – a thing of local legend and continued adoration.

Iglesia Preciosa Sangre de Cristo
The Precious Blood of Christ Church in Teotitlán del Valle is built atop a still-visible prehispanic structure. It is named for a storied painting with a dark past, venerated annually in July.

Museo Comunitario Balaa Xtee Guech Gulal
This museum tells the story of Teotitlán del Valle's Zapotec heritage, including its languages, arts and traditions. It's also a good place to book guides for local archaeological sites.

of wild agave, which should be allowed to mature for as many as 25 years before it can be harvested.

If you're lucky, you might see the process of mastication by horse-drawn stone wheel, but visitors can almost always view vats in fermentation, and can often taste mezcal as it is just completing distillation. For a sweet treat, ask to try the herbal or fruity *cremas* (liqueurs), spiked with espadin to 14% ABV.

CASA HERRADURA

Doña Gabriela Pena Lozada 405, Amatitán, Jalisco; www.herradura.com; +52 33 3942 3900

◆ Food   ◆ Tours   ◆ Bar
◆ Distillery ◆ Shop   ◆ Transport

One of the most unique aspects of a visit to this tequila distillery is that you can get there by a special train that allows visitors to take in the beautiful rolling hills and fields of blue agave in and around the valley of Tequila. It runs to and from Guadalajara, the central city in Jalisco, with three levels of VIP service for those who want a streamlined and upmarket visit to this large-scale operation. The experience takes a full day and includes a tour of the modern and colourful distillery as well as lunch with live music; tequila and cocktails are abundant throughout.

Walk-up tours are also offered at different levels for those who are staying in the region. Be sure to taste the premium tequilas, some of which are exclusively offered to guests visiting the premises.

THINGS TO DO NEARBY

Tacos Tacos
Where tequila flows there will be people hungry for tacos, which is exactly what is served up hot and fresh from this food stand near Casa Herradura on the street Dona Gabriela Pena Lozada.

Cementerio De Amatitán
A traditional Mexican cemetery, where the ornate monuments and beautiful colours show a distinct aspect of the local culture. Visitors are able to walk through at their leisure.

SIETE LEGUAS

Ave Independencia 360, San Felipe, Atotonilco, Jalisco; www.casasieteleguas.com; +52 391 917 0996

◆ Distillery   ◆ Transport
◆ Tours

Located along the main road in the town of Atotonilco El Alto, Siete Leguas is one of the most time-honoured tequila distilleries in Mexico, backed by 65 years of operating heritage. With staunch commitment to an authentic process and sourcing the highest-quality agave possible, there is pride in the air.

The distillery itself has two main areas: the smaller original distillery, and the larger adjacent addition. Chances are good that you'll see their horses in action pulling the tahona, a large stone wheel that crushes

cooked agave hearts. Each tour includes a tasting, which may end with a special bottle that they happen to be working on. A sample of all three expressions of tequila during the tasting is essential.

THINGS TO DO NEARBY

La Capilla
The bar in Tequila that agave nerds from all over the world make pilgrimage to, this highly acclaimed venue is famous for having created the Batanga cocktail: lime, coke and tequila.

Parque Reforma
A serene park, this landscaped area in Atotonilco El Alto offers shade and murals on the walls of an open-air museum. It makes a good place to explore local history.

LA ROJEÑA

José Cuervo 33, Centro, Tequila, Jalisco;
mundocuervo.com; +52 374 742 6717

◆ Food   ◆ Tours   ◆ Bar
◆ Distillery   ◆ Shop   ◆ Transport

As one of the oldest tequila houses, La Rojeña is an important place for historic reasons. The most iconic brand produced here is Jose Cuervo, and the tours offer an opportunity to taste your way through its premium tequilas that are rarely found outside Mexico. Customisable tours can include a demonstration of harvesting an agave heart, lunch, music, games and entertainment.

With a 250-year-old legacy, and the current best-selling tequila in the world, the Cuervo family's influence cannot be underestimated. It was largely because of their political action to get royal approval at the turn of the 17th century that tequila was able to flourish and become a global success story. Tasting the premium family reserve will change how you think about tequila.

THINGS TO DO NEARBY

La Cata
This highly regarded tequila tasting room and restaurant is popular among locals and visitors alike. It offers one of the best selections of the spirit in the world.
www.lacatatequila.com

Tacos Con Licho
A local stalwart for tacos, this food stand just south of the main highway on Filosofos St serves up the real deal. Aside from being delicious, it is well liked for being clean and hygienic.

SAUZA

Calle Luis Navarro 70, La Villa, Tequila, Jalisco;
www.casasauza.com; +52 374 742 1432

◆ Food   ◆ Tours   ◆ Bar
◆ Distillery   ◆ Shop

Casa Sauza offers a long list of tours at its tequila estate with optional add-ons such as three-course meals, visiting its antique bottle collection and having cocktails at the hacienda. The highly customisable experience offers everyone the opportunity to find the right fit, even if that includes arriving in a private helicopter.

Its impressively kept grounds offer a first-class view of the modern tequila industry. The list of brands produced on the property include Sauza, Tres Generaciones and Hornitos, all of which can be the focus of different tours.

On offer for all the branded tours is the opportunity to taste fresh agave juice, which is an experience as memorable and delicious as it is important in deepening your understanding of tequila.

THINGS TO DO NEARBY

Museo Los Abuelos
A charming museum exploring the history of the region with a focus on the agave and tequila industries. Inside, a small gift shop offers locally made crafts. *www. museolosabuelos.com*

Restaurante Fonda La Cholula
This restaurant is geared towards tourists who want to experience the authentic flavours of the region in a comfortable setting, often accompanied by live music. *www.lafondacholula.mx*

LA COFRADIA

Calle La Cofradia 1297, La Cofradia, Tequila,
Jalisco; tequilacofradia.com.mx; +52 374 742 6800

◆ Food   ◆ Tours   ◆ Bar
◆ Distillery ◆ Shop

Best known for its flagship brand Casa Noble,
La Cofradia distillery makes many tequilas, but
a visit to this estate is an immersive Mexican
experience rather than simply a brand push. It is something
of an agave theme park, with regional food, themed
lodgings and a large range of tours and experiences.

As well as tours and tastings, hands-on experiences include
harvesting agave, fermenting and distilling, and blending your
own bottle. Visitors can also design their own bottle and go
horse riding through agave fields.

THINGS TO DO NEARBY

El Meson Del Mezcal
Expect typical regional
food at very low prices
at this restaurant and bar,
which includes a generous
selection of Mexican
spirits to leisurely taste
your way through.

Mayahuel Landmark
This centrally located
monument is in honour
of the goddess of agave,
Mayahuel. It features
historical information
about the region and a
touristy photo opportunity.

**Tortas Ahogadas Donde
Tú Ya Chávez**
A small local cafe
specialising in the saucy
sandwich that the region is
known for. The cash-only
spot opens early morning
and closes mid-afternoon.

Balneario Los Patos
This public water park has
multiple pools where you
can relax and take a swim.
There's even a bar serving
beer, while the live DJs
create a hip environment.

The beautiful buildings and large rustic wooden furniture
create a Mexican wonderland of rich colour to wander
through and, within the estate, La Cofradia operates the
only hotel in the world that's integrated into a tequila
factory. Boutique cottages and barrel-shaped hotel pods are
available for overnight guests, and the full-service restaurant
and bar also mean it's a good destination for day-trippers.

Whether you come for the day or stay overnight, it's the
speciality activities like blending or designing a bottle that
are a once-in-a-lifetime opportunity.

NICARAGUA

How to ask for a spirit without mixers? Un trago solo, or 'un shot'

Signature spirit? Rum

What to order with your spirits? Coca-Cola or juice if the rum is white; nothing but ice if it's aged

Do: Say 'salud!' – good health – and raise your glass before you drink

Nicaragua's go-to spirit is rum, with one homegrown brand standing above the rest. Flor de Caña is one of the most-awarded premium rums in the world with a trophy room to prove it, and in 2017 it was named Global Rum Producer of the Year at the International Wine and Spirit Competition.

The story of this single-estate rum began in 1875, when Francisco Pellas left Genoa, Italy, for Nicaragua to take over his family's shipping company. But after Cornelius Vanderbilt gave us his plan to build a Nicaraguan inter-oceanic canal, in 1890 Pellas set up a sugar mill in the fertile volcanic soil around Chichigalpa. Today, after many trials and tribulations, it's run by the fifth generation of the family, Carlos Pellas.

The sugarcane spirit is influenced by terroir, technique and tradition and each country has its own style – Flor de Caña slow-ages its rum in American white oak barrels previously used to age bourbon to give it its complex flavours.

Nicaragua's bartenders blatantly borrowed from Cuba, adding Coca-Cola to rum and dubbing it a Nica Libre, so in 2006 there was a competition to create a national cocktail. The winning Macuá – named after a tropical bird – is strong, fruity and sweet, mixing white rum with guava and lemon juice, shaken and poured over ice, with sugar to taste.

While there's no shortage of bars serving top-quality rum, especially in popular tourist hangouts such as Granada and San Juan del Sur, the locals tend to drink their Flor de Caña – both white with mixers and aged sipping rum – en familia (with family) at fiestas.

FLOR DE CAÑA

Carretera a Chinadenga Km 120, Chichigalpa;
www.tourflordecana.com; +505 89 66 82 00

◆ Distillery ◆ Shop
◆ Tours

Nicaragua's premier distillery has an undeniably spectacular location, sitting among tall green shoots of sugarcane under the still-smoking San Cristóbal volcano. Its 90-minute tour is rum 101, as you're guided around six interactive stations showcasing more than 125 years and five generations of award-winning rum-making.

Proceedings start with a look at the 19th-century train that used to transport molasses to the distillery, and end at a small museum inside the world's largest rum barrel. In between, there's a rundown of the family-run company's history, before a visit to the cellars and the Family Reserve, where the finest rums are stored, for Flor de Caña's signature sensorial tasting session. You'll explore the colour, from crystal clear to rich amber, the aroma and finally the taste of the distillery's fine aged rums, with a shot of Rum Centenario 18 and Gran Reserva 7 to finish.

Flor de Caña still handcrafts its barrels without nails or glue, using plantain leaves to seal the American white oak barrels, and its rums are naturally slow-aged without sugar or additives, then five-times distilled using 100% renewable energy.

If you're serious about rum, sign up for the VIP tour, which gets you a private guide, a tasting of the distillery's longer-aged rums and a personalised bottle of 18-year-old rum to take home.

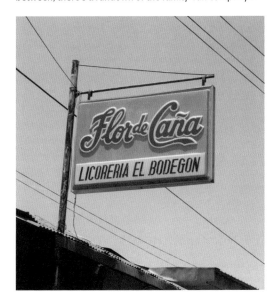

THINGS TO DO NEARBY

Las Peñitas
When the cities sizzle, head to the coast and the white-sand beaches of Las Peñitas, where the gentle rollers are ideal for novice surfers.

Reserva Natural Isla Juan Venado
The sandy beaches and black mangroves of this nature reserve are a haven for wildlife, including a bevy of birds and nesting turtles from July to January.

Léon
The former capital has the lively feel of a university city and the biggest cathedral in Central America, as well as numerous colonial churches and quirky museums.

Cerro Negro
Adrenaline-seekers can don an orange jumpsuit and volcano-board at high speed down the black ash slopes of the still-active Cerro Negro volcano.
leon.quetzaltrekkers.org

PERU

How to ask for a spirit without mixers? Un trago puro
Signature spirit? Pisco
What to order with your spirits? Cancha (roasted and salted giant corn)
Do look your drinking partner in the eye when you say salud (cheers) – it's bad luck otherwise

The story of pisco, Peru's national spirit, begins in 1553, when grape vines arrived in the luggage of a Spanish conquistador who intended to make his own wine, first planting them in the Andes and then, with more success, in the sun-baked coastal valley of Ica. No one knows for certain how the brandy-like pisco came about. One theory is that when Spain imposed heavy taxes on South American wine, the locals turned to distilling, fermenting the grape must in the local clay vessels to create a spirit that became known as 'pisco', after the valley, the vessels and the port from where it was shipped.

Pisco was all the rage in San Francisco during the California Gold Rush (when many Peruvians immigrated there to seek their fortunes), but post-Prohibition it was consigned to oblivion, at best seen as a worker's tipple. Now it's undergoing a renaissance with mixologists worldwide, including in the capital's trendy cocktail bars. Always popular along the south coast, now it's overtaken wine, beer and whisky as the drink of choice for young Limeños.

Peru's Ruta del Pisco is centred on Ica's small, artisanal distilleries that still use traditional methods and adhere to strict rules: pisco must be distilled from wine from one or more of eight grape varietals, should be single distilled in a copper still, distilled to proof and must remain unaltered and unaged.

It's the key ingredient in the ubiquitous Pisco Sour, along with egg white, lime and a dash of Angostura bitters, or the lighter Chilcano, paired with ginger ale and a squeeze of lime that locals drink from lunchtime onwards.

Neighbouring Chile also claims pisco – and the Pisco Sour – as its own. But in 2013, Peru won a major battle in this long-standing war when the European Commission ruled that it originated in Pisco, Peru.

■ **BAR**

MUSEO DEL PISCO

Santa Catalina Ancha 398, Cuzco, Peru;
www.museodelpisco.org; +51 84 262 709

◆ Food   ◆ Shop   ◆ Transport
◆ Tours   ◆ Bar

Founded by three passionate 'pisqueros' in 2012, there are now four Museo del Pisco branches (one other in Arequipa and two in Lima) but the original in Cuzco is still the best place for everything pisco-related.

Postcards explain the distillation process and the subtle differences between the three types of pisco, while Tasting Immersions take you on a pisco journey, by geography, distillery or grape. The bar serves local tapas and there's live music every night from 9pm.

You can learn to rustle up your own pisco sour with a master mixologist, or try one of their creative cocktails such as the Cocamanto, with coca leaf-macerated pisco, goldenberry juice, lime juice and ginger syrup, topped with ginger ale.

THINGS TO DO NEARBY

Peruvian Tasting Explorer
Take a sensory voyage of discovery around three of Peru's flagship products at Cuzco's ChocoMuseo and Museo del Café, rounding off at the Museo del Pisco.
www.museodelpisco.org

San Pedro Market
There's everything from exotic fruit and freeze-dried potatoes to maca root (Andean ginseng) and dragon's blood – the resin from the *croton lechleri* (dragon's blood tree).

HACIENDA LA CARAVEDO

Salas Guadalupe, Panamericana Sur alt. km 241, Fundo La Caravedo; www.lacaravedo.com; +51 1 711 7800

◆ Food   ◆ Distillery   ◆ Bar
◆ Tours   ◆ Shop

Founded in 1684, Hacienda La Caravedo is the oldest working distillery in the Americas, in Peru's arid coastal desert region near the town of Pisco. Home to award-winning Pisco Portón, it is two distilleries in one: the original with its ancient falcas – subterranean stills encased in brick – where distillation runs on gravity, and a state-of-the-art facility that uses Cognac-style alembic copper stills.

Officially, there are eight grape varietals that can be used in pisco; *puro* (pure) is made from one, while *acholado* is a blend of two or more, and *mosto verde* is made with grapes that haven't fully fermented. After discovering the pisco process you'll get a taste of Caravedo's premium pisco *puros*, developed by master distiller Johnny Schuler, regarded as the world's leading authority on Peruvian pisco.

THINGS TO DO NEARBY

Nazca Lines
Etched into the parched earth, the best views of these mysterious geoglyph lines are from the air, or get up close to three of the figures from the Mirador Observation Tower.

Ballestas Islands
The rocky cliffs of this mini-Galapagos are covered in thousands of seabirds, including the Peruvian booby and Guanay cormorant, along with Humboldt penguins and sea lions.

USA

How to ask for a drink without mixers? Neat, please
Signature spirit? Whiskey and bourbon, often in expertly crafted cocktails
What to order with your spirits? Elevated bar food, like ground chuck hamburgers or truffle mac and cheese
Do: Tip $1 per drink when ordering from a bar; table service warrants a 20% tip on the total bill

What's the trendiest word in an American barkeep's dictionary? It's probably 'speakeasy' – a secret liquor outfit open during the Prohibition. The recent resurgence of faux-clandestine watering holes has been so pronounced in the past decade that it's starting to feel like there are just as many hidden bars as there are establishments in plain sight. Whatever the gimmick – bouncers in suspenders, passwords to enter, or slippery bookcases – the throwback to the 1920s is a fun way to couch the US's rampant cocktail craze. Another trendy term, 'mixology', comes to mind, which sounds like your bartender had to earn a doctorate before stirring your beverage.

America has entered a golden age of home-grown spirits – customers are not only interested in the provenance of what they imbibe, but they want to understand its method and materials. Everyone's reaching for the top of the shelf, too. And it's not just whiskey and bourbon that are riding high; gin drinking is also on the rise, and there are dozens of distilleries experimenting with unusual spirits – moonshine, too, is being resurrected.

Yet historically the nation's relationship with alcohol could best be described as complicated. America's foundation was laid by pilgrims seeking religious freedom, because England was just too profane. However, by the time the first settlers overcame frostbite, a rum distillery had opened in every colony along the Atlantic Coast – rum was Boston's most profitable industry by the end of the 1600s. That so-called Tea Party of theirs? Yeah, that was alcohol.

In the 1800s, immigrants pushed westward to fulfil their Manifest Destiny, and the bourbon industry took off in Kentucky. But by the end of the century the moral core of the country was rotting – poisoned by what had become an overindulgence in alcohol, or so said the voices of the Temperance Movement who dug up the ghosts of pilgrims

"We are watching what has traditionally been an oligopoly bloom into a thriving market full of diverse ideas, approaches, and innovations"
– BRYAN DAVIES, LOST SPIRITS

TOP 5 SPIRITS

- **1776 Rye** James E. Pepper Distillery, Kentucky
- **Abomination, Crying of the Puma Malt** Lost Spirits Distillery, California
- **Breakfast Gin** FEW Spirits, Illinois
- **Vodka** New Deal Distillery, Oregon
- **Blade & Bow Bourbon** Stitzle-Weller Distillery, Kentucky

past and pushed America towards its infamous Prohibition. From 1920 to 1933 America was dry. Enter the speakeasy – historians believe there were anywhere from 30,000 to 100,000 in New York City alone – and moonshine, or mash liquor, produced illicitly in kind with high alcoholic proofs. The ban may have been a win for conservative citizens, but the dissolution of one of the country's pillars of industry meant a stark reduction in tax money the government could acquire, which ultimately led to the Great Depression.

After the austerity of World War II, alcohol resumed its place as a fashionable fixture of the American life (cue Don Draper and his whiskey). While the trajectory hasn't been perfectly linear – the US did have its 'bigger is better' moment in the 1950s and beyond – the country is now firmly aboard the craft distillery express, producing some of the best tipples in the world and regularly winning awards at international spirits competitions.

CHARBAY DISTILLERY

3001 South State St 48, Ukiah, Mendocino;
www.charbay.com; +1-707-462-2249

◆ Distillery   ◆ Transport
◆ Tours

Distilling and winemaking have been in the blood of the Karakasevic family for more than 250 years. Their story starts in former Yugoslavia, but since 1983 they have been distilling in Californian wine country as Charbay – given their location, it's no surprise that their reputation was founded on caramel-and-toasty-vanilla-hinted brandies. The family is especially proud of their alambic charentais pot stills.

More recently vodka, whiskey, rum and black walnut liqueur have been added to the production line. Tour Charbay's distillery (by appointment), set in an unpresuming industrial space in a Mendocino village, and you'll learn about the passion that goes into the family's victuals. Its vodkas – including green tea and blood orange flavoured – are award winning; but don't miss the green tea, white wine and brandy aperitif.

THINGS TO DO NEARBY

Wine tasting
Around Charbay there are more than 500 wineries, from back-alley operations to some of the world's biggest names in wine. Visiting is one of the area's greatest experiences.
www.mendowine.com

Napa Valley Tequila Train
The ultimate in luxury, this rolling restaurant takes you through the beautiful Napa countryside. Along the way, you'll sample local fare and try some of the world's best tequilas.
www.winetrain.com

HANGAR 1

2505 Monarch St, Alameda, California;
www.hangarone.com; +1-510-871-4951

◆ Distillery ◆ Shop
◆ Tours ◆ Transport

Hangar 1's head chemist Caley Shoemaker cut her teeth on whiskey at Stranahan's in Colorado, but at this Bay Area boutique distillery it's vodka in the stills. Aromatic, farm-foraged ingredients infuse the spirits' flavours with notes of fruit. Equally spiriting are the sweeping San Francisco views across the water that visitors are treated to as they sip their taste-testing samples.

No visit would be complete without trying the Hangar 1 Fog Point flight, called the Aviation School, which takes a wine tasting approach to vodka swigging. The session starts with a straight vodka, then graduates through infusions – including a California rosé blend – and culminates with the illumination of an abstract concept: 'water terroir', which is the idea that fog and dew can have different flavour profiles.

THINGS TO DO NEARBY

Rake at Admiral Maltings
Swap distilling for brewing at the Admiral Maltings, whose bar, the Rake, is a low-key space overlooking the malting room. More than 20 beers are on draft. *www.admiralmaltings. com/#rake*

Robert W Crown Memorial State Beach
At this quiet spot it's hard to believe you're less than 10 miles as the crow flies from central San Francisco – until you look up and see the skyline. *www.ebparks. org/parks/crown_beach*

DRY DIGGINGS DISTILLERY

5050 Robert J Mathews Pkwy, El Dorado Hills, California;
www.drydiggingsdistillery.com; +1-916-542-1700

◆ Distillery ◆ Shop ◆ Transport
◆ Tours ◆ Bar

Located in the beautiful rolling hills near Northern California's Gold Country, Dry Diggings Distillery is building a strong name for itself – not just in California, but across the US. The main focus here is on connecting locally produced fruits and grains with uniquely Californian takes on vodka, whiskey, brandy and bourbon.

Gold Country is an unexpected treat for visitors – it's less visited than California's Wine Country, but you can still find amazing wine and spirits here, plus there's easy access to

THINGS TO DO NEARBY

Calaveras Big Trees State Park
Commune with the giant sequoias before heading out for an afternoon paddle on the North Fork tributary of the Stanislaus River. **www.parks.ca. gov/bigtrees**

Lake Tahoe
Two hours west of Dry Diggings, crystal-clear Lake Tahoe provide a million-and-one adventures by water. Come in winter to ski the Sierra Nevada's best resorts, such as Heavenly. **www.visitinglaketahoe.com**

Yosemite National Park
Cruise through Gold Country on a long day trip to this remarkable national park with its majestic granite domes, cascading waterfalls and spectacular vistas at every corner. **www.nps.gov/yose**

Highway 49
For a day of shopping and food sampling, head down historic Highway 49 to the main Gold Country towns of Auburn, Coloma, Placerville and Sutters Creek.

the Sierra Nevada Mountains, Lake Tahoe and Yosemite National Park. Not far from the Dry Diggings tasting room you'll find awesome shopping for jewellery, antiques and locally made crafts and fine art in the historic township of Placerville. The town started out as a gold mining camp on Hangtown Creek in 1848. The locals named it Old Dry Diggins, finally changing the name to Placerville in 1854 after millions were taken from nearby mines.

OLD HARBOR DISTILLING CO

270 17th St, San Diego, California; www.oldharbor
distilling.com; info@oldharbordistilling.com

◆ Distillery ◆ Shop
◆ Tours ◆ Transport

San Diego's craft booze scene was founded on beer, but today a fast-paced evolution is adding off-the-charts spirits to the city's much-lauded brewing scene. Old Harbor Distilling Co was one of the city's first liquor distilleries and is still one of its best-loved.

Located in the steampunk-inspired warehouse district known as the East Village, Old Harbor's signature offerings include San Miguel Southwestern gin, flavoured with locally grown lime, cucumber, cilantro and sage, and the local favourite, Navy Strength rum, which has superb notes of vanilla and coconut, with dark molasses and herbal elements of earth and grass. Try Old Harbor's Ampersand cold-pressed coffee liqueur with gin, rum, simple syrup and bitters for a radical take on a traditional Old Fashioned.

THINGS TO DO NEARBY

Tijuana
Hopping across the border to the ever-evolving Mexican town of Tijuana is a must for any visitor to southern California.

Balboa Park
Art and nature collide in San Diego's Balboa Park – home to museums, performing arts venues, gardens, pop-up dance exhibitions and a million ultra-tanned roller skaters. *www.balboapark.org*

LOST SPIRITS

1235 E 6th St, Los Angeles, California;
www.lostspirits.net; +1-213-505-2425

◆ Distillery ◆ Shop
◆ Tours ◆ Transport

'The artistic application of genetic engineering makes me laugh,' says Bryan Davis, who definitely has more fun at work than you do. In October 2014, Davis recreated the chemical signature of 20-year-old Port Morant rum in a laboratory in only six days. The discovery quite literally disrupted the spirits industry and Silicon Valley came a-knockin'. Now in LA, Davis' distillery-cum-laboratory has evolved into a speakeasy wonderland offering real-deal tours for enthusiasts.

It's safe to say that it'll be the most memorable distillery visit of your life – think *Island of Dr Moreau* meets *Heart of Darkness* with a generous smattering of *Charlie and the Chocolate Factory*. And, of course, you'll exit through the gift shop where you can purchase Davis' engineered tipples.

THINGS TO DO NEARBY

OUE Skyspace
LA's version of the Empire State Building has an observation deck with a yoga studio, a Hollywood museum, and a glass slide that protrudes 1000ft above ground. *www.oue-skyspace.com*

ROW DLTA
Reclaiming one of the last derelict quarters of Downtown Los Angeles, ROW is a redevelopment project turning empty factory space into a hip collection of small brands. *www.rowdtla.com*

BRECKENRIDGE DISTILLERY

1925 Airport Rd, Breckenridge, Colorado;
www.breckenridgedistillery.com; +1-970-547-9759

◆ Food   ◆ Tours   ◆ Bar
◆ Distillery ◆ Shop   ◆ Transport

Pulling its inspiration from the skyrocketing Rocky Mountains, Breckenridge Distillery is turning heads in the whiskey world and disrupting an industry that's been around for hundreds of years in the US.

The key is the water from the Blue River, which runs clear with unique mineral components of dolomite, limestone and quartz, giving this craft bourbon a unique structured mouth and strong finish. The distillery makes vodka, rum and gin too, but its whiskey is the real star of the show.

You'll want to stay after the free tour and tasting to have a pig roast on the wide-open patio and play some cornhole. Breckenridge Distillery's owner and chief mixologist are both huge Star Wars fans: try the Obi Wan Old Fashioned, made with Breckenridge bourbon and in-house whiskey bitters.

THINGS TO DO NEARBY

Breckenridge Ski Resort
Breckenridge has some of North America's best skiing and snowboarding with glorious mountain peaks topping 12,998ft. Summer fun includes alpine rollercoasters and biking.
www.breckenridge.com

Mohawk Lakes Trail
This steep trail takes you past a series of waterfalls, an abandoned turn-of-the-century mine and about a million wildflowers to a picture-perfect alpine lake.

MONTANYA DISTILLERS

212 Elk Ave, Crested Butte, Colorado;
www.montanyarum.com; +1-970-799-3206

◆ Food   ◆ Tours   ◆ Bar
◆ Distillery ◆ Shop   ◆ Transport

For years, rum-making has been an all-boys club, but Montanya's co-owner Karen Hoshkin is trying to change that image through her founding role in the Women's Distillery Guild, which is fostering unique talents. Her distillery uses non-GMO sugar cane from Louisiana farmers and is run on 100% wind power. Whiskey-barrel aging and water sourced from local snowmelt-fed aquifers add a distinct finish to Montanya's well-structured and perfectly balanced rum.

One of its biggest draws is the idyllic setting 9000ft above sea level in one of America's last great ski towns, Crested Butte.

Montanya's tasting room ignites the Rocky Mountain nights with live bluegrass music, craft cocktails and excellent farm-to-table bites. Tours are free, but stay longer to do a full rum flight and grab a bowl of pho or ramen – perfect après ski.

THINGS TO DO NEARBY

Crested Butte Mountain Resort
In winter you'll get some of Colorado's most extreme ski runs; in summer it's about mountain-biking – take the lift up and ride back into town. *www.skicb.com*

Three Lakes Trail
This iconic trail amid a massive forest of quaking aspen outside Crested Butte takes you past thundering waterfalls to three pristine alpine lakes.

STRANAHAN'S

200 South Kalamath St, Denver, Colorado;
www.stranahans.com; +1-303-296-7440

◆ Distillery ◆ Shop ◆ Transport
◆ Tours ◆ Bar

THINGS TO DO NEARBY

Denver Art Museum
This visually arresting museum has rotating multimedia exhibits, world-class contemporary art and one of the US's finest collections of Western art. *www. denverartmuseum.org*

Bike Denver
Denver is a very bike-friendly city. Grab a bikeshare and head out to explore the 85 miles of paved bike trails that run along waterways such as Platte River and Cherry Creek. *www.bikedenver.org*

Jefferson County Open Space parks
The Open Space system encompasses 54,000 acres of preserved land – great for year-round hiking and just minutes from downtown Denver. *www.jeffco.us/open-space*

Colorado Spirits Trail
There are more than 70 distilleries in Colorado and this guided route covers 50 of the best; far-off ones, in places like Ouray and Palisade, offer unique tippling adventures. *www. coloradospiritstrail.com*

A groundbreaker in every sense of the word, Stranahan's started in 2004 with just three employees. It was Colorado's first distillery and, if you can believe it, just the 22nd recipient of a distilling permit in the United States since the days of prohibition.

It is now a juggernaut of an operation with an uproarious steampunk-meets-Wild-West bar, and one of America's best-loved single malt whiskies, yet Stranahan's still manages to hold on to its handcrafted roots and attention to detail.

On the tasting tour you will learn about the entire distillation process, which starts with 100% Colorado malt barley that's milled on-site and some of the world's best spring water sourced nearby in Eldorado Springs. The process ends with ageing in new white American oak barrels. The

unique flavour profile has notes of vanilla, oak and even Werther's caramel. Master distiller Rob Dietrich is working hard to establish an internationally recognised category for American Single Malts – as Scotland and Japan have done.

Stranahan's has a cult following in Colorado. People camp out for days in the Colorado cold to get Rob's special small batch in December, which he calls 'Snowflake'. It's a new flavour every year so try it if you can – no two are alike.

HAWAII SEA SPIRITS

4051 Omaopio Rd, Kula, Maui, Hawaii;
www.hawaiiseaspirits.com; +1-808-877-0009

◆ Food   ◆ Tours
◆ Distillery   ◆ Shop

THINGS TO DO NEARBY

Surfing Goat Dairy
This neighbouring farm produces more than 30 types of goat-milk cheeses, plus goat-milk chocolate truffles. Take a tour to feed the goats and try the cheese. *www.surfinggoatdairy.com*

Ulupalakua Vineyards
Maui's only winery produces estate-grown table wines and pineapple wines from island fruit. The vineyard's tasting room was once a vacation cottage for Hawaii's King Kalākaua. *www.mauiwine.com*

Paia
Shop the boutiques, stop for coffee or fresh fish, or check out the surfers challenging the waves in this funky North Shore town. *www.paiamaui.com*

Haleakalā National Park
Drive the winding road up Maui's volcano to watch sunrise or sunset from the 10,000ft Haleakalā summit – a bucket-list experience. *www.nps.gov/hale*

Sugar cane was once a traditional crop across Hawaii, contributing a significant component of the islands' economy for much of the 19th and 20th centuries. The islands' last commercial sugar plantation closed in 2016, but the crop has found a new life on Maui thanks to the family who launched Hawaii Sea Spirits in 2013.

On 80 acres of rolling red-earth farmland near Maui's Upcountry town of Kula, the distillery is organically growing more than 30 species of Polynesian sugar cane and crafting vodka from a blend of this sugar coupled with desalinated deep-sea water. The solar-powered facility produces its spirits in a 60ft-tall column still that rises over the fields, and its Ocean Vodka is put on the shelves in unusual blue glass bottles modelled after Hawaii's historic glass fishing net floats.

The property has great views across the island and daily tours include a walk through the sugar cane fields, a guided visit to the distillery for an education on its production process, and tastings of its vodka – a delicious way to experience the island's spirit of aloha.

FEW SPIRITS

918 Chicago Ave, Evanston, Illinois;
www.fewspirits.com; +1-847-920-8628

◆ Food ◆ Tours ◆ Bar
◆ Distillery ◆ Shop ◆ Transport

First you have to find FEW Spirits, which hides in an alleyway in Evanston, Chicago's neighbour 15 miles to the north. The wee distillery occupies a low, white-washed building that used to be a chop shop and stripped illicit automobiles of their parts. It still feels clandestine, and though the gin and whiskey produced here are perfectly legal, that's only because distiller Paul Hletko got a century-old prohibition law revoked so he could begin operations in 2011.

Evanston was a hub of the Women's Christian Temperance Movement, launched in the late 1800s and presided over by

THINGS TO DO NEARBY

American Toby Jug Museum
This quirky venue in Evanston holds the world's largest collection of character-shaped jugs. See Barack Obama, Mick Jagger and R2-D2 among the 8000 pieces on display here.
www.tobyjugmuseum.com

Peckish Pig
Trivia nights, live jazz, lamb burgers with cumin French fries, and nine house-made ales are on tap at this brewpub close to FEW distillery, amid homey, exposed-brick environs.
www.thepeckishpig.com

Baha'i House of Worship
This striking white structure, surrounded by public gardens, is one of nine temples belonging to the monotheistic Baha'i faith. Guests are free to explore the complex.
www.bahai.us/bahai-temple

Grosse Point Lighthouse
Built in 1873 after several ships sunk in the shallow waters of Lake Michigan just offshore, this picture-perfect beacon in Evanston is now a national landmark. *www. grossepointlighthouse.net*

Frances Elizabeth Willard (note the initials). Thanks to Hletko the town is dry no more. FEW makes just a handful of spirits including a rye whiskey, bourbon whiskey and single-malt, Scottish-style whiskey. The gin line-up is a smoky barrel-aged gin and orange-y breakfast gin infused with Earl Grey tea.

The no-frills tasting room lets you sample widely. Come for the Thursday vinyl nights to sip bourbon to a DJ's soul tunes.

BUFFALO TRACE DISTILLERY

113 Great Buffalo Trace, Frankfort, Kentucky;
www.buffalotrace.com; +1-800-654-8471

◆ Food ◆ Tours
◆ Distillery ◆ Shop

Even on a bustling tour, the dark and cramped confines of Warehouse C will give you pause. The 24,000 weathered oak barrels here, stacked high across several floors, are portals to the past, each date-stamped vessel waiting patiently to share the secrets of whiskies distilled in years and decades past. On a breezy day you might even catch the scent of bourbon floating past, a product of evaporation poetically dubbed the Angel's Share.

The name Buffalo Trace comes from the fact that the distillery borders a path, or trace, once travelled by buffalo to reach the Kentucky River. Distilling began on this Frankfort property in the mid-1800s, with innovative craftsmen producing quality bourbons here over ensuing decades. Their names – Col EH Taylor, George T Stagg, Pappy Van Winkle and Albert Blanton – grace the labels of the finest brands made on-site today. The Sazerac Company purchased the distillery in 1992 and introduced its flagship Buffalo Trace Bourbon in 1999. Kentucky's pure, nutrient-filled limestone water is a prized ingredient.

Tours and tastings are free. Many of the hard-to-get brands, including the elusive Pappy Van Winkle – produced in partnership with the Van Winkle family – are not available for tasting or purchase here. But no matter, the Buffalo Trace Bourbon is always a welcome gift. Especially if the recipient is you.

THINGS TO DO NEARBY

Proof on Main
The wild art inside this devilishly fun bar flips from intriguing to mind-bending after that second Buffalo Trace cocktail. Trust us.
www.proofonmain.com

Crittenden Rawlings
Gentlemen come to this classic Midway menswear store to dapper up their wardrobe before a big Kentucky horse race – the sports coats are affordable, and classic Kentucky. *www. crittendenrawlings.com*

Keeneland
You might see champions while touring these racing grounds, and world-class races are a fine distraction in April and October.
www.keeneland.com

Brown Hotel
Birthplace of the hot brown sandwich (a deliciously messy turkey sandwich with bacon and Mornay sauce), this Louisville grand dame is also a festive spot for sipping bourbon.
www.brownhotel.com

JAMES E PEPPER

1228-100 Manchester St, Lexington, Kentucky;
www.jamesepepper.com; +1-859-309-3230

◆ Distillery ◆ Shop
◆ Tours ◆ Bar

A passion for history and an expertise in whiskey was a potent cocktail for Amir Peay. It led him from his home in Maryland down to Lexington, Kentucky, where he stumbled upon the relics of the James E Pepper bourbon empire, which thrived for more than a century before falling into obscurity. Peay resurrected the brand in 2008, making boutique batches of whiskey and rye under the Pepper name and winning coveted blind-tasting competitions, including a Double Gold medal at both the San Francisco and New York City World Spirits Competitions.

In the summer of 2018, Peay reopened the distillery on its original site and unearthed the site's limestone spring, both of which had been abandoned for more than 50 years. Today, a visit not only includes a detailed look at traditional bourbon-making methods, but offers insights

THINGS TO DO NEARBY

Crank & Boom
Have your bourbon by the scoop instead of the glass at Lexington's favourite ice-creamery, right next door to the James E Pepper distillery.
www.crankandboom.com

Wallace Station
James Beard award–nominee Ouita Michel holds court as regional Kentucky's top restaurateur. Her no-frills sandwich shop slings dripping meat melts and homemade cookies.
www.wallacestation.com

Gainesway
A tour of Gainesway, owned by the Beck family of South African wine fame, will illuminate the ultra-lucrative world of racing and selective breeding.
www.gainesway.com

Dudley's On Short
When the horse racing bigwigs are in town, they all dine at this Lexington institution, which has been showcasing local flavours with a French twist for almost 40 years.
www.dudleysonshort.com

into the history of local spirit production from the American Revolution, through the Prohibition Era, and up to the 1950s. You'll also learn about the Colonel himself – a larger-than-life horseman who proudly carried on the distilling traditions of his grandfather, but preferred socialising with American industrialists in New York City.

Try the Old Fashioned, mixed on-site, which – according to legend – was invented as a tribute to the Colonel. Buy a bottle of the 1776 rye to continue the experience at home.

BOURBON 101

Although the name is French in origin, bourbon – like whiskey – was probably introduced to the US by Scottish immigrants in the 1700s. The word 'bourbon' surfaced in the 1800s around the same time the area of present-day Kentucky was established as the best place to create what would become America's trademark tipple.

The state's name roughly means 'the prairie field' in the Iroquois language and its lands fattened hordes of grazing animals. It turns out a massive substructure of limestone lurked beneath Kentucky, giving extra potency to the local grass (bluegrass!) and purifying the artesian water with its porous stone. Good water and potent corn are the cornerstone ingredients of bourbon; pour it in a new, charred oak barrel, wait two years and voila: a world-class spirit is born. Today, Kentucky is still the source of 95% of the world's bourbon supply.

But it's been a bumpy road for bourbon from farmer's brew to esteemed beverage. Few industries have ridden America's volatile swing of the industrial pendulum like bourbon distillation, which has savoured the perks of being a cherished luxury item and also experienced the bitterness of having the government quash its very existence.

First came the Whiskey Rebellion in the 1790s when distillers quarrelled with the government for imposing massive excise taxes. Then, of course, there was the Prohibition, which pushed production underground for all of the 1920s. Only a handful of distilleries in the US were allowed to produce bourbon for medicinal purposes at the time, leaving hundreds of distillers bankrupt.

By the 1960s a reverence for bourbon was restored, and Congress declared it a 'distinctive product of the United States'. Its popularity has been cyclical over the past five decades, but in 2009 an interest in imbibing top-shelf bourbon soared (a reaction to the global financial crisis, perhaps?) – the industry has experienced exponential growth ever since.

Kentucky Bourbon Trail

Originally created by the Kentucky Distillers' Association as a marketing tool to help stimulate interest at a time when sales of the spirit were slumping, the Kentucky Bourbon Trail has now become a veritable pilgrimage, in the way people flock to Bordeaux or Napa to taste the literal fruits of vintners' labour.

Today the trail links both big and boutique distilleries and there are around two-dozen pitstops spread across the entirety of Kentucky, from the Tennessee border all the way to Cincinnati, illuminating the importance of the state's massive amount of rippling subterranean limestone in creating a world-class beverage.

You need roughly a long weekend to properly dig into Kentucky's finest distilleries, pairing a few of the bigger name brands like Buffalo Trace and Maker's Mark with some smaller brands that warrant discovery; perhaps the all-female-owned Jeptha Creed? Fly into Louisville and out of Cincinnati if you don't want to backtrack, making sure to stop in Lexington on the way to dip into the world of horse racing and rearing, a passion in Kentucky.

In order to properly indulge and really get the most out of each tasting, it would be worth booking a chauffeured tour with Mint Julep (www.mintjuleptours.com) based out of Louisville. The service has partnered with the distilleries on the trail to offer one-of-a-kind experiences – they're well worth the price – and having a personal driver is a better plan than trying to moderate yourself in the tasting room.

BY BRANDON PRESSER

The Trail

1. **Four Roses Distillery** –Lawrenceburg, KY
2. **Heaven Hill** –Bardstown, KY
3. **Woodford Reserve** –Versailles, KY
4. **Wild Turkey** –Lawrenceburg, KY
5. **Town Branch**–Lexington, KY
6. **Angel's Envy** –Louisville, KY
7. **Jim Beam** –Clermont, KY
8. **O.Z. Tyler** –Owensboro, KY
9. **Lux Row** –Bardstown, KY
10. **Old Forester** –Louisville, KY
11. **Maker's Mark** –Loretto, KY
12. **Bulleit**–Louisville, KY
13. **Evan Williams** –Louisville, KY
14. **Bardstown Bourbon Company** –Bardstown, KY

JEPTHA CREED

500 Gordon Lane, Shelbyville, Kentucky;
www.jepthacreed.com; +1-502-487-5007

◆ Food   ◆ Tours   ◆ Bar
◆ Distillery   ◆ Shop

While Joyce Nethery was cooking up plastic monomers at a chemical engineering plant, she never dreamed that she'd one day run the only all-female-owned spirits distillery in the heart of Kentucky bourbon country. It was a circuitous path, which included a stint as a high-school chemistry teacher, but after graduating from a five-day course at Moonshine University (yes, that place really exists), her passion for engineering was rekindled. She approached her then 19-year-old daughter about partnering on a bourbon project, and the rest is history.

Jeptha Creed uses a special red-tinged varietal of corn known as Bloody Butcher that's grown in the distillery's backyard for the full 'ground-to-glass' experience. The organic produce is the secret sauce that gives their two-year four-grain mash its exceptional flavour and taste. After your tour, pause in the capacious bar for a seasonal cocktail;

although the Nethery family has made its name with boutique bourbon, its vodka (the only one on the planet made exclusively from 100% Bloody Butcher) is top-shelf too – it's the official vodka of the Kentucky Derby.

THINGS TO DO NEARBY

Louisville Mega Cavern
The rich network of Kentucky's subterranean limestone is largely responsible for giving the region's bourbon is great taste – there are also massive cave systems to explore, including the so-called Mega Cavern, where you can zip line underground. *www. louisvillemegacavern.com*

21c Museum Hotel
Originally conceived as a project to help revitalise Louisville's bleak downtown streets, this accommodation-cum-gallery concept has been such an undisputed hit that a handful of satellite properties have swung open their doors in other regional towns such as Cincinnati and Nashville. *www.21cmuseumhotels.com*

Hell Or High Water
Secreted in the basement of an historic building in Louisville's cobblestoned core, this speakeasy bar goes full-blown Prohibition-chic with suspender-ed waiters spinning sweet cocktails. Reservations recommended. *www. hellorhighwaterbar.com*

Monnik Beer Co.
Tired of bourbon? This brewery, in a working-class neighbourhood of Louisville, takes its beers as seriously as the surrounding distilleries – you can even opt into a tasting menu that pairs bar food with a flight of homemade brews. *www.monnikbeer.com*

STITZEL-WELLER DISTILLERY

3860 Fitzgerald Rd, Louisville, Kentucky; www.bulleit.
com/stitzel-weller-distillery; +1-502-810-3800

◆ Distillery   ◆ Shop
◆ Tours   ◆ Transport

Sparked by Thomas E Bulleit Jr's desire to revive his great-great-grandfather's high-rye whiskey recipe, America's favourite cocktail bourbon is neatly paired with an immersive distillery tour at the Stitzel-Weller compound. Every person that has visited the site over the past four decades has met gatekeeper Carroll Perry at the iron gates. He is so beloved, in fact, that the campus entryway was renamed in his honour: Perry Lane. Inside, visitors have guided access to the experiments lab and historic cooperage before reaching the tasting salon.

Try Stitzel-Weller's premium label, Blade and Bow Kentucky Straight Bourbon, which blends some of the distillery's original stock with younger whiskey using the solera method, an ageing technique typically found in the rum industry.

THINGS TO DO NEARBY

**Mammoth Cave
National Park**
Kentucky's bourbon prowess is largely due to its subterranean limestone, and Mammoth Cave lives up to its name: it's the longest limestone cave on the planet. ***www.nps.gov/maca***

Bar Vetti
Housed on the ground floor of a retro-mod apartment building, this haute pizza joint prides itself on fare wages, its diversity employment strategy, and brightly flavoured veggie starters. ***www.barvetti.com***

WOODFORD RESERVE

7855 McCracken Pike, Versailles, Kentucky;
www.woodfordreserve.com; +1-859-879-1812

◆ Food   ◆ Tours
◆ Distillery ◆ Shop

Thoroughbred racehorses graze on lush pastures in Woodford County, the landscape framed by tidy wooden fences. It's a fitting backdrop for the drive to Woodford Reserve, established in 1996 and named the presenting sponsor for the Kentucky Derby in 2018 – a five-year gig. The swanky horse-country vibe continues as you step into the stone-and-wood visitor's centre, where a sparkling fire adds intimacy to the glossy lounge and tasting room.

The distillery is a national historic landmark with a bourbon-making history stretching back to 1812. Tours swing past the distillery's copper pot stills and a 500ft-long gravity-fed barrel run. The one-hour option ends with samples of the Distiller's Select Kentucky Straight Bourbon and the Double Oaked Bourbon – the latter is a rich, twice-barrelled wonder.

THINGS TO DO NEARBY

Coolmore at Ashford Stud
Triple-Crown-winning race horse American Pharoah and other retired stallions get frisky with the world's most eligible mares at this stud farm, where you can take a tour. ***www. visithorsecountry.com***

Heirloom
This modern restaurant in the charming town of Midway serves delicious seasonal fare. Dishes run the gamut from spinach salad to crispy buttermilk-fried chicken. ***www.heirloommidway.com***

CASTLE & KEY

4445 McCracken Pike, Frankfort, Kentucky;
www.castleandkey.com; +1-859-873-2481

◆ Food   ◆ Tours   ◆ Bar
◆ Distillery   ◆ Shop

With a rich history dating back to 1887, Castle & Key's grounds were always envisaged as a destination for visitors; its manicured gardens and hundred-year-old mock castle created expressly to lure leisure travellers. A century later the site was abandoned and sat filled with nothing but cobwebs until 2014, when a lawyer with a bourbon hobby decided to turn his passion into his practice. The current spirits scientist – who makes everything from scratch on the 113-acre estate – is also Kentucky's first female bourbon master distiller since the Prohibition era.

The most recent addition to the estate's tourist-facing facilities is the transformation of the on-site train depot into the Taylorton Station Café, where visitors can stroll over to the ticket window and order cocktails and snacks.

THINGS TO DO NEARBY

Midway
A manicured manifestation of a Kentuckian one-horse town, Midway is an idyllic pit stop. Its main street features a popcorn shop, soda fountain, bakery, art gallery and antiques. *www. meetmeinmidway.com*

Middle fork
A so-called 'kitchen bar', Middle Fork is lending Lexington's revitalised Distillery District some gravity. Diners regularly orbit for the ever-changing array of sharable plates. *www.middleforkkb.com*

VIKRE DISTILLERY

525 S Lake Ave, Duluth, Minnesota;
www.vikredistillery.com; +1-218-481-7401

- ◆ Food
- ◆ Tours
- ◆ Bar
- ◆ Distillery
- ◆ Shop
- ◆ Transport

Emily and Joel Vikre want you to taste northern Minnesota in their products, so they use grains from local farmers, water from Lake Superior crashing just outside the door, and botanicals they've foraged from the surrounding North Woods.

The distillery's aquavit is its masterwork. Generations of Norwegian and Swedish descendants live in the area, so these folks know their Scandinavian booze. Vikre's Øvrevann mends the typical caraway bite of aquavit with cardamom, pink peppercorn and citrus peels, while its Voyageur aquavit is aged in cognac barrels for a floral finish. The small distillery also cooks up gin, vodka and whiskey, all prime for sampling in the rustic cocktail room. Settle in at a barrel table, order an Aquavit Old Fashioned, and you're steeped in northern flavour.

THINGS TO DO NEARBY

Aerial Lift Bridge
The distillery sits right at the foot of Duluth's main landmark, the Aerial Lift Bridge, which raises its mighty arm frequently to let horn-bellowing cargo ships into port.

Duluth Experience
This company gets you into Duluth's renowned outdoor scene with tours paddling on Lake Superior and mountain biking on the Duluth Traverse. *www. theduluthexperience.com*

KINGS COUNTY DISTILLERY

299 Sands St, Brooklyn, New York;
www.kingscountydistillery.com; +1-347-689-4211

◆ Distillery ◆ Shop ◆ Transport
◆ Tours ◆ Bar

Kings County Distillery has two main buildings: the street-facing bar that looks like a castle, and the actual distillery that is just inside the Brooklyn Navy Yard. The historic buildings include many of the original details and are an architectural treat in and of themselves. The tour of the facility starts in the 'boozeum', which offers an account of distilling in the early United States, as well as specifically in New York City. Proudly, Kings County is the first whiskey distillery to open in the city since the end of prohibition.

THINGS TO DO NEARBY

Jane's Carousel
This ornate carousel is fun for people of all ages. It is situated on a park overlooking the river with streamlined views of lower Manhattan.
www.janescarousel.com

Vinegar Hill House
In an all-but-forgotten neighbourhood of Brooklyn, this gem of a restaurant offers the highest quality of new American cuisine, with beverages to match.
www.vinegarhillhouse.com

Building 92
Located in the Navy Yard with the distillery, this restored building houses a museum, with exhibitions about the history of the site.
www.brooklynnavyyard. org/visit/bldg-92

Brooklyn Bridge Park
A favourite perch for locals and tourists alike, this park is prime real estate for a picnic, photos of the NYC skyline and relaxing.
www.brooklynbridge park.org

The tour, which lasts about 90 minutes, goes into the nitty-gritty details of the artistry of distillation, as well as some of the science behind it. Production here is rooted in tradition, but stirred up a bit – like with its peated bourbon, which is a hybrid spirit honouring both bourbon and scotch.

The small distillery is operating continuously to keep up with demand, which means spirits with new age statements are being released almost every year. Its lineup of whiskies includes seasonal infusions such as grapefruit jalapeño and bitter chocolate; taste them neat or in a house cocktail.

NEW YORK DISTILLING COMPANY

79 Richardson St, Brooklyn, New York;
www.nydistilling.com; +1-718-412-0874

◆ Distillery   ◆ Shop   ◆ Transport
◆ Tours   ◆ Bar

A true urban distillery, this Brooklyn warehouse operation is sandwiched in between Greenpoint and Williamsburg – two bustling areas of what has become New York's most dynamic 'boro. Like most things in New York City, space is at a premium, meaning the tasting room is compact and right on the floor of the distillery. Its attached bar, The Shanty, is a local watering hole that offers cocktails made from the distillery's own line of gins and whiskies, as well as beer.

The vibe is decidedly industrial, modern and artist-driven, with occasional live music, film screenings and other events. To get the full experience, drink like the locals and opt for the beer and a shot deal, featuring the house pink gin served from an antique still.

THINGS TO DO NEARBY

MOFAD

Housed in a cute urban space, the Museum of Food and Drink is dedicated to rotating curated series plus special events that feature the food and drink culture of New York and beyond.
www.mofad.org

Union Pool

A performance venue and local dive bar, this Williamsburg institution also hides one of the best taco trucks in the city in its back yard.
www.union-pool.com

VAN BRUNT STILLHOUSE

6 Bay St, Brooklyn, New York;
www.vanbruntstillhouse.com; +1-718-852-6405

◆ Distillery   ◆ Shop   ◆ Transport
◆ Tours   ◆ Bar

In a quiet part of Brooklyn, a nondescript warehouse emits the sweet aroma of ageing whiskey. Speakeasy-like signs escort guests to an industrial-chic bar and tasting room. With accents of vintage glass and furniture fashioned from barrels, it feels like a secret hideaway in an otherwise uneventful part of town. The small distillery is just down the hall and can be seen through a glass window from the bar.

A sampling of Van Brunt's spirits – all whiskey – show a grain-forward flavour profile that is accomplished by using a lighter char on its barrels than most other brands. To get a sense of how important grain is to the operation, be sure to try Van Brunt's rye moonshine, made with heirloom danko rye.

THINGS TO DO NEARBY

Valentino Pier
This open-air waterfront park is a place to relax while taking in views of the Hudson River and snapping photos of Lady Liberty.
*www.nycgovparks.org/
parks/valentino-pier*

Fort Defiance
A mainstay for high-end American food and a thoughtful drinks program, this is the neighbourhood go-to for cocktails and a hearty meal.
*www.fortdefiance
brooklyn.com*

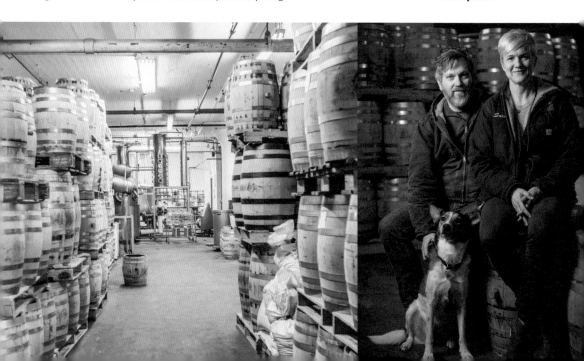

WIDOW JANE

214 Conover St, Brooklyn, New York;
www.widowjane.com; +1-347-225-0130

◆ Food   ◆ Tours   ◆ Bar
◆ Distillery   ◆ Shop   ◆ Transport

THINGS TO DO NEARBY

Hometown Bar-B-Que
Often referred to as New York's best barbecue restaurant, the rich, meat-focused menu is exactly what you want after a day of tasting whiskey.
www.hometown barbque.com

Red Hood Waterfront Museum
Built on an actual barge, this maritime museum is a visually impressive and interactive way to take in local history and lore.
www.waterfront museum.org

Red Hook Lobster Pound
The original go-to for lobsters and shellfish in New York City, this picnic-style restaurant is the place for a full lobster dinner.
www.redhooklobster.com

Steve's Key Lime Pie
With something of a cult following, the key lime pies and treats from this small shop are famous, and live up to the hype.
www.stevesauthentic.com

Unusually, Widow Jane is the by-product of Cacao Prieto – a small-batch chocolate factory that sources single-origin cacao beans to make a line of silky dairy-free bars. On a visit to its industrial production facility, it's the gorgeous German roaster and other machines used to make its beans-to-bar chocolate that you'll encounter first. This flows organically into the whiskey portion of the operation, creating a heavenly world of aromas.

There is a ton of education packed into this compact and highly efficient space in Brooklyn, but the small team at Widow Jane is welcoming and humble, creating a laid-back atmosphere that is completely free of pretension. One of the major points of pride behind the distillery's whiskey is using heirloom non-GMO corn as well as proprietary grains bred specifically for its small-batch spirits. Another hallmark of Widow Jane's flavour profile is using limestone water from the Hudson Valley to balance the alcohol of its spirits, some of which take inspiration from the chocolate business, such as the chocolate malt bourbon whiskey.

While the facility itself technically only includes the chocolate and whiskey production plus a tasting room, the company also runs a restaurant and bar next door where a full menu of small bites and cocktails is served daily. The generous line-up of whiskey is delicious from start to finish, but the 10-Year Bourbon is a must-try for its deep and rich flavour.

HILLROCK ESTATE DISTILLERY

408 Pooles Hill Road, Ancram, New York;
www.hillrockdistillery.com; +1-518-329-1023

◆ Distillery   ◆ Shop
◆ Tours   ◆ Bar

A small sign on a windy country road is the only indication Hillrock Estate exists in the hills of Hudson Valley. It may be easy to miss, but this high-end distillery is worth the journey. It's a field-to-glass operation that uses estate-grown grain and smokes its own malt, housed in buildings designed to mimic a 19th-century malt house – in the century before Prohibition, New York state was full of farm distilleries and produced half the US's barley and rye.

In addition to a particular fondness for rye-based spirits, the distillery is known for finishing its ultra-premium whiskies in fortified and dessert wine barrels, and for ageing its whiskey using the traditional solera method of fractional blending. Try the solera-aged whiskey for a unique flavour profile with hints of fortified wine on the finish.

THINGS TO DO NEARBY

Suarez Family Brewery
This laid-back brewery is known for crisp beers such as unfiltered lagers and clean pilsners, offered by the pint to drink in or by the growler for takeaway.
www.suarezfamily brewery.com

Fish & Game
Located in the newly trendy town of Hudson, this upscale restaurant is housed in a former blacksmith's shop. Local fare is the speciality here.
www.fishandgame hudson.com

HUDSON VALLEY DISTILLERY

1727 US Route 9, Germantown, New York;
www.hudsonvalleydistillers.com; +1-518-537-6820

◆ Food   ◆ Tours   ◆ Bar
◆ Distillery   ◆ Shop

The old barn that contains this compact distillery, bar and lounge looks like a farm stand from the road. Inside, the authentic country flavour is enhanced by 1800s-era exposed beams and there's a welcoming atmosphere with evenings of live music, trivia and, of course, spirit and cocktail tastings.

The charming husband-and-wife team who run the distillery offer intimate tours and tastings of their spirits, which range from vodka and gin to whiskey and applejack (a whiskey-like spirit made with apples and aged in white oak barrels). Unapologetically experimental, the unique spirits all use local products such as apples, grain, wine, beer and honey as their base. Don't miss the Old Tom Gin, made with honey from the winery across the street.

THINGS TO DO NEARBY

Tousey Winery
A premier winery of the Hudson Valley, Tousey has a well-earned reputation for making delicious cassis using estate-grown blackberries. There's also an on-site cafe.
www.touseywinery.com

Sloop Brewing Co
This trendy brewhouse in the countryside is rooted in traditional brewing with added twists along the way. Communal picnic tables and an old barn set the vibe.
www.sloopbrewing.com

TUTHILLTOWN DISTILLERY

14 Grist Mill Lane, Gardiner, New York;
www.tuthilltown.com; +1-845-419-2964

◆ Food   ◆ Tours   ◆ Bar
◆ Distillery   ◆ Shop

Beyond charming, this Hudson Valley distillery started as a family passion project in 2003, and produced its first distillates in 2005. It specialises in sourcing local grain and fruit to make its range of small-batch spirits, such as apple vodka and rye whiskey, and was one of the first New York state farm distilleries to reappear after Prohibition, blazing the trail for what is now a region full of craft spirits. The family estate, situated among rolling hills and sprawling farmlands, encompasses the distillery and visitors' centre as well as a B&B and restaurant, all popular destinations for visitors from New York City. Five handcrafted spirits are available to taste, but it's the iconic Baby Bourbon with round supple sweetness that's not to be missed.

THINGS TO DO NEARBY

Hudson Valley Wine Market
This small shop specialises in local wines, but also carries a wide range of local spirits, making it a one-stop shop to taste the region.
**www.hudsonvalley
winemarket.com**

Shawangunk Grasslands National Wildlife Refuge
This public nature reserve tucked into the Catskill mountains offers a taste of the nature that makes the Hudson Valley so precious.
**www.fws.gov/refuge/
shawangunk_grasslands**

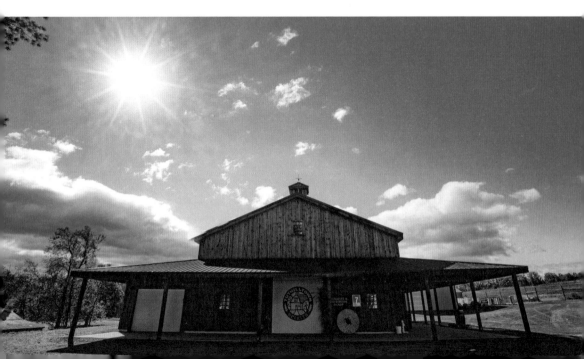

ASHEVILLE DISTILLING CO

12 Old Charlotte Hwy, Suite 140, Asheville, North Carolina;
www.ashevilledistilling.com; +1-828-575-2000

◆ Distillery ◆ Shop
◆ Tours

THINGS TO DO NEARBY

Blue Ridge Parkway
This 469-mile scenic byway links Shenandoah National Park in Virginia with the eastern entrance of Great Smoky Mountains National Park in North Carolina. Trails and views abound. *www.nps.gov/blri*

Biltmore Estate & Gardens
This grand chateau on the outskirts of Asheville has ornate rooms and gorgeous gardens worth touring. It was completed in 1895 for shipping-and-railroad heir George Vanderbilt. *www.biltmore.com*

Limones
Traditional Mexican dishes get a modern spin at this downtown restaurant, which serves a Moonshine Margarita with Troy & Sons' heirloom moonshine. *www.limonesrestaurant.com*

Asheville Ale Trail
Home to nearly 30 breweries and nicknamed Beer City, Asheville is a destination drinking spot for craft beer fans across the South. The Ale Trail provides the map. *www.ashevillealetrail.com*

Bags of heirloom grits and photos of crop-dotted fields in Asheville Distilling's tasting room evoke the feel of a cosy Appalachian barn. This rustic look aligns with the goal of founder Troy Ball: to produce an authentic Scots-Irish un-aged white whiskey (aka moonshine). To replicate the 19th-century taste, Troy uses heirloom white corn that dates back to the 1840s. But unlike the original moonshiners, who often sold the bad-tasting heads and tails and kept the heart for themselves, at Asheville Distilling Troy ensures it's only the heart that makes it into the bottle for sale.

After tours, visitors sample five whiskies. They also learn about the inspiring Ball, who moved to Asheville with husband Charlie in 2004 from Texas, seeking a better climate for her three sons, two of whom have special needs. She took an interest in un-aged whiskey after neighbours from her rural community brought welcoming gifts of moonshine. An energetic entrepreneur, Ball soon realised that there were no quality white whiskies on the market. She decided to fill that niche with artisan moonshine, becoming the first female founder of a whiskey distillery in modern times. Celebrate her persistence with a smooth cocktail made from Troy & Sons Platinum American Moonshine.

NEW DEAL DISTILLERY

900 SE Salmon St, Portland, Oregon;
www.newdealdistillery.com; +1-503-234-2513

◆ Distillery   ◆ Shop
◆ Tours   ◆ Transport

A pioneer of North America's artisanal distillery scene, New Deal began making spirits in 2004 in the southeast Portland neighbourhood now known as Distillery Row. Owner Tom Burkleaux says: 'We were mad scientists, learning our craft in this idyllic wilderness', nostalgically describing a time when fewer than two dozen craft spirits makers operated across the US.

Today, the distillery's flagship New Deal vodka is a grain-to-glass product, made from locally grown winter white wheat. Also in its line-up are gins, whiskies and a ginger liqueur.

In the tasting room, which looks into the production facility, you can sample the spirits straight up or in mini cocktails and chat with the staff about how the products are produced. The must-try drink is the spicy-sweet ginger liqueur.

THINGS TO DO NEARBY

Kachka Restaurant
Raise a glass of vodka at this Russian-themed eatery specialising in zakuski (small plates) such as herring salad, blini with caviar, and pelmeni (dumplings).
www.kachkapdx.com

Portland Art Museum
See what's on view at the city's art gallery, which often showcases Native American works as well as regional and international contemporary artists, and photography. ***www. portlandartmuseum.org***

VINN DISTILLERY

222 SE 8th Ave, Portland, Oregon;
www.vinndistillery.com; +1-503-807-3826

◆ Shop   ◆ Transport
◆ Bar

Run by five Chinese-Vietnamese siblings, Portland's Vinn Distillery draws on the family's Asian heritage to produce rice-based spirits. While the family had been distilling at home for generations, it was the siblings' father who conceived the idea of a commercial distillery as a family project: Vinn is the middle name that the siblings all share.

Today they're crafting traditional Chinese baijiu (white liquor), as well as the first rice vodka and rice whiskey produced in the USA, and blackberry liqueur that infuses their vodka with Oregon berries. Bonus: these spirits are all gluten free.

The distillery tasting room is in southeast Portland's Distillery Row, where more than 10 producers have set up shop. Tasting flights includes sips of the spirits plus sample cocktails. Don't miss the hand-to-find bracing baijiu.

THINGS TO DO NEARBY

Steven Smith Teamaker
Portland's local tea specialist operates a tea bar in a revamped eastside warehouse, where you can pop in to sample a tasting flight of various different brews.
www.smithtea.com

Cartopia Food Cart Pod
Many of Portland's street-food carts cluster into 'pods' around the city, like this collection of mobile munch wagons at Southeast Hawthorne Boulevard and 12th Avenue. ***www. foodcartsportland.com***

OLE SMOKY MOONSHINE DISTILLERY

903 Parkway Suite 128, Gatlinburg, Tennessee;
www.olesmoky.com; +1-865-436-6995

◆ Distillery ◆ Transport
◆ Shop

Musicians play bluegrass on the patio and the moonshine comes in mason jars at 'The Holler', the nickname for Ole Smoky Moonshine Distillery in downtown Gatlinburg. Passels of different flavoured hooch cost $5 and if you ask, staff might also give an impromptu tour.

Ole Smoky was the first distillery to open in Tennessee after a law was passed in 2009 allowing commercial distilling in 41 counties (from only three). Founder Joe Baker is a Gatlinburg native whose ancestors were living in East Tennessee before it even became a state in 1796. Pre-2009, some of Joe's relatives made illegal whiskey and he can recall seeing stills and helping to make grain mash growing up. 'I have a certain sense of pride coming from the mountains and those traditions,' he says. Experience that pride with a sip of his tasty Apple Pie hooch.

THINGS TO DO NEARBY

Great Smoky Mountains National Park
Head into the hills and hollers (valleys) of America's most visited national park for hiking, history and wildlife watching. Waterfalls run best in spring. ***www.nps.gov/grsm***

Peddler Steakhouse
Sip an Ole Smoky moonshine cocktail with your prime rib at this stone-and-wood steakhouse near the Gatlinburg entrance to Great Smoky Mountains National Park. ***www.peddlergatlinburg.com***

SEVIER DISTILLING CO

745 Old Douglas Dam Rd, Sevierville, Tennessee;
www.sevierdistilling.com; +1-865-366-1772

◆ Distillery ◆ Shop
◆ Tours

A ninth-generation East Tennessean with a passion for maths, Chris Yett dubs himself a 'scientific redneck'. You can thank that combination of personality traits for Sevier Distillery's Real Deal Shine, an un-aged corn whiskey that's fermented, distilled and bottled on site. Chris, the distillery's founder, swears by what he calls a 'full-grain conversion process' – a fancy term for a production method used by early pioneers. No outside sugars are pumped into the fermenting tanks, which is what often happens at larger distilleries.

The distillery's 1000-gallon still is dubbed 'The Colonel' as a homage to Colonel Valentine Sevier, who was a relative of Chris's. See it on a tour, before sampling spirits such as vodka, gin and Yenoh – an unusual spirit distilled from 100% honey.

THINGS TO DO NEARBY

Dollywood
Sevier is the hometown of country music legend Dolly Parton, and her roots are celebrated with roller coasters, Southern food and live country music at her namesake theme park. ***www.dollywood.com***

Local Goat
Skip the many national food chains in favour of locally sourced dishes that spotlight East Tennessee and the South. Sevier Distilling cocktails are served, too. ***www.localgoatpf.com***

HERITAGE DISTILLING COMPANY

3207 57th St Ct NW, Gig Harbor, Washington;
www.heritagedistilling.com; +1-253-509-0008

◆ Distillery   ◆ Shop
◆ Tours

Most Pacific Northwest visitors who venture outside Seattle to the small waterside town of Gig Harbor will see the small Heritage tasting room along the main street in town, but it's worth heading out of downtown to taste at the source inside the distillery itself. Here, the tasting room's walls are lined with 10-litre casks ageing private whiskey blends made by Heritage Distilling fans – an atmospheric spot to sip the small-batch whiskies and vodkas that have made Heritage one of the most awarded distilleries in the country.

Tours allow visitors to survey the stills. Whiskey connoisseurs and sceptics alike should try the wildly popular Brown Sugar Bourbon, with a flavour that evokes Pacific Northwest campfires and mountaintop summits.

THINGS TO DO NEARBY

Harbor History Museum
An architecturally modern museum that honours the history and waterways of South Puget Sound. Exhibits are stuffed with artefacts and there are live boat restorations. *www. harborhistorymuseum.org*

Netshed No 9
Named for the net repairs that used to occur on this pier, here you can tuck into American breakfast and lunch dishes while admiring the view from Netshed's harbourfront patio. *www.netshed9.com*

MOONSHINE 101

If you take away the bad boy reputation, moonshine is nothing more than un-aged whiskey, often sourced from corn. But where's the fun in that? Hooch. White Lightning. Mountain Dew. It's the outlaw history that adds mystique to this uniquely American spirit, conjuring visions of hidden copper stills, bearded mountain men and wild car chases with revenuers in hot pursuit of Depression-era bootleggers.

However, the story of moonshine begins well before the 1930s Depression. It can be traced back to the Scots-Irish settlers who followed the Great Wagon Road south from Pennsylvania in the mid-1700s. These hardy pioneers built small farms across the valleys and foothills of the Appalachian mountains, settling the region that now comprises Pennsylvania, West Virginia, Virginia, Tennessee and the Carolinas. Many of these families, particularly in the southern Appalachians, distilled spirits for medicinal purposes. And yes, sometimes 'medicine' included whiskey – for personal consumption or sold for extra income. Since corn grew so well on mountain slopes, it was the default grain in much of the whiskey.

Conflict between Appalachian distillers and the government dates as far back as the 1794 Whiskey Rebellion in western Pennsylvania. After the Revolutionary War, many states were in debt. The young federal government agreed to assume this debt, but imposed an excise tax on whiskey producers to help the states pay it off. This tax was wildly unpopular with Appalachian farmers, and mob violence ensued. President George Washington led a 13,000-strong militia force into Pennsylvania to quash the rebellion (the first and last time a sitting US president led military forces). The rebels backed down, but the unpopular tax was repealed a few years later.

Moonshine earned its modern reputation during Prohibition, when the production and consumption of alcohol in the US was banned by Constitutional amendment in 1920. Enforcement, however, was difficult, and illegal whiskey production became a good source of extra income for Appalachian home distillers. To hide the smoke from their stills, the distillers – also known as bootleggers – made their corn liquor at night, under the light of the moon, hence

From left: ©GL Archive/Alamy Stock Photo; ©Valery Rizzo/Courtesy Kings County Distillery(2)

the name moonshine. This primitive un-aged whiskey, also called white whiskey, earned a reputation for its rough taste, or burn.

Dividing Tennessee and North Carolina, the Smoky Mountains have deep ties to Depression-era moonshine. There are rumours that mobster Al Capone spent time in Johnson City, Tennessee, while running moonshine from the Smokies back to Chicago. The city even earned the nickname 'Little Chicago'.

Although Prohibition was repealed in 1933, moonshining was a good way for families to make extra cash during the Great Depression, which continued during the 1930s. NASCAR racing is a descendant of the wild automobile chases of the era, when federal agents chased the souped-up cars used by the bootleggers to deliver their product.

For decades, strict alcohol laws prevented the legal production of distilled spirits across much of southern Appalachia. A recent loosening of these laws – plus the popularity of the Discovery Channel show *Moonshiners* – has spurred a slew of new distilleries to open, and sales of 'legal' moonshine have sky-rocketed.

BY AMY BALFOUR

GLOBAL DISTILLERY TOUR

ASIA

KYŪSHŪ

Fancy sampling *shōchū* in a vinyl-spinning distillery bar, or sipping whisky over lunch with a traditional Japanese garden in the background? Kyūshū is the place to come for some of Japan's most enthralling distillery experiences, parcelled into a mainland coastal region of lush volcanic peaks.

BANGKOK

The craft spirits movement is still in its infancy in Southeast Asia, but Bangkok's pre-eminence on the cocktail bar scene has paved the way for one notable pioneer: Iron Balls gin. It was founded by an Australian bar designer making waves in Asia; his distillery serves a unique tropical G&T.

UBUD

Between thrashing surf beaches and new-age hangouts, Bali's culture capital is building on its new-found reputation as a foodie haven with a backyard distillery attached to one of the town's most progressive cocktail dens. Night Rooster is house-infusing gins, and making vermouths and arak.

SOUTHEAST ASIA

How to ask for a spirit without mixers? Neat (in English)
Signature spirit? Arak straight up in Indonesia; an ice-cold
beer and Mekhong chaser in Thailand; gin & tonic in Malaysia
What to order with your spirits? East Imperial Tonic, inspired
by Asian tastes and ingredients, pairs perfectly with a craft gin
Don't: Be surprised if prices seem very cheap; some bars put
local spirits in branded bottles like Gordon's or Johnnie Walker

Southeast Asia is an emerging region in terms of
homegrown artisan distilleries, but a long-standing
culture exists here of drinking imported spirits.
Today, that culture is mushrooming into one of the world's
most exciting bar scenes for experimental cocktails and
cutting-edge speakeasy watering holes.

For years, Thai farmers have distilled their own moonshine
spirits, primarily from rice, while any backpacker will have
tried the iconic Mekhong, a rough industrially produced
whisky. Recently though, small-batch producers are popping
up all over the country. Local sugar cane is being artisan-
distilled in Phuket, Koh Samui and Issan to produce Thai
rums, while in Chiang Mai you will find rice vodka and
distilled coconut flowers. Bangkok's top cocktail bar, A R
Sutton Engineers Siam, has its own copper still making Iron
Balls Gin – a blend of lemongrass and passion fruit with
traditional juniper berries.

Both Malaysia and Singapore are renowned as key markets
for top-end premium spirits, with huge sales of the world's
most expensive cognac, XO (Extra Old). XO is the ultimate
wealth status symbol, ritually drunk at Chinese wedding
banquets and business dinners after a shout of *yam sing*
(bottoms up), or even with ice and Coca-Cola – total heresy
back in France where it was produced. Here too, times have
changed, with the emergence of hip speakeasies where the
emphasis is on craft spirits mixed with exotic ingredients,
including locally distilled tuak from Borneo in cocktails.

In Indonesia the local speciality is arak, a local firewater
made from fermented coconut and palm nectar, but it can
be tricky to sample: beware the plastic bottles produced by
bootleg village distillers, because they often add methanol to
up the alcohol content, which can lead to serious health risks.
Stick to ordering arak from the menus of restaurants and bars,
especially in Bali, and you will discover a unique local spirit.

Courtesy of Night Rooster (3)

■ BAR
NIGHT ROOSTER

10 Jalan Dewi Sita, Ubud, Bali; www.locavore.co.id/
nightrooster; +62 3619 777 33

- ◆ Food
- ◆ Bar
- ◆ Distillery
- ◆ Transport

Created by the owners of Locavore, Ubud's top-rated restaurant, Night Rooster has branched out from being Bali's coolest cocktail bar into a garage distillery using a homemade alembic to experiment with naturally fermented tropical fruits, traditional Brem rice wine, and arak, the local firewater.

The bar showcases the talents of Balinese mixologist Raka Ambarawan, an alchemist bartender who makes his own vermouth and bitters, gin and rum infused with jackfruit and fragrant kemangi leaves from Locavore's herb garden.

Going one step further, in 2018 he asked a local artisan to make a handcrafted copper still, and today a beautiful five-litre alembic sits on Night Rooster's bar.

Beginning with fermented fruits, Raka then learnt a family recipe from his mother to make cloudy Brem rice wine, usually used in religious ceremonies, and these distillations add a new dimension to his already creative cocktails. The challenge now is to make his own arak, a potent alcohol from fermented coconut and palm nectar. To taste the influence of arak in a cocktail, just order Raka's Northern Bramble: a concoction of pickled grape brine, mace jam, arak infused with wood and spices, sour candy and kampung chicken egg white.

THINGS TO DO NEARBY

Goa Gajah
Known as the Elephant Cave, Goa Gajah is a 9th-century religious sanctuary of pools, fountains and a meditational cave whose entrance is covered in intricate stone carvings.

Campuhan Ridge Walk
To escape Ubud's crowds, head to Gunung Lebah Temple where a 9km hill track begins. It's the perfect spot for walking or jogging through lush jungle landscapes.

Ali Antiques
This Ubud shop is a dusty emporium of hidden treasure, including ceremonial sarongs, graphic Balinese scenes painted on mirrors and jewellery.
www.facebook.com/ali.artshop.3

The Yoga Barn
The perfect detox to recover from Night Rooster's cocktails is a class at Ubud's oldest yoga centre, whose spa also offers Ayurveda and wellness treatments.
www.theyogabarn.com

■ **BAR**

MBAR

6 & 7 Main Bazaar, Kuching, Sarawak, Borneo;
www.theranee.com; +60 82 258833

◆ Food ◆ Bar
◆ Shop ◆ Transport

Travel upriver to the world's oldest rainforests in Borneo's Sarawak and the traditional drink in a tribal Long House will be tuak, a heady moonshine brew of fermented glutinous rice. But in the urbanised environment of Sarawak's capital Kuching, it can also be sampled in very different circumstances in The Ranee, a chic boutique hotel fashioned out of two 19th-century shop houses.

Light wine tuak can be sampled in The Ranee's popular bistro, but the serious distilled tuak, known as *langkau*, is left in the hands of the mixologist of the hotel's MBar. This clear distilled spirit features in half a dozen exotic cocktails. While the easy drinking Orang Utan Swing mixes the potent alcohol with tangy tropical fruits, adventurous drinkers order Borneo Black Magic, blending the jungle spirit with Guinness.

THINGS TO DO NEARBY

Borneo Headhunter
Local Iban tribesmen are renowned for distinctive tattoos, and Ernesto Kalum is one of the world's most famous tattoo artists. Be brave and book an inking at his studio. **www. borneoheadhunter.com**

Top Spot Food Court
Every evening the open-air roof of a concrete car park becomes a teeming foodie paradise, with stalls cooking spicy dishes of crabs, squid and prawns. It's in the historic centre, just off Jalan Padungan.

■ **BAR**

PS150

150 Jalan Petaling, Chinatown, Kuala Lumpur;
www.ps150.my; +60 3 76228777

◆ Food ◆ Transport
◆ Bar

Hidden behind the false entrance of a retro Chinatown toy shop, PS150 typifies Kuala Lumpur's booming speakeasy cocktail bar scene. A long passageway with opium den booths leads to a neon-lit bar echoing the decadent Suzy Wong world of the 1960s. But what's special here is that tattooed barista Angel Ng is adding a twist to her cocktails using tribal tuak shipped from Sarawak.

Tuak starts out as cooked glutinous rice, fermented with a secret yeast concoction, ragi, containing galangal and ginger. It gets increasingly alcoholic as it ages, especially when the producer distills the spirit, making it the perfect ingredient for Angel's Rumble in the Jungle, where tuak blends with coconut and pandan-infused rum, tropical juices, bitters and gula melaka syrup.

THINGS TO DO NEARBY

Heritage Walk
Discover old colonial Kuala Lumpur on free walking tours that pass the swirling minarets of fairytale Jamek mosque and the lavish Moorish railway station. **www.visitkl.gov.my**

No Black Tie
In the backstreets of Bukit Ceylon's nightlife quarter sits a world-class jazz club, featuring Asian musicians and international stars jamming 'til the early hours. **www.noblacktie.com.my**

IRON BALLS DISTILLERY

Park Lane, Soi 63/Ekkamai, Thanon Sukhumvit 63,
Bangkok; www.ironballsgin.com; +66 2 714 2269

◆ Distillery ◆ Shop ◆ Transport
◆ Tours ◆ Bar

In Thailand, spirits are produced by massive conglomerates or domestic operations, with little in between. Iron Balls, concealed in a strip mall in Bangkok, is one of the few exceptions. The distillery specialises in gin, made here from a base of coconuts and pineapples before being seasoned with 15 botanicals, including lemongrass, Cambodian pepper, coriander seeds and ginseng. The result has the sun-baked, tropical character of its home: notes of mango and pineapple, with a background of ginger and cinnamon. To suit its unique profile, the attached bar – which, with its retro baubles, pipes, wheels and fittings, resembles the temple of a steampunk overlord – has created its own riff on the gin and tonic, serving it with a pineapple spear and Thai basil leaves.

THINGS TO DO NEARBY

Soul Food Mahanakorn
If you're new to Bangkok – and Thai food – there's no better introduction than this restaurant, where ingredients familiar to the west mingle with Thai flavours. *www. soulfoodmahanakorn.com*

Kamthieng House
The Sukhumvit area is more about entertainment than sightseeing, but this traditional Thai house, dating to 1848, shows how much Bangkok has changed. *www.siam-society.org/ facilities/kamthieng.html*

ISSAN RUM DISTILLERY

Khai Bok Wan, Nong Khai province;
www.issan-rum.fr, +66 80 525 7592

◆ Distillery
◆ Shop

Of the distillers returning rum to its roots in Southeast Asia, perhaps none is more passionate or intrepid than David Giallorenzo. The transplanted Frenchman crafts his award-winning *rhum agricole* (a perfect base for tropical cocktails) in a simple village in Thailand's remote northeastern Isan region, surrounded by the sugarcane fields that feed the copper still.

Getting there is a bit of an adventure, but anyone stopping by (8am to 5pm) will get a genuine Isan welcome and can take a taste in the distillery's little lounge. The team always presses the sugar cane the same day that it's cut, so it's only possible to see the full-blown production process between about late October and early April, during the sugarcane season, but visitors are welcome to drop in any time.

THINGS TO DO NEARBY

Sala Kaew Ku
A must-see for anyone visiting Nong Khai, this surreal religious centre features a bizarre and enthralling mix of Buddhist, Hindu and other concrete sculptures, many of them massive.

Phu Phrabat Historical Park
A wonderful mix of history and beauty, this quiet park 60km west of Nong Khai has prehistoric rock paintings and carvings, plus lots of oddly eroded stone towers.

JAPAN

How to ask for a spirit without mixers? Sutoreito (straight)
Signature spirit? Whisky
What to order with your spirits? Peanuts –
they'll generally just appear
Don't: Pour your own drink; pour for others (unless there
is a dedicated pouring person assigned to your table) and
without doubt, someone will fill your glass for you. If you
can't drink any more, leave your glass full so that no one
can put any more in it!

Anybody who thinks the Japanese are strait-laced
obviously hasn't had a good look behind the
tatemae, the public face of Japan. This is the land
of the love hotel and where idiotic misbehaviours performed
while boozed out of the brain are explained away (and almost
instantly forgiven) with the words – 'Sorry, I'd been drinking!'
Alcohol is an accepted release from daily pressures. Those
from countries with conservative liquor policies are often
shocked how booze plays such an important part in society.
And it has been doing so for a long time: in the 3rd century,
Chinese historians noted that the people of these islands were
into excessive drinking.

While beer arrived in Japan via Dutch traders stationed
in Nagasaki in the 17th century, it was when Japan reopened
to foreign trade in the Meiji period from the late 1860s that
western-style spirits appeared. Whisky was first produced
in 1870, while the first commercial distillery opened in
1924. Consumption was mostly domestic until the early
2000s, when Japanese whiskies started winning major
international awards and garnering enthusiastic acclaim
overseas. The bulk of Japanese blended whisky is consumed
in cocktails, notably as 'whisky highballs' (whisky with soda),
which can even be found in cans in convenience stores. Fine

"*The proliferation of craft whisky distillers in Japan in recent years is a welcome development, even for established distillers like myself. The new distillers are stimulating people's interest in Japanese whisky*"

—ICHIRO AKUTO, CHICHIBU DISTILLERY

TOP 5 SPIRITS

- **Peaty & Salty single-malt whisky** Yoichi Distillery, Hokkaido
- **Yamazaki 18 single-malt whisky** Yamazaki Distillery, Osaka
- **55 Junmai Ginjō Blue sake** Daimon Brewery, Osaka
- **Satsuma Shiranami shōchū** Satsuma Distillery Kagoshima
- **Hakuryu awamori** Zuisen Distillery, Okinawa

whisky is mainly ordered straight or on the rocks (*rokku*). It is often mixed with hot water (*oyu-wari*), a favourite in winter, or cold water (*mizu-wari*), popular in summer. Most recently, Japan has also started to dabble with craft gins using local botanicals such as yuzu peel and the sakura flower (cherry blossom). At the time of writing, these fledgling distilleries were not open to the public, but look out for brands such as Roku, Jinzu and Ki No Bi at bars both in Japan and overseas.

In the Japanese language, sake can refer to any alcoholic beverage, and the Japanese will use the word *nihonshu* to refer to what English-speakers think of as sake. It is served chilled (*reishu*), at room temperature (*jōon*), or heated (*atsukan*), depending on the drinker's preference, quality of the sake, and the season. Despite its international reputation as a relatively potent alcohol, sake is actually brewed rather than distilled and the fermentation process technically makes it more like a beer than a wine or spirit. Typical alcohol percentages are in the 14% to 18% ABV range. However, for most drinkers, for all intents and purposes sake delivers very much like a spirit, which is why it's been included in this book.

Japan's love affair with alcohol doesn't stop there though, and there are a couple of traditional spirits also worth your time. Originally from Kyushu, *shōchū* is distilled from rice, barley, sweet potatoes, buckwheat or brown sugar and typically contains 25% alcohol. This spirit hit boom times early this century with the opening of countless *shōchū* bars as the drink became trendy, particularly with young women. It is often consumed with soda as *chūhai*.

The oldest type of distilled liquor in Japan, however, is said to be Okinawan *awamori*. It's distilled from long-grain indica rice and can be anywhere in the 25% to 60% ABV range. The most popular way to drink it is with water and ice, though it can also be consumed neat, on the rocks or in cocktails.

MASUMI BREWERY

1-16 Motomachi, Suwa, Nagano Prefecture;
www.masumi.co.jp; +81 266-52-6161

◆ Food   ◆ Tours
◆ Brewery   ◆ Transport

Masumi Brewery sprung into life near the shores of Lake Suwa in 1662, surrounded by mountains at 759m above sea level. The Miyasaka family who established it found Suwa's clean air, pure waters and long cold winters perfect for sake brewing, and they work with local rice farmers to produce award-winning sake with pride.

They don't stop there, either: the brewery also produces a tasty yuzu citrus liqueur, *shōchū*, *umeshu* (plum liqueur) and sparkling sake. Always innovative, Masumi was the birthplace of *nana-gō*, a yeast used today in 60% of sake breweries throughout Japan. The brewery, housed in traditional buildings with sake barrels out front, is 2.5 hours west of Tokyo by train. Reserve ahead for tastings with English explanations at the brewery's elegant Cella Masumi cafe, shop and gallery.

THINGS TO DO NEARBY

Matsumoto Castle
Known as 'Crow Castle' because of its black exterior, spectacular Matsumoto-jō has gorgeous grounds, walls and moats, and houses an impressive weapons museum.
www.matsumoto-castle.jp

Yatsugatake
The impressive Yatsugatake mountain range is criss-crossed with popular hiking trails. Its name means 'eight peaks' – Aka-dake, the highest mountain, stretches to 2899m.

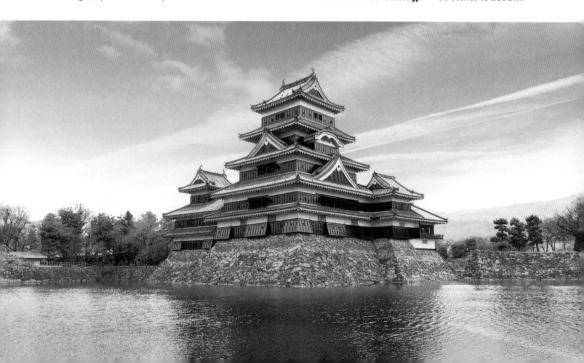

YOICHI DISTILLERY

7-6 Kurokawa-cho, Yoichi-cho, Yoichi-gun, Hokkaido;
www.nikka.com/eng/distilleries/yoichi; +81 135-23-3131

◆ Food   ◆ Tours   ◆ Bar
◆ Distillery ◆ Shop   ◆ Transport

THINGS TO DO NEARBY

Yoichi Winery
There are half a dozen wineries in Yoichi, but most of them are not open to the public. This one is and offers tours and tastings, plus there's a cafe, bakery and restaurant.

Old Shimoyoichi Unjoya
This 19th-century herring trading post is the only remaining building of its kind. Displays give an insight into how the locals lived and worked at the time.

Sushi In Otaru
Otaru is famous for its fresh seafood, so sushi or sashimi is what you go for. Try Otaru Masa Sushi or Kukizen – the latter is the only 2-star Michelin restaurant in Hokkaido.

Bar Hatta
A good starting point for some bar-hopping in Otaru. There are 28 warehouses at Yoichi distillery and this bar is nicknamed 'No.29', so that should give you an idea of what to expect.

In 1934, Masataka Taketsuru left the company now known as Suntory and founded his own business. He called it The Great Japan Juice Co – Nikka, for short – and set up shop in the coastal town of Yoichi in Hokkaido. He did dabble in apple juice and cider for a few years, but the real juice he was after was whisky, of course. He was convinced that the climate and natural features of the area, similar to the Scottish Highlands, made it the ideal location to make quality whisky.

The distillery as it is today feels like its own little village, with beautiful stone buildings of the type one sees in the nearby historic port town of Otaru. Visitors can take a guided tour or just wander around freely. The stillhouse is one of the big attractions at Yoichi, as this is the only working distillery in the world where the pot stills are still heated with coal. You can also see Taketsuru's old residence here, which was moved from the countryside nearby to the distillery grounds. Those eager to drop some cash are spoiled for choice: there's a well-stocked whisky bar where different drams can be sampled, a large distillery shop with some exclusive bottlings (if you're lucky) and a restaurant (the herring soba is to die for). Yoichi single malt is at its best when it's peaty, so try the 'Peaty & Salty' distillery exclusive.

HAKUSHU DISTILLERY

2912-1 Torihara, Hakushu-cho, Yoichi-gun, Hokkaido;
www.suntory.com/factory/hakushu; +81 55-135-2211

◆ Food   ◆ Tours   ◆ Bar
◆ Distillery   ◆ Shop   ◆ Transport

THINGS TO DO NEARBY

Jissoji Temple
In the grounds of this temple you'll find the oldest cherry blossom tree in Japan and likely worldwide. Catch it when it's in full blossom in April.

Bar Perch
This bar is part of Moegi-no-mura, a western-style rustic theme park in Kiyosato. The whisky selection is definitely worth the detour.

Shichiken Sake Brewery
Run by the same family for 12 generations, this sake brewery is a must-visit. There's also a restaurant and a cafe on site.

Ojiragawa Valley
Near the distillery, a leisurely walk through this valley will give you a good feel for the majestic natural beauty of the area.

Hakushu is nicknamed 'the forest distillery' and you'll understand why when you make the trek out here. When whisky behemoth Suntory acquired the 200-square-acre site in the early 1970s, it left more than 80% of it undeveloped. Part of it even includes a wild-bird sanctuary. The original distillery was completed in 1973 and expanded four years later, making it the biggest whisky distillery in the world at the time. In 1981, a completely new distillery – the one that you'll see today – was built on site and the older one abandoned: instead of quantity (big stills and lots of whisky of the same type) it went for diversity, meaning a variety of still shapes and sizes.

Hakushu distillery is a popular destination so it's essential to book your tour well in advance. Your walk-around will start in the museum, which focuses on the history of distilling in general and the craftsmanship involved in making whisky, so it pays to show up a little earlier. You'll also want to set some time aside for the bar and the shop. Whatever you do, don't skip the restaurant; nothing beats a selection of local, seasonal fare with a refreshing Hakushu highball, enjoyed al fresco, surrounded by the forest.

DAIMON BREWERY

3-12-1 Mori-minami, Katano City, Osaka;
www.daimonbrewery.com; +81 72-891-0353

◆ Food   ◆ Tours   ◆ Bar
◆ Distillery   ◆ Shop   ◆ Transport

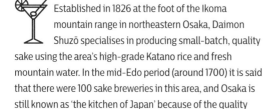

Established in 1826 at the foot of the Ikoma mountain range in northeastern Osaka, Daimon Shuzō specialises in producing small-batch, quality sake using the area's high-grade Katano rice and fresh mountain water. In the mid-Edo period (around 1700) it is said that there were 100 sake breweries in this area, and Osaka is still known as 'the kitchen of Japan' because of the quality food and drink.

The kanji characters for Daimon (大門) mean 'big gate' and the brewery is proud that its gate is always open to welcome visitors to the world of sake – its motto is 'brew well, drink well, live well!'. Daimon produces an eponymous series of

THINGS TO DO NEARBY

Daibutsu (Giant Buddha) in Nara
With Daimon Brewery between Osaka and Nara, consider visiting on your way back from seeing the 16m-high bronze Daibutsu at the Tōdai-ji in Nara Park. *www.todaiji.or.jp*

Osaka Castle
A visit to Osaka Castle, its museum and surrounding park is a must. It may be a reconstruction, but the castle is a dramatic symbol of the city. *www.osakacastle.net*

Shinsaibashi
Stroll down Osaka's bustling central shopping arcade and spot all the latest trends at Ebisubashi bridge. Restaurants, bars and nightclubs line the side streets. *www. shinsaibashi.or.jp*

National Museum of Art
Underground on the small island of Nakanoshima between two rivers in central Osaka, this museum houses a fabulous collection of modern art. *www.nmao.go.jp*

premier sake, as well as the Rikyubai series of traditional Kansai sake; the latter is best served warm or at room temperature. The brewery also has a traditional restaurant, Mikune-tei, overlooking a 300-year-old Japanese garden.

Daimon is a 40-minute train ride from central Osaka and offers tours in English that include viewing the production and tasting – check its website and reserve ahead. Be sure to try the 55 Junmai Ginjō Blue, a full-bodied, unpasteurised sake in a startling pale blue bottle, best served chilled.

YAMAZAKI DISTILLERY

5-2-1 Yamazaki, Shimamoto-cho, Mishima-gun, Osaka;
www.suntory.com/factory/yamazaki; +81 75-962-1423

◆ Distillery ◆ Shop ◆ Transport
◆ Tours ◆ Bar

Yamazaki, between Osaka and Kyoto, is an area steeped in history. It's also the birthplace of Japanese whisky. It was here that an entrepreneur by the name of Shinjiro Torii decided to build the first malt whisky distillery in Japan: construction began in 1923 and the stills were fired up on November 11, 1924. Over the years, the distillery has grown and now there are 17 fermenters and 16 different stills in a variety of shapes and sizes. The distillery is very much part of the town – in fact, a public road runs through the middle, so don't be alarmed when you see kids walking through the distillery in the morning or late afternoon.

There are a few old-style warehouses with casks stacked three high and a few racked warehouses at Yamazaki distillery, but 90% of the whisky produced here is aged in a

THINGS TO DO NEARBY

Sanshotei

The best-kept secret near Yamazaki distillery, this family-owned restaurant offers exquisite seasonal tempura prepared right in front of you.

Asahi Beer Oyamazaki Museum Of Art

There's a lot for fans of visual beauty to enjoy here: architecture, fine art and a 4000-acre garden. This was originally the country villa of wealthy businessman Shotaro Kaga – one of the first investors in what would later become Nikka Whisky Distilling. **www.asahibeer-oyamazaki.com/english/**

Ryōan-ji

A Unesco World Heritage Site since 1994, this Zen temple in the northwest of Kyoto is famous for its rock garden, thought to have been built in the 15th century.

Taian Teahouse

Located in the Myokian temple, this teahouse is said to be the creation of legendary tea master Sen no Rikyu. It's the oldest teahouse in Japan and one of three designated as a National Treasure. By appointment only.

large warehouse complex 40 miles northwest. It's essential to reserve tours in advance online. There's also an interesting museum with historical Suntory artefacts. However, the real gold can be found at the bar, where you can try rare whiskies at unbeatable prices.

GEKKEIKAN SAKE MUSEUM

247 Minamihama-chō, Fushimi-ku, Kyoto City; www.
gekkeikan.co.jp/english/kyotofushimi; +81 75-623-2056

◆ Brewery ◆ Transport
◆ Shop

Fourteen generations of the Okura family are behind Gekkeikan, which was founded in 1637 and today is one of Japan's biggest sake producers. In the township of Fushimi, famous for its important Inari shrine, Gekkeikan's museum explains the history of sake and the processes of making it. There are English-language descriptions and an English brochure that can be downloaded for self-guiding. Included in the 400 yen entry fee is a 180ml bottle of Gekkeikan sake and the opportunity to taste three of the brews, making it an excellent deal for visitors.

Next to the museum is the Gekkeikan Sake-kōbō mini-brewery, which brews sake and can be visited by making a reservation at least a day before your visit. When it comes to tasting, don't miss the Gekkeikan Retro-Bottle Ginjō-shu.

THINGS TO DO NEARBY

Fushimi Inari Taisha
Endless red torii gates stretching up the mountain is one of the classic images of Japan; this is the shrine headquarters of 30,000 Inari shrines throughout the country.
www.inari.jp/en

Tsuki-no-Kurabito
In a building that housed a Gekkeikan brewery rice-polishing plant during the Taishō period (1912-26), this stylish restaurant has a wonderful ambience. **www.19an. com/kurabito**

MATSUOKA BREWERY

7-2 Shimo-furutera, Oaza, Ogawa-machi, Saitama
Prefecture; www.mikadomatsu.com; + 81 493-72-1234

◆ Brewery ◆ Shop
◆ Tours ◆ Transport

An hour northwest of Tokyo's Ikebukuro station, Matsuoka Brewery was established in the Chichibu mountains in 1851, an area known for its mineral-rich water. The company's award-winning sake is made using time-consuming, low temperature fermentation that produces sake with a fruity aroma and a unique, mild taste. Matsuoka has carved a niche for itself with other products, too – shōchū and yuzu-flavoured liqueur (yuzu is like a small grapefruit), but also a mind-numbing choco-liqueur, recommended by the brewery as a Valentine's Day gift. In

the brewery shop, popular non-alcoholic sake ice cream is on offer, as are cosmetics made from sake kasu, the leftover product of the rice mash. Book ahead for free English-language tours; try the Daiginjō sake, an eight-year winner at the National Sake Competition.

THINGS TO DO NEARBY

Ikebukuro
Your train to Matsuoka leaves from Ikebukuro station, used by more than a million people a day. Take time to explore the area's department stores and down-to-earth alleyways.

Chichibu Pilgrimage
Nearby Chichibu is known for its 34-temple pilgrimage, with temples dedicated to Kannon the goddess of mercy. Pilgrims have been coming here since the 14th century.

ISHIKAWA BREWERY

1 Kumagawa, Fussa City, Tokyo;
www.tamajiman.co.jp; +81 42-553-0100

◆ Food ◆ Tours ◆ Transport
◆ Brewery ◆ Shop

In a cluster of buildings built next to the Tama River from the 1880s, Ishikawa Brewery is known for its range of Tamajiman (Pride of Tama) sake, made with traditional techniques and all-natural, local ingredients from the Tama region. Its standard sake is labelled as Junmai, its premier Daiginjō range uses rice milled to less than 50% of its original size, and the brewery also produces a couple of interesting liqueurs including *umeshu* (plum liqueur).

After government deregulation in the early 1990s, Ishikawa decided to branch out into brewing beer and is now also known for its range of Tama-no-Megumi (Tama's blessing) and Tokyo Blues range of beers.

Even though it's just an hour west of Tokyo's Shinjuku station, Ishikawa has the feel of a peaceful oasis, away from the capital. Tours take a walk around the brewery buildings, including the historical museum in the original rice storehouse, the sake cellar and beer factory, and involve tastings.

For free tours and tastings in English, check the website and book at least one day ahead. Visitors can buy sake, beer and souvenirs from the cellar door, and dine at the on-site Italian restaurant, Fussa-no-Birugoya. Ask to try the Tokyo-no-Mori (Tokyo Forest liqueur), a tipple that's unique to Ishikawa Brewery, made by adding wood chips of mountain cedar to sake.

THINGS TO DO NEARBY

Tokyo Skytree
For unbelievable views of the capital, head to the upper observatory floor (450m above ground level) at Tokyo Skytree, designed to resemble a five-storey pagoda. *www.tokyo-skytree.jp*

Shinjuku Station
Enjoy finding your way (or getting lost!) in the world's busiest transport hub, used by a mind-boggling four million people each day. *www.shinjukustation.com*

Takao-san
Get your nature fix on Takao-san's hiking trails, ride its cable car and visit its temple – all within easy access of Tokyo and the Ishikawa Brewery. *www.takaosan.or.jp*

Shibuya Crossing
Known as 'the scramble', test your urban skills as traffic stops and pedestrians surge from all directions into the infamous intersection outside Shibuya station.

KANOSUKE DISTILLERY

845-3 Kaminokawa, Hiyoshi-cho, Hioki City,
Kagoshima; www.kanosuke.com; +81 99-201-7700

◆ Distillery ◆ Shop
◆ Tours ◆ Bar

Parent company Komasa Jozo has been making liquor in Kagoshima for well over a hundred years, specialising in barrel-aged *shōchū*, but as far as whisky is concerned, it's the new kid on the block – or more specifically, the new kid on Route 270, with Tsunuki distillery 20 miles further south.

Whisky production started at the end of 2017, so it's still early days for this new player. The best part of your visit will be the Mellow Bar, which overlooks Fukiage beach and the East China Sea beyond. It is the only distillery bar in Japan where you'll find vinyl spinning on the sound system to accompany your drinking. What's not to love?

Its whisky needs time to mature; don't leave without trying Mellowed Kozuru, its signature barrel-aged rice shochu.

THINGS TO DO NEARBY

Araki Toyo
There's a high concentration of Satsuma pottery artisans in Hioki. The Araki Toyo kiln specialises in black Satsuma ware and is well worth a visit.

Midoriso
Kagoshima is blessed with an abundance of natural volcanic hot springs. Midoriso is hands-down the most beautiful one in the area, especially in the fall.

TSUNUKI DISTILLERY

6594 Kaseda Tsunuki, Minami Satsuma City,
Kagoshima; www.hombo.co.jp; +81 99-355-2121

◆ Food ◆ Tours ◆ Bar
◆ Distillery ◆ Shop

In 2016, Hombo Shuzo made the bold move of becoming the first craft producer in Japan to set up a second whisky distillery, to cash in on the resurgence of Japanese whisky. For this one, the Hombo family went back to its roots in Tsunuki, Kagoshima – its historical home.

What Hombo Shuzo is after is diversity of character. Its original distillery, Mars Shinshu, is at high altitude between Japan's Central and Southern Alps. Mars Tsunuki, on the other hand, is a stone's throw from the sea. There's a self-guided tour where you can wander around the facilities, but the real draw is the old family home next door, which has been remodelled into the most beautiful visitor centre in Japan. Reserve ahead for lunch or dinner, then finish in style with a limited-edition single malt overlooking the Japanese garden.

THINGS TO DO NEARBY

Mt Kamegaoka
With stunning views of the Fukiagehama sand dunes to the north and the coastline of Bonotsu to the west, this is an ideal hike to burn some of those whisky calories off.

Akime Bay
007 fans will recognise this idyllic fishing village from the Bond movie *You Only Live Twice*. Mercifully, not much has changed in the intervening 50 years since filming took place.

SATSUMA SHUZŌ

26 Tategami-honmachi, Makurazaki, Kagoshima
Prefecture; www.satsuma.co.jp; +81 993-72-4741

◆ Food ◆ Tours ◆ Transport
◆ Distillery ◆ Shop

Satsuma Shuzō, in southern Kyūshū, is a superb place to learn about *shōchū*. The atmospheric white-walled, black-roofed factory and museum buildings, collectively known as Meijigura, are open to the public for free tours. The name Meijigura means 'distillery of the Meiji period' and Satsuma Shuzō uses traditional methods for making *shōchū* from that era (1868-1912), distilling from barley, rice, buckwheat, sugar cane and locally grown sweet potatoes; Satsuma Shuzō also uses the latter to brew tasty craft beer.

The on-site Kedogawa Beer House sells meals, *shōchū* and beer. Reserve your tour at least two days in advance, and ask to try the Satsuma Shiranami – it's a full-bodied and aromatic *shōchū* made from local Satsuma-imo sweet potatoes.

THINGS TO DO NEARBY

Kaimon-dake
This perfect-cone 924m-high volcano, known as 'Satsuma Fuji' because of its resemblance to Fuji-san, makes a great four- to five-hour return hike offering superlative views.

Ibusuki Sand Bath
Join the crowds being buried in the sand at Ibusuki's beach, warmed from below by natural hot springs, then wash off in the regular onsen (hot spring). www.sa-raku.sakura.ne.jp

ZUISEN DISTILLERY

1-35 Shuri, Sakiyama-cho, Naha City, Okinawa;
www.zuisen.co.jp; +81 98-884-1968

◆ Distillery ◆ Shop
◆ Tours ◆ Transport

Awamori is considered the oldest type of distilled liquor in Japan and Zuisen is one of the oldest producers. Its distillery is in beachy Okinawa, the southernmost part of Japan to which *awamori* is indigenous – an area that was once its own kingdom with a distinct cultural identity. *Awamori* is made using Thai-style long-grain indica rice, fermented using a unique, local black koji mold, distilled in pot stills and (some of it) aged in clay pots.

Because of Zuisen's age, it's a good place to get the whole then-and-now picture. There's a lot to see and absorb, and

staff are exceptionally keen to let your taste buds explore their 50-plus range of *awamori*: set aside some time. It's an acquired taste, so start out with a mild expression such as the Hakuryu on the rocks, or diluted with water.

THINGS TO DO NEARBY

Shuri-jō Castle
Once the centre of the Ryūkyū Kingdom and now a Unesco World Heritage Site, you can easily spend a whole day here, even you're not a history buff. www.oki-park.jp/shurijo/en/

Ryukyu Sabo Ashibiuna
A traditional Okinawan restaurant with a stunning garden. It's near the castle, reasonably priced and the food is top-notch, so you may have to wait a bit.

MIYAGIKYO DISTILLERY

1 Nikka, Aoba-ku, Sendai City, Miyagi; www.nikka.com/
eng/distilleries/miyagikyo; +81 22-395-2865

◆ Distillery   ◆ Shop   ◆ Transport
◆ Tours   ◆ Bar

THINGS TO DO NEARBY

Umami Tasuke
Grilled beef tongue is a
Sendai speciality. There is
a plethora of restaurants
to pick from, but if you
only have time to visit one,
make it Umami Tasuke.

Kamakura
Not to be confused
with the seaside city
south of Tokyo, this
mountain is a popular
hiking spot near
Miyagikyo distillery.

Sakunami Onsen
Easily accessible from
Sendai, this onsen district
has various outdoor baths
that allow you to take in
the spectacular scenery.
Seek out Ichinobo – a
particularly nice one that's
open to the public.

Le Bar Kawagoe
Old liqueurs, antique
glassware, beautifully
crafted cocktails and
an interesting selection
of whiskies: this bar in
Sendai is the perfect
place to start (and/or
finish) the night.

In the mid-1960s, Masataka Taketsuru felt the need to expand the range of malt whiskies available to him to make more complex blended whiskies. In Scotland, producers swap stock so diversity is relatively easy to accomplish. In Japan, there was (and still is) no such tradition so the only way to increase diversity is to produce it in-house – hence the idea of setting up a second distillery in a completely different environment.

Miyagikyo is the yin to Yoichi's yang: light, fruity and floral versus robust, oily and often smoky. The atmosphere is very different, too. Miyagikyo is a beautiful example of a distillery coexisting with nature. Red-brick buildings following the natural undulation of the terrain are tucked away between two rivers, and it's not unusual to be greeted by a wild monkey when approaching the distillery. Grain whisky, gin and neutral spirits are also produced on site, but those facilities are not open to the public.

Tours are in Japanese only, but there's a handy smartphone/tablet app you can use to get the info in a number of different languages. There's a great bar and distillery shop on site, so you'll leave in good spirits. Try the Miyagikyo 'Sherry & Sweet' whisky, a distillery exclusive.

EUR

OPE

BURGUNDY

France is a boozy bottomless bowl when it comes to spirits, producing an astounding breadth of tipples. It's in Burgundy that you'll find some of the most interesting: Pontarlier is the home of absinthe, whose production is once again thriving. And in between the vines there's also crème de cassis.

AMSTERDAM

Dutch jenever is the spirit that inspired London's gin, and Amsterdam is crammed with creaky tasting houses dating back to the 17th and 18th centuries, still distilling to original recipes. Some, like House of Bols, now combine that heritage with thoroughly modern tasting experiences.

LONDON

The global gin revival was arguably kick-started in London, when craft brand Sipsmith received a landmark distilling licence that turned the industry on its head. Visit this distillery and many others in the Brit capital, hopping between heritage dens, derelict car parks and warehouses.

GLOBAL DISTILLERY TOUR

BELGIUM

How to ask for a spirit without mixers in the local language? Puur or sec

Signature spirit/spirit style? Genièvre

What to order with your spirits? Kip-kap (pork brawn), cheese and salami cubes

Don't: ever drink an aged genièvre chilled

The Belgians are friendly people, proud of their hospitable drinking culture where everyone is welcomed in even the tiniest village cafe or bar, known as 'estaminets'. Internationally renowned for its hundreds of different beers, Belgium has also produced the distinctive spirit genièvre for centuries. A first distillation of grain mash undergoes a second distillation with aromatic juniper berries, producing genièvre, the historic forerunner of today's gin (and the same spirit as Dutch jenever).

At the end of the 19th century, personal consumption hit an outrageous peak of nine litres per year in Belgium, though that changed with the Germans melting down distilleries' copper stills for armaments during WWI, followed by a severe 1919 Temperance. Today, however, genièvre is enjoying a popular resurgence. This is a complex country, hopelessly divided on nationalist and linguistic lines between Dutch-speaking Flanders and French-speaking Wallonia, but Belgians are united in drinking the national tipple, which goes under several different names thanks to Belgium's linguistic tapestry – genièvre, jenever, peket.

Everyone loves a glass; an aged jenever sipped by Flemish aficionados in specialist Antwerp bars, mixed as a cocktail in a hip French-speaking Brussels speakeasy, or chugged down on riotous Saturday nights in €1 shot glasses of lemon, chocolate or peach-flavoured varieties by festive students in university towns like Mons and Liège. More recently, a new generation of artisan distillers are looking beyond genièvre, creating craft gins, like Heynsquared's Ginderella, made from foraged wild herbs in Ghent, while others have taken the pioneering path to create Belgian whisky, absinthe and even rum. It's not always possible to visit these distilleries, but look to Belgium's bars and you'll find their wares.

■ BAR

'T DREUPELKOT

12 Groentenmarkt, Ghent; www.dreupelkot.be;
+32 9 2242120

◆ Shop ◆ Transport
◆ Bar

Ghent's most famous watering hole sits on a picturesque river bank in the historic centre, with a dark, cosy salon packed to bursting from sunset to the early hours. The bar is dedicated to Belgium's national drink: genièvre for French-speakers, or jenever in Flemish – the precursor of modern gin. This aromatic alcohol, initially distilled from wheat or barley mash, is distilled again with juniper berries and other botanicals.

It is said to have been accidentally discovered in 1303 by a Brussels alchemist searching for gold. The Dutch then commercialised it to the world, and England demonised it as 'Mother's Ruin'. There is a daunting list of 215 to choose from here, including traditional stone bottles of 10-year-aged genièvre, as highly prized as single malt.

The genial owner, Pol, holds court behind a minuscule bar as he has for 33 years, performing the Dreupelkot ritual of lining up tiny shot glasses, filling them to the brim, and waiting for customers to bow their heads and take a little sip before raising the glass. Working with a local distiller, Pol himself oversees the production of 50 different spirits – any serious drinker should try a glass of his fiery red pepper genièvre.

THINGS TO DO NEARBY

Design Museum
Hidden down a medieval backstreet in Ghent, ancient and modern blend in this cutting-edge design museum with contemporary exhibitions showcased in a grand 18th-century mansion. *www.designmuseumgent.be*

De Charlatan
The Ghent nightlife scene is legendary, and since the days of techno this labyrinthine bar, concert venue and dance club has been the place for partying. *www.charlatan.be*

St Jacobs Flea Market
The square surrounding the medieval church St-Jacobskerk is invaded by teeming flea market stalls every Friday, Saturday and Sunday morning, brimming with bric-à-brac bargains.

Canal Boat Trip
There's no better way to get a feel for Ghent than a romantic boat ride along criss-crossing canals and rivers lined with ornate medieval guild houses. *www.debootjesvangent.be*

BELGIAN OWL

Fexhe-le-Haut-Clocher, Meuse Valley, near Liège;
www.belgianwhisky.com; +32 4 2230717

◆ Distillery   ◆ Shop   ◆ Transport
◆ Tours   ◆ Bar

Whisky is not what most people expect in beer-loving Belgium, but master distiller Etienne Bouillon has won global awards for his Belgian Owl, including European Single Cask Whiskey of the Year at the World Whiskies Awards. And surprises keep coming for enthusiasts that make a pilgrimage to his state-of-the-art distillery near Liège.

Spread over an entire 17th-century enclosed hamlet, the distillery is dominated by two immense 1898 copper stills that Etienne miraculously persuaded the Scottish Caperdonich distillery to sell him – unheard of in the closed world of Scottish whisky. This was the final part of his jigsaw necessary to make a remarkable single malt. The two-hour 'from the field to the bottle' tour takes visitors outside to see the barley growing, the crucial primary ingredient of Belgian Owl, while

THINGS TO DO NEARBY

Le Pot au Lait
Conservative Liège has a hidden secret: one of the most surreal bars imaginable. Prepare for irreverent psychedelic murals, sculptures, art installations, great cocktails and DJ sets. *www.potaulait.be/en/*

Le Ratin-Tot
In the heart of medieval Namur, Le Ratin-Tot is a traditional pub that dates back to 1616 – perfect for sampling traditional Trappist ales. *www.facebook.com/ratintot/*

La Closerie des Prébendiers
No one imagines wine from Belgium, but high above the Meuse river, vineyards date back 1000 years. Try its crisp white müller thurgau and pinot gris. *https://en.liegetourisme.be/closerie-des-prebendiers.html*

Namur's Citadel
Trek up though the wooded slopes of this immense military fortress, which towers over the picturesque city of Namur and has panoramic views across the snaking Meuse and Sambre rivers.

the hamlet's ancient well pumps out the perfect pure water to distil along with the mash of fermented malted barley. The result is an authentic, quality Belgian whisky.

As production is relatively small, specific vintages are quickly sold out, so ask to taste Monsieur Bouillon's personal selection, Belgian Owl Passion, which is aged for three years in a single numbered cask.

FRANCE

How to ask for a spirit without mixers? Say 'sec' if you want it neat, or 'avec des flacons' for on the rocks
Signature spirits? Calvados or cognac, both served neat
What to order with your spirits? Nothing – French spirits are best appreciated when drunk as digestifs after a meal
Do: Try a Ti'-Punch, a delicious but lethal mix of rhum agricole from the French Caribbean, sugar cane syrup and lime juice

The French spirits scene is unparalleled when it comes to the key combination of variety, quality and heritage. Drinking a strong distilled liqueur after a meal – the classic 'digestif' – is the perfect way to digest the nation's gourmet cuisine, a gesture imbibed in the Gallic personality. And just as the secret behind French gastronomy lies in the different regional influences, so each spirit is uniquely tied to the region where it is produced, be it cognac, armagnac, calvados or chartreuse.

The history of distilling here stretches back to the 14th century, when the usual suspects – monks and abbots – experimented with handmade copper alembics to distil wine and fruits into alcohol, creating mysterious medicinal elixirs treating an encyclopedia of ailments. It did not take long for these miracle cures to be appreciated by the population at large, and the first brandy – literally 'burnt wine' – was born in the Armagnac region of southwestern France. Soon distillers in the vineyards around Cognac were transforming wine into a unique amber nectar aged in wooden casks. Across the country, vignerons developed their own tradition of 'marc', distilling not wine but the leftover grape pomace in the same manner as Italy's grappa producers. And not wanting to be left out, farmers in Normandy, Alsace and the east of France created their own distinctive fruit *eaux de vie* (fruit brandies)

by distilling apples into calvados, cherries into kirsch, and experimenting with potent herbs and plants to create the legendary absinthe.

However, this is not a nation to rest on its laurels, basking in the world's never-ending love affair with cognac and calvados, Bénédictine or Cointreau. The reality is that there are a lot of exciting new spirits arriving in bars here every year. What makes the French stand out on the global distillation scene is that when they decide to do something new, they display a single-minded pursuit of excellence to become the best. No one would ever have thought of drinking a vodka or gin 'made in France', but in just a few years, Grey Goose became one of the leading international vodkas, while artisan distilleries are producing quality craft creations like Fair's Quinoa Vodka or Citadelle, a flowery

TOP 5 SPIRITS

- **Poire Williams** Distillerie Miclo, Alsace
- **La Libertine absinthe** Distillerie Paul Devoille, Burgundy-Franche-Comte
- **Réserve du Château calvados** Château du Breuil, Normandy
- **Bénédictine** Palais Bénédictine, Normandy
- **Noces d'Or Sublime** Hardy Cognac, Grande Champagne

botanical gin made in a Cognac still. High-quality whisky is being produced in the wilds of Brittany. And the Jura single malt found in a swish Paris cocktail bar may not hail from Scotland's famous Hebridean island. Instead, it's distilled in the Jura region in eastern France, historically known for its fruit brandies and absinthe.

France remains a country where everyone still enjoys *la goutte* (a drop of alcohol); be it in a rural restaurant, where after dessert and cheese *le patron* brings out his precious 30-year-old bottle of Poire Williams pear brandy; in an elegant Michelin-starred dining room whose sommelier tempts diners with a snifter of 1949 armagnac; or at the bistrot's classic zinc bar, where early-morning workers order a café calva – an espresso lined up alongside a shot of calvados.

"France has a long heritage of distilling spirits in a variety of styles and categories whose excellence has created icons across the globe"

—RENAUD FILLIOUX DE GIRONDE, HENNESSY

DISTILLERIE G MICLO

Lieu-dit Gayire, Lapoutroie, Alsace;
www.distillerie-miclo.com; +33 3 89 47 50 16

◆ Distillery   ◆ Shop
◆ Tours

In the 1950s Gilbert Miclo travelled around Alsace for his wine merchant father, buying up artisan *eaux de vie* (fruit brandies) direct from farmers who were distilling the produce of their orchards. Determined he could do better himself, Gilbert set up two alembics in his front room and Distillerie G Miclo was born. Today it is the biggest producer of *eaux de vie* in Alsace, family-run by Gilbert's grandson, and its modern distillery is in the Vosges mountains.

An hour-long visit includes a stroll through an educational garden with plants and fruits used to make the brandies, then a film explaining the mysterious process of distillation, with ripe fruit fermented then distilled in metal vats before bottling. It is this process that gives *eau de vie* its distinctive

THINGS TO DO NEARBY

Château du Haut-Koenigsbourg
One of France's most awesome fortress castles, the medieval ochre-coloured Koenigsbourg sits atop a 700-metre rocky outcrop, overlooking rolling hills covered with picturesque vineyards.
www.haut-koenigsbourg.fr

Col du Bonhomme
A steep zigzag route climbs up this 950-metre peak, a mythical venue for the Tour de France bike race, as well as a base for paragliding and cross-country skiing.*www.tourisme-alsace.com*

Sainte-Marie-Aux-Mines
Nicknamed 'Silver Valley', in Sainte-Marie-Aux-Mines you can explore the narrow galleries of a 16th-century silver mine guided by volunteer speleologists, or visit nearby Tellure – a silver theme park.
www.asepam.org

Musée Albert Schweitzer
The picturesque medieval village of Kaysersberg was once home to the musicologist, medical doctor and 1952 Nobel Peace Prize laureate Albert Schweitzer (1875–1965), and this museum is dedicated to his life.

clarity compared with amber spirits such as cognac, which are aged in barrels. Tastings begin with fruit specialities – kirsch, Poire Williams, raspberry, damso – then move on to stranger spirits made from quince, cumin or holly. As long as there is a designated driver, finish with its single-malt Alsatian whisky.

MUSÉE DES EAUX DE VIE

85 rue du Général Dufieux, Lapoutroie, Alsace;
www.musee-eaux-de-vie.com; tel:+33 3 89 47 50 26

◆ Tours ◆ Bar
◆ Shop ◆ Transport

Driving through the sleepy village of Lapoutroie, it's impossible to miss the yellow 18th-century coaching post that today houses this staggering private collection dedicated to the art of distillation. The wood-beamed museum is crammed with rare collectibles, from art nouveau Poire Williams posters to Pastis water carafes and thousands of vintage bottles of brandies and liqueurs. Above all, there are historical examples of all the weird and wonderful paraphernalia used in distillation: stills, presses, juice extractors, barrels and corking apparatus, bottles and glasses. Jovial owner René de Miscault holds court in the on-site bar, enthusiastically pouring *eaux de vie* and absinthe. As a souvenir, take home a jar of juicy *griottes* (cherries in kirsch liqueur).

THINGS TO DO NEARBY

Fromagerie Haxaire
This working dairy farm produces Alsace's famous Munster cheese. Come for a gourmet visit to watch the complex fabrication, then taste this creamy, pungent fromage. *www.facebook. com/haxaire*

Lac Blanc Bike Park
A tailor-made park offering adventurous mountain biking in the Vosges mountains. The rough wooded trails are graded and surround the waters of White Lake. *www. lacblanc-bikepark.com*

ESPACE PAGÈS MAISON VERVEINE DU VELAY

29 place du Breuil, Le Puy-en-Velay, Auvergne;
www.verveine.com; +33 4 71 03 04 11

◆ Food ◆ Bar
◆ Shop ◆ Transport

In France's Auvergne region, there's no sweeter medicine than verveine liqueur. Created in 1859 as a tonic to soothe the nervous and digestive systems, this viridescent liqueur is a blend of 32 plants including fragrant verveine citronnelle, which gives the elixir its name.
Distillerie Pagès, where the liqueur is bottled, offers 45-minute guided tours, but verveine's bright-green heart is 8km west at the Espace Pagès in Le Puy-en-Velay. Within this tasting room and boutique, nostrils flare over samples of the liqueur's varieties: the radioactive-green original, with notes of nutmeg and mint; coppery brown 'Extra', strengthened by cognac; the lighter 'Gold' verveine and perfumed 'Petite Verte'. At the adjoining Pub la Distillerie, try it muddled into a mojito.

THINGS TO DO NEARBY

Chapelle St-Michel d'Aiguilhe
Le Puy-en-Velay owes its rugged skyline to dormant volcanoes and plumes of volcanic rock. One such rocky crag is crowned with this 10th-century chapel. *www.rochersaintmichel.fr*

Cathédrale Notre Dame
Grand arches frame the entryway to Le Puy-en-Velay's own Notre Dame, bedecked with Roman frescoes. Its the starting point of the French Way of St James pilgrimage route. *www.cathedraledupuy.org*

CAVES DE LA CHARTREUSE

10 boulevard Edgar-Kofler, Voiron, Auvergne-Rhône-Alpes; www.chartreuse.fr; +33 4 76 05 81 77

◆ Distillery ◆ Shop ◆ Transport
◆ Tours ◆ Bar

In 1605, a Carthusian monk inscribed a herbal tonic recipe onto parchment. More than four centuries later, the liqueur – famous for its greenish, gold-flecked colour – is sipped around the world.

To safeguard the precious recipe during the French Revolution, monks smuggled it out of the country. Thanks to their efforts the fragrant formula, comprising 130 herbs and roots, has remained unchanged. Liqueur production, which began in earnest in 1737, still takes place under the watchful eyes of monks who live amid the steep, forested land now gazetted as Chartreuse Regional Park.

West of the park in Voiron are the Caves de la Chartreuse: a museum revering the liqueur's long history and a warren of cellars where the cool air is tinged with Chartreuse's minty, vegetal aroma. Guides lead visitors past huge oaken barrels and, with a raised eyebrow, offer a dab of 69%-alcohol Elixir Végétal – still a staple in French grandmothers' medicine cabinets. More drinkable are vert (green) and jaune (yellow) Chartreuse: the former is grassy-hued with a sharp herbal kick, the latter a floral concoction that slips down the throat like honey.

After the tour, most visitors haul a clanking box of bottles home. Instead, linger to enjoy the perfect sweet-sour balance of Chartreuse with ice-cold pineapple juice.

THINGS TO DO NEARBY

Musée de la Grande Chartreuse
Want to peer into the lives of the Carthusian monks at the helm of Chartreuse liqueur production? Head to this museum, 24km east of the cellars. *www.musee-grande-chartreuse.fr*

St-Pierre-de-Chartreuse–Le Planolet
Skiers seeking low-key thrills will delight in Le Planolet's 35km of mostly easy, tree-lined runs. Not recommended after too many sips of Chartreuse liqueur. *www.ski-alpin-chartreuse.com*

Parc Naturel Régional de Chartreuse
More than 1300km of walking trails spider through this dramatic regional park, a 767 sq km wilderness of forests, limestone caves and razor-edged cliffs. *www.parc-chartreuse.net*

Fort de Bastille
Some 25km southeast of Voiron is the bubbly city of Grenoble, whose centrepiece, a looming 19th-century fortress, has peerless mountain views, as well as museums and cafes on-site. *www.bastille-grenoble.com*

DISTILLERIE DES MENHIRS

Pont Menhir, Plomelin, Brittany;
www.distillerie.bzh; +33 2 98 94 23 68

◆ Distillery   ◆ Shop
◆ Tours

Celtic culture abounds in the region of Finistère and that includes the water of life, whisky. While there are a few distilleries in Brittany, the Distillerie des Menhirs – named after the huge standing stones opposite – is the only one offering whiskies made entirely with buckwheat, a grain used in Brittany's galette pancakes.

The distillery is run by the fifth generation of the Le Lay family, who produce a number of different whiskies under the Eddu label, as well as ciders and *lambig* (Breton cider brandy). The heady scents of apple and barley hit you as you enter the warehouses. In the cellars, hundreds of barrels are overlooked by a stained glass window of Queen Anne, who first brought buckwheat to Brittany. Try the Silver blend, which is like no other whisky and glides down like honey.

THINGS TO DO NEARBY

Quimper
With its colourful timber-framed buildings and mighty twin-spired cathedral, Quimper is the perfect place to soak up Breton culture and scoff galettes in the town's Place au Beurre.

Beaches
The south Finistère coast is a delight, especially the charming fishing harbour of Le Guilvinec to the wild and windswept beaches of Pointe de la Torche, where you can surf the rolling Atlantic waves.

DISTILLERIE LES FILS D'EMILE PERNOT

18 au Frambourg, La Cluse-et-Mijoux, Burgundy;
http://en.emilepernot.fr; +33 3 81 39 04 28

◆ Food   ◆ Bar
◆ Shop   ◆ Transport

This grand 19th-century distillery oozes history. The moment France re-legalised absinthe in 2009, the descendants of Emile Pernot, one of the pioneer distillers of the original recipe of The Green Fairy created by Dr Pierre Ordinaire, resurrected production with their original century-old copper alembics. The result is an exceptional selection, ranging from the traditional 1797 – an intense herbal recipe with hints of wormwood, anise and fennel – to more sophisticated absinthes such as Cousin Jeune, perfect for cocktails.

The distillery is famous for Vieux Pontarlier, an artisan *pastis* (anise-flavoured aperitif) and its aromatic Gentiane, distilled from a mountain plant. Don't miss the shop's absinthe accessories: specialist spoons, absinthe fountains, you name it.

THINGS TO DO NEARBY

Château de Joux
This ornate chateau fortress has protected Pontarlier's strategic mountain pass between France and Switzerland for 1000 years, and now houses a museum of rare weapons. **www.chateaudejoux.com**

Musée Gustave Courbet
Overlooking Ornan's meandering Loue river, the grand home of 19th-century Neo-Realism painter Gustave Courbet houses a remarkable collection of his paintings. ***https://musee-courbet.doubs.fr***

ABSINTHE: THE GREEN FAIRY THEN & NOW

The word absinthe strikes fear into the heart of even a hardened drinker. Its shady reputation as the mind-bending tipple that sent Van Gogh mad and inspired the delirious scribblings of Rimbaud has lingered for a century, yet a foray into its heartland – on the border between eastern France and Switzerland – reveals absinthe to be a much-misunderstood drink.

It is still on the strong side – around 50% to 60% ABV – but with botanicals such as aniseed, lemon balm, mint and Melissa, which temper the bitterness of the wormwood (named absinthe in French), it is refreshing, floral and easy to drink.

In the late 1980s, tests proved that the ingredient thujone in wormwood wasn't as toxic as believed in the early 20th century.

Back then, the 'scientific' evidence of its toxicity came after injecting thujone into mice's brains, which gave ammunition to a terrifying propaganda campaign from the church. With vineyards only just recovering from the ravaging effects of the phylloxera virus, wineries, too, were happy to put an end to its popularity and supported the campaign.

So, in 1910 in Switzerland and 1915 in France, absinthe was banned. Distilleries in France shut or diversified into spirits such as pastis, another aniseed-flavoured drink. In Switzerland's Val de Travers, which had its own thriving industry, production went underground, giving birth to a clandestine industry.

Fast-forward about 100 years, with the ban overturned, and many of these former bootleggers are at the heart of the drink's renaissance (albeit using a lower permitted level of thujone). Dozens of small, artisan distilleries can now be found throughout Val de Travers in Switzerland and around Pontarlier in France. They form part of the official Route de l'Absinthe (www.routedelabsinthe.com), a cross-border trail between museums, distilleries, fountains and other historic sites that demystify the drink, and tell of times during the ban when locals distilled and drank absinthe in secret – stashing bottles in the woods and drinking it al fresco with natural spring water.

Today, remarkably few bars serve absinthe, so the best place to try it is at the distilleries. It is often served *à la Parisienne* – an elaborate ritual centred around a glass fountain with spigots that slowly drip iced water through a sugar cube placed on a slotted spoon resting on the rim of the glass, until the glass is around one part absinthe, three or four parts water. Keep your eyes peeled for when the water first hits the transparent or green-tinted absinthe and begins to turn it cloudy. That first twist of colour was known as 'the Green Fairy', the moment when the aromas from the herbs are liberated. In the 19th century this was thought to be when the madness began, though more likely it came from the drinker's side order of opium.

BY CAROLYN BOYD

ARTISAN DISTILLERY PAUL DEVOILLE

9 rue des Moines Haut, Fougerolles, Burgundy-Franche-Comte;
www.devoille.com; +33 3 84 49 10 66

◆ Distillery   ◆ Shop
◆ Tours   ◆ Transport

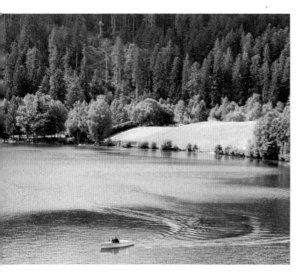

THINGS TO DO NEARBY

L'Auberge des Mille Etangs
This 18th-century auberge
has four private lakes
that can be reserved for
fly-fishing, plus a gourmet
restaurant serving locally
caught crayfish, eels
and perch-pike. *www.
aubergedesmilleetangs.fr*

La Rochère
A historic glass works
dating back to 1475,
renowned for architectural
glass tiles. Visit the
furnaces for free to
witness traditional glass-
blowing techniques.
www.larochere.com

La Chaloupe, Gérardmer
Gérardmer's idyllic lake
nestles in the Vosges
mountains and is best
explored by pedalo or
canoe, or by hiking through
thick forests surrounding
the water's edge. *www.
lachaloupe.free.fr*

**Les Thermes de
Luxeuil-les-Bains**
Luxeuil's Roman baths date
back 2000 years; visit the
18th-century municipal spa,
with its pools, Jacuzzis and
modern treatment centres.
*www.chainethermale.fr/
luxeuil-les-bains.html*

The sleepy village of Fougerolles is France's cherry
capital, surrounded by orchards of 10,000 trees that
have been distilled into *kirsch* (cherry brandy) since
the founding of Paul Devoille's distillery in 1859. Its ground
floor is where mashed, fermented cherries and other fruits,
such as plum and pear, are double-distilled in traditional
alembics. Things get interesting when the visit moves up to
the vast attic, where hundreds of wickered glass demijohns
are stacked high to the rafters. This is the Devoille system of
ageing. For two to six years, the pure fruit alcohol sits here
through intensely hot summers and freezing winters – perfect
conditions to produce an exceptional *eau de vie* (fruit brandy).

When absinthe fever was at its height at the end of the 19th
century Devoille was a major producer, and now that it's back
in demand the distillery is again bottling an unusually made
absinthe, La Libertine. Each type of plant used to make it is
dried, macerated and distilled separately, secretly blended,
then bottled without ageing. Walk through Le Jardin Secret to
discover the plants used in Devoille's absinthe recipe, such as
wormwood, fennel, hyssop, speedwell and chamomile.

CASSISSIUM

8 Passage Montgolfier, Nuits-Saint-Georges,
Burgundy-Franche-Comté; www.cassissium.fr; +33 3 80 62 49 70

◆ Distillery ◆ Shop
◆ Tours ◆ Bar

Burgundy is better known for its wine than anything else and the vineyards around Nuits-Saint-Georges are home to some of the world's most expensive vintages, but between the Chablis and Pinot Noirs there lies the story of crème de cassis, a blackcurrant liqueur much loved in Burgundy and in France beyond. At Cassissium, the museum and distillery of the Védrenne brand, the story of the humble blackcurrant is told in detail through engaging interactive displays, vintage equipment and a film. The museum covers everything from its botany to how it's farmed, and also shows the history of crème de cassis.

The liqueur pops up time and again in the local cocktail 'kir', which is blended with white wine and was named after the

THINGS TO DO NEARBY

Nuits-Saint-Georges
The charming little town huddles around a narrow central square overlooked by the 17th-century belfry, which chimes at each quarter hour. Visit the wine boutiques and wineries for tastings.

Beaune
Foodies will love Beaune for its buzzing Saturday market, fromageries and wine boutiques. It also offers excellent restaurants with local-produce menus. Don't miss the Hotel Dieu, a medieval hospital.

Cycling in the vineyards
The vineyards outside Nuits-Saint-Georges are perfect cycling country, with pretty lanes between vineyards and sleepy villages – Route des Grands Crus is one of the world's most famous wine routes.

Ferme Fruirouge
To see a smaller, more rustic producer of crème de cassis, visit this small farm and its salon de thé to see how it macerates the blackcurrants in its copper pans to make liqueurs sold in dainty bottles. **www.fruirouge.fr**

post-war mayor of Dijon, Félix Kir, a church canon and former resistance fighter who championed the drink. The museum visit leads on to a tour of the distillery and then finally to the tasting bar adorned with vintage posters, where visitors can try Védrenne's products, including several crème de cassis and other fruit liqueurs, as well as cordials and brandies. The pièce de résistance is the Marcassin – a woozy blend of marc eau de vie and Védrenne's best crème de cassis.

DISTILLERIE GUY

49 rue des Lavaux, Pontarlier, Burgundy-Franche-Comté;
www.pontarlier-anis.com; +33 3 81 39 04 70

◆ Distillery   ◆ Shop
◆ Tours

THINGS TO DO NEARBY

Musée Municipale de Pontarlier
A whole floor of Pontarlier Town Museum is given over to the history of absinthe in the town, including its wealth of factories and distilleries. *www.routedelabsinthe.com*

Château de Joux
Towering high above the dramatic Doubs countryside just outside Pontarlier, this 12th-century fortress hosts evening shows, concerts and falconry displays. *www.chateaudejoux.com*

Au Bon Echanson
This bijou wine boutique in Pontarlier's main street is part of the absinthe trail and sells French and Swiss varieties, as well as paraphernalia such as absinthe fountains. *www.routedelabsinthe.com*

Jura mountains
The town of Pontarlier makes a good base for hikes in the Jura mountains, with trails leading up peaks and along ridges, past lakes and forests. *www.rando-jura.com*

In absinthe's heyday, Pontarlier was home to some 25 distilleries and dozens of bars employing around 3000 people, so when the ban came in the town was hit badly. One of the few distilleries to survive was Distillerie Guy, which was founded in 1890 by Armand Guy: after the ban, it concentrated on making other spirits.

Distillerie Guy's aniseed-based spirit Anis was created in 1921 in a bid to replace absinthe. It contains all the ingredients of the popular spirit, except for the absinthe plant itself. Alongside it, the aromatic Vert Sapin – the alcoholic equivalent of a walk in the forest – is still made to a recipe that dates from 1902, using the buds of the fir tree. These, along with other fruit liqueurs (still produced today), enabled the distillery's operation to survive after the absinthe ban.

Distillerie Guy is now run by the fourth and fifth generations of the Guy family. Tours explore the stages of absinthe's production, including the grand copper stills and oak casks, before absinthe tasting, complete with traditional perforated spoon, sugar cube and water fountain.

©Hemis/Alamy Stock Photo

DELAMAIN

7 rue Jacques & Robert Delamain, Jarnac;
www.delamain-cognac.fr; +33 5 45 81 08 24

◆ Tours   ◆ Transport

◆ Shop

This tiny outfit has a loyal following of connoisseurs, and with good reason. Still in the hands of its artistic founding family, visits are led by whoever is available, be it the cellar master, the master assembler or even the owner himself. Extremely specialised in Grande Champagne Vieilles Vignes, the brand does not do its own distilling, but distinguishes itself through its unique ageing process in the seasoned barrels of its medieval *chais* (ageing cellars). For the most part, it omits the prevalent technique of adding water to accelerate evaporation.

Tours are led as an olfactory initiation, using only the sense of smell to compare the *eaux de vie* (fruit brandies) that are ceremoniously gathered in a test tube (called a 'proof') from increasingly aged barrels. Try the award-winning Vesper blend.

THINGS TO DO NEARBY

Maison Natale de François Mitterand
François Mitterand, France's president from 1981 to 1995, was born in this house; it's now an archive of family memorabilia.
www.maison-natale-francois-mitterrand.org

La Ribaudière
A little further up the river from Delamain, in Bourg Charente, this quiet, chic restaurant has a Michelin star and offers menus that expertly pair each dish with cognac.
www.laribaudiere.com

HENNESSY

8 rue de la Richonne, Cognac; www.lesvisites.
hennessy.com; +33 5 45 35 06 44

◆ Distillery   ◆ Shop

◆ Tours   ◆ Transport

The unquestioned world leader (representing almost 50% of the global market) in Cognac was founded by a plucky Irishman in the 18th century, with an early flair for international sales. After a float down the river Charente, past the château where King François 1 was born, the main tour plunges visitors into the darkness of the newly renovated *chai*, celebrating the brand's rich history and influence in a modern, multisensory, interactive experience.

A more exclusive and immersive tour leads aficionados through the experimental vineyard to see the stunning 10

copper alembics still in use in the private distillery – it's an in-depth, half-day exploration with a glimpse of the choreography of cognac actually being made, and a taste of the brand's pride and joy, Paradis Impérial.

THINGS TO DO NEARBY

L'atelier des Quais
This romantic bistro facing the old king's château has a patio on the riverfront and a simple three-course lunch menu that's hard to beat.
www.atelierdesquais.fr

Cognac Canoë Club
Rent a canoe, stand-up paddleboard or small, easy-to-drive electric boat and follow the Charente river to discover the area from the water. **www.cognaccanoeclub.com**

MARTELL & CO

16 avenue Paul Firino Martell, Cognac;
www.martell.com; +33 5 45 36 34 98

◆ Food   ◆ Tours   ◆ Bar
◆ Distillery ◆ Shop   ◆ Transport

THINGS TO DO NEARBY

Musée des Arts du Cognac
Dedicated to the art of making cognac, this is a good place to get a global overview of the entire industry, from grape to bottle design.
www.musees-cognac.fr

Bar Luciole
Discreet cocktail bar with an innovative list of creations, all based around – can you guess? – cognac. The ambience is trendy, the drinks are divine.
www.bar-luciole.com

Marché Couvert
A 19th-century covered market hall in Cognac where you'll find everything you need for a picnic by the Charente. Open every morning except Mondays.

Chateau Royal de Cognac
A visit to see where King François 1 was born will also introduce you to the cognac of Baron Otard, who bought the chateau after the French revolution.
www.baronotard.com

A visit to the oldest of the 'big four' cognac producers begins in a suave room decorated with the amber colours of a good cognac, with touches of the indigo blue from the brand's bestselling Cordon Bleu XO, which is a throwback to founder Jean Martell's initial career in the trade of colour pigments. A wooden-clad tunnel moulded into the shape of an old *gabare* (a 19th-century boat used to transport barrels down the river) leads visitors back in time to the courtyard where, in 1715, a young man from Jersey sold cognac to everyone from the Duke of Orléans to George Washington.

The tour progresses through a diorama of the area's soils to the thousands of samples of *eaux de vie* in the assembly room, and a look into an ageing cellar that is now protected as part of France's industrial heritage. Finally, a poetic and passionate bartender will teach you to read the 'tears' on the side of the glass and taste the crescendo 'peacock's tail' of flavours on the tongue.

As well as the main site in town, a more in-depth tour to the Borderies site can be arranged to see the largest alembic in the region, as well as a VIP day within its Chanteloup estate for a more immersive, gastronomical experience. The latter includes an entire meal planned around the brand's signature XO, L'or de Jean Martell.

MICHEL FORGERON

Chez Richon, Segonzac; www.cognacforgeron.com;
+33 5 45 83 43 05

◆ Distillery   ◆ Shop
◆ Tours

 The drive through the vines to this independent winegrower, distiller and distributor is magical in itself, but the main reason to visit is family matriarch Francine, whose raw storytelling talent reveals the beauty of making cognac with complete sincerity and humour. Before getting up close with the harvesting machines and ageing tuns, Francine begins by sticking your nose in the grapes, the varieties of which include the pre-phylloxera folle blanche, which is notoriously difficult to grow. From there, hands on hips, Francine walks visitors through the process, shining the copper on the alembic as she goes. Visits are free and can last anything from 30 minutes to three hours. Don't miss the *barriques* (barrels), which are each guaranteed to contain a blend of cognacs from a single year between 1965 and 1996.

THINGS TO DO NEARBY

La Vue
A great base in the heart of the Grande Champagne region, this charming B&B with luxury gîtes is set high on a hill overlooking the vines. *www. lavuefrance.com*

Le Baume de Bouteville
Find out more about Cognac's local balsamic vinegar, reduced in the vineyard's alambic before ageing in barrels previously used for *eaux de vie*. *www. lebaumedebouteville.com*

REMY MARTIN

Avenue de Gimeux, Merpins;
www.visitesremymartin.com; +33 5 45 35 76 66

◆ Food   ◆ Tours   ◆ Bar
◆ Distillery   ◆ Shop

The original site of this 300-year-old big shot provides a good introduction to its famed fine champagne cognac, but families favour the varied and interactive pace of the Merpins site, just outside Cognac – especially the little train that whisks visitors between cellars.

In the tasting room, while the guide explains how to 'make the cognac dance in your glass', scrummy bites such as blue cheese and pear on a hazelnut biscuit, or a passionfruit and chocolate macaron, give a good introduction to food and cognac pairing. Keener fans should plump for the six-hour extravaganza exploring the creation of house jewel (and Churchill's favourite cognac) Louis XIII, which blends more than 1200 *eaux de vie* (fruit brandies), some of which are more than 100 years old.

THINGS TO DO NEARBY

Taransaud Cooperage
Rival brand Hennessy buys traditional barrels from this 400-year-old cooperage, which recently invented an egg-shaped barrel sought after by the region's winemakers. *www.taransaud.com*

Base Aérienne 709 Cognac-Châteaubernard
The French Air Force's initial pilot training school is based here in Cognac. If you are lucky enough to catch them, practice sessions can be quite spectacular.

■ **BAR**

L'ABSINTHE BAR

25 cours Massena, Antibes, Côte D'Azur;
www.facebook.com/AbsintheAntibes; +33 4 93 34 93 00

◆ Shop   ◆ Transport
◆ Bar

THINGS TO DO NEARBY

Musée Picasso
Picasso's Antibes studio, in the imposing 14th-century Château Grimaldi overlooking the sea, is now a splendid museum offering an intimate insight into his art. *www.antibesjuanlespins.com*

Jazz à Juan Festival
The world's greatest jazz musicians have gathered at this glamorous festival in a unique outdoor setting overlooking the Mediterranean every summer since 1960. *www.jazzajuan.com*

Chemin des Douaniers
This picturesque 5km ramble or bike ride from Cap D'Antibes' Plage De La Garoupe follows an old smugglers' trail along white sandy beaches, past cliffs and hideaway millionaires villas.

Thuret Botanical Garden
Victorian botanist Gustave Thuret bequeathed his Antibes villa to the nation, and his luxuriant gardens are landscaped with some 1600 exotic trees, flowers and plants. *www.sophia.inra.fr/jardin_thuret*

Few visitors wandering through Antibes' bustling Marché Provençal realise that tucked away in an ancient vaulted cellar below a touristy boutique lies a legendary bar-museum devoted to absinthe, the favourite hallucinatory tipple of Baudelaire, Rimbaud and Oscar Wilde that was banned for almost a century. Owner Daniel Rosenfelder is a fanatic and has created a buzzing locale where most evenings, accompanied by jazz musicians, the ambience heats up as absinthe puts everyone in a party mood.

Sitting around a *bistrot* table, Daniel initiates new devotees like a ceremonial high priest, filling an ornate art nouveau fountain with chilled water, beginning the slow drip-drip onto a sugar cube delicately balanced on a perforated spoon, and then down into the glass where the crystal-clear absinthe turns first cloudy, then faintly green. Order a second glass, and Monsieur Rosenfelder will jovially treat you like a local, making you put on one of his collection of hats. Choose a third from the 50 different absinthes, such as the 76° Résurrection, and it will be your last; house rules limit consumption, otherwise no one remembers much more of the evening.

DISTILLERIE LOUIS ROQUE

41 avenue Jean Jaurès, Souillac, Dordogne;
www.lavieilleprune.com; +33 5 65 32 78 16

◆ Distillery ◆ Shop
◆ Tours ◆ Transport

Walnut groves have peppered the banks of the Dordogne Valley since the 10th century, and the area's delectable walnut aperitifs and liqueurs are a local speciality. At family-run Distillerie Louis Roque, which dates from 1905, a large museum room displays antique copper alambics, vintage bottles and other memorabilia, including the horse-drawn stills that once went between orchards and groves, distilling farmers' fruit and nuts in situ.

The distillery seals its fruit and nut liqueurs with wax, bottling and labelling them on site. Its most successful product is La Vieille Prune, a plum liqueur for which the original Louis Roque became well known. But especially worth trying is the walnut liqueur Vieille Noix, great as a Christmas tipple, with a sweet and nutty flavour and retro brown-paper label.

THINGS TO DO NEARBY

Souillac market
Tucked away in the narrow streets of the old town, Souillac market offers the best of the Dordogne valley's local produce, from walnut oil to foie gras.

Dordogne Valley
Souillac makes a good base for exploring the imposing chateaux, fascinating gardens and golden-stone villages that lie either side of the sinuous Dordogne River, which is itself great for canoeing.

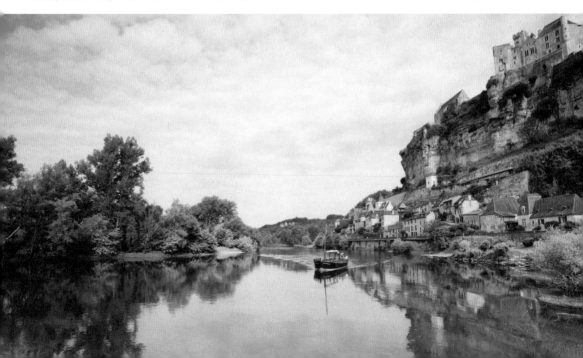

COINTREAU DISTILLERY

Boulevard des Bretonnières, Saint-Barthelemy-D'Anjou,
Angers, Loire; www.cointreau.com; +33 2 41 31 50 50

◆ Distillery ◆ Shop
◆ Tours ◆ Bar

Few French liqueurs embody the glamour that comes with Cointreau, which has maintained an exotic allure since its invention in Angers in 1875 when oranges were a rare and precious fruit. A visit to the distillery just outside Angers celebrates everything from its history and ingredients to its advertising heyday, as well as the classic cocktails – such as the Cosmopolitan and the Sidecar – in which it plays a starring role.

Expect all five senses to be indulged as you get to smell the bitter orange peels that form Cointreau's central flavour and tour the jaw-dropping giant orange stills with their

THINGS TO DO NEARBY

Château d'Angers
This mighty fortress has 17 towers that punctuate its mighty 2.5-metre-thick walls. Take a walk around its ramparts for a bird's eye view of the city.
www.chateau-angers.fr

Tapestry of the Apocalypse
Inside the chateau, this work of medieval art is an attraction in itself. Created in 1375, the 104-metre tapestry charts the battle between good and evil in the Bible's book of Revelations.

Terra Botanica
This gentle theme park celebrates all aspects of plant life with stunning gardens and rides including a tethered hot air balloon that rises over the site. *www.terrabotanica.fr*

Cathédrale Saint-Maurice
Angers' attractive 12th- and 13th-century cathedral sports some impressive stained glass windows, and makes a good starting point for exploring the city.

intricate copper piping. Sunglasses may be required – not for the hangover that may ensue, but rather to counteract the dazzling orange colour scheme that is carried through the whole experience to chime with the drink's branding.

The tasting (with nibbles) is the highlight. In the stylish bar at the end, staff present both classic cocktails as well as more unusual concoctions using lesser-known products such as the tangy Blood Orange Cointreau or the indulgent Cointreau Noir, which is blended with cognac to wonderfully woozy effect.

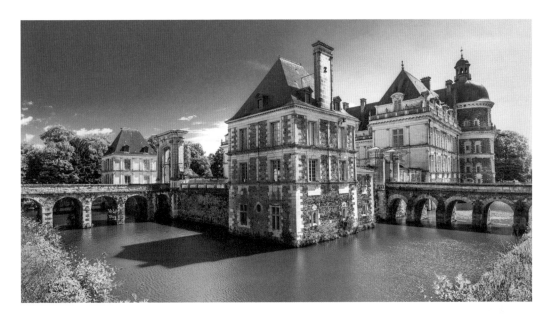

DISTILLERIE GIFFARD

Giffard Chemin du Bocage, Avrillé, Angers, Loire;
www.giffard.com; +31 2 41 18 85 00

◆ Distillery ◆ Shop
◆ Tours

It's better known in France as the home of Cointreau, but Angers in the Western Loire is also the city where crème de menthe has its roots. The Giffard distillery's most famous product is the mint liqueur Menthe-Pastille, which was created by pharmacist Emile Giffard in 1885 when Angers was hit by a heatwave and locals craved a drink to cool them down. The small museum at the distillery in the suburbs of the city celebrates the history of this refreshing liqueur, used in such cocktails as the original White Lady and the Stinger, and features posters, display boards and a cool little tasting bar with a sensory experience to test your olfactory skills. The distillery also creates a huge range of other cocktail ingredients, from fruit liqueurs to cordials, including another local speciality, Guignolet d'Angers – a sweet cherry brandy.

THINGS TO DO NEARBY

Château de Serrant
Angers is at the far western end of the chateaux-filled Loire Valley and this majestic moated château just outside the city is enchanting, particularly its library and vaulted kitchens.
www.chateau-serrant.net

Les Guinguettes bars
Hire a bike or float a canoe down the Mayenne and Loire rivers that surround Angers to discover the riverside bars known as Les Guinguettes – the new incarnations of 17th-century drinking cabarets.

CHÂTEAU DU BREUIL

14130 Le Breuil en Auge, Normandy;
chateau-breuil.info; +33 2 31 65 60 00

◆ Distillery   ◆ Shop
◆ Tours   ◆ Bar

Between the hills and woodlands of Pays d'Auges lie Normandy's apple orchards. It's here the region's ciders, apple brandy calvados and aperitif pommeau are produced by dozens of farms and distilleries. Among the best set up for visitors is Château du Breuil, a 16th- and 17th-century manor house south of Pont L'Evêque, producing calvados and other spirits such as whisky, gin and cognac.

Visits include a look at the grand stills once used to create its calvados and a glimpse into the atmospheric cellars where the heady aroma of sweet apples permeates the air, and where the ancient oak casks of ageing calvados are arranged in neat rows. Look up to admire the wooden-beamed roof built by Normandy's best ship-builders; it looks like a boat's upturned hull. When it comes to the tasting, you may be offered the vanilla-infused calvados, which is a twist on the tradition. More interesting for those new to calvados is to taste the different aged varieties, from two to 20 years old, which shows how the flavours become more complex as each vintage matures.

THINGS TO DO NEARBY

Pont L'Évêque
Famous for its eponymous pungent cheese, the town of Pont L'Évêque has colourful, timber-framed buildings and a vibrant market. The nearby lake is a good spot for watersports.

Cerza Safari park and zoo
Home to some 1500 wild animals from all over the world, this animal park is one of France's best and has around 120 different species to admire in the spacious enclosures. *www.cerza.com*

Calvados Experience
This multimedia visitor centre, part of the Pére Magloire distillery, opened in March 2018 and celebrates the region's history of calvados with multisensory exhibits. *www.calvados-experience.com/en/*

Deauville
This ritzy resort was the place to see and be seen in the early 20th century. Walk the seaside boardwalk, where each cabin is named after a famous movie star, and lounge on the beach, known for its colourful tents and parasols.

PALAIS BÉNÉDICTINE

110 rue Alexandre Le Grand, Fécamp, Normandy;
www.benedictinedom.com; +33 2 35 10 26 10

◆ Food ◆ Tours ◆ Bar
◆ Distillery ◆ Shop ◆ Transport

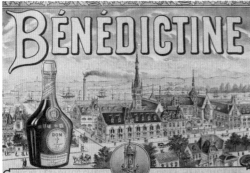

THINGS TO DO NEARBY

Chez Nounoute

Overlooking Fécamp's port, the seafood in this classic brasserie comes straight from local boats, selected by Madame Nounoute herself – a former fishmonger and married to a fisherman. *www.cheznounoute.com*

La Ferme aux Escargots

Tour a traditional Normandy farm breeding snails to discover the strange secrets of this French foodie delicacy, and take home a jar of delicious escargots. *www.fermeauxescargots.com*

La Mer Pour Tous

Sail from Fécamp along the white chalk cliffs of the Alabaster coast to the spectacular 70-metre Needle, rising out of the sea at Étretat. *www.sites.google.com/site/lamerpourtous*

MuMa

This part of Normandy was beloved by Impressionist painters, and there is a stunning collection in the Modern Art Museum overlooking the harbour of Le Havre. *www.muma-lehavre.fr*

Bénédictine used to be known as an obscure herbal liqueur, the dusty bottle stuck at the back of grandma's drinks cabinet. Today it has been rediscovered as a novel ingredient for cocktails and has become a firm favourite among mixologists.

While many ancient spirits were first distilled in monasteries and abbeys, none can boast the magnificent Palais on Normandy's coast where Bénédictine has been made for more than 200 years. Apparently invented in 1510 as a medicinal elixir by a Venetian monk in Fécamp's Bénédictine abbey, the secret recipe of 27 herbs and spices was lost when the abbey was destroyed during the French Revolution, only to be miraculously rediscovered by a local wine merchant in 1810 who built the palais as Bénédictine's home. This new distillery was a folly of neo-gothic and mock-renaissance architecture, and with Alexandre Le Grand as master distiller – and master storyteller – the aromatic liqueur rapidly became a bestseller.

Touring the original 19th-century copper stills today, visitors will learn that nothing has changed in Bénédictine's unique production of multiple distillations and cask-ageing. And while we know some ingredients – nutmeg, tea, honey, saffron, pine cones and vanilla – the full recipe remains a hotly guarded secret. After the tasting room, visit the Palais's splendid gallery of artworks collected by Monsieur Le Grand.

COGNAC 101

The process required to make a cognac was invented by Dutch sailors, who favoured this *brande-wijn* (brandy) for its stability during long journeys. Like brandy, cognac is a result of the double distillation of wine through the round belly and swan's neck of a copper alembic, which becomes a clear 70 proof alcohol, of which only the heart is put aside for ageing.

For every eight litres of wine that go in, only one litre of *eau de vie* (spirit) comes out – it's then up to the cellar master's nose to decide whether it is worthy of being placed into oak barrels to gain colour and flavour from the wood's tannins and the varying levels of humidity in the *chais* (cellars).

Once its aromas have revealed themselves, the *eau de vie* can be removed from the barrel and blended with others at various stages of the ageing process. A blend that has *eaux de vie* as young as two years will be labelled as VS (Very Special), and it will take four years to make the youngest VSOP (Very Superior Old Pale), or anything from 10 years for an XO (Extra Old).

But cognac is not your average brandy. Just as every sparkling wine does not a champagne make, for a brandy to become a cognac its grapes must grow within the confines of a certain terroir. Encompassing climate, know-how and, crucially, soil composition, the cognac terroir was locked down by official decree in

1909 and divided into six areas, all of which provide a different signature taste. The appellation's limited area (75,000 ha) means that all of its vines are sought after, but those from the Grande Champagne and Petite Champagne are considered to be the most prestigious.

The number one big-shot producer is Hennessy, claiming almost half the market. However, even the big names can't meet their entire demand alone, and must rely on the know-how of other winegrowers and distillers for up to 97% of their production.

The good news is, as soon as it leaves its barrel, cognac is as old as it will ever get. There's no need to squirrel it away like wine; just enjoy it.

BY JESSICA KNIPE

Barrel makers

All of the winegrowers' and distillers' hard work would be nothing without a good barrel in which to age their *eaux de vie*. It's worth visiting a cooperage to gain some insight into what, arguably, has one of the biggest influences over the colour and flavour of the final cognac blend. Watching a master cooper season, mould, bend and toast the staves into a barrel that might be in action for almost 100 years is a humbling experience, and a good reminder of the artisanal know-how that goes into each part of the process of making a good cognac.

More than 4000 winegrowers provide the grapes used to make cognac each year, but between them just four distilleries control more than 80% of the global market

GERMANY

How to ask for a spirit without mixers? Pur, bitte
Signature spirit? Fruit schnapps/brandy
What to order with your spirits? Schwarzwälder schinken (smoked Black Forest ham) with a hunk of crusty bread
Do: When saying prost or zum wohl (cheers), always clink glasses and look your drinking partner in the eye. Lore has it that not to do so means you'll be cursed with seven years of bad sex

The Germans only drink foamy beers in glasses that are bigger than their heads, right? Wrong. That would be Bavaria. Over in the southwest, in that deep and darkly wooded slice of Germany that is the Black Forest, you enter micro-distillery country. Like something out of a Grimm fairy tale, this region is riven with valleys where streams run swiftly, brushed with forests of fir and spruce, and sprinkled with half-timbered towns of such ludicrous loveliness they almost don't look real. Then there are orchards, where cherries, pears, apples, plums, apricots, quinces and other fruits ripen in the warm months – this is where the spirits come in.

After all, the winters up in these hills are often bitterly cold and snowy, so for centuries locals have needed something to warm the cockles – a *wässerli* (little tipple) perhaps. The tradition of distilling goes back donkeys years in the Black Forest. It's most famous for its *kirschwasser* (the brandy that gives the gateau its unique cherry kick), but pretty much every other fruit that grows here is also made into a fiery spirit at small, family-run *brennereien* (distilleries), of which there are officially 14,000 – and unofficially double that.

As tastes change, the Black Forest too is embracing the zeitgeist, with craft gins tanked with local botanicals that can easily compete with the world's finest. So are you ready to raise a toast? Prost! Remember, eye contact...

ALDE GOTT

Sasbachwalden, Baden-Württemberg;
www.aldegott.de; +49 7841 20290
◆ Distillery ◆ Bar
◆ Shop

Often ranking highly in polls of Germany's prettiest villages, Sasbachwalden is particularly *herrlich* (glorious) after a gulp of good forest air, an invigorating hike and a snifter or two of the finest schnapps and brandies at Alde Gott. This distillery has been fermenting and bottling the likes of *kirschwasser*, with a snappy cherry bite, *waldhimbeergeist* (raspberry spirit), *zibärtl* (wild plum schnapps) and local digestif *tobinambur* (Jerusalem artichoke) since the 16th century.

Hour-long guided tastings are available to groups only, but no matter: all are welcome at the shop and tasting room, a rustic-cool space in stone, wood and glass. Sample the schnapps, but also ask to try its single malt whiskies.

THINGS TO DO NEARBY

Schnapsbrunnenweg
What a clever idea: a 7.6km circular trail connecting distilleries and self-service schnapps stations, deep in the forest or high on the hills. We (hic...) love it.

Hornisgrinde
Stretch your legs on the nearby wooded slopes of 1164m Hornisgrinde, the highest peak in the Northern Black Forest. Walking trails abound.

EMIL SCHEIBEL SCHWARZWALD BRENNEREI

Grüner Winkel 32, Kappelrodeck, Baden-Württemberg;
www.scheibel-brennerei.de, +49 7842 94980
◆ Distillery ◆ Shop ◆ Transport
◆ Tours ◆ Bar

On clear days you can pick out the spire of Strasbourg Cathedral in neighbouring France from Kappelrodeck's vine-striped hills and orchards. It's a view worth toasting – and luckily there are abundant distilleries where you can do just that. Emil Scheibel has been in business since 1921 and has an extensive range of schnapps, brandies and spirits. The rambling half-timbered house in which it's based hides a modern shop and tasting room.

What to try? The *obstbränden* (fruit brandies), of course, which are sharp, tangy and intensely aromatic. Go classic,

say, with *kirschwasser* (cherry), *nussler* (a spirit made from walnut kernels) or Elixier 26, a 26-blend herbal liqueur. Other knockouts include rose-tinted gin, aged in cherry brandy oak barrels, and Woodka, a honey-laced vodka liqueur.

THINGS TO DO NEARBY

Baden-Baden
This nearby spa town is the go-to place for a grand splash around in old-world and ultramodern bathhouses. Try the domed 19th-century Friedrichsbad.
www.carasana.de

Kappelrodeck
Go for a stroll in the vineyards reaching above Kappelrodeck, best known for their Pinot Noir reds. They are particularly glorious on a golden autumn day.

MONKEY 47

Äusserer Vogelsberg 7, Lossburg, Baden-Württemberg;
www.monkey47.com, +49 7455 946870

◆ Distillery   ◆ Shop
◆ Tours   ◆ Bsr

THINGS TO DO NEARBY

Schiltach
With its half-timbered houses staggering up a wooded hillside and pretty riverside, Schiltach is every inch the Black Forest of bedtime stories.

Triberg
A scenic drive winds south to this town of giant cuckoo clocks, Germany's highest waterfall and must-try Black Forest gateau (head to Café Schäfer for the real deal).
www.cafe-schaefer-triberg.de

Gengenbach
Lovely Gengenbach combines a medieval Altstadt (Old Town) with a backdrop of orchards and vineyards, which are easily explored on foot.

Alpirsbach
A Benedictine monastery lords it over this quaint Black Forest town, and indeed monks were the first to brew here. Join a tour to sample Alpirsbacher Klosterbräu beers, brewed from pure spring water.
www.alpirsbacher.de

You might well associate the Black Forest more with cuckoo clocks and *kirschwasser* than sexy craft gins, but this funky monkey has worked its distilling magic to create one of the world's most raved-about hand-crafted gins. Three-time winner at the World Gin Awards, Monkey 47 is one of the finest spirits in this neck of the woods. It takes its name from its 47 botanicals and the fact it's bottled at 47 per cent in old-fashioned stills. Combine that with the pure, silky-soft water drawn from local springs and you can see why this botanically complex gin packs one heck of a punch – brace yourself for the Black Forest in a bottle.

Distillery tours take place at an old farmstead set amid woods, orchards and meadows. They are limited in number and the early monkey gets the banana – it's by appointment only, so check online and book ahead. The classic tipple has to be the dry gin, with an initial burst of citrusy, palate-awakening aromas giving way to pine, lingering pepperiness and hits of botanicals like cranberry, bramble, angelica root, spruce shoots, liquorice and cardamom. Sip it with tonic or mixed into a cocktail at the quirkily rustic, wood-panelled Wild Monkey Inn, which you can visit on a tour.

SCHWARZWALDBRENNEREI MARKUS KALMBACH

Stöckerweg 16, Baiersbronn, Baden-Württemberg;
www.schwarzwaldbrenner.de, +49 7442 604056

◆ Distillery   ◆ Shop   ◆ Transport
◆ Tours   ◆ Bar

The village of Baiersbronn is the Black Forest's gourmet holy grail, shining with eight Michelin stars. But this is also serious fruit brandy country. At Markus Kalmbach's rustic farmhouse, the stables have been converted into a tasting room – choose your tipple and pair with smoky *Schwarzwälder schinken* (Black Forest ham), or hook onto a tour for a sneaky peek at how locally picked pears, apples, cherries, sloe berries and raspberries go into high-quality spirits and brandies. Top marks go to the mouth-puckering *kirschwasser* (cherry water) and delight-fully smooth *mirabellenwasser* (mirabelle plum brandy). The small family-run distillery also has an outdoor *schnapps-brunnen* (self-service schnapps fountain) on the forest fringes – perfect for warming the cockles after a bracing hike.

THINGS TO DO NEARBY

Schwarzwaldhochstrasse
The ravishingly scenic Black Forest High Road is 60km of hairpin bends, glacial lakes, waterfalls and mist-wreathed mountains, with endless forest-vaulted kitchens.

Nationalpark Schwarzwald
Strap on your boots and strike out on the blissfully peaceful trails of the 100 sq km Black Forest National Park.
www.nationalpark-schwarzwald.de

HUNGARY

How to ask for a spirit without mixers? Kérek szépen egy pálinkát

Signature spirit? Pálinka (fruit brandy)

What to order with your spirits? Pálinka is drunk neat; with other drinks, a typical bar snack is körözött, a cream cheese and paprika dip

Do say cheers – egészségére (literally, 'to your health') – in a Hungarian bar, and be sure to look the person in the eye when your glasses clink

Hungary boasts one spirit that has made it famous in bars the world over. Unicum, created in the 18th-century glory days of the Austro-Hungarian Empire, is an intensely bitter herbal concoction that is not for the faint-hearted, perhaps explaining why the Hungarians love describing Germany's similar Jagermeister as 'Unicum with sugar'. But proud Magyars will tell any visitor that the national drink is pálinka (fruit brandy), whose production began in the Middle Ages. Traditional home distillation and popular mass consumption of pálinka is imbued in the national character, covering the panorama of Hungarian fruits – plum, apricot, pear, apple, sour cherry – that are left to ripen and ferment before being double distilled.

Budapest is famed for 'ruin pubs' such as Szimpla Kert and Fogasház, which will have at least a dozen commercially produced pálinkas on the menu, usually knocked back straight as a shot. Refined city locales like Mester Étterem és Pálinkaház offer a more sophisticated choice, with the spirit served in a tulip-shaped glass and sipped like a brandy, while the ultimate shop in which to choose a bottle to take home is Magyar Pálinka Háza.

For travellers, the danger with pálinka is that there is a huge home-brew market, where the spirit can leap stratospherically to as high as 86 proof (43% ABV). Stay with a local family in a Budapest B&B or at a rural inn out in the countryside, and be prepared for the hosts to proudly bring out the family's moonshine pálinka. You can't refuse, so drink one glass for politeness but carry on at your own risk.

ZWACK UNICUM HERITAGE VISITORS' CENTRE

Dandár utca 1, Budapest;
www.zwackunicum.hu; +36 1 476 2383

◆ Distillery ◆ Shop
◆ Tours ◆ Transport

Packaged in an orb-shaped bottle with a medicinal cross, you'll find Unicum on virtually every bar shelf in Hungary, and the history of this unusual spirit makes a visit to the Budapest distillery a fascinating experience. The Zwack family still keeps the Unicum recipe, made of 40 herbs and spices, under lock and key. Dr Zwack, a royal physician to the Habsburg court, concocted this black herbal liqueur in the 18th century as an indigestion tonic for Emperor Joseph II, who allegedly christened it by exclaiming: 'Das ist ein Unikum!', meaning 'this is unique' in German.

The Zwacks, Hungarian-Jews, converted to Christianity in 1917, but still only narrowly escaped the concentration camps thanks to Swedish diplomat Raoul Wallenberg. The distillery didn't escape the bombs of WWII and the family worked among the ruins, rebuilding bit by bit, until the distillery was confiscated by the communist state in 1948. The Zwacks emigrated to the US – leaving an inferior, fake recipe behind – until they bought the distillery back in the 1990s.

Today, you can visit the distillery and taste Unicum from the red and black barrels in the cellars under the factory. If you find the original version too bitter, try the fruity Unicum Szilva, which was aged on a bed of dried plums.

THINGS TO DO NEARBY

Szimpla Kert Ruin Bar
You can also try Unicum at Budapest's most famous ruin bar, a formerly abandoned apartment complex now filled with art, fairy lights and mismatched furniture.
www.szimpla.hu

Rudas Thermal Baths
Lounge in a 16th-century bath built during the Ottoman occupation, filled with thermal water from one of Budapest's many geothermal springs.
www.en.rudasfurdo.hu

Gellért Hill
Get the best views over Budapest from the top Gellért Hill. You can hike up from the river, following the paths up to the Citadel.

Danube cruise
Take the tram one stop to Müpa – Nemzeti Színház and get the local BKK boat for a Danube cruise on a budget. *www.bkk.hu*

IRELAND

How to ask for a spirit without mixers? Neat, thanks

Signature spirit? Whiskey

What to order with your spirits? Tayto crisps are a popular bar choice

Do: Be flattered not alarmed if the pub owner suddenly locks you inside. Welcome to the 'lock-in'. It's usually for friends/regulars to continue drinking at the owner's discretion when the pub's officially closed

We have a lot to thank the Irish for in the drinking world: the word 'whiskey,' for example, derives from the Gaelic *uisce beatha*, which means 'water of life'. There is much debate as to whether whiskey/whisky originates with the Irish or Scots. The Irish have been making spirits as far back as the 6th century. Poitín, aka Irish moonshine (distilled from locally produced grain, barley then, later, potatoes), was created by an Irish monk in 584 AD. For centuries it was illegal under British rule and became symbolic of Irish pride and independence. Some believe whiskey was discovered from poitín; others think it has magical qualities. Since 2008 it has had protected status and can only be made in Ireland.

The first licensed distilleries opened in Northern Ireland in 1608, followed by a production boom in Dublin, hastened by competition from the Scottish whisky industry. It was the 18th century by the time parliament figured out they should tax the distillers and regulate the industry. This, combined with the Irish famine then the 1920s Prohibition era, slowed things down significantly.

International acclaim for Irish spirits took a while to arrive, but in 1973 a drink called Baileys Irish Cream was invented, and now it'd be hard to find a bar without it. And the whiskey industry is making up for lost time: Irish whiskey is currently the fastest-growing spirit category in the world.

Visitors can expect a genuine welcome in Ireland's distilleries, many of which are located in idyllic green pockets: rustic converted sawmills or 18th-century country estates, where even your slightest interest in the distilling process will generate hearty discussion and generous pours.

MIDLETON DISTILLERY

Distillery Walk, Midleton, County Cork;
www.jamesonwhiskey.com; +353 21-461 3594

◆ Distillery ◆ Shop ◆ Transport
◆ Tours ◆ Bar

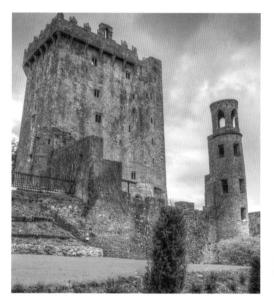

THINGS TO DO NEARBY

Ballymaloe Cooking School
If you want to learn to
cook, multi-award-winning
Ballymaloe is the place to
learn. Classes range from a
few hours to three months,
and it has its own organic
farm. *www.cookingisfun.ie*

Ichigo Ichie
Takashi Miyazaki opened
Ireland's first Japanese
haute-cuisine restaurant
to great acclaim in summer
2018 and it's a must-do
for all food-loving Cork
visitors. *www.ichigoichie.ie*

Blarney Castle
Get the gift of the gab
by hanging upside down
and kissing the Stone
while visiting the grounds
and the castle ruins,
founded in 1446.
www.blarneycastle.ie

The English Market
The most famous covered
market in Ireland, full
of local produce as well
as delis, bakeries and a
fish aisle. It's been in
business since 1788.
www.englishmarket.ie

The Midleton distillery is a production house for many of the big Irish whiskey brands, including Redbreast, Tullamore Dew and Jameson. It's a modern complex that opened in 1975 and heavily expanded in 2010; it would be no understatement to say that Midleton really is the centre of the Irish whiskey industry. It uses a combination of three pot and three continuous stills and has a production capacity of 64 million litres per year.

The old Midleton distillery, built in the 1700s in the same grounds, has been turned into the visitor centre. Tours to suit every level of interest are on offer here. The introductory guide to Irish whiskey includes a tour of the cooperage, where you can see barrels being reconditioned to be refilled with spirit. Another option involves tasting whiskey straight from different casks, and there's also a full-on Irish Whiskey Academy experience lasting two days.

While the shop stocks all the bands produced by the distillery, due to high Irish taxes it may well be a lot cheaper to buy bottles at the airport or online in your home country. Come for the experience, rather than to shop.

TEELING WHISKEY

13-17 Newmarket, Dublin; www.teelingwhiskey.com;
+353 1-531 0888

◆ Distillery ◆ Shop ◆ Transport
◆ Tours ◆ Bar

THINGS TO DO NEARBY

Guinness Storehouse
Although it's no longer brewed on site, Guinness has created a showcase for its beer that feels like it could have been thought up by Disney, complete with a bar with 360-degrees views. *www.guinness-storehouse.com*

Guinness Open Gate
Guinness's experimental lab is open Thursday to Sunday if you want to try its beer offerings, and the website lists partner pubs where you can find its unusual beers the rest of the week. *www.guinnessopengate.com*

Liberty Market
Full of all kinds of essentials for locals, who prefer it to expensive stores, this 40-year-old market is a taste of real Dublin. *www.libertymarket.ie*

Mannings Bakery
This Dublin institution has been selling sandwiches and cakes for more than 60 years and is still popular with Dubliners. *www.manningsbakeryshops.ie*

The first new distillery in Dublin in more than 125 years is owned by the sons of Dr John – the man responsible for Cooley's distillery, the flag bearer for Irish whiskey since 1985. The family connection with whiskey goes back to the 18th century, when ancestor Walter Teeling opened a distillery in Marrowbone Lane in Dublin in 1782.

Located near Marrowbone Lane in the Liberties, an area once known as the 'golden triangle' due to the number of distilleries there, Teeling brought distilling back to Dublin in 2015 after an absence of more than 40 years. The last distillery closed in 1976 but in the industry's heyday there were 37 in the city. To mark this heritage, the distillery's brand symbol is a phoenix rising from the ashes. The owners follow the old traditions but also keep innovation at the heart of the business.

While most of the Teeling bottlings up until 2018 have comprised whiskey from Bushmills distillery, spirit made on site has now started to be released. Up to 25% of its production is being kept for experimentation, and its releases so far have already been experimental, with the whiskey being finished in, among others, cognac casks. The small-batch whiskey, with its traditional Irish smooth taste, is the one to try.

DINGLE WHISKEY DISTILLERY

Farranredmond, Dingle, County Kerry;
www.dingledistillery.ie; +353 86-777 5551

◆ Distillery ◆ Shop
◆ Tours ◆ Transport

Built in 2012 by the owners of Porterhouse brewing company, Dingle was the first of the new wave of distilleries in Ireland. Determined to be a boutique, artisan distillery, the whiskey production is just two barrels a day and Dingle has only ever bottled and sold what has been produced by the distillery, which makes gin and vodka as well.

The distillery prides itself on having shaped stills modified to make an especially smooth and soft whiskey, and it is also just the second distillery in Ireland to produce a pot still whiskey made from a mixture of malted and unmalted barley.

Its tour only offers tasting shots of its gin and vodka. Don't miss the gin with its Kerry heather flavour, best served on ice with a slice of orange; then head to Dingle's many pubs to try the whiskey.

THINGS TO DO NEARBY

Murphy's Ice Cream
Owned by American-Irish returnees, the Murphy brothers almost exclusively use local ingredients to make their renowned ice cream. They also serve the best coffee in Dingle. *www. murphysicecream.ie*

Inch beach
This 5km long sand-duned beach, a 30-minute drive from Dingle, is ideal for walking, surfing, kayaking and swimming. There's a lifeguard on duty during the summer season.

KILBEGGAN DISTILLERY EXPERIENCE

Lower Main St, Aghamore, Kilbeggan, County Westmeath;
www.kilbeggandistillery.com; +353 57-933 2134

◆ Distillery ◆ Shop ◆ Transport
◆ Tours ◆ Bar

A small pot still distillery, Kilbeggan has been licensed to distil since 1757 but closed completely in 1957. In 1982 the townspeople took over the building, and soon after managed to restore the waterwheel and get it turning again. In 2007, using antique copper stills, they restarted distilling whiskey and in 2010 installed mashing and fermenting equipment. The distillery is basically a working museum, demonstrating old techniques and methods of whiskey making, and is one of the few places in the world where you can see such old-fashioned methods still being

used. The production is small and the whiskey produced here is not actually for the Kilbeggan whiskey brand, which is now made by Cooley's. The bar sells mostly whiskey, including the Kilbeggan brand – this is a good chance to try it.

THINGS TO DO NEARBY

Kilbeggan Races
The Irish are famous for their horse racing, and this is an ideal place to watch the races in the locals' famously friendly, laid-back style. *www. kilbegganraces.com*

Victorian Escapade
If you and a group fancy playing at Downton Abbey with costumes and parlour games as well as period food, Clonard House is for you. *www. victorianescapade.com*

GLENDALOUGH DISTILLERY

Glendalough Valley, County Wicklow;
www.glendaloughdistillery.com

◆ Distillery ◆ Shop
◆ Tours ◆ Bar

Ireland's first craft distillery has come a long way since 2011. It started as a pipe dream for five mates from Dublin and County Wicklow; first they made *poitín* (an ancient Irish spirit), then whiskey, and finally gin. The latter has become Ireland's best-selling gin in the UK and the US, and with new, expanded premises on the way Glendalough Distillery is proof of gin's recent boom in Ireland.

Until its new home is ready, public access is only possible as part of a Meet the Makers day with tour company Brewery Hops (www.breweryhops.com). Go foraging in the gorgeous Glendalough Valley to gather wild botanicals that go fresh into the still the same day, then taste the four seasons of Glendalough in the Wild Botanical Gin, starting with spring and pine on the nose through to a spicy, fruity winter finish.

THINGS TO DO NEARBY

Wicklow Mountains National Park
This tranquil 200 sq km of mountainous heath and bog has birdwatching, walking trails, and glorious picnic areas at the Upper Lake.
www.wicklowmountains nationalpark.ie

Wicklow Heather
This restaurant's Irish Writer's Room offers first editions of Wilde, Yeats and Joyce alongside an extraordinary collection of Irish whiskies. Try the premium tasting tray.
www.wicklowheather.ie

WALSH WHISKEY DISTILLERY

Royal Oak, Clorusk Lower, County Carlow;
www.walshwhiskey.com; +353 59-918 6653

◆ Distillery ◆ Shop ◆ Transport
◆ Tours ◆ Bar

Located in an 18th-century country estate, this distillery was the brainchild of Rosemary and Bernard Walsh, who had run the Hot Irishman company making Irish cream and then moved on to bottle their own-label Irish whiskies, The Irishman and Writers' Tears.

The duo opened their own distillery at Royal Oak on Easter Sunday 2016 – the 100th anniversary of the Easter Rising. Walsh Whiskey is the only independent distillery to produce all three types of whiskey – pot still, malt and grain – and has the capacity to produce six million litres of spirit at a time. The light, sweet-tasting, easy-drinking Writers' Tears is their most successful brand to date and the one to try on your visit.

THINGS TO DO NEARBY

Carlow Brewing Company
One of Ireland's first modern craft breweries, Carlow brands its beer as O'Hara's and brews traditional Irish stout and beer using local wheat. Tours are available on Fridays.
www.carlowbrewing.com

Visual Centre for Contemporary Art
Ireland's largest contemporary art space has ever-changing modern art exhibitions as well as live comedy, theatre, film, music and workshops for all ages. *www.visualcarlow.ie*

> *"Thanks to continuous technological innovation and superb raw materials, distilling – especially of grappa – has moved from an ancient rural tradition to a noble art: a symbol of Italian excellency"*
>
> **—CHRISTINA NARDINI, GRAPPA NARDINI**

ITALY

How to ask for a spirit without mixers? Vorrei una grappa liscia, per favore

Signature spirit? Grappa, served neat, sometimes chilled

What to order with your spirits? Bars will often offer free olives, crisps and nuts, then there are regional specialities like local salami or cheese

Do: Order limoncello when in the south. It's one of Italy's most popular after-dinner drinks, and the best is made from southern lemons. Beware of chemical-tasting imitations served in the rest of the country

Walk into any Italian bar early in the morning and a group of workers will be ordering *caffe corretto*, an espresso topped with a large dash of grappa, industrially produced and a real throat-burner. At the same time, the sommelier in one of the country's numerous Michelin-starred restaurants proposes a selection of exquisite cask-aged grappas as an alternative after-dinner tincture to the classic cognac or single malt.

Grappa production dates back to the Middle Ages, when winemakers in the north of Italy, anxious to waste nothing, began distilling, by steam or bain-marie, the skins, pulp, stems and pips of grape pomace left over after wine fermentation. While today every famous winemaker from Sassicaia in Tuscany to Gaja in Piedmonte proposes their own boutique grappas, the region that remains the heart of production is the Veneto and Bassano del Grappa in particular, where locals in an osteria request a *resentin* – a tot of grappa drunk after coffee, never together.

Today, grappa is just the tip of Italy's mountain of diverse spirits. This is a country that was united barely 150 years ago, a kaleidoscope of regions that speak their own dialect, proudly cook a local cuisine and moreover all have their own particular digestivo – from *filu 'e ferru* (moonshine grappa), and *mirto* in Sardinia to anise-flavoured Sambuca, drunk with a coffee bean in Rome. Then there's fragrant lemon zest limoncello from the Amalfi coast and the new trend of artisan-distilled gins set in Italy by brands such as Roby Marton in Treviso and Rivo on Lake Garda. Many distilleries are not open to the public, but the spirits culture is there: you just have to take to Italy's cafes, bars and restaurants to find it.

■ BAR
LIQUORIFICIO ARTIGIANALE PIOLO&MAX

Via Felice Venezian, Trieste, Friuli;
www.pioloemax.it; +39 040 24 60 223

◆ Shop   ◆ Transport
◆ Bar

The majestic maritime city of Trieste, once part of the Habsburg Empire, is more Mitteleuropa than Italian. Inspired by this special heritage, two friends, Piolo Basolo and Max Zocchi, began producing artisan liqueurs using the ancient art of infusion, popular in Austria and Hungary, macerating organic plants, spices and local grappas and bottling the results under the label Piolo & Max.

A tiny boutique is open to the public, but serious enthusiasts call ahead to visit their cellar, where hundreds of bottles are stored for ageing, infused with secret formulas of fruits, plants and spices. Try their signature Amaro di Erbe Trieste, an incredibly intense herbal liqueur with flavours ranging from orange peel, wild hops and dandelion root to gentiane, eucalyptus, wormwood and cinnamon.

THINGS TO DO NEARBY

Piazza Unita d'Italia
This monumental square, one of the largest in Europe, is lined on three sides by grand palatial buildings and spectacularly opens up onto the Bay of Trieste.

Antico Caffè San Marco
Trieste is famed for its opulent literary cafes, and this favourite haunt of James Joyce oozes Belle Epoque grandeur and serves delicious *sachertorte* (chocolate gateau).
www.caffesanmarco.com

FRATELLI BRANCA DISTILLERIE

Via Resegone 2, Milan;
www.brancadistillerie.com; +39 02 851 31

◆ Distillery   ◆ Shop
◆ Tours

THINGS TO DO NEARBY

Torre Branca
Restored by the Branca
distillery, this 108m-high
steel tower designed by Giò
Ponti in 1933 sits in Milan's
largest park, affording
views over Napoleon's
'Peace Arch' and the castle.

Triennale
Milan is Italy's design city
par excellence and knows
how to market itself. Step
into this design museum
for insights into the magic
of this couture fashion city.
www.triennale.it

Il Duomo
Milan's magnificent
cathedral is a fitting symbol
of the city's creative brio.
Climb to the rooftop where
you can walk within its
forest of spires and get
views of the Alps.
www.duomomilano.it

Pasticceria Marchesi
Contemporaneous with the
distillery is this beautiful
wood-panelled and painted
bakery on Via Santa Maria
alla Porta, which serves
the city's best pastries
with perfect coffee. ***www.
pasticceriamarchesi.it***

Neuroscientists will tell you we have taste receptors
on our tongues tuned to seven flavours: sweet, sour,
salty, bitter, umami, kokumi (calcium) and fat. Of
them, bitterness is the most complex, because it is a biological
trigger for poisonous or unhealthy substances. Strangely, as
we age, we acquire a love-hate hankering for it, hence our
addiction to coffee and bittersweet digestifs like amaro.

King of the amaros is Milan's Fernet Branca. In business
since 1845, the distillery takes up an entire city block, its
halls filled with old presses, stills, production tools and
vintage advertising artwork produced by the company over
the past 170 years. It was savvy originator Bernardino Branca
who came up with the idea of marketing the bitter liqueur as
a healthy tonic, validated by physicians as a preventative for
cholera, which regularly laid the city low.

The tour, led by museum curator Marco Ponzano, is full
of fascinating anecdotes like this, and talks you through the
27 active ingredients – including myrrh, grains of paradise,
cinchona bark and cardamom – while stepping through
historic offices, tailoring studios where factory uniforms were
made, and a vast cellar of 800 Slovenian oak barrels where the
amaro sits marinating. At the end, Marco pours tasters of the
entire line – the Branca Menta, created in 1960 for American
opera singer Maria Callas, is one of the most interesting.

■ BAR
CAMPARI ACADEMY

Via Davide Campari 23, Sesto San Giovanni, Milan;
www.campariacademy.it; +39 02 6225 278

- ◆ Food
- ◆ Bar
- ◆ Shop
- ◆ Transport

The key component in some of the world's most beloved cocktails – the Negroni, Garibaldi, Americano and spritz – Campari is Milan's most famous liqueur, with 3.3 million cases shipped to 190 countries each year. That's quite an achievement for a company founded by the 10th child of a farmer, Gaspare Campari, in 1860, and a drink originally dyed with carmine from crushed cochineal insects.

But Gaspare was a visionary. When Europe's first shopping mall, the Galleria Vittorio Emanuele II, opened in Milan in 1867 he opened his first bar there. His son, Davide, installed a hydraulic system to guarantee a flow of iced *seltz* (soda water) to the bar – introducing the world to the first spritz.

Campari Academy is part of a reimagining of the family's former summer house, Villa Campari, where star-architect Mario Botta has installed a beautiful gallery exploring the liqueur's history and production. Upstairs, lectures and bartending courses are hosted. Try the city's classic Aperitivo (one part Campari to three parts soda, garnished with a slice of orange) at the restaurant or period bar.

THINGS TO DO NEARBY

Galleria Vittorio Emanuele II
So much more than a shopping arcade, the Galleria is the city's finest drawing room, and marks the *passeggiata* (promenade) from the Duomo to Teatro alla Scala.

Camparino
Gaspare Campari's original bar still serves his signature cocktails amid gorgeous art-noveau décor including iridescent, Klimt-inspired mosaics of flowers and birds.
www.camparino.it

Museo del Novecento
Milan's dynamic museum of modern art offers an insight into the energy and creativity of the 19th-century city when Gaspare Campari was cutting his entrepreneurial teeth.
www.museodelnove cento.org

Cimitero Monumentale
Milan's city cemetery is filled with extravagant mausoleums where the city's great families are interred. The Campari tomb, depicting a Last Supper-style table of diners, is jokingly referred to as the 'Last Aperitivo'.

■ BAR
GRAPPERIA NARDINI AL PONTE

2 Ponte Vecchio, Bassano del Grappa, Veneto;
www.nardini.it/en/corporate/places; +39 0424 227741

◆ Distillery   ◆ Shop
◆ Tours

The Nardinis are the aristocracy of Italian grappa, pioneering family production since 1779 and now in their seventh generation. Their distillery can only be visited by groups, so the showpiece for most visitors is this snug, wood-panelled bar at the foot of Palladio's red wooden Ponte degli Alpini across the Brenta river. While their classic clear grappa is found in restaurants and cocktail bars across the globe, here in Bassano visitors will discover a range of bitters and liqueurs, including Tagliatella – a secret recipe of grappa with hints of orange, sour cherry, cinnamon and cloves.

After tasting amber oak-aged grappa, join the locals for a glass of everyone's favourite, Mezzoemezzo, a bittersweet rhubarb-based Aperitivo, served with a splash from a soda siphon.

THINGS TO DO NEARBY

Museo Civico di Bassano del Grappa
Bassano's surprising municipal museum offers a serious Old Masters collection and a modern wing for avant-garde shows.
www.museibassano.it/ sedi/museo-civico

Taverna al Ponte
This typical rustic osteria sits on Palladio's Bridge. Downstairs there's a fascinating museum about Italy's legendary Alpine mountain soldiers.
www.facebook.com/ tavernaalponte

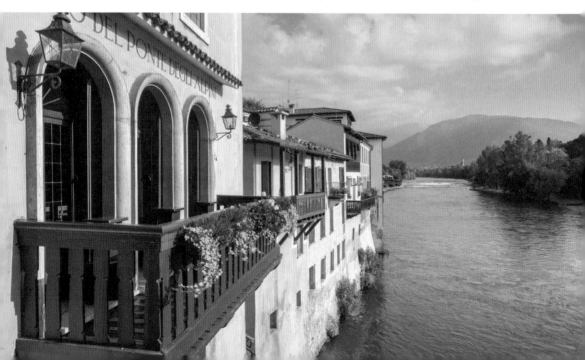

POLI DISTILLERY

46 Via Marconi, Schiavon, Veneto; www.poligrappa.com;
+39 0444 665007

◆ Distillery   ◆ Shop   ◆ Transport
◆ Tours   ◆ Bar

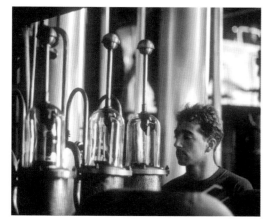

THINGS TO DO NEARBY

Ristorante Birraria Ottone
Opened when Bassano
was part of the Habsburg
Empire, this cosy 150-year-
old tavern at 50 Via
Matteotti serves local
specialities such as white
asparagus topped with
chopped eggs.

Piazza Castello, Marostica
Medieval Marostica boasts
a fortress castle with a
majestic piazza that
every other September
becomes Piazza Degli
Scacchi – an unforgettable
human chess game.
www.marosticascacchi.it

Birrone Bassano
Artisan ale lovers head
for this modern brew pub,
specialising in hoppy weiss
beer and a dark porter
known by the very non-
Italian name of 'Fuckin'.
www.birrone.it

La Cantina Maculan
Stop off in the nearby
vineyards of Breganze
for a tasting of the
excellent Vespaiola and
Torcolato wines at the
Maculan family winery.
www.maculan.net

The Poli family have a small museum in Bassano, but to understand the mysteries of grappa, head to their distinctive red-brick distillery in the nearby Veneto hills. Today's master distiller, Jacopo Poli, whose great-grandfather started the business in 1898 by taking a handcart alembic from village to village, presents his awesome personal collection in a museum that houses ancient stills, some 2,000 bottles of vintage grappa and a historical library on distillation.

Entering the distillery itself is like stumbling into a mad scientist's laboratory crammed with shining copper stills, cooling pipes, steel vats and oak barrels. Here the guide will perfectly explain the complex stages of making grappa, from the arrival of grape pomace – the key ingredient of skins and pips left over after the pressed grape is fermenting into

wine – through to the subtle difference in artisan distilling between pot stills, where steam flows directly through the pomace, and 'bain-marie', where hot water gently warms up a double boiler.

The last stop is a tasting room with some 40 grappas and liqueurs. Nobody has ever managed to try all of them, but one not to miss is the fruity, elegant Torcio d'Oro, distilled from luscious dessert-wine Torcolato grapes grown in the surrounding Breganze vineyards.

NETHERLANDS

How to ask for a spirit without mixers? Een jenever, alsjeblieft

Signature spirit? Jenever – Dutch gin, drunk neat

What to order with your spirits? Bittenballs (deep-fried meatballs) are the quintessential Dutch bar snack, but some old-school bars keep hard-boiled eggs behind the bar

Don't: Down a jenever shot in one. It's supposed to be sipped, otherwise a burning sensation and rapid drunkenness are potential outcomes

It's believed the Netherlands gave us gin. Plaudits go to Dutch physician and scientist Franciscus Sylvius, who, it's said, in around 1650, had the bright idea of combining juniper berries with the local brandy-wine to create a herbal, medicinal drink, though the historical evidence for his involvement is sketchy. Gin's origins are in truth less tidy than the alchemical touch of an experimental medic, but the influential spirit definitely emanated from somewhere in the Low Countries. 'Jenever' is the Dutch for juniper, hence the name. The Netherlands' traditional tastings bars still resemble old-school, wood-and-bottle-lined pharmacies, reflecting the drink's medicinal origins.

During the Golden Age in the 17th century, the glory days when the Dutch were the dominant force in international trade, distilleries opened in all the larger cities. During the Thirty Years War (1618-1648), the English discovered the spirit when they saw their fellow Dutch soldiers taking a sip of 'Dutch courage' before launching into battle. English speakers shortened 'jenever' to gin.

However, English and Dutch gin are markedly different, both in process and in taste. The Dutch version is based on malt wine, and not eminently mixable. Jenever is drunk neat and has a far maltier, robust and sweet taste than English gin. In the Netherlands, it's common to drink it alongside a beer, a practice evocatively named *kopstootje* (headbutt).

TOP 5 SPIRITS

- **Bols Barrel Aged Genever Gin** House of Bols , Amsterdam
- **Ketel 1 Originale Graanjenever** Nolet Distillery, Schiedam
- **Van Wees 15 Year Old Zeer Oude Jenever** A Van Wees, Amsterdam
- **Ketel 1 Graanjenever** Nolet Distillery, Schiedam
- **Zuidam 5 Year Old Zeer Oude Genever** Zuidam Distillery, Baarle-Nassau

"Such is the importance of distilleries in the Netherlands, Distillery Van Kleef was the first place with a telephone in The Hague in 1883, their number simply being 1"

— **FLEUR KRUYT, VAN KLEEF DISTILLERY & MUSEUM**

From left: Courtesy of House of Bols; ©Matt Munro/Lonely Planet

Traditionally, it is sipped neat from a narrow tulip-shaped glass, to enhance the scent and thus the flavour, and is filled until it's brimming, so that you have to bow to take the first sip.

There are two different recipes: *oude* (old) jenever includes at least 15% malt wine. It's yellower, stronger and yeastier than the younger version, and usually sipped at room temperature. *Jonge* (young) jenever is slightly less alcoholic (but still 35%), and has not more than 15% malt wine. It's distilled twice, using grains infused with botanicals, and usually drunk chilled. It's better for mixing than the old version, and more likely to be served as an aperitif.

As well as distilleries in Amsterdam, and a distillery-museum in the Hague, the town of Schiedam, near Rotterdam, is a historic home to the spirit industry, and there's another gin museum there. There are also annual gin festivals in Amsterdam, Rotterdam and Utrecht.

Jenever is not a drink that the local youth will typically order on the rocks at their favourite bar. That said, this spirit has lately had a renaissance and, as well as historic distilleries with atmospheric tasting rooms, there is a smattering of places that have opened in the past decade.

Jenever's historic ties to the Netherlands makes it the easiest spirit to taste at the source in open distilleries, but there are other local spirits, including rum and some superb vodkas. The Nolet Distillery produces Ketel One, an internationally respected vodka that has had the same recipe for more than 300 years. House of Bols, Van Gogh Vodka, and Vodka/Amsterdam are other tipples worth seeking out.

HOUSE OF BOLS

Paulus Potterstraat 14, Old South, Amsterdam;
www.bols.com; +31 20 5708575

◆ Food ◆ Shop ◆ Transport
◆ Tours ◆ Bar

Bols started distilling in 1575, in 'Het Loosje' (the 'little shed') in central Amsterdam. Today it's a huge commercial operation, and this is Amsterdam's most cutting-edge distillery experience. On a self-guided, high-tech tour, you'll learn about the history of Lucas Bols – big gun in the all-powerful East India Company, who took over the business in the 17th century and began distilling jenevers. The company has been going strong ever since.

In the Hall of Taste, you can sample 38 different liqueur flavours, and see how your other senses affect your sense of taste, with the help of sounds and flashing lights. In the

THINGS TO DO NEARBY

Rijkmuseum
The Rijkmuseum is packed full of Dutch masterpieces, from Rembrandt's *Night Watch* to the intimate interiors of Vermeer and the expressionistic brushstrokes of Van Gogh.
www.rijksmuseum.nl

Vondelpark
Amsterdam's favourite place to kick back and relax, this pretty, lozenge-shaped park has teahouses, cycle paths, lakes, concerts in summer, and a Picasso sculpture.
www.hetvondelpark.net

Van Gogh Museum
With more than 200 paintings, this museum traces Van Gogh's life and work, his prior lack of success forming a poignant contrast with the queues to enter the museum today.
www.vangoghmuseum.nl

Stedelijk Museum
An excellent art museum where bright, light galleries are filled with major international artists' work from the 20th century to the present day.
www.stedelijk.nl

glitzy Mirror Bar, you can create your own personal cocktail with the help of one of Bols' mixologists, who train at the upstairs bartenders' academy.

You can also arrange private tours that include jenever tastings of five different varieties, accompanied by Reypenaer cheeses. Sample the many-layered complexity of Bols Genever, which is based on the original 1820 recipe used in many cocktails in the 19th century.

T'NIEUWE DIEP

Flevopark 13, Oost, Amsterdam; www.nwediep.nl;
+31 6 25378104

◆ Distillery   ◆ Shop   ◆ Transport
◆ Tours   ◆ Bar

THINGS TO DO NEARBY

Tropenmuseum
Fabulous eclectica from the tropics forms the permanent collection of this magnificent museum at the edge of Oosterpark, while cool temporary exhibitions cover anything from international conflicts to tattoos.
www.tropenmuseum.nl

Dappermarkt
The clothes, knick-knacks, food and electronics on sale at this untouristy market on Dapperstraat seem to draw the entire diverse neighbourhood of Oost out to browse. People-watching heaven. exclusive Cap d'Antibes.
www.dappermarkt.nl

Hortus Botanicus
One of the world's oldest botanic gardens, Hortus has beautiful greenhouses, including a butterfly house, and houses more than 4000 different species of plants.
www.dehortus.nl

Roest
Roest is a wonderfully counter-culture waterside bar and entertainment venue in a former industrial zone, with an artificial beach, hammocks, and regular live music and DJs.
www.amsterdamroest.nl

There is no lovelier setting for a distillery than this, in eastern Amsterdam's Flevopark, which runs along the side of the 'Nieuwe Diep harbour. Here a former archaeologist, Kees Filius, and his business partner have revived long forgotten recipes for jenevers, bitters, *eaux de vie* (clear spirit distilled from fermented fruit) and liqueurs, distilling them in traditional ways.

They opened the t'Nieuwe Diep distillery in 2010 in this frilly edged, greenery-shrouded former pump house, dating from 1880. It has a glorious terrace on the water's edge in the up-and-coming district of Oost; on balmy days you can drink with a view of gliding swans, reflections and fruit trees.

The distillery uses organic products to concoct sweet liqueurs and jenevers flavoured with fresh juices, as well as young and aged jenevers, but also offers beer and wine. Tours are available weekly, but the tasting room opens daily. It is particularly renowned for fruity flavours: try the lemon jenever, which rocks the taste buds like a punchier limoncello.

WYNAND FOCKINK

Pijlsteeg 31, Centrum, Amsterdam;
www.wynand-fockink.nl; +31 20 6392695

◆ Distillery   ◆ Shop   ◆ Transport
◆ Tours   ◆ Bar

THINGS TO DO NEARBY

Royal Palace
The King's Palace looks grand enough outside, but wait until you step into the interior, where it's full-throttle neo-classical. It's still in use for state occasions. *www.paleisamsterdam.nl*

Magna Plaza
Facing the Royal Palace across Dam Square, this piece of 19th-century fabulousness was possibly the world's fanciest post office. Now it's been turned into a glitzy shopping mall. *www.magnaplaza.nl*

Red Light District
The infamous area where women flaunt their wares behind pane-glass windows lines several canals in the city centre, and has a testosterone-charged yet unthreatening atmosphere.

Blauw aan de Wal
Sandwiched between sex shops, this French–Italian restaurant has a serene whitewashed 17th-century interior, offers a great wine list and gets creative with fantastic seasonal produce. *www.blauwaandewal.com*

Wyand Fockink (try saying it after a few tastings...) opened his liqueur distillery in 1679 at the height of the Netherlands' booming Golden Age. A bar was soon added, where customers could sample the wares. It's kept the winning format of distillery and tasting room for more than 300 years, fronted by ancient panelled windows. Many of the recipes to its 70 liqueurs and jenevers date back to its 17th-century origins. The spirits' names evoke the past, such as Bride's Tears (an orange-flavoured liqueur with flakes of silver and 22-karat gold, traditionally served at weddings), and Naked Belly Button (once served when an expectant mother showed off her belly to her nearest and dearest).

Inside, the bar is lined with shelves groaning with antique bottles and ceramic pots, enthusiastic bartenders wear leather aprons, and it's standing-room only. Tastings are limited to small groups, to preserve the intimate atmosphere. Tours of the next-door distillery illustrate how the liqueurs are made, and show off metal vats that contrast starkly with the bar's heritage image. When tasting, as per tradition, you drink from a tulip glass filled to the brim: make sure you bow for the first sip.

■ BAR

PROEFLOKAAL A VAN WEES

Herengracht 319, Jordaan, Amsterdam;
www.proeflokaalvanwees.nl; +31 20 6254334

◆ Food ◆ Tours ◆ Bar
◆ Distillery ◆ Shop ◆ Transport

Ooievaar is one of Amsterdam's original jenever distilleries – dating to 1782 – and Proeflokaal A Van Wees is its twinkling gem of a tasting house. The distillery itself is closed to the public, but contains gleaming 240-litre copper kettles that make the base *brandewijn* (brandy wine) used for its jenever. Its malt wine is sourced from local makers, then juniper berries and herbs are added in the later stages to make the flavours increasingly complex.

Learn about the process from the knowledgeable bar staff at Proeflokaal A Van Wees on Herengracht, in a room lined with carved wooden cabinets full of bottles – old liqueur bars of this kind resemble old-fashioned pharmacies, echoing the

THINGS TO DO NEARBY

Museum Van Loon
For the full Golden Age experience, visit this splendid private townhouse turned museum, which proffers an insight into the life of the Dutch glitterati, 18th-century style.
www.museumvanloon.nl

Foam
An elegant canal house turned cutting-edge photography gallery, this has some fabulous exhibitions, from photographs of the Gold Rush era to portraits from 1950s Mali. ***www.foam.org***

Hermitage Amsterdam
Yes, an off-shoot of the St Petersburg great, with marvellous changing exhibitions from the masterpiece-packed Russian collection.
www.hermitage.nl

Dignita Hoftuin
A glasshouse cafe-restaurant in the grounds of the Hermitage Museum, Dignita is ideal for a light and lazy lunch before basking on the grass.
www.eatwelldogood.nl

spirits' original functions as digestives for stomach disorders. The bar has been here for centuries, but in 1973 changed its name from 'the Admiral' when the Van Wees family took it on.

The family offers more than 60 different old-Dutch liqueurs, as well as a fine selection of authentically distilled jenevers. Try either Zeere Oude ('very old'), which is distilled twice with 100% malt wine and herbs, then aged for a year in oak barrels, or its heavenly distilled rose liqueur, the 'Rose without Thorns'.

■ **BAR**

PROEFLOKAAL DE DRIE FLESCHJES

Gravenstraat 18, Centrum, Amsterdam;
www.dedriefleschjes.nl; +31 20 6248443

◆ Food ◆ Bar
◆ Shop ◆ Transport

Dating to 1640, Proeflokaal de Drie Fleschjes ('Three Little Bottles') is one of Amsterdam's oldest tasting rooms and was once attached to the Bootz distillery next door, which was later converted into what is now the Best Western Hotel.

The room has one wall lined by rows of oak casks, with taps on each of them: these are rented by locals (there's a long waiting list) who have them filled with their favourite spirit and can unlock their supply with their own private keys. What was once the back office, with stained-glass windows, has been turned into a cosy snug. It's now owned by Bols, so you can taste Bols jenevers and liqueurs here: ask for the citroen jenever, which used to be supplied to sailors to ward off scurvy.

THINGS TO DO NEARBY

Oude Kerk
The 14th-century 'old church' has some fine, notably risqué, gothic carving. Take a map to scout out famous tombs or reach for the sky by climbing the tower.
www.oudekerk.nl

Scheepvaarthuis
An astounding building, this is the pinnacle of the neo-Gothic Amsterdam school. It's now the Grand Hotel Amrath: step in to see the magnificent stained glass inside. ***www. amrathamsterdam.com***

VAN KLEEF

Lange Beestenmarkt, Centrum, the Hague;
www.vankleef.eu; +31 70 3452273

◆ Food ◆ Tours ◆ Bar
◆ Distillery ◆ Shop ◆ Transport

Van Kleef is a thriving steam distillery in the Hague, producing liqueurs and jenevers since 1842. It's said that Van Gogh may have frequented the distillery bar, as he lived only a few doors down from here for a time. Today it's now also a museum, with fascinating archives that include an incredible resource of liqueur and jenever recipes dating to before 1900.

The modern Van Kleef distillery attempts to revive many of these vintage recipes, using all-natural ingredients. Book a tour that includes a themed food tasting menu paired with selected jenevers and liqueurs. Don't miss the drankorgel (barrel organ) – there's a wall of barrels and if you tap them, they'll make different sounds according to how full they are, demonstrating that empty vessels do make the most noise.

THINGS TO DO NEARBY

Mauritshuis
The lavish 17th-century mansion of Johan Maurits, governor-general of Dutch Brazil and Count of Nassau Siegen, has magnificent architecture and interiors hung with Golden Age art.
www.mauritshuis.nl

Gemeentemuseum Den Haag
In an art deco building with mind-bendingly geometric interiors, the Hague's municipal museum has masterpieces by Mondrian, Macke, Schiele and more.
www.gemeentemuseum.nl

NOLET DISTILLERY

Hoofdstraat 14, Schiedam;
www.noletdistillery.com; +31 10 2462929

◆ Distillery   ◆ Transport
◆ Tours

Quaint canals, gin distilleries galore and the tallest windmills in the world. Welcome to Schiedam, which lives and breathes jenever. This old Dutch town on water, just 10 minutes from Rotterdam, was once home to 392 roasters and distilleries and jenever has been distilled here for hundreds of years. The city was once known as 'Black Nazareth' because of the intense pollution from its working distilleries.

Ironically, the town's most famous distillery, Nolet, is best known internationally for its Ketel One vodka, though it also produces jenevers. Here, craftsmanship is key. Owned by the same family since 1691, Nolet sets a rare example of combining centuries of family tradition with state-of-the-art technology.

THINGS TO DO NEARBY

Lucas Drinkwinkel
Located in a former police station in the city centre, Lucas Drinkwinkel is one of Schiedam's hippest bar addresses, serving ice-cold gin and tonics made with both heritage and contemporary gin labels.
www.lucasdrinkwinkel.nl

Jenever Festival
With an abundance of tastings, workshops and tours, the annual National Gin Festival in June is a two-day jamboree of Schiedam's centuries-old fine jenever. *www.jeneverfestival.nl*

Molenmuseum De Nieuwe Palmboom
For a real-life demo of millers grinding, head to the museum in De Walvisch mill (1794), where a wooden veranda flaunts views to the other Schiedam windmills. *www.jenevermuseum.nl/museummolen*

Nationaal Jenevermuseum
The only one of its kind in the Netherlands, this jenever museum boasts its own distillery where Old Schiedam is distilled from 100% malt wine, following a 300-year-old recipe. *www.jenevermuseum.nl*

Located in the De Nolet tower mill, the tallest windmill in the world, the weekday two-hour tours showcase the distillation process and bottling plant up close.

Following a walk through the sophisticated family museum, indulge in the refined aromas of Turkish rose, peach and raspberry that characterise Nolet's Silver Gin, before moving on to Ketel 1 Matuur Jenever, which has a fuller flavour.

PORTUGAL

How to ask for a spirit without mixers? Simples (pronounced 'sim-plesh')

Signature spirits? Bagaço and aguardente (the hard stuff) and ginja (the crowd pleaser)

What to order with your spirits? Ask for your ginja 'com elas' (with drunken cherries) or 'sem elas' (without cherries)

Do: Drink up but don't get sloshed. Pacing oneself is a Portuguese art that ensures happily protracted drinking sessions

Life in Portugal pivots around a schedule of family gatherings, long lunches and late-night get-togethers, where a carafe of wine, glass of beer or shot of liqueur is never out of place. Despite a healthy appreciation for alcohol, consumption is sensible and oils good conversation, much like oxygen enhances a good wine.

When the international stage spotlights Portuguese booze, port is the clear victor (and for those of a certain vintage, retro-trend Mateus Rosé might also ring a bell). But Portugal has many other potions pegged to its timeline, and liquors such as bagaço, aguardente and ginja have been produced and consumed domestically for centuries, while herby licor beirão has more recently raised its status as a pharmaceutical-turned-recreational tonic.

Bagaço and aguardente are geared towards hardened drinkers (they don't call the latter 'firewater' for nothing), but ginja is a palatable all-rounder, softened with a hit of sour cherry. This ruby-red liqueur, sometimes nicknamed ginjinha, is thought to trace back to 17th-century monks who mixed fruit with sugar and alcohol for medicinal purposes and also fancied the syrupy liquid as a digestif.

Ginja is made and consumed across Portugal, but the microclimate of Óbidos yields a fine varietal of the small ginja fruit (which are an inedible bee-sting on their own), hence the town is considered the country's eminent locale for ginja production.

The time to sip a shot of ginja is whenever you please, but it is known to round out a meal particularly well.

▣ BAR
A GINJINHA

8 Largo Sao Domingos, Barrio Rossio, Lisbon; www.facebook.com/GinjinhaEspinheira; +351 21 8145374

◆ Shop   ◆ Transport
◆ Bar

Legend recounts that in the 1800s, Francisco Espinheira, a friar in Lisbon's San Antonio church, infused *ginja* (morello cherries) in a powerful mix of *aguardente* (wine brandy), sugar and cinnamon. The result was a unique liqueur, swiftly commercialised as ginjinha. The first location to serve what is now the national drink was A Ginjinha, and it's been packed to bursting from morning until night ever since that day in 1840.

To describe it as a hole-in-the-wall bar is flattering – small is not the word to describe a locale where no more than three people can squeeze up at the counter, sipping from tiny glasses filled to the brim. Either drink it neat or with an alcohol-soaked sour cherry floating in it.

THINGS TO DO NEARBY

Mercado da Ribeira
This 1900s covered market is perfect for local food specialities, but it's also a street-food centre serving everything from fusion sushi to *pasteis de Belem* custard tarts. **www.timeoutmarket.com/lisboa**

Elevador de Santa Justa
As well as iconic trams, this hilly city has an awesome system of lifts and funiculars, including this monumental 1902 iron elevator, still operating perfectly. **www.carris.pt/en/elevador**

FRUTÓBIDOS

Estrada Nacional 114, Amoreira, Óbidos; www.frutobidos.pt; +351 262 969 479

◆ Distillery   ◆ Shop
◆ Tours

The secret behind Frutóbidos' signature spirit was whispered into the ear of Marina Brás when she acquired the ginja distillery from its original owner in 2001. The sweet velvety liqueur's name – Vila da Rainhas – means 'Queen's Village' and honours the area's former esteem among nobility.

To see how this nectar is made, call ahead to arrange a countryside facility tour and enjoy a tasting on the house. Frutóbidos is a 10-minute drive from Óbidos and has its own crop of fruit trees on the property, so a visit showcases a true plant-to-bottle experience. Satiate your new-found appreciation of the ginja art by purchasing a bottle from the on-site store – if you're feeling fancy, splash out on a reserve ginja aged in oak for a hint of vanilla and spice.

THINGS TO DO NEARBY

Nazaré
In winter you can witness the world's biggest waves just 30 minutes' drive from Óbidos in the seaside resort of Nazaré. Surf aside, there's culture galore and perpetually splendid views.

Igreja de Santa Maria
This lovely little 16th-century Christian church stands on the site of a former Moorish mosque in Óbidos and represents the city's capture by Dom Afonso Henriques in 1148.

©Michael Robertson/Alamy Stock Photo

OPPIDUM

Rua da Escola, Sobral da Lagoa, Óbidos;
www.ginjadeobidos.com; +351 262 969 109

◆ Distillery   ◆ Shop
◆ Tours

Portuguese grandfolk have been bottling sweet cherry ginja for eons but, at the opposite end of the spectrum, Oppidum has established a firm reputation for quality, large-scale production that remains true to its roots. Dário Pimpão started this distillery near the lovely town of Óbidos – widely considered the home of ginja – in 1987 and now manages the company with his daughter Marta.

Although Oppidum's operation upscales grandma's kitchen, the company fosters analogous charm by accepting sour ginja cherries from around 100 local community farmers, including

THINGS TO DO NEARBY

Óbidos city walls
A fear of heights and lack of barriers may discourage some from trotting the exceptionally well-preserved walls of Óbidos, but the views are outstanding.

Porta da Vila
Inside the city gates is a chapel adorned with blue and white *azulejo* tiles. Snap a selfie then enter the town: Portuguese royalty love it so much that a 13th-century king once gifted it to his queen.

Mercado Biológico
Óbidos is a Unesco-designated literary town so a bookstore visit is fitting. Here you can peruse floor-to-ceiling bookshelves with a side of organic produce. *www.obidosvilaliteraria. com/en/mercado-biologico*

Pousada de Óbidos
Although you can roam Óbidos in a few hours, consider bunking in the swish castle-turned-hotel Pousada de Óbidos. The town is adorable. You'll want to stay. *www.pousadas.pt*

one with a lone backyard tree. The public are welcome to arrange ad-hoc facility tours and informal tastings. Tours highlight Oppidum's simple blend of fruit, alcohol, water and sugar, and meticulous four-year process to fuse these ingredients into its signature sticky red liqueur. Ginja can be sampled traditionally in a small glass, or in a tiny chocolate cup – a practice that has become a year-round custom. Don't miss Oppidum's chocolate-flavoured ginja and ginja-injected Belgian chocolates; they're as indulgent as they sound.

RAKIJA 101

Rakija's secrets are hidden behind the twinkly smiles of many a Balkan grandparent. Variously rakija, rakia or rakı, depending on whether you're drinking with Serbs, Bulgarians or Turks, this fruit-based firewater is a source of immense pride: it underpins regional identities, lubricates weddings, funerals and everything in between, and has a role in various histories and legends.

What unites different types of rakija is the preference for traditional production methods – it's difficult to find distilleries in which to taste this spirit, as it is often homemade in small batches using seasonal fruits to flavour it. Innocent plums, pears and apples, or sometimes cherries and grapes, are double-distilled to produce an almost clear brandy. A whisper of the source fruit is present in its scent, but a sip of rakija is like a bolt of pure, cleansing fire in the throat. It's an appetite stimulant, a cure-all, and something to take the edge off a bitter Balkan winter.

Archaeologists unearthed 11th-century distilling equipment at Bulgaria's Lyutitsa Fortress, leading Bulgarians to claim they were first to master the art of rakija. Numerous written sources suggest

that medieval Bulgarians drank it before going into battle; their Ottoman opponents are said to have remarked upon the fortitude of Bulgarian fighters under the influence of this beastly liquor.

But no single nation can lay claim to rakija, contrary to what they'll opine after a glass or two. Serbia claims the greatest rakija production per capita, but locals sip it delicately from a tapered glass called a *čokanj*. When drinkers in Turkey huddle together, the setting is referred to as the 'locksmith's table', a nod to the way in which the brandy unlocks meaningful conversation.

To Romanians it's *rachie*, while the plum version goes by the name *ţuică*. Unusual flavours include floral *giulovitsa* from Bulgaria's Rose Valley; *mrtina* (myrtle)-infused rakija from Croatia's Hvar Island, and nutty *orahovica* from Dalmatia.

One thing that all nations can agree on: rakija is best drunk unadorned, though in winter it can be served 'cooked' with spices and honey. Homemade varieties can be up to 60% abv (compared with 40% for store-bought rakija). Cancel all plans for the next morning if a local starts pouring their own family recipe.

BY ANITA ISALSKA

THE BEST RAKIJA BARS

RAKETA RAKIA BAR, BULGARIA
Communist decor, a big rakia selection, and many meaty accompaniments... yes, it sounds like a tick-list of Eastern European clichés, but this bar in Sofia is enormously satisfying.
www.facebook.com/raketarakiabar

BALIKÇI SABAHATTIN, TURKEY
Turkish rakı is best accompanied by mountains of mezze, especially melon and *bayaz peynir* (white cheese). This chic Istanbul spot's well-chosen menu complements the fine raki.
www.balikcisabahattin.com

RAKIA BAR, SERBIA
Serving firewater neat, in cocktails or mulled as a winter warmer, this unimaginatively named bar in Belgrade, Serbia, is popular with tourists but 30 varieties of rakija bring locals flocking, too. *www.rakiabar.com*

BRETTOS, GREECE
A big spread of fruity spirits is available at this Athens distillery and bar, including raki from Crete and *rakomelo* – raki boiled with cinnamon and honey (practically medicinal, if you ask us).
www.facebook.com/brettos.plaka

MUSIC PUB, ROMANIA
Live bands and retro rock tunes liven up this brick-lined boozer in Sibiu, Romania. The convivial vibe invites a *ţuică* or two, while a burger-heavy menu soaks up the damage. *www.facebook.com/musicpubsibiu*

RUSSIA

How to ask for a spirit without mixers? Odna vodka, pozhaluysta (pronounced vot-ka)

Signature spirit? Vodka

What to order with your spirits? Traditionally vodka is drunk with a plate of zakuska (snacks such as pickles, herring or rye bread) to nibble on in between shots

Do: Say 'pyey da dna' as you down your shot of vodka – it means 'drink to the bottom!'

There's nothing more quintessentially Russian than a bottle of vodka shared among comrades. It forms not only an integral part of the country's social fabric, but also its cultural heritage. This is the land from which Smirnoff originated in the 19th century. And though that brand is now produced by British drinks giant Diageo, there are some 3000 Russian vodkas on the market and entire supermarket aisles dedicated to elegant bottles with grand motifs.

Distilled mainly from fermented grain (usually wheat, rye or barley, and sometimes potato) vodka was first produced in the country around the 16th century. While there's been a shift among the younger generation to drinking more beer and mixer drinks (or less booze in general since anti-alcoholism campaigns), vodka remains synonymous with Russia as its national drink.

You'll find the spirit served in bars across the country, but for a more authentic, memorable experience try it in the more local-style taverns (ryumochnaya) or restaurants serving Russian food. It's best served chilled at 10°C, and etiquette dictates it be drunk neat and downed in one shot; locals consider it cowardly to sip your vodka. In between shots, it is custom to graze on a plate of *zakuzi* ('vodka' snacks). If you're not so much into the idea of slamming down straight vodka, opt for the more palatable flavoured varieties – instilled with anything from cranberry, apple, cloves to horseradish – which are more acceptable to sip.

Vodka is the most known of Russia's spirits, but also look out for other traditional herbal liqueurs such as *nastokya*, distilled with cranberry, cinnamon or juniper.

ALKON

b2 Str Germana, Veliky Novgorod;
www.alkon.su; +7 8162 77 94 03

◆ Food ◆ Shop ◆ Transport
◆ Distillery ◆ Bar

THINGS TO DO NEARBY

Cathedral of St Sophia
The gleaming golden dome of Russia's oldest church, completed in 1050, sits within the kremlin and houses the icon of Novgorod's patron saint, Our Lady of the Sign.

Dom Berga
Dine on hearty traditional classic Russian dishes at this well known restaurant set in a 19th-century former merchant's home. *www.domberga.ru*

Novgorod State United Museum
Also within the city's kremlin, this absorbing museum has one of the world's largest collections of Russian icons, and exhibits covering local history. *www.novgorodmuseum.ru*

Yaroslav's Court
Across the river from the kremlin, this historic site features remnants of an 18th-century market arcade, churches and the 12th-century St Nicholas Cathedral.

Founded by the merchant IA Korsakov in 1897, Alkon distillery has been producing some of Russia's finest vodkas for more than 120 years, surviving the Russian Revolution and two World Wars. Located in the beautiful town of Veliky Novgorod in the country's west – a popular getaway for St Petersburg residents – it is well known for the quality of its spirits, made using centuries-old classical techniques. The spring water that forms the basis of its vodka is said to be a secret of its success – it is drawn from nearby Lake Ilmen and goes through three natural filters during the purification process. Traditional fruit and berry liqueurs, known as *nastoykas*, and balsams are also made here; the on-site gift shop has an English-language pamphlet and helpful staff to help you choose your tipple to take home.

Attached to the distillery is a restaurant-bar with crackling log fire, dark wood and exposed brick walls, creating the ultimate cosy atmosphere to settle in for a night of spirits tasting. Knock back shots of crisp, cold premium Sadko vodka or thyme-infused vodka paired with delicious homemade *pelmeni* (dumplings). Try Alkon's famous traditional cranberry liqueur early in the night – while your tastebuds are still intact.

SWEDEN

How to ask for a spirit without mixers? 'Snaps', or (more casually) a 'nubbe'

Signature spirit? Aquavit, a type of brännvin, also called snaps

What to order with your spirits? Pickled herring, ideally with Swedish hardbread and various accompaniments (red onion, sour cream, chives)

Do: Toast with a song! Aquavit lends itself to drinking songs – called snapsvisor – whose lyrics often revel in the effects, good and bad, of the drink at hand

Sweden has always had a complicated relationship with alcohol. The legal drinking age is 20, and the only way to buy alcohol is through the state-run monopoly Systembolaget, which for decades was a notoriously draconian regime that made the purchase of booze a difficult and discouraging errand. Regulations softened and prices dropped substantially when Sweden joined the EU, and these days shopping at Systemet, as it's fondly called, is a pleasant experience, with helpful service and a great selection.

Liquor is still relatively expensive in bars, and Swedes today drink more beer and wine. The old-fashioned Swedish beer hall is a thing of beauty; after-work drinks are a popular casual alternative. In winter, people walk through Christmas markets holding mugs of *glögg* (hot spiced wine).

But there's nothing like a *snaps* – shot of vodka or aquavit

– to warm you on a chilly day, or to wash down a plate of pickled herring at Midsummer or pile of crayfish on a long August night. One of the world's most famous vodka brands was conceived in Sweden: though it has been owned by French drinks giant Pernod Ricard since 2008, Absolut Vodka was born in Åhus, southern Sweden, in 1879, and is still produced here. Aquavit, meanwhile, has recently found favour with mixologists in New York and has been experiencing a renaissance both at home and abroad, helping to raise the profile of Scandinavian spirits.

On weekends and summer holidays, Swedes party hard. At parties and celebrations, *snaps* are accompanied by a toast and boisterous drinking songs. Among the most popular is *Helan Går*, or 'The whole goes down' – bottoms up, in other words.

BAR
SPRITMUSEUM

Djurgårdsvägen 38, Djurgården, Stockholm;
www.spritmuseum.se; +46 8 12 13 13 00

◆ Food   ◆ Bar
◆ Tours   ◆ Transport

Stockholm's Museum of Spirits is an educational and entertaining temple to the subject of Swedish booze, but it is also one of the most convenient and knowledgeable places in Sweden to sample a range of aquavit. This Swedish spirit – whose Latin name translates quite literally as 'water of life' – is traditionally spiced with caraway, fennel and aniseed, and it's a variety of *brännvin*, a category of clear, grain-based alcohol that also includes vodka.

Inside the Spritmuseum, sniff at various aquavit spices in the scent organ, relax in a darkened theatre with overhead projections that make you feel like you've had a few, then face your regrets with a simulated headache in the Hangover Room. Finish at the small, classy bar, which offers a sampler of three types of aquavit and a Swedish *punsch* made with arrack.

The Spritmuseum also houses a collection of art created

for Absolut Vodka marketing campaigns; in 1986 Andy Warhol was the first of several big artists to collaborate with the Swedish brand. Other exhibits walk you through Sweden's complex relationship with alcohol and the history of local distilling. When you reach the bar, start your aquavit tasting with O.P. Anderson – first made in 1891 and the closest in flavour to the original 15th-century recipe, with its emphasis on caraway.

THINGS TO DO NEARBY

Vasamuseet
Next door to Spritmuseum on the parklike island of Djurgården, this museum houses the spectacular engineering failure that is Sweden's great battleship Wasa, and brings 17th-century Stockholm to life. **www.vasamuseet.se**

Nordiska Museet
A huge museum housing a variety of art and artefacts related to Swedish cultural history, from the Vikings and August Strindberg to Sami handicrafts and industrial design. **www. nordiskamuseet.se**

Skansen
Sweden in miniature, this open-air museum has examples of traditional life from every part of the country, plus a Nordic zoo. **www.skansen.se**

Abba The Museum
This relatively new, flashy museum is dedicated to the Swedish pop supergroup, complete with costumes, gossip, audio clips and a sound stage. **www. abbathemuseum.com**

HERNÖ GIN

Dala, Härnösand, Västernorrland;
www.hernogin.com; + 46 611 505 770

◆ Food ◆ Tours ◆ Bar
◆ Distillery ◆ Shop

It's quite a trek to Sweden's first gin-only distillery, yet many make the pilgrimage for a special guided tour and tastings of one of the world's most-awarded gins. Located in a little village called Dala near Härnösand, around a five-hour train journey north of Stockholm, Hernö launched in December 2012 with the visitor centre opening in 2015. Founder and master distiller Jon Hillgren (trained at the Institute of Brewing and Distilling in London) uses only certified organic botanicals, macerating a wheat-based spirit in juniper and coriander before adding native lingonberries, meadowsweet, black pepper, vanilla and lemon peel. The spirit is cut with water from the distillery's own well before Jon hand-labels and signs each bottle.

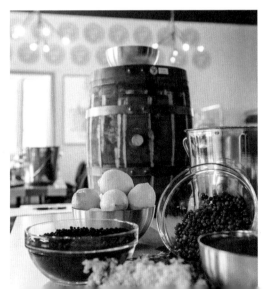

THINGS TO DO NEARBY

Västanåfallets Naturreservat
A scenic BYO picnic spot, with tables set alongside a gushing waterfall. Or follow one of the walking trails for a bit of wildlife spotting.

Royal by Mathias
A friendly lunch spot in Härnösand focusing on fresh, healthy ingredients (cod with dill, ratatouille and almond potatoes) where you could be served by chef Mathias himself. *www.royalbymathias.se*

Murberget
Visiting this open-air museum (open mid-June to mid-August only) is like stepping back in time to the 1920s. Expect traditional farmhouses and guides in authentic costume. *www.murberget.se*

Härnösand Stadsfest
Visit Härnösand in July for this two-day music extravaganza where around 13,000 people party in the streets. Tickets must be booked well in advance. *www. harnosandsstadsfest.se*

Distillery visits need to be booked in advance unless you pop into the 'open day' held on 1 July each year. Experiences on offer include a 45-minute guided tour and a tasting of either four or six gins. As well as the classic London Dry, there's Navy Strength, Old Tom, a Juniper Cask-Aged Gin, the Blackcurrant Gin and limited editions. Also keep an eye out for special events, such as the Hernö Gin cruise – a cocktail extravaganza sailing around the Stockholm archipelago.

SWITZERLAND

How to ask for a spirit without mixers? 'Pur', but if you want ice say either 'our' or 'auf eis', or use the English 'on the rocks'

Signature spirit? Schnapps, which vary region to region depending on the ingredients available.

What to order with your spirits? Like locals, drink them as a digestif, or mixed with coffee

Do: Cheer! The Swiss tend to cheer when each new round of drinks is served, and don't drink until you've chinked glasses with everyone at the table, using their name and looking them in the eye as you do so

In the mountains and valleys of the Alps, the Swiss are fond of a tipple or two – how better to defrost from a day on the ski slopes than a warming shot of schnapps? Many are fruit-based and with those long winters, it's little wonder the Swiss turned their summer harvests into something that would warm the cockles when the snow began to fall.

In the Valais canton, in the southwest of Switzerland, the apricot schnapps abricotine is the one to seek out as a shot or a digestif (or drink it with a mixer). Meanwhile, in the Graubünden canton to the east, it is sweet cherries that take centre stage, blended with spices such as cinnamon, cloves and vanilla in the traditional *röteli* liqueur. Many fruit schnapps are used in coffee, (like an

Irish coffee) as *kaffee schnapps*. *Plümli* (plum schnapps) is one of the most popular used this way: order it by its charming name, *schtümli pflümli*.

Herbal schnapps are also popular; *alpenbitter* is a digestif produced by a few different distilleries throughout the country. The most popular is Appenzeller, which is often compared to Jägermeister. It is made with 42 mountain herbs and its recipe is said to be known by only two people.

By far the best globally known herb-based spirit – though possibly for all the wrong reasons and more for its French history – is absinthe, which originates in the Val de Travers west of Neuchatel. Despite its shady reputation, this refreshing spirit – served with chilled water – is now enjoying a renaissance thanks to the clandestine distillers who kept it going during its century-long ban. Add to that the birth of Swiss craft gin, with brands like Gin Bisbino in the southernmost Italian-speaking canton of Ticino now taking advantage of mountain herbs to create local botanical flavour profiles, and this small European country is becoming an increasingly interesting place to drink.

■ BAR
MAISON DE L'ABSINTHE

10 Grande Rue, Môtiers, Val de Travers;
www.maison-absinthe.ch; +41 32 860 1000

◆ Tours   ◆ Bar
◆ Shop

At the heart of the Val de Travers absinthe trail, this museum and visitor centre tells the scintillating history of the forbidden spirit. Ironically, it is set in the former judges' offices where so many absinthe bootleggers were brought under charges during its century-long ban. It has been transformed into an architecturally striking space with an alluring bar, and showcases the myriad distillers now making the infamous spirit without fear of prosecution.

Displays cover absinthe's manufacture, its various herbal ingredients and the propaganda-fuelled prohibition; the most fascinating exhibits are dedicated to how distillers kept their product secret – from distilling it in hidden rooms to distributing it in reused pineapple tins. Book ahead for aperitif snacks, or to try an intriguing absinthe-based cookery course.

THINGS TO DO NEARBY

Fontaine à Louis
During the absinthe ban, bottles were hidden near mountain springs so it could be mixed with spring water. Walk through forest outside Môtiers to this spring to drink like locals did. *www. routedelabsinthe.com*

Creux du Van
Hike into the Jura mountains to admire this kilometre-wide natural amphitheatre, with cliffs rising 160 metres. The area is home to wildlife, too, including marmots and deer. *www.val-de-travers.ch*

ABSINTHE LA VALOTE MARTIN

10 rue du Quarre, Boveresse, Val de Travers;
www.absinthe-originale.ch; +41 32 861 2654

◆ Distillery ◆ Shop
◆ Tours ◆ Bar

As the son of a former absinthe bootlegger, Philippe Martin, who runs La Valote Martin, has long had connections to the infamous drink. As a child, his father and uncle would use the family bathtub as a cooling system for the stills, and mysterious phone calls would command orders for absinthe using code words.

Philippe's tales add a fascinating dimension to a visit to his distillery, set in a creaking, green-shuttered chalet in the village of Boveresse. It is the only one in the area involved in every stage of creating absinthe. Tours start in the small walled garden; climb the crooked stairs into the attic and you'll see the plants drying, pinned to the beams. In the small bar, try Philippe's signature brand Bacchus – an amber blend with woody notes, showcasing how sophisticated absinthe can be.

THINGS TO DO NEARBY

Robella
This Val de Travers adventure park in Buttes offers a host of activities, from mountain-biking to a toboggan track in the summer, and skiing and snowshoeing in the winter. *www.robella.ch*

Musée de l'Officine de Verre
This glass museum in Couvet is set in a former pharmacy that once supplied clandestine absinthe traders with ingredients. It also houses an absinthe distillery. www. routedelabsinthe.com

GIN BISBINO

Via dell'Unione, Sagno, Muggio Valley, Ticino;
www.bisbino.ch; +41 79 967 5736

◆ Distillery ◆ Shop
◆ Tours ◆ Transport

The first gin from Ticino – Switzerland's southernmost, Italian-speaking canton – was born in the bucolic Valle di Muggio, the brainchild of four friends. Everything about it is local; after playing around with the recipe they settled on seven herbs, including coriander, Melissa and one secret ingredient, all plucked from their terraced garden in the village of Sagno on the slopes of Mount Bisbino.

They took over a distillery used for grappa, the region's more traditional tipple, and the result is a 100% organic dry gin, with light citrusy overtones. Tours visit the gardens and distillery, followed by tastings. Don't leave without trying a true Ticinese G&T – fizzy *gazzosas* have been produced in Ticino since 1883 and now the oldest brand, Noé, makes tonic.

THINGS TO DO NEARBY

Cycling
Ticino's landscape is a mountain-biking paradise and Switzerland's Route 66 stretches for 120 stunning kilometres from the lakeside city of Lugano to Ponte Tresa. *www.ticino.ch*

Bellinzona market
The Saturday morning market in Ticino's historic capital is a showcase for the region's must-try goodies, including cold meats and cheeses, polenta and traditional Swiss cakes.

UNITED KINGDOM

How to ask for a spirit without mixers? A shot (or a dram for whisky). Ordering neat gin will probably raise some eyebrows

Signature spirit? London Dry gin and Scotch whisky

What to order with your spirits? Order a gin and tonic, but try tonics with aromatic flavours or bitters, and add a garnish like citrus or dried juniper berries to bring out the best in the spirit

Don't be surprised to receive just ice and a slice when you order a G&T down the pub

The UK is often regarded as a nation of drinkers, but who can blame them when they're so very spoilt – from world-famous Scotch, to gin made in its historic home of London. It's not always been that way. In the past five years, distilleries in the UK have more than doubled, with the 'ginaissance' playing no small part in the country's craft booze boom. Before that, you wouldn't have been wrong to assume the British drinking scene was all about two pints of lager and a packet of crisps, but these days even the more upmarket pubs offer a range of artisan gins, whiskies and quirkily flavoured spirits, while top bars are exploring uncharted territory on creatively put-together cocktail lists.

The last time the UK had it this bad for spirits was in the 18th century, during a period often referred to as 'the Gin Craze'. The nation went nuts for the juniper-based spirit after they got a taste for Dutch jenever under the influence of their ruler William of Orange. Gin became so popular that soon one in four London homes were said to be making moonshine, often to catastrophic ends. The phrase 'to be blind drunk' was coined in this time, and gin became known as 'mother's ruin' – neither were ironic statements. As such, parliament introduced a series of Gin Acts that cracked down on small-batch distillation and practically outlawed the spirit. Inevitably, beer made its return as the people's champion.

Meanwhile, up in Scotland, barley was being used for other purposes, with Scotch whisky production reaching a refined

"Securing the first small-batch distilling licence in London for nearly 200 years helped to pave the way for the 315 gin distilleries now in the UK, and the wider craft spirits renaissance we're experiencing across the UK, with new distilleries opening almost weekly"

—JARED BROWN, DRINKS HISTORIAN & MASTER DISTILLER, SIPSMITH

point by the 17th century, when its popularity began to soar. As such, Scottish parliament introduced heavy taxation into the industry, forcing distillers to move underground – or even to hide their stills in the heather – and use smuggling practices to get their product to market. The drink persisted this way for 150 years until a change of law in the early 1800s, but it's fair to say the struggle paid off. Scotch whisky is now of world-renown, accounting for around 20% of all food and drink exports from the UK. This is perhaps to the chagrin of the Irish, who it's thought invented the drink some 100 years before the Scots raced ahead with production.

With practices and methods firmly in place thanks to this long and rich history, experimentation in distillation is now booming. The floodgates for this new chapter of drink geekery opened in 2009, when London-based gin-maker Sipsmith was granted a licence to distil after two years of lobbying parliament for a change in laws that had been in place since the Gin Act's inception. Small batch distillation was finally back on the agenda and a resurgence in craft booze-making took off. You'll now find distilleries in unlikely spots – from the edges of the Brecon Beacons and John o' Groats, to a car park in east London.

Distilleries that started with gin then explored vodka and are now moving on to the darker spirits. It's an exciting time in UK spirit making, and a time when asking for a G&T at the bar will probably be met with the response: 'which gin?'

TOP 5 SPIRITS

- **Sipsmith London Dry Gin** Sipsmith Distillery, London, England
- **Salcombe Gin Finisterre** Salcombe Distilling Company, Devon, England
- **Chase Marmalade Vodka** Chase Distillery, Hereford, England
- **Aberlour A'Bundah Whisky** Aberlour Distillery, Speyside, Scotland
- **Springbank 12 Year Old Whisky** Springback Distillery, Campbeltown, Scotland

SALCOMBE DISTILLING COMPANY

The Boathouse, 28 Island St, Salcombe, Devon;
www.salcombegin.com; +44 1548 288180

◆ Distillery ◆ Shop
◆ Tours ◆ Bar

THINGS TO DO NEARBY

Salcombe Maritime Museum
Take in the area's seafaring past with artefacts, paintings and models that bring to life Salcombe's maritime traditions. *www.salcombemuseum.org.uk*

Salcombe Brewery
Sample a range of locally produced real ales at this craft beer brewery, built on the site of a decommissioned water reservoir. *www.salcombebrewery.com*

Sea Kayak Salcombe
Less of the sailing – the more modern way to tackle Salcombe's waters is by kayak. Or sign up for paddleboarding if you feel even more adventurous. *www.southsandssailing.co.uk*

The Millbrook Inn
You'll have to take a boat from Salcombe to access this traditional pub in nearby South Pool. Its menu champions the local catch of the day. *www.millbrookinnsouthpool.co.uk*

We doubt there's a more beautiful place to make gin than at this Devon distillery: a boathouse in an old smuggler's cove transformed into a light-filled space, with plenty of nods to the area's seafaring past. In the 1800s, schooners known as Salcombe Fruiters voyaged across the seas to bring dried fruit to English soil. In more modern times, this stretch was home to Island Cruising Club, where Salcombe Gin's founders Angus Lugsdin and Howard Davies met as young sailing teachers. They'd lap up sundown G&Ts at the end of their working days at Salcombe Yacht Club, a venue overlooking the estuary's waters that has clearly inspired the pair. In 2016, they took over a boat repair yard that had belonged to the club where they'd met, launching Salcombe Distilling Company and its bar looking out to sea.

Their copper still, Provident, is named after a local trawler, but you'll get more up-close with mini equipment at Salcombe's Gin School, making a batch you can then sample on the balcony of the bar. While there, order a G&T made with Salcombe Start Point, a gin playing on that fruity heritage with its citrusy botanicals. They've also made a limited-edition gin aged in sherry barrels, Finisterre – with the bar often the testing ground for future limited runs.

BOMBAY SAPPHIRE DISTILLERY

London Rd, Laverstoke, Whitchurch, Hampshire;
www.distillery.bombaysapphire.com; +44 1256 890090

◆ Food ◆ Tours ◆ Bar
◆ Distillery ◆ Shop ◆ Transport

One of the world's most famous gin bottles – that sparkly blue Bombay Sapphire – set up home in Hampshire in 2014, taking over the site of a former paper mill that used to produce notes for the Bank of England. It's now churning out gin by the bucketload as well as welcoming daily groups of visitors as one of the area's most popular tourist attractions. You can shell out for a personalised tour with one of the brand ambassadors, but the standard tour is just as insightful, with audio points in several languages allowing you to tap into the story.

Although it's illuminating to see these large-scale stills in action, it's actually the two glasshouses sitting above the River Test that garner the most attention. Designed by

THINGS TO DO NEARBY

Blackwood Forest
Hire a bike and do a circuit of this enchanted patch of woodland. Or make a night of it by hiring a wood cabin with its own hot tub. *www.forestholidays.co.uk /blackwood-forest*

Whitchurch Silk Mill
Move from the former paper mill to a silk manufacturer – this mill is the oldest of its kind in the UK, filled with Victorian machinery and looms still producing fabulous fabrics. *www. whitchurchsilkmill.org.uk*

Highclere Castle
Have your Lady Mary moment at the location where Downton Abbey is filmed. The castle is also home to a museum of Egyptian curiosities. *www. highclerecastle.co.uk*

Overton
This nearby village has been inhabited since the Stone Age and offers picturesque walks past its pretty white buildings and between its four pubs.

Heatherwick Studio (which also designed London's Olympic velodrome), the domes made from curved glass are a beauty to behold and offer two separate climates for growing all the botanicals used within the gin (purely for demonstration purposes, mind).

Visit a mini gin museum, sniff a range of botanicals in the dry room and finish up at the Mill Bar, where gin cocktails are lapped up by thirsty day-trippers – try The Laverstoke, a refreshing gin fizz with lime, ginger and elderflower cordial.

CHASE DISTILLERY

Chase Farm, Rosemaund, Hereford;
www.chasedistillery.co.uk; +44 1432 820455

◆ Distillery   ◆ Shop
◆ Tours

Chase Distillery is more than 10 years old, and has come a long way since humble beginnings as a producer of vodka on a remote Hereford farm. The range now includes a fleet of flavoured gin and vodka as well as an elderflower liqueur. William Chase was the potato farmer behind Britain's Tyrrells crisps, who had a vodka epiphany when researching crisp production. He sold the crisp empire in 2008 and, before long, Chase became home to the largest copper-rectifying column in the world – one that juts from the roof of the barn. The ethos has always been about sustainability (Chase has bought a biomass boiler in its quest for carbon neutrality) and 'field to bottle' production – see potatoes grow before mashing, fermenting and distilling. Try Williams Elegant 48 Gin, which uses apples from the orchard.

THINGS TO DO NEARBY

Verzon House
Also owned by the Chase family, this country house hotel will lay on transport to the distillery. Naturally, its restaurant's a la carte menu includes Hereford beef. *www. verzonhouse.com*

Mappa Mundi, Hereford Cathedral
Marvel at what is believed to be the world's largest surviving medieval map, which charts humanity in both a geographical and a spiritual sense. *www. herefordcathedral.org*

BERMONDSEY DISTILLERY

55 Stanworth St, Bermondsey, London;
www.bermondseygin.com; +44 20 7237 1500

◆ Distillery   ◆ Shop   ◆ Transport
◆ Tours   ◆ Bar

Christian Jensen took his obsession with old-style gin to new heights in 2004, taking a vintage bottle to Charles Maxwell, master distiller at Thames Distillery (one of just two places making gin in London at the time). He persuaded him to create 1200 bottles of Bermondsey Gin, sticking closely to that vintage recipe, which he would then whip out at bars for the perfect martini. The popularity of Jensen's gin spread, and a distillery followed in 2012.

At weekends, drop by for tipples or pre-batched cocktails to take away, or get a history of gin on a tour bookended by a G&T and a martini. This is gin-making that shies away from new-fangled botanicals, or as they say, 'gin as it was, gin as it should be' – best seen in Jensen's Old Tom Gin, devised from an 1840s recipe.

THINGS TO DO NEARBY

Maltby Street Market
A heaving weekend market filled with street food stalls and a rival bar operated by Peckham's Little Bird Gin, serving hot cocktails in winter. *www.maltby.st*

Bermondsey Beer Mile
Crawl along the many craft beer distilleries that fill the area's railway arches – from Anspach & Hobday to Fourpure Brewing Co. Hop to it!

CITY OF LONDON DISTILLERY

22-24 Bride Lane, City of London;
www.cityoflondondistillery.com; +44 20 7936 3636

◆ Food   ◆ Tours   ◆ Bar
◆ Distillery   ◆ Shop   ◆ Transport

Not only was the City of London Distillery the first to make gin within the Square Mile in over 200 years when it launched in 2012, but as it is the last remaining manufacturer of anything within the City, it is allowed to bear the area's crest on its posh-looking bottles.

Celebrate the team's success from the bar, a smart-looking space filled with brown leather armchairs and fit for the neighbourhood. Punters drink cocktails with a view of two copper stills behind glass, named after British TV's *Two Fat Ladies*' chefs, Clarissa and Jennifer. Tours are guided by London experts – including blogger and World Gin Day founder 'Gin Monkey' – and include a stiff G&T using the distillery's London Dry. Back at the bar, don't miss a Martinez cocktail made with its Old Tom Gin.

THINGS TO DO NEARBY

Ye Olde Cheshire Cheese
Forget the landmarks; you'll get more of London's history from sipping underground at this Victorian pub, which Charles Dickens is said to have frequented. It's on Fleet Street, a five-minute walk from the distillery.

Museum of London
From temporary exhibitions to year-round displays, the Museum of London captures life through the ages, dating all the way back to prehistoric times. *www. museumoflondon.org.uk*

EAST LONDON LIQUOR COMPANY

Unit GF1, Bow Wharf, 221 Grove Rd, Bow, London;
www.eastlondonliquorcompany.com; +44 20 3011 0980

◆ Food ◆ Tours ◆ Bar
◆ Distillery ◆ Shop ◆ Transport

Could this be London's hippest distillery? Based in a former glue factory in a derelict car park near Victoria Park, we reckon so. But it's got heart for sure, with a welcoming team throughout its bottle shop, restaurant and exposed-brick bar – from where you can peer at shiny stills, accessible on one of ELLC's tours. The distillery makes vodka, gin and rum, and is soon to launch London's first whisky – a trend that's set to spike in surrounding distilleries.

Grab a pizza from the Italian kitchen or something hot off the summertime barbecue, all washed down to perfection with a negroni made using its London Dry gin – there's a very good reason this cocktail is pre-batched and served at so many London bars, who've sensibly chosen to install their own ELLC taps.

THINGS TO DO NEARBY

Victoria Park
Get active on the boating lake, check out a library on a canal barge, find peace in the shade of a Chinese pagoda or just saunter through this large London park.

Renegade London Wine
For more craft booze making, this Bethnal Green bar doubles as an urban winery producing London's first-ever sparkling wine.
***www.renegadelondon
wine.com***

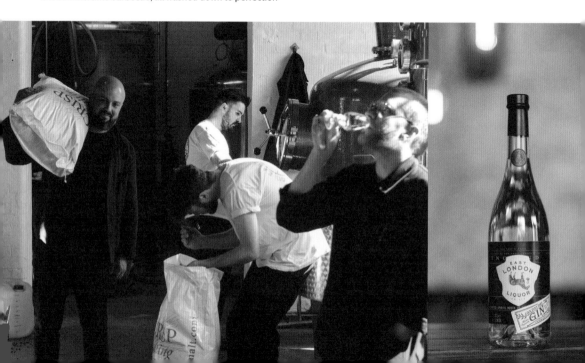

HALF HITCH GIN

Unit 53, West Yard, Camden Lock Place, London;
www.halfhitch.london; +44 20 3096 3027
◆ Distillery   ◆ Shop
◆ Tours   ◆ Transport

Even as a Camden native who'd worked on the market before moving into the drinks trade, Half Hitch Gin's founder Mark Holdsworth admits he knew nothing of the North London area's gin heritage when he discovered Camden had been home to Gilbey's gin and its vast booze empire in the late 1800s.

Half Hitch isn't quite so sprawling, a micro-distillery by The Lock producing less than 15,000 bottles a year since 2014. The gin itself gets its unique Earl Grey flavour from bergamot and black tea sourced from Malawi. The process is interesting too, blending distillates and tinctures using the cold vacuum method. Experimentation is also encouraged at Half Hitch Gin School, where punters bring their own flavours to gin making – pickled onions included.

THINGS TO DO NEARBY

Kerb Camden Market
From vegan tacos to sourdough pizzas and hawker-style grub, you'll be spoilt for choice at this street food market, open seven days a week.
www.kerbfood.com

The Cheese Bar
Cheese is served every which way at this quirky Camden restaurant, which attracts a fair few fanatics. Stuff your face with truffled Baron Bigod from Suffolk.
www.thecheesebar.com

HAYMAN'S DISTILLERY

8a Weir Rd, Balham, London; www.haymansgin.com;
distillers@hayman.co.uk
◆ Distillery   ◆ Shop
◆ Tours

Hayman family ancestor James Burrough invented Beefeater Gin, one of the UK's best-selling gin brands. This heritage has led Hayman's to dub its style of mother's ruin 'a true English gin', staying loyal to recipes devised by the family more than 150 years ago.

Hayman's production facility in a Balham warehouse, on the other hand, was shiny and new for 2018. The family owners use a small-batch, two-day process across three copper stills – Marjorie, the eldest, and Karin and Miranda, named after Christopher Hayman's mother, wife and daughter, respectively.

Join a 90-minute tour or get to grips with gin cocktails through the centuries in a drink-making masterclass. The distillery's most unique feature is 'ginema' – a pop-up cinema pairing gin-loving movies with cocktails and London Dry Gin popcorn.

THINGS TO DO NEARBY

The Exhibit
For more big-screen action, venture to Balham's Exhibit – pub meets cinema, with a full range of events to boot.
www.theexhibit.co.uk

Brother Marcus
Do brunch the right way at Brother Marcus, a local cafe that does fritters, eggs and avocado every which way.
www.brothermarcus.co.uk

Courtesy of East London Distillery (2)

SIPSMITH GIN DISTILLERY

83 Cranbrook Rd, Chiswick, London;
www.sipsmith.com; +44 20 8747 0753

◆ Distillery   ◆ Shop
◆ Tours   ◆ Transport

If the 'ginaissance' could be credited to one distillery, it would be West London's Sipsmith. Its founders, Sam Galsworthy and Fairfax Hall, lobbied UK parliament for a change in legislation that had restricted small-batch distilling since the Gin Act of the 1800s. They received a licence to distil at their Hammersmith premises in 2009, opening the floodgates for others to follow suit.

Sipsmith's modus operandi has helped them continue to stand out from the crowd, with a gin that reflects distilling heritage and stays loyal to classic London recipes. This is in part thanks to the expertise of drinks historian Jared Brown, who they met at a negroni party. He offered to join as master

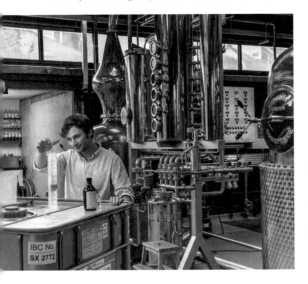

THINGS TO DO NEARBY

Chiswick House and Gardens
There are 65 acres to explore in Chiswick House's lush gardens, and there's a companion podcast you can download to help guide you through its leafy history. *www. chiswickhouseandgardens. org.uk*

Griffin Brewery
London's historic brewer Fuller's has been active in Chiswick since 1816 – tour its brewery to see a different scale of drink making. Beyond hops, it's also home to the UK's oldest wisteria plant. *www.fullers.co.uk*

Hogarth's House
Eighteenth-century artist William Hogarth played his part in spreading gin's bad reputation with his depiction of 'Gin Lane', so it feels right to pay his former house a visit. *www. williamhogarthtrust.org.uk*

Evans and Peel Pharmacy
After visiting Sipsmith to sip a gin that honours the Victorian era, step back in time at this Chiswick speakeasy bar, fronting as an old-fashioned pharmacy. *www. evansandpeel.com*

distiller if they promised to honour the historical roots of distilling. Since then, they've graduated to larger premises in Chiswick and have been bought by drink giant Beam Suntory.

Come for a G&T or visit for the Sipsmith Sipper Club, which includes a tutored tasting followed by a gin-paired dinner at nearby Charlotte's Bistro. In colder months, try the Hot G&T – a unique winter warmer devised from a Victorian recipe.

THE DISTILLERY

186 Portobello Rd, Notting Hill, London;
www.the-distillery.london; +44 20 3034 2233

◆ Food   ◆ Tours   ◆ Bar
◆ Distillery   ◆ Shop   ◆ Transport

THINGS TO DO NEARBY

Portobello Road Market
Antiques, knick-knacks,
fruit and veg; but mostly
an opportunity to marvel
at an old-school market
on a colourful street.
Visit on a Saturday when
it's at its best. **www.
portobelloroad.co.uk**

108 Garage
Contemporary cuisine,
a pulsating setting and
charming staff make 108
a standout restaurant
in the area. Visit at
lunchtime when it's
way more affordable.
www.108garage.com

Electric Cinema
Catch a movie in West
London luxury – this
cinema from the Soho
House group has luxurious
red velvets sofa beds for
your viewing pleasure, and
its own retro diner.
www.electriccinema.co.uk

The Churchill Arms
If you thought Portobello
Rd was full of hashtaggers,
visit the Churchill Arms,
a traditional pub decked
in flowers – sure to get
you snapping too. **www.
churchillarmskensington.
co.uk**

Welcome to the world's first gin hotel. The Distillery threw open its doors to great fanfare at the end of 2016, in a prime position on West London's Instagram-ready Portobello Road. It's brought to you by the team behind Portobello Road Gin, a well-known brand conceived in 2011 just down the road. As well as three boutique rooms (just imagine those mini bars), a couple of restaurants, a bar and a shop, the basement houses a museum dedicated to the juniper spirit. They call this the Ginstitute, and it's down here that the team also make gin under 'The Distillery' name.

The Ginstitute is the ideal place to learn the chequered history of mother's ruin, with knowledgeable tutors showing off artefacts including bottles of gin so old, they advise consuming as a 'stimulant for the liver'. Then take a gin-making class, blending pre-distilled botanicals – from traditional bitter orange and liquorice to the likes of asparagus and Yorkshire tea. Should you like your own batch enough, you can re-order using your bottle's unique number. Book seriously far in advance for a stay in one of those boutique rooms – then order a red snapper at the bar the morning after, the gin alternative to a Bloody Mary.

MANCHESTER THREE RIVERS

21 Red Bank Parade, Manchester; www.mancheste
threerivers.com; info@manchesterthreerivers.com

◆ Distillery ◆ Shop
◆ Tours ◆ Transport

Distilling under the arches of a disused railway track, if any further proof were needed that Manchester Three Rivers is a truly urban distillery, its copper still is named 'Angel' after Angel Meadow – the notoriously brutal 19th-century slum that once stood nearby.

Paying homage to the diet of the mill workers who would have scraped by there, its hand-blended London Dry gin uses porridge oats as one of its 11 botanicals, which impart a sweet kick and also give off oils that add viscosity for an incredibly smooth gin. To get a seat at the bar inside the red-brick distillery chamber, you have to book the 'Gin Experience' – a three-hour immersion that starts with a film about Manchester's industrial heritage and a potted history of gin, and ends with you making your own gin in a 1L alembic still.

THINGS TO DO NEARBY

Manchester United Museum

It might just be the world's most famous football club, and even if you're not a fan it's a thrill to tour Old Trafford's changing rooms and walk on the hallowed turf. ***www.manutd.com***

Curry Mile

Lit up like Christmas with plenty of neon, more than 70 South Asian restaurants are crammed into Manchester's Curry Mile, a five-minute taxi ride south from central Manchester to Wilmslow Road.

ST GEORGE'S DISTILLERY

Harling Rd, Roudham, Norfolk;
www.englishwhisky.co.uk; +44 1953 717939

◆ Food ◆ Tours
◆ Distillery ◆ Shop

When the English Whisky Company founded St George's in 2006, it was the first dedicated malt whisky distillery to open in England in more than 100 years. Using local Norfolk barley and water from an aquifer that comes directly into the distillery, the company sells its whisky by chapter, indicating which year in its lifespan each whisky has been released, rather than by age, to allow customers to taste how the distillery's output changes.

All the distillery tours offer a warehouse visit, while special tours include lunch and there are also monthly tastings of whisky from around the world. The shop offers all of the St George expressions as well as some very unusual whiskies from elsewhere, such as New Zealand's Dunedin DoubleWood.

THINGS TO DO NEARBY

Norfolk Broads

Famous for boating holidays since the late 19th century, the broads are actually flooded medieval peat excavations – ideal for the sailing whisky fan. ***www.visitnorfolk.co.uk/ explore/broads.aspx***

Winbirri Vineyard

It's rare to be able to combine a whisky distillery with a vineyard visit, but in Norfolk it's possible. Award-winning Winbirri Vineyard is a mere 30-minute drive away. ***www.winbirri.com***

HARROGATE TIPPLE

Main St, Ripley, North Yorkshire;
www.harrogatetipple.com; +44 1423 779915

◆ Distillery ◆ Shop
◆ Tours ◆ Bar

'I adore otters. They're playful, cute. They only live in clean water and they live in all the rivers around here. So it sort of clicked.' Harrogate Tipple founder Steven Green talks about moving his distillery to Ripley Castle estate as if it was fate. The otter branding on his spirit bottles dovetails nicely with the animals' presence around the estate, his gin botanicals are now being grown in the castle's Victorian hothouse and gardens, and the wildflower honey used in his award-winning rum comes from Lady Emma's bee hives.

Steven's distillery is in 19th-century stables on the castle's doorstep. Short tours finish with tastings of rum, classic gin and popular blueberry and gooseberry gins (all made with 100% Harrogate spring water). Don't miss the gin school: gather botanicals from the castle gardens, then distil in the map room.

THINGS TO DO NEARBY

RHS Garden Harlow Carr
The botanical gardens where Harrogate Tipple sources its lavender are a year-round riot of colour and life. Innovative displays open up through a series of walking trails. *www.rhs. uk/gardens/harlow-carr*

Boar's Head
Country charm envelops Ripley village's old coaching inn. Those staying at the pub get free entry to the castle gardens and the added bonus of sleeping on the distillery's doorstep. *www. boarsheadripley.co.uk*

WARNER EDWARDS DISTILLERY

Falls Farm, 34 High St, Harrington, Northamptonshire;
www.warneredwards.com; +44 1536 710623

◆ Distillery ◆ Shop
◆ Tours

A picturesque farm in Northamptonshire, once the parks of a medieval manor house, is the home that livestock farmer turned spirit-maker Tom Warner shares with Warner Edwards Distillery. He and Sion Edwards, friends from agricultural college, acquired their copper still with the idea of making essential oils from plants on their farms, but discovered a better use for it: booze. Water from the farm's spring is used at the core of Harrington Dry Gin, and the farming duo use plenty of local produce, making elderflower gin and an expression using rhubarb that's put through a cider press. The most recent acquisition is an apiary, helping to create Harrington Honeybee Gin – a smooth, floral style that 'recreates the feelings of bee foraging season', according to the master distillers. Make a beeline for it on the Curiosity Tour.

THINGS TO DO NEARBY

The Tollemache Arms
Affectionately known as The Tolly to locals, Harrington's thatched-roof pub serves up a slice of country life, as well as hefty Sunday roasts. *www.thetolly.co.uk*

Kelmarsh Hall and Gardens
The heritage-listed gardens at Kelmarsh Hall, designed by famed inter-war gardener Norah Lindsay, are just as bucolic as Warner Edwards' patch of land. *www.kelmarsh.com*

BATH GIN COMPANY

2-3 Queen St, Bath, Somerset;
www.thebathgincompany.co.uk; +44 1225 462457

◆ Distillery   ◆ Shop   ◆ Transport
◆ Tours   ◆ Bar

Drink from bottles labelled with a winking Jane Austen – sorry, 'Gin Austen' – at the Bath Gin Company, a multistorey experience just off Bath Spa's cobbled streets. Despite the historic setting and literary reference, this gin veers away from tradition, dialling down juniper and amping up botanicals like kaffir lime and liquorice.

While a tour of the basement distillery is short and sweet, it can be combined with a botanicals workshop in the first-floor Distiller's Bar, a colourful space for gin blending – and you'll leave with a filled hip flask. However, it's the Canary Bar that attracts the attention – a cocktail joint with a mildly Victorian aesthetic and 230 gins in stock (including Bath's own). The drinks are as playful as that bottle; try the Harlem Shake, where gin meets piña colada.

THINGS TO DO NEARBY

The Jane Austen Centre
While clueing up on the life and times of the historic author is commendable, it's really all about the Regency tearoom, where you can order 'tea with Mr Darcy'. **www.janeausten.co.uk**

Thermae Bath Spa
If you're going to spa while in Bath Spa, do it at this spot with a jaw-dropping infinity pool on its roof, in among the ancient architecture. **www.thermaebathspa.com**

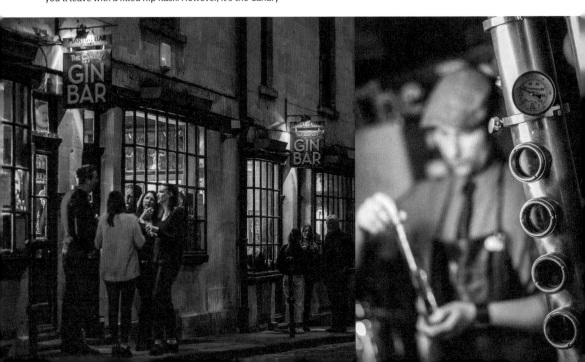

ADNAMS COPPER HOUSE DISTILLERY

Sole Bay Brewery, Southwold, Suffolk;
www.adnams.co.uk; +44 1502 727200

◆ Distillery ◆ Shop
◆ Tours

THINGS TO DO NEARBY

Southwold Pier
Go for an old-fashioned
saunter along this classic
waterfront marvel, filled
with shops, chip shops and
fairground attractions.
www.southwoldpier.co.uk

Southwold Lighthouse
Adnams has named one
of its ales after this iconic
Southwold building, built
in 1887. The visitor centre
operates tours for a taste
of local history.

**Southwold Boating Lake
and Tearoom**
A 1940s-themed tearoom
sits in the middle of a
boating lake and elevates
the humble cream tea to
a real occasion, in among
the splashing wildlife.
*www.southwoldboating
lakeandtearoom.co.uk*

**Walberswick Circular
Walk**
The mostly flat terrain
near Southwold makes for
perfect walking conditions.
Tackle forestland by the
seaside on this 7.6-mile
circuit that starts and ends
in Walberswick.

When you hear the Adnams story, it's surprising
that other breweries in the UK aren't attaching a
distillery to their headquarters. In Jonathan Adnams'
words, 'distilling spirits is really just one process on from
having fermented a beer'. Attracted by the US trend of micro-
distilling, the Copperhouse was founded in 2010, where staff
now use the same grains to make spirits as they use to make
beer, including rye grown on the surrounding fields.

The brewery produces a 'wash' – essentially a beer with
no hops – that spends a week in fermentation before being
pumped from brewery to distillery. This low percentage
spirit can then be tinkered with, first using a beer-stripping
still (as you'd find in American bourbon houses) to increase
the alcohol percentage and create the base for Adnams
whisky, vodka and gin, as well as limoncello and other
liqueurs. Experimentation has even led to an Adnams Rising
Sun gin made from matcha tea and lemongrass.

Coupled with the distillery's prize-winning sustainable
ethos (its warehouse has a green roof, solar panels and
lime/hemp walls), Adnams HQ makes for an interesting day
out. Start with a brewery tour, then visit the distillery and
taste the range. Check out the Spirit of Broadside, described
as an '*eau de vie de biere*', perfectly demonstrating the
duality of Adnams' output.

SILENT POOL DISTILLERS

Shere Rd, Albury, Surrey; www.silentpooldistillers.com;
+44 1483 229136

◆ Distillery   ◆ Shop
◆ Tours

THINGS TO DO NEARBY

Newlands Corner
You're totally spoilt for choice for stunning walks in this area, but this one tops the list. Climb to the top of the hill and marvel at magnificent views of the North Downs.

Albury Vineyard
An organic winery just moments from the distillery – in fact it's staggering distance. Sample a drop of its famous blanc de blancs. *www.alburyvineyard.com*

The Onslow Arms
An all-weather pub with gorgeous garden space and cosy winter nooks. You're sure to find something you'll love on the menu or behind the bar. *www.onslowarmsclandon.co.uk*

Shere
Take in the splendour of this chocolate-box village, often named the prettiest in Surrey. No wonder it's a famed film location – see *Four Weddings and a Funeral* and *The Holiday*.

The legend goes that King John kidnapped a woodcutter's daughter before she met her fate in Surrey Hills' Silent Pool, a practically turquoise body of water that sits below this diminutive craft distillery. The maiden is said to haunt the lake by night, but during the day it's a hive of activity – Silent Pool Distillers has had to scale up production to satisfy demand for its pretty blue bottle of gin, which uses that pool as a natural spring for its spirit. Its botanicals (and there's a whopping 24 of them) are just as local, from honey and lavender to pear and rose.

On a weekend tour (which hardly warrants the name, the site is so small), you'll gaze down at that lake before being led to a boiler room to meet The Major – a steam engine salvaged from Liverpool's docks and reclaimed for a new, boozy purpose. It's powered by logs from the surrounding forest, and is used to heat a still named Juliet. They'll talk you through production – from maceration to vapour distillation – before offering tasters of the complete range, including a vodka and liqueur. Silent Pool's blackberry gin cordial is delicious neat and available in the gift shop with a discount to tour-goers.

COTSWOLDS DISTILLERY

Whichford Rd, Stourton, Shipston-on-Stour, Cotswolds;
www.cotswoldsdistillery.com; +44 1608 238 533

◆ Distillery ◆ Shop
◆ Tours

The middle of the Cotswold countryside, with few amenities for miles around, seems an unlikely place for a distillery, but when you hear that the founder was inspired to start making craft whisky by the rippling fields of golden barley around his home, it couldn't be more perfect. The first casks of ex-financier Dan Szor's smooth and fruity single malt were laid down shortly after opening in 2014, and so were ready for release in autumn

THINGS TO DO NEARBY

Rollright Stones
This ancient site features a 4000-year-old stone circle, known as the King's Men, and a 5000-year-old burial chamber with standing stones known as The Whispering Knights.

Daylesford Organic
This organic farm shop and complex offers everything from fresh fruit and veg, meat and dairy, to workshops on cooking, floristry and interiors.
www.daylesford.com

Cotswold villages
Wander the lanes and admire the stone cottages of Bourton-on-the-Water, Stow-on-the-Wold and Chipping Campden before a pint in a charming old pub.

Stratford-Upon-Avon
The home of the one and only William Shakespeare; visit his birthplace, his wife Anne Hathaway's cottage and take in a play at The Swan theatre.

2017. Made with exclusively Cotswold barley, which has been malted by hand at Britain's oldest working maltings in Warminster, Wiltshire, the whisky has a depth of flavour that is more mature than it should be given its young age.

While the casks of whisky were ageing, the distillery began producing its own award-winning gin, which put it on the map. Part of this distillery's appeal, though, is how much fun the staff are having creating a huge variety of unusual spirits. Popular distillery tours finish in its comfortable bar area: start with the rose gin, or maybe the strawberry-and-chocolate liqueur, or the absinthe, or calvados-inspired apple spirit...

GIN 101

There are a whole heap of misconceptions when it comes to gin. But in the past few years, gin education has come on in leaps and bounds and most avid drinkers will be able to tell you at least this one fact about mother's ruin: it must contain juniper in order to be called gin. Juniper is an evergreen shrub producing the piney-scented berries that go into this clear spirit, and although its plants are found in all parts of the world, many modern craft producers champion Macedonian crops.

But sticking to this fact alone would be to underplay the complexity of a spirit that has risen up through the ages. The first record of gin – like many a good drink – lies with the Benedictine monks. In 12th century Salerno, this religious crowd were using distillation for medicinal purposes. Juniper was known as a diuretic, and wine-based juniper infusions were used to treat kidney, stomach and liver (yes, really) troubles.

By the mid 1500s, this juniper-based spirit had taken on new meaning in the Low Countries, where records show recipes for a medicinal tonic known as jenever. It was popularised among the English during years of support for the Dutch during the Eighty Years' War (1568–1648) against Spanish rule, where they'd have a tot before battle to steady their nerves – hence the term 'Dutch courage'. Over time – and through lazy pronunciation – jenever became known as gin in London, where its popularity reached fever pitch during London's gin craze (see page 172). Regulations for distilling had been thrown out the window by William of Orange in the 1600s, and people took to creating their own versions of the jenever they'd embraced on the battlefields. Gin was finally born.

Nowadays, you're likely to see a broad spectrum of botanicals blended with juniper. You can usually expect to find coriander seed, adding a citrus-like spice and aroma to the drink. More subtle but often present are angelica root – grown in Scandinavia and Europe – and orris root, taken from the iris plant. Both are commonly used as fixatives, helping bind and preserve fellow botanical aromas (fun fact: orris root is also often used in perfume for this very purpose).

From there, it's anyone's guess what else is in your gin of choice, but common flavours include citrus (lemon peel, grapefruit), earth (wormwood, mace), flowers (rosehip, elderflower), and spice (cinnamon, peppercorn). Many distillers choose to include between six and 10 botanicals but, in recent years, that rule has definitely not been hard and fast. Young distillery upstarts all over the world are choosing to push this boundary in order to find their gin a USP – often using locally grown botanicals that are an ode to the place where the gin is being made. Many distilleries share the botanicals they've chosen to include, although they'll stay guarded about the specific measures used in their secret formula.

The end product is the combination of these botanicals with a neutral spirit base, hence why gin is sometimes considered to be essentially a flavoured vodka – albeit a very fancy one.

BY LAURA RICHARDS

What is London Dry gin?

First things first, London Dry gin can be made anywhere in the world – there's no geographical designation to the category at all. In fact, it's more of a quality designation. Any gin labelled as London Dry must be above 37.5% abv, botanicals must be added through re-distillation and no flavourings can be added after the distillation process takes place.

BUSHMILLS DISTILLERY

2 Distillery Rd, Bushmills, County Antrim;
www.bushmills.com; +44 28 207 33218

◆ Food   ◆ Tours   ◆ Bar
◆ Distillery   ◆ Shop   ◆ Transport

Although often seen as the smaller, less successful sibling to giant Jameson, Bushmills is still a well-respected long-standing Irish whisky and even mentioned in James Joyce's *Ulysses*, so worth investigating.

The oldest distillery on the island of Ireland, Belfast's Bushmills was founded in 1784, although the date on the whisky labels refers to the year (1608) that the landowner was given a royal licence to distil. The most recent rebuild of the distillery was in 1885 after a fire destroyed the building and, apart from a break during the Second World War, it has been in continuous production since then. The site's five-storey old brick building is a reminder that warehouses

THINGS TO DO NEARBY

Giant's Causeway
A wonder of nature, made from cooled lava. Legend is that giant Finn MacCool built it to go to Scotland to fight Benandonner. *www.nationaltrust.org.uk/giants-causeway*

Dark Hedges
Many Northern Ireland landscapes featured in *Game of Thrones*. Fans will recognise this avenue of 18th-century beech trees in Ballymoney as King's Road. *www.discovernorthernireland.com*

The Crown Bar, Belfast
Justifiably the most famous bar in Northern Ireland, with ornate carvings, polychromatic tiles and proper Victorian snugs. *www.nationaltrust.org.uk/the-crown-bar*

Dunluce Castle
One of the iconic ruins of Northern Ireland, this castle on the Antrim coast has a tumultuous history, including having its kitchen blown away in a storm. *www.discovernorthernireland.com*

were once places of work rather than trendy flats.

With a range of triple-distilled malt and blended whiskies, Bushmills has expanded its signature range of whiskies to include aged statement blends and cask finishes such as sherry, bourbon and port, all with the Bushmills signature light fruity taste. A seat at the distillery bar and a taste of the range is a must – the bar staff will even mix you a cocktail of your choosing so don't miss your chance to try their whisky margarita.

SPRINGBANK DISTILLERY

85 Longrow, Campbeltown; www.springbankwhisky.com;
+44 1586 552 2009

◆ Distillery   ◆ Shop
◆ Tours   ◆ Transport

THINGS TO DO NEARBY

Cadenhead's Shop

The legendary independent bottling company Cadenhead's occupies part of the Springbank whisky shop; book a famous warehouse tasting here.
www.cadenhead.scot

Campbeltown Picture House

Opened in 1913 and recently restored, the 'Wee Pictures' is worth a visit to see old-style cinema glamour, even if you don't watch a film.
www.campbeltownpicture house.co.uk

Ardshiel Hotel

With more than 700 malts, the Ardshiel is one of the best-stocked bars in Scotland and the best place in town to stretch your taste buds.
www.ardshiel.co.uk/bar

Shark and whale watching

The Mull of Kintyre sea-tour company offers wildlife-watching boat trips around the Kintyre coast, with minke whales, basking sharks and porpoises. *www.mull-of-kintyre.co.uk*

Campbeltown's largest distillery produces three whisky brands: Springbank, Longrow and Hazelburn. Family-owned, it was founded in 1828 and is the only Scottish distillery that continues to malt, distil, mature and bottle on the one site with almost no automation. The main brand is the slightly peated Springbank; Longrow is the heavily peated expression of the distillery and Hazelburn the unpeated, triple-distilled expression.

The owners, the Mitchell family, take their role as heirs to Campbeltown's whisky legacy very seriously – at its height Campbeltown had more than 30 distilleries – and won't change the way they run the Springbank distillery. They employ 70 people to make less whisky than other distilleries that employ no more than 20, and don't want to expand production as they have lived through too many whisky booms and busts, so just keep it the way it is.

Springbank offers one of the few chances to see an old-style working distillery completely integrated into a town. There's no visitor centre: you buy the tour tickets and have all the tastings in the whisky shop around the corner from the distillery. Look out for one-off bottlings unique to the shop.

BOWMORE DISTILLERY

School St, Bowmore, Isle of Islay; www.bowmore.com;
+44 1496 810 441

◆ Distillery   ◆ Shop   ◆ Transport
◆ Tours   ◆ Bar

THINGS TO DO NEARBY

Big Strand Beach
The longest beach on Islay, usually deserted, can be accessed via a track between Port Ellen and Bowmore, from Kintra farm, or via a track beside the airport.

Kilarrow Parish Church
Overlooking the rest of the village, this church was built in 1767 and is completely round so that the devil couldn't hide in the corners. *www. theroundchurch.org.uk*

Loch Gruinart RSPB Reserve
The other major attraction on Islay is bird watching. It's possible everywhere but especially at the Loch Gruinart RSPB reserve, with weekly guided walks available. *www.rspb.org. uk/reserves-and-events*

Islay Woollen Mill
This island tweed-making business uses Victorian hand looms. The mill is open for visitors to explore and you can also see the pattern books from closed-down mills. *www.islaywoollenmill. co.uk*

One of the oldest distilleries on the island of Islay and a legend in the whisky world, Bowmore is one of the few distilleries with its own malting floor still in use. It claims to have been founded in 1779 (though it wasn't legal at the time, so this is hard to verify) and has had a distilling licence since 1816.

Located in the coastal village of Bowmore, the island's capital and one of its biggest villages, the distillery is an integral part of the village; its surplus energy is used to heat the village swimming pool.

To really give yourself a feel for the Islay life, you can stay in the grounds of the distillery in one of five former workers' cottages, which range from one to four bedrooms, or just beside it at the newly refurbished Harbour Inn. The tours themselves range from a distillery visit and a taste of the whisky to a Secret Vault tasting tour, where you get a special cask tasting as well as tour of the malting floor and the kiln.

The tasting bar, which is open all day, is the ideal place to try the unusual Bowmore Vault Edition with its characteristic peaty taste while looking out to the sea loch.

KILCHOMAN DISTILLERY

Rockside Farm, Bruichladdich, Isle of Islay;
www.kilchomandistillery.com; +44 1496 850011

◆ Food ◆ Tours ◆ Bar
◆ Distillery ◆ Shop

When owner Anthony Willis bought the farm on which Islay Distillery was founded in 2005, the aim was to find a place where as much as possible could be carried out on-site. Kilchoman has its own malting floor that makes medium-peated malt, while heavily peated malt is brought in from Port Ellen. Once distilled, the spirit is matured in high-quality bourbon and sherry casks.

Held in high regard by whisky geeks for the mature taste in such a relatively young product, the distillery is a must-visit if you're on Islay. Just getting there is an adventure: it's located five miles off the main road along one of Scotland's legendary single tracks with passing places. As well as a cafe, the shop offers all of the Kilchoman range – look out for limited editions exclusive to the shop.

THINGS TO DO NEARBY

Loch Gorm
The largest inland loch on Islay offers some of the best brown trout fishing on the island, and the overgrown ruins of Loch Gorm castle perch on the southeast corner.

Glenegedale Guesthouse
Islay isn't known for its food, but this multi-award-winning B&B has some of the best accommodation, great food and the most epic breakfasts in Scotland. ***www.glenegedale guesthouse.co.uk***

ISLE OF ARRAN DISTILLERY

Lochranza, Isle of Arran;
www.arranwhisky.com; +44 1770 830 264

◆ Food ◆ Tours ◆ Bar
◆ Distillery ◆ Shop ◆ Transport

The first legal whisky distillery on Arran in more than 150 years was built in 1992; in the 19th century, most of Arran's whisky was smuggled up the Clyde river to Glasgow and sold illegally. The distillery sits on the north side of the island, but the owners recently acquired a site at the other end so it can start making a peaty version of its whisky.

The distillery famously had to temporarily halt construction because of a pair of nesting golden eagles on the hill behind them. Because of this encounter, the bird became part of the signature design of the Arran label. What sets Arran apart from other distilleries is the variety of the whisky offer in the Casks cafe-bar – where you can sip whisky with a view – as well as its shop range. Try the cafe's limited-edition whisky flight, showcasing the light, sweet Arran taste.

THINGS TO DO NEARBY

Golf at Lochranza
Arran is a famous golfing destination and the nine-hole Lochranza course is well known for its stunning views and course invasions by deer. ***www. lochranzagolf.com***

Holy Isle
Just off the coast at Lamlash, this island is home to a Tibetan Buddhist retreat centre that runs courses from April to October and is open to visitors. ***www.holyisle.org***

OBAN DISTILLERY

Stafford St, Oban; www.malts.com/en-us/distilleries/oban; +44 1631 572 004

◆ Distillery   ◆ Shop
◆ Tours   ◆ Transport

Standing in the middle of Oban, this distillery was established in 1799 and rebuilt in 1883, and actually pre-dates the town that was later built around it. Today, Oban is the seafood capital of Scotland and the main port for ferries to the Western Isles of Mull and Iona. The distillery's position makes it impossible to expand, which means it is likely to always remain one of the smallest distilleries in Scotland. It's now owned by international drinks giant Diageo and is part of the company's Classic Malt series.

To keep the whisky's characteristic light fruitiness, the team doesn't run the stills every single day. Look out for the Distillers Edition, which has a second maturation in fino sherry casks and is one of the shop's highlights.

THINGS TO DO NEARBY

Seafood shack
The green shack beside the CalMac ferry office on the pier is the best place in Oban to eat fresh seafood, although there's no indoor seating so the experience is best enjoyed on sunny days.

McCaig's Folly
This unmissable Colosseum-of-Rome-like structure dominates the town and is great to climb. Wealthy banker John Stuart McCaig died before he could finish it, in 1902.

ANNANDALE DISTILLERY

Northfield, Annan, Dumfriesshire; www.annandaledistillery.com; +44 1461 207817

◆ Food   ◆ Tours   ◆ Transport
◆ Distillery ◆ Shop

Opened in the Lowlands in 1830 by George Donald, Annandale Distillery was bought by Johnnie Walker in 1893 and used as part of that whisky's famous blend until the distillery closed in 1918.

In 2007 Teresa Church and David Thomson purchased the site and, after extensive restoration to the 19th-century red sandstone buildings, resumed whisky production in 2014. They are now bottling both an unpeated Man O' Words and, unusually for a modern-day Lowland distillery, a peated Man O' Swords.

The foundations of the original distillery chimney have been uncovered and left in view, and there's now a well-stocked shop and restaurant in the building. Because the distillery is so young its bottlings are pretty rare, so buy one if you see it.

THINGS TO DO NEARBY

Gretna Green
The runaway marriage border village of Gretna Green with its famous blacksmith's shop is just 9 miles away from the Annandale Distillery, if you want to tie the knot.

Devil's Porridge Museum
Learn about the largest munitions factory in the world during WW1 ('devil's porridge' being the paste used in the process) and the role of the Solway coast during WWII. *www.devilsporridge.org.uk*

Courtesy of Edinburgh Gin (2)

EDINBURGH GIN

1A Rutland Place, Edinburgh;
www.edinburghgin.com; +44 131 656 2810

◆ Food   ◆ Tours   ◆ Bar
◆ Distillery   ◆ Shop   ◆ Transport

In the Scottish capital's West End, Edinburgh Gin's arch-filled spirits cellar lies beneath a maze of Georgian buildings and modern boutiques, watched over by two gin stills – Flora and Caledonia. Although 'Gin Jeanie', the larger still responsible for most of Edinburgh Gin's output, resides at its headquarters in Leith, this central atmospheric visitor-centre-cum-bar called Heads & Tales is where the public can sample the distillery's spirits range – five gins plus colourful gin liqueurs mixed into cocktails – or settle in for the evening with snacks to boot.

Edinburgh Gin is in partnership with Heriot-Watt University (home to a famed brewing and distilling course) so it makes sense to join a gin-making class. Afterwards, reward yourself with a Cannonball Martini, made with navy-strength gin.

THINGS TO DO NEARBY

Dean Village
Just minutes from the West End is Edinburgh's historic milling area, a surprisingly green space by the Water of Leith with a bridge designed by Thomas Telford.

Panda & Sons
This Scottish speakeasy serves cocktails in playful ways – including a drink that looks like Chinese noodle soup – and has plenty of darkened corners for a late-night gin tipple.
www.pandaandsons.com

EDEN MILL

Main St, Guardbridge, St Andrews, Fife;
www.edenmill.com; +44 1334 834 038

◆ Distillery   ◆ Shop   ◆ Transport
◆ Tours   ◆ Bar

This new Lowland distillery and brewery in Fife is built on the site of one of very first grain whisky distilleries established by the legendary Haig whisky-making family. Businessman Paul Miller started the brewery in 2012 and began distilling malt whisky in 2014, making it the first combined brewery and distillery in Scotland.

Currently in the process of a £4 million refurbishment and moving to a bigger site next door, the distillery makes gin, beer and whisky, all of which will be available as part of in-depth tastings when the new distillery opens. The whisky output is limited to eight barrels a day and uses three different types of barley that become three distinct malt whiskies; tasting all three is a unique opportunity to judge the importance of barley variety on taste.

THINGS TO DO NEARBY

St Andrews Links
Regarded as the 'home of golf', the game started here in the 15th century, making it the oldest golf course in the world. It's still open to the public; places are hard to get. *www.standrews.com/ play/courses/old-course*

West Sands Beach
The famous beach from the film *Chariots of Fire* is a 15-minute drive from the distillery – great for walking, running and (very cold) swimming. There's a lifeguard on duty in summer.

THE CLYDESIDE DISTILLERY

100 Stobcross Rd, Glasgow; www.theclydeside.com;
+44 141 212 1401

◆ Distillery   ◆ Transport
◆ Tours

Opened in November 2017 on the banks of the Clyde in central Glasgow, this is one of the most attractive distilleries in the Lowlands, with glass walls that show off its stills to passing trains and give visitors a spectacular view of the Clyde river.

Owner Morrison Glasgow Distillers isn't planning to bottle until 2020 – because by law whisky has to be aged for three years and a day in an oak barrel – so until the whisky is available the visitor experience focuses on the history of the whisky industry and its relationship with Glasgow.

The visit offers a tasting of whisky from three different regions of Scotland, enabling you to find out what your tastes are. With your new-found knowledge, you can buy a bottle at the distillery.

THINGS TO DO NEARBY

Ben Nevis Bar
No music, a coal fire, comfortable seats and one of the best whisky pubs in Glasgow; an ideal way to start an evening in Glasgow's hip Finnieston area (you'll find it at 1147 Argyle Street).

Kelvingrove Art Gallery
The city's top gallery houses works by the Impressionists and Salvador Dali, and has an area dedicated to local Charles Rennie Mackintosh and the Glasgow Style. *www.glasgowlife.org.uk/ museums*

TALISKER DISTILLERY

Carbost, Isle of Skye; www.malts.com/en-gb/
our-whisky-collection/talisker; +44 1478 614308

◆ Distillery   ◆ Shop
◆ Tours

Founded in 1830 by the MacAskill brothers, but now owned by Diageo and part of its Classic Malts series, Talisker was Scottish writer Robert Louis Stevenson's favourite whisky. The distillery is on the west coast of the popular inner Hebridean island of Skye and uses the sea water to cool the condensers. Environmental concerns are front of mind here, and the distillery recently managed to double its production time without increasing its carbon footprint.

The shop sells an extensive Talisker range, including distillery exclusives, and there's a cafe called The Oyster Shed a five-minute walk up the hill behind the distillery, with a view out to the bay. It is well work hiking up here to buy takeaway oysters to drink with some smoky briny Talisker bought from the distillery.

THINGS TO DO NEARBY

Three Chimneys
This restaurant, open since 1985, kick-started Skye's food revolution. It was voted UK Restaurant of the Year in 2018 and now also has rooms.
www.threechimneys.co.uk

Point of Sleat
There are many places to go for wild swimming on the Isle of Skye, but by far the most beautiful is here, with views onto the isles of Rum, Canna and Eigg.

THE MACALLAN DISTILLERY

Easter Elchies, Craigellachie; www.themacallan.com/en/
the-distillery; +44 1340 872 280

◆ Food   ◆ Tours   ◆ Bar
◆ Distillery   ◆ Shop   ◆ Transport

After a recent £125 million refurbishment, Macallan's new state-of-the-art distillery, which produces one of the biggest malt whiskies in the world, now has the most cutting-edge distillery in Scotland to date.

Designed by internationally acclaimed architect firm Rogers Stirk Harbour + Partners, the new building is cut into the slope of the land, to emulate Scottish hills and maximise the beauty of the building while minimising the visual impact on the landscape. The undulating timber roof structure is one of the most complicated of its kind in the world, comprising 380,000 individual components; the top of the roof is covered in turf to further blend into the landscape.

THINGS TO DO NEARBY

Speyside Way
A 65-mile walk from Buckie through the Speyside region to Aviemore. It's less well known than sibling West Highland Way, but is becoming increasingly popular for walkers. *www.speysideway.org*

Spirit of the Spey
Offers a range of canoeing experiences on the Spey river, with either wild camping or B&Bs and hotel accommodation, and you can whisky-taste as you go. *www.spiritofthe spey.co.uk*

Elgin cathedral
One of Scotland's most beautiful ruins and one of the country's few cathedrals. Two towers can still be climbed, rewarding you with a view of Elgin. *www. visitscotland.com*

Drouthy Cobbler
The Elgin hotspot for beer, whisky and decent food, this is the place to go when you have drouth (thirst) on you. There's also live music and comedy upstairs. *www. thedrouthycobbler.uk*

The tour gives a 360-degree view of the distillery via a walkway, as the building has been designed specifically with visitors in mind. There's a Macallan museum, including a collection of decanters, four flasks and 398 bottles that have never been previously displayed, and several interactive exhibits showcasing how Macallan's signature sherry-cask-influenced taste came about. The restaurant and bar offer a wide range of whiskies: try the rare M and No 6 expressions.

CAORUNN

Balmenach Rd, Cromdale, Grantown-on-Spey, Speyside;
www.caorunngin.com; + 44 1479 874933

- ◆ Tours
- ◆ Distillery
- ◆ Shop
- ◆ Bar

Balmenach Distillery has been making single malts since 1824, but it was only in 2009 that the distillers decided to try their hand at gin. And so Caorunn was born, partly out of a desire to make use of the Celtic botanicals growing wild around the rural Highland distillery. The five-pointed star on Caorunn bottles represents the five local ingredients: rowan berry, coul blush apples, bog myrtle, heather and dandelion – patches grow right outside the door.

Tour-goers get to see the unusual copper berry chamber still where botanicals are layered in trays during distillation, but the most unique element is the master distiller's challenge to nose the essences of Caorunn's London Dry and work out the flavour scales of its 11 botanicals. Afterwards you'll get slipped an envelope with the exact formula. Finish in the Bothy with a G&T garnished with apple slices; it enhances the coul blush zing.

THINGS TO DO NEARBY

Craigellachie Hotel
This chic 19th-century country hotel is the perfect base for touring Speyside's distilleries. Its whisky bar, The Quaich, has one of the world's best selections of single malts – more than 900. *www. craigellachiehotel.co.uk*

Hire a Caterham
Embrace the crystal-clear Scottish air and gorgeous scenery by road-tripping the Highlands in an open-top Caterham Seven, one of the icons of British sports car design. *www.highlandcaterham hire.co.uk*

GLENFIDDICH DISTILLERY

Dufftown, Banffshire; www.glenfiddich.com;
+44 1340 820 373

◆ Food   ◆ Tours   ◆ Bar
◆ Distillery   ◆ Shop   ◆ Transport

Dufftown is home to nine visitable distilleries and is said to raise more money per head for the Exchequer than any other place in the UK. Its most famous inhabitant is undoubtedly Glenfiddich. The distillery was founded by William Grant in 1887 and hand-built by him, his wife and their nine children. Buying second-hand stills, worms, water mills and mash tuns, the set-up costs came in at £800, which is a fun fact given that Glenfiddich is now one of the world's biggest malt whisky producers. Still owned by the family, its whisky has a traditional Speyside sweetness.

The visitor centre is geared up for the international luxury market with cashmere knitwear, tweed and crystal glasses for sale, as well as special distillery-only bottlings. Personalised labels make great presents.

THINGS TO DO NEARBY

Keith & Dufftown Railway
The 11-mile heritage train track from Dufftown to Keith runs on select weekends each summer, with 1940s carriages and special events.
www.keith-dufftown-railway.co.uk

Speyside Cooperage
if you've ever wondered how bourbon and sherry barrels are reconditioned, the cooperage has a visitors' gallery and you can see exactly how it's done. *www.speysidecooperage.co.uk*

HIGHLAND PARK DISTILLERY

Holm Rd, Kirkwall, Orkney; www.highlandparkwhisky.com/distillery; +44 1856 874 619

◆ Distillery   ◆ Shop
◆ Tours   ◆ Transport

Founded on the Orkney Isles around 1798, Highland Park retains its malting floor using local peat from Hobbister Moor to dry the malt and is one of the few distilleries where you can see malting taking place in the original 18th-century greystone buildings.

Its whisky is a major component of the Famous Grouse blend, and a rebrand has emphasised the Orkney islands' – and therefore the whisky's – connection with the Vikings, going so far as to get a Danish descendent of the first Earl of Orkney to help design the packaging.

There's no bar or cafe here – the best thing to do is one of the more in-depth tours to give you a real appreciation of its whisky range, then buy one of the unusual bottlings from its shop.

THINGS TO DO NEARBY

Ring of Brodgar
One of the the most famous standing stone circles in the British Isles, not to be missed on a visit to Orkney, along with other Neolithic sites. *www.historicenvironment.scot*

The Italian Chapel
Built and decorated by Italian prisoners of war in WWII using old Nissan Huts in a pre-Renaissance style, the Italian Chapel is an Orkney highlight. *www.visitorkney.com/listings/history/the-italian-chapel*

ISLE OF HARRIS DISTILLERY

Tarbert, Isle of Harris, Outer Hebrides;
www.harrisdistillery.com; +44 1859 502 212

◆ Food ◆ Tours ◆Transport
◆ Distillery ◆ Shop

THINGS TO DO NEARBY

Scarista House
This former manse
has been turned into a
three-star hotel with
stunning views and highly
recommended dining (open
to non-residents) – expect
local lamb and seafood to
always be on the menu.
www.scaristahouse.com

Isle of Skye
A seven-minute walk from
the distillery, the CalMac
ferry from Tarbert to Uig
on Skye runs twice a day
in high season and once at
other times. *www.calmac.
co.uk/ports/tarbert-harris*

Harris tweed
Find out the story and
method behind the famous
Harris tweed, which has
graced the shoulders of
countless celebrities, from
one of the many family
businesses on Harris.
*www.harristweed.org/
find-tweed/*

St Kilda
Two companies run day-
long cruises from Harris to
this uninhabited double
Unesco World Heritage
Site that is a bucket-list
experience for nature
lovers. *www.kilda.org.uk*

The first commercial distillery on the island of
Harris was the brainchild of musicologist Anderson
Bakewell and took seven years to become a reality,
with the help of various investors including the Scottish
government. Based in the port village of Tarbert, it is a social
enterprise and was built by the islanders. It has 20 employees
– a huge number for this sparsely populated area. The distillery
hosts regular gatherings for local people, gives the draff (the
residue left over from the distilling process) to farmers to feed
their cows, and offers work experience for local schoolchildren.

When it launched in 2015 ,it started off distilling the hugely
popular sea-kelp-flavoured Harris Gin and later, in 2017,
Hearach whisky, which will be ready in 2020. The distillery
offers regular tours and there's a constantly burning peat
fire, even in the height of summer. The visitor centre prides
itself on having no public wi-fi nor interactive displays, thus
encouraging real-life interaction. There's also a cafe that serves
soups, sandwiches and cakes, and is popular with Tarbet locals.
Don't miss the rare opportunity to buy Harris Gin in the shop.

GLENGOYNE DISTILLERY

Dumgoyne, near Killearn, Stirling;
www.glengoyne.com; +44 1360 550 254

◆ Distillery   ◆ Shop
◆ Tours   ◆ Transport

In continuous production since 1833, available as single malt since the early 1990s and originally marketed as an unpeated Highland malt, Glengoyne sells itself as the most beautiful distillery in Scotland, but this claim may have more to do with the surprise of discovering such rural tranquillity a mere 15 miles from the centre of Glasgow.

Located right on the Highland line, owner Ian MacLeod makes a big deal of the fact that his spirit is made in the Highlands but the storage warehouse across the road is in the Lowlands.

The tours include tastings of a range of ages of Glengoyne bottlings – do take up the opportunity to personalise the whisky labels to take home as souvenir bottles or presents.

THINGS TO DO NEARBY

West Highland Way
The most popular hiking trail in Scotland stretches 96 miles from Milngavie to Fort William and passes by Glengoyne Distillery on the first leg from Milngavie. *www. westhighlandway.org*

Finnich Glen
This moss-covered, 100ft-deep sandstone gorge, just east of the Finnich bridge on the A809, is hard to find but a stunning place to visit. Wear shoes suitable for climbing down a worn stone staircase.

SNOWDONIA DISTILLERY

Tal-y-cafn, Colwyn Bay;
www.snowdoniadistillery.co.uk

◆ Distillery
◆ Tours

THINGS TO DO NEARBY

Palé Hall Hotel
Head to this five-star hotel
in Wales for luxurious
dining or a 'Ginventure'
gourmet package,
including a Snowdonia
Distillery visit and a Raw
Adventures foraging hike.
www.palehall.co.uk

Surf Snowdonia
The only guaranteed surf in
the UK: this huge outdoor
artificial wave pool is ideal
for all skill levels, offering
everything from beginner
white-water waves to
point breaks. ***www.
surfsnowdonia.com***

Snowdonia Mountains
North Wales' mountain
range (peaking at
1085m-high Snowdon)
is idyllic for hikes
encompassing Snowdonia
National Park, castles,
craggy coast and heritage
train lines.

Zip World
Home to the world's fastest
zip wire, the old Penrhyn
slate quarry, at 360m
deep, is a magnet for the
adventurous. Fancy soaring
at 125mph over a lake?
www.zipworld.co.uk

'Did you see any yellow gorse on the mountains?'
The underlying sense of urgency in Chris Marshall's
question becomes crystal clear when he explains
the painstaking methods involved in handcrafting his
(exclusively small batch) Foragers Gin. Snowdonia Distillery's
founder, owner and head distiller spent six years researching
(with the help of a botanist) how he could make a gin from
foraged, fresh and exclusively local botanicals. There's nothing simple, easy – or, indeed, quick – about it.

The yellow gorse flowers in question are only at their
peak for two weeks of the year, for example. And Chris, citing
one of the world's best chefs Massimo Botturi as one of
his inspirations, won't settle for less than authenticity. He
wanted to make a gin that truly tells the story of North Wales.
The result? Forager Yellow Label's combination of juniper,

sea buckthorn, apple, elderflower, gorse flower and heather
handpicked from the Snowdonia mountains, cut with pure
Welsh mountain water – a gin that won silver at the World
Gin Awards. The actual distillery, located two miles down
the road from the tasting rooms, isn't open to the public and
there's no mass-marketed tours – that's just how they like it.
Instead, book ahead for a cocktail masterclass or embark on a
Ginventure (see Palé Hall Hotel, Things To Do Nearby).

WHISKY 101

No records exist of the beginnings of whisky, but it's thought that monks brought distilling technology, first developed in the Arab world, to Ireland and Irish refugees then brought it to the west coast of Scotland. In Ireland, you'll find whiskey is always spelt with an 'e' whereas in Scotland it's always without. Elsewhere, the spelling can differ.

The world's favourite distilled drink, Scotch whisky mostly comes in two main types: blended and malt. Malt whisky is made from malted barley in pot stills, while blended whisky is a mixture of grain and malt whisky, produced by fractional distillation, a process where the liquid is separated by a column still into fractions with different boiling points. Single grain Scotch whisky is increasingly available, notably from Haig Club and Ailsa Bay, but unlike malts and blends there isn't a wide variety of single grain Scotch.

A single malt whisky is whisky made from malted barley and all at the same distillery. If a malt or blended whisky bottle has an age on it, for example Highland Park 12, it means the youngest whisky in the bottle will have been aged in an oak barrel for at least 12 years.

Blends contain grain whisky and often more than 30 different malts in the one blend, therefore the taste varies greatly between brands, from the sweet Famous Grouse to the smoky, heavy Johnnie Walker Black. Single malt whiskies, on the other hand, can be generalised according to region.

Although there are always exceptions to the rule, especially now as new distilleries are popping up like mushrooms, generally in Scotland the softest, lightest, sweetest whiskies are in the Lowlands, then they get stronger as you move northeast across Speyside and start becoming peaty and smoky as you move west and north. The strongest, heaviest and peatiest whiskies come from the Hebridean island of Islay.

Irish whisky, while only about one tenth of the size of Scotch production, is the fastest growing industry in the world. Here you'll find malt, blended and grain whisky as well as 'pot still' whisky, which is made using both malted and unmalted barley. The main difference between Irish and Scotch whiskies is that when making whisky in a pot still, Irish is mostly triple distilled, making for a soft, light liquid, whereas Scotch is generally distilled twice.

Japanese whisky, first made in 1923, needs to be aged in Japan rather than distilled, so spirit from Scotland can be aged in Japan and barrels other than oak can be used. Along with the lower pressure distilling of Japanese spirit and the climate with four distinct seasons, these production factors give Japanese blenders the chance to engineer a distinctive range of tastes within each brand – very different to how the Scottish labels work. **BY RACHEL McCORMACK**

How should you drink your whisky?

The shortest answer is the way you like it. A good-quality whisky should be sipped and savoured rather than downed in one. Anything over 40% almost certainly needs a few drops of water, but whether you like it in cocktails, with fresh coconut water like the Brazilians, with green tea like the Chinese or even with cola like the Spanish, the most important thing is to grab all the pleasure from it you can.

OCEA

NIA

TASMANIA

Australia's island state is widely considered to be the home of Australian craft distilling, largely down to one man, Bill Lark, who breathed new life into Australian whisky distilling in the 1990s. Fast forward to 2018 and Tasmania is picking up 'World's Best' awards for intriguing vodka and whisky.

VICTORIA

The best known craft spirit to come out of Australia? It's got to be Four Pillars gin, from the Yarra Valley wine region near Melbourne. But there are dozens of craft distilleries in Victoria: whisky enthusiasts operating out of sheds in rural outposts, and state-of-the-art gin palaces using native botanicals.

NZ SOUTH ISLAND

It may come as a surprise, but the sparsely populated South Island of New Zealand has become a hotbed for fledgling distilleries. Many are inspired by European ancestry and are capitalising on their proximity to pure mountain water in a land of curvaceous peaks and glacial lakes.

AUSTRALIA

How to ask for a spirit without mixers? G'day, just a whisky thanks, mate

Signature spirit style? Gin and tonic

What to order with your spirits? Fresh oysters or a locally sourced cheese board (actually, any local produce will be divine)

Don't: Be a 'bludger'. If you've accepted a drink, you're caught in a 'round' (a shout) and it's un-Australian to leave until you've bought everyone else in the round a drink

Australia has come a long way from the colonial days of the early 1800s, where spirits were used as payment for commodities. While the 1807 'Rum Rebellion' – a fierce resistance against Governor Bligh's attempts to prohibit such practices that saw him overthrown from office – was essentially more about a power play between government and local entrepreneurs, the legend does tend to paint Australians as a nation of die-hard, unsophisticated drinkers. It's a stereotype that some visitors may encounter in remote rural pockets of the vast nation (ask for 'two Margaritas' in some bars and you may be surprised by a 20-minute wait and the arrival of two pizzas: true story). Yet today, the craft distillers of Australia are winning global accolades, such as World's Best Vodka 2018 (Hartshorn Distillery, p225) or World's Best Single Cask Single Malt 2018 (Sullivans Cove, p228) and the cities' cocktail bars hold their own in international rankings. So how did these unruly rum rebels become discerning drinkers?

Australia's new wave of craft distillers all speak reverentially about one man: Bill Lark (p224), aka the godfather of Australian whisky, who brought the industry back to life after distilleries were outlawed between 1838

and 1992. He was the first to question why Australia wasn't following Scotland's lead and making whisky when it had the same, if not better, natural resources.

Then the drinking scene started to change, as liquor licensing laws started loosening up in Victoria in the late 1990s; suddenly, small cocktail bars appeared. It was no longer necessary to order a meal to have a glass of wine or go to a beer-swilling pub. Bar culture had arrived and the rest of the nation overthrew a few monopolies and got on that bandwagon. The next questions being asked: if Australia can make excellent wine, then why not all of the spirits too?

Today, the rest of the world is enjoying the answers to these questions. Australian whiskies are unique, in part because of Australia's successful wine industry; whiskies here are aged in high-quality barrels of different wine styles, unlike many whisky-producing countries that use an abundance of cheap ex-bourbon barrels or casks that are just 'conditioned' for a short time with sherry. Here, the flavours of apera (sherry) and tawny (port) come from barrels that have aged these spirits for decades. Australia's whiskies are also considered 'legal' before the rest of the world: the new make has to live in oak barrels for a minimum

"The spirit scene in Australia is probably where the Aussie wine industry was 35 to 40 years ago. With the botanicals from this incredible country, we can make stuff that is unique and delicious"

—STUART GREGOR, AUSTRALIAN DISTILLERS ASSOCIATION & FOUR PILLARS GIN

of two years here, whereas it's three years' minimum maturation time elsewhere.

Yet, despite the accolades, vodka, whisky and rum consumption is in decline in Australia. Much like the rest of the world, the nation is in the grip of a love affair with gin. Consumption grew 16% from 2016 to 2017, but, importantly, consumption of locally made gin grew faster: up 33%. Take a trip out to Four Pillars in Healesville (p233) for gin tasting paddles in wine country, or to Adelaide Hills Distillery (p221) for a startling green ant concoction – you'll soon see why such a fuss is being made about indigenous botanicals. Cheers, mate.

TOP 5 SPIRITS

- **Bloody Shiraz Gin** Four Pillars Distillery, Victoria
- **Federation Gin** McHenry Distillery, Tasmania
- **Sheep Whey Vodka** Hartshorn Distillery, Tasmania
- **French Oak Single Malt Whisky** Sullivans Cove Distillery, Tasmania
- **Green Ant Gin** Adelaide Hills Distillery, South Australia

CAPE BYRON DISTILLERY

80 St Helena Road, McLeods Shoot, NSW;
www.capebyrondistillery.com; +61 2 6684 7961

◆ Distillery   ◆ Shop
◆ Tours   ◆ Bar

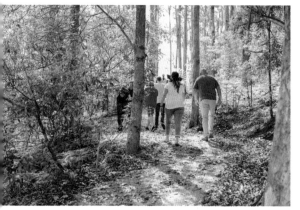

'We start with a blank canvas and paint it with a picture of the rainforest' is how the 'spiritual advisors' at Cape Byron Distillery describe their craft. Unlike most gins flavoured with a handful of botanicals, Cape Byron's signature Brookie's Dry Gin is infused with no less than 26 plants, many foraged from the distillery's own lovingly regenerated, 96-acre 'backyard'.

The property was covered in grass and noxious weeds when the Brook family purchased it 30 years ago. They've since planted more than 35,000 rainforest trees and 4500 macadamia trees, giving them a broad palette to paint with.

Visit the sleek, corrugated steel distillery nestled in the Byron Bay hinterland and you'll be able to see, touch and taste many of the unusual botanicals flavouring this spirit. The tour begins with a relaxing G&T on the veranda overlooking the macadamia orchard before wandering

THINGS TO DO NEARBY

Cape Byron Track
Walk this scenic route in Byron Bay to the historic lighthouse looking out to sea. The track ticks off secluded beaches, rare littoral rainforest and magical views. *www. nationalparks.nsw.gov.au*

Stone & Wood Brewery
Another delicious local drop with a sustainable ethos, Stone & Wood in Byron Bay hosts regular tours and serves up tasting paddles in its cheery, industrial-style brewery. *www. stoneandwood.com.au*

Harvest
Continue down Hinterland Way to Newrybar to sample Harvest's innovative menu (plus Brookie's Gin cocktails), or raid its historic bakery for a gourmet picnic. *www. harvestnewrybar.com.au*

Cape Byron Kayaks
Paddle the calm waters of Byron Bay on a kayak for a close-up look at the locals: dolphins, green sea turtles and, in the winter months, you might even see migrating whales. *www. capebyronkayaks.com*

into the rainforest to seek out goodies such as native raspberries, white aspen berries and Davidson plums. Back in the distillery you'll meet George, the copper pot still, and learn how the botanicals are used to impart delicate, nuanced flavour in the dry gin, and deep colour and sweetness in the 'slow' gin. When the lesson's over, pull up a stool at the recycled timber bar and test your newly awoken palate with a rainforest martini.

ARCHIE ROSE DISTILLING CO

85 Dunning Ave, Rosebery, Sydney, NSW;
www.archierose.com.au; +61 2 8458 2300

◆ Food ◆ Tours ◆ Bar
◆ Distillery ◆ Shop ◆ Transport

The first distillery to open in Sydney in 160 years, Archie Rose launched in 2015 with a young and ambitious team who quickly began impressing judges worldwide. It has picked up a number of world's best unaged whisky awards overseas, poured as 'white rye' in Australia because, by law, it ain't whisky until it's been aged for at least two years. Impressive gin and vodkas are also served at its popular and welcoming distillery bar.

Behind a gleaming copper bar, surrounded by hand-crafted barrels, chatty staff offer cocktail recommendations, fix up nibble platters and dispense Sydney distilling factoids: did you know Sydney's hot weather means that 8.5% of the

THINGS TO DO NEARBY

Three Blue Ducks
Rosebery is a 'hood of warehouse conversions and a great place to graze. Try Archie's neighbour, Three Blue Ducks, with its Argentinian grill and wood-fired oven. *www.threeblueducks.com*

Sydney Opera House
Sydney's best-looking venue hosts world-class opera and ballet, but touring rock bands, circus shows and Aboriginal Australian dance companies regularly perform here too. *www.sydneyoperahouse.com*

Go sailing
Whether it's a romantic sunset sail or an adrenalin-fuelled ride, Sydney Harbour is an incredible yachting spot for water lovers. Learn the ropes with Sydney by Sail. *www.sydneybysail.com*

The Rocks
The fledgling colony that became Australia began here as a shanty town on the harbour. Today its atmospheric convict-built pubs still stand proud beside the skyscrapers. *www.therocks.com*

batch evaporates each year, compared with only 2% to 3% in Scotland? It all adds to the complex flavour profile in the glass.

Archie Rose provides many experiences that peek behind the curtain at the distillery wizardry. There are tours, blend-your-own-gin or -vodka days (book online) and, unusually, well-heeled whisky lovers can tailor their own cask (from A$4000 for 20L) with the option to muck in with the mashing, pitching the yeast and distillation processes over a few days.

MANLY SPIRITS CO

4A/9-13 Winbourne Rd, Brookvale, Sydney, NSW;
www.manlyspirits.com.au, +61 2 8018 5144

◆ Food   ◆ Tours   ◆ Bar
◆ Distillery   ◆ Shop   ◆ Transport

Gin and yoga, anyone? In Manly, every second Sunday offers the chance to unroll your mat among the barrels at this distillery, with poses chosen to achieve the balance and poise necessary to sip your glass of gin through a straw during the class – it's Sydney to a tee.

Asanas aside, the spirits distilled here are well worth a swish – its Australian Dry Gin took double gold at the 2018 San Francisco World Spirits Comp. Inspired by the nearby ocean, husband and wife founders David Whittaker and Vanessa Wilton include sustainably foraged marine botanicals such as seaweed in their recipes. Unusually, even the distillery's vodka is infused with botanicals, meaning it takes on the slight taste and smell of the ocean – a feature that unsurprisingly pairs extremely well with seafood.

THINGS TO DO NEARBY

Manly Ferry
The best way to get to your gin-yoga class: from Circular Quay you pass the Harbour Bridge and the Opera House. From Manly Wharf it's a 25-minute bus ride to the distillery.

Curl Curl Beach
One of many local beauties, nearby Curl Curl Beach on Sydney's north shore is a gorgeous arc of golden sand, with a stunning rock pool. Surf's pretty good too.

YOUNG HENRYS

76 Wilford Street Newtown, Sydney, NSW;
www.younghenrys.com; +61 2 9519 0048

◆ Distillery   ◆ Shop   ◆ Transport
◆ Tours   ◆ Bar

Young Henrys beer is on tap at pubs all over Sydney, but its brews have a spiritual home in the alt-hip, make-it-yourself inner west where its brewery and distillery are based. Collaborations with local artists, theatres and bands (as well as some not-so-local stars like the Foo Fighters) have embedded Young Henrys in the hearts of the city's beer-loving urban tribes. So when the team expanded into distilling, it was only natural that hops were incorporated.

Mashing up brewing and distilling techniques, its Noble Cut gin is brewed from scratch and cut with Tasmanian-grown Enigma hops. Reviewers agree it has personality – in a good way. Plus, a visit to Young Henrys' tasting room might involve punk rock, food trucks, street art and an escalation of your street cred.

THINGS TO DO NEARBY

Enmore Theatre
One of Sydney's premier indy stages, hosting events such as the Sydney Comedy Festival, FIFA World Cup nights, and touring international cool kids. **www.enmoretheatre. com.au**

White Rabbit Gallery
With its cutting-edge collection of contemporary Chinese art, White Rabbit is one of the best places in Australia to experience the edgiest artists from the People's Republic. **www. whiterabbitcollection.org**

HUSK DISTILLERS

1152 Dulguigan Rd, North Tumbulgum, NSW;
www.huskdistillers.com

◆ Food   ◆ Tours   ◆ Bar
◆ Distillery   ◆ Shop

Vast fields of sugar cane are a familiar sight across northern NSW, but one plantation, nestled in the fertile caldera of Mt Warning, is doing things differently. Here, Husk Distillers is growing, crushing and fermenting sugar cane to make Australia's only agricole rum.

It's the brainchild of scientist Paul Messenger, who was inspired to make paddock-to-bottle rum with an Australian accent after holidaying in the Caribbean. Eight years after his initial experiments in a modest shed, Messenger has produced award-winning unaged, spiced and barrel-aged rums, and the passion project has blossomed into a custom-built sugar mill and distillery with a stately cellar door, bar and cafe on the idyllic family farm.

Rum may be the focus, but it's another adventurous tipple, concocted between cane harvests, that's made Husk a star. Its Ink Gin is flavoured with native and traditional botanicals then infused with blue butterfly pea flowers, resulting in a vibrantly coloured but soft-tasting spirit that's pH sensitive – it turns a delightful shade of lavender when mixed with tonic and lemon. After trying it, stay for a picnic in the landscaped grounds, washed down with a refreshing North Coast caipirinha.

THINGS TO DO NEARBY

Osteria
Treat yourself to a long lunch that showcases local produce at this relaxed, rustic-chic Italian a 15-minute drive from Husk Distillers. *osteriacasuarina.com.au*

Cabarita Beach
Fling out your towel at this beautiful beach surrounded by a nature reserve, paddle out for world-class waves, or stroll around the pretty Norries Headland. *www.destinationtweed. com.au*

Tropical Fruit World
Follow the giant avocado to a sub-tropical oasis that's home to more than 500 varieties of fruit, ripe for the tasting. Ice-cream bean, anyone? *www. tropicalfruitworld.com.au*

Wollumbin National Park
Explore the ancient Gondwana rainforest covering this now-extinct volcano and pay your respects to Wollumbin, a sacred place for the Bundjalung people. You can even stay in the park. *www. nationalparks.nsw.gov.au*

PROHIBITION LIQUOR COMPANY

22 Gilbert St, Adelaide, South Australia;
www.prohibitionliquor.co; +61 8 8155 6007

◆ Food   ◆ Shop   ◆ Transport
◆ Distillery   ◆ Bar

THINGS TO DO NEARBY

Adelaide Central Market
One of the largest
undercover fresh-food
markets in the southern
hemisphere, Adelaide
Central Market is the
perfect showcase of
South Australian produce.
*www.adelaidecentral
market.com.au*

**National Wine Centre
of Australia**
Nestled in Adelaide's
Botanic Gardens sits this
massive wine-barrel-shaped
building where visitors can
explore Australia's relatively
young wine history and
sample its spoils. *www.
wineaustralia.com.au*

Adelaide Oval
One of Australia's premier
sporting grounds, offering
a roof climb and housing
the Bradman Collection,
dedicated to, arguably, the
world's best cricketer. *www.
adelaideoval.com.au*

Osteria Oggi
Oozing with atmosphere
and design cred, this
award-winning restaurant
offers a delicious Australian
spin on Italian favourites.
The wine list is killer.
www.osteriaoggi.com.au

A massive black claw-foot bathtub takes pride of place behind Prohibition Liquor Co's slick bar, hinting at the period from which the distillery has lifted its name. Yet the tasting room, housed in a former gym and garage, has a contemporary feel and encourages drinkers to immerse themselves in gin culture.

The lads behind Prohibition are gin enthusiasts and that plays out in their gin-tasting flights, which are a homage to contemporary Australian gin rather than merely a means of displaying their own products – South Australia's small-batch offerings take centre stage. For those brave of heart there's the Aussie Muscle flight, featuring three over-proof gins including Prohibition's own Bathtub Cut (69%). Questions are encouraged during the flights and paddles are presented laden with native Australian botanicals such as lemon myrtle.

Unafraid of one-off experimental gins, as noted by the bottles of kumquat gin with hand-scrawled labels that sit behind the bar, the collective behind Prohibition Liquor has embraced the spirit of the 1920s. Celebrate the clandestine era that inspired the distillery by finishing with an Australian negroni, featuring Prohibition's Bathtub Cut gin and Adelaide Hills-based Applewood Distillery's amaro, Økar.

TWENTY THIRD STREET DISTILLERY

Cnr 23rd Street and Renmark Ave, Renmark, South Australia;
www.23rdstreetdistillery.com.au; +61 8 8586 8500

◆ Food   ◆ Tours   ◆ Bar
◆ Distillery   ◆ Shop

The reinvention of Twenty Third Street Distillery's century-old site, a 3.5-hour drive from Adelaide, is a heartening success story. It was established in the early 1900s as a distillery and winery, but became an eyesore and embarrassment for the town after its closure in 2004. Many locals petitioned to have it levelled, but in 2014 it was acquired by South Australian beverage brand Bickford's and the cobwebs were dusted off to reintroduce distilling.

Today, Twenty Third Street Distillery is a contemporary facility producing award-winning gin, vodka, brandy and whisky made from locally sourced ingredients. The history of this brilliant landmark is brought to life during the 45-minute

THINGS TO DO NEARBY

Arrosto Coffee
Housed in Renmark's former fire station, this boutique operation is the Riverland's only small-batch coffee roaster. The perfect place to pick up a brew for the road.
www.arrostocoffee.com.au

Canoe the Riverland
One of the best ways to see the Riverland is from the waters of the mighty Murray River, and this company organises self-guided canoeing adventures. *www. canoetheriverland.com*

Wilkadene Woolshed Brewery
This zero-waste brewery operates out of a former woolshed, and its pinging Firehouse Coffee Stout (a collaboration with Arrosto Coffee) is required drinking.
www.wilkadene.com.au

Murray River Queen
The largest side paddle boat in Australia, moored at the Renmark wharf, offers overnight accommodation and regional wine tasting at its unique floating cellar door. *www. murrayriverqueen.com.au*

guided tour, which shows off the stills and allows for a sniff of the angel's share in the barrel room. The tour ends with a tasting flight that includes its award-winning Signature Gin and the cleverly named Not Your Nanna's Brandy.

Don't leave without downing the distillery's take on a Cosmopolitan made with its Riverland Rose Vodka, whose pink hue comes courtesy of an infusion of valentine-red petals from locally grown Mr Lincoln roses.

ADELAIDE HILLS DISTILLERY

68 Chambers Road, Hay Valley, South Australia;
www.adelaidehillsdistillery.com.au

◆ Food ◆ Tours ◆ Bar
◆ Distillery ◆ Shop

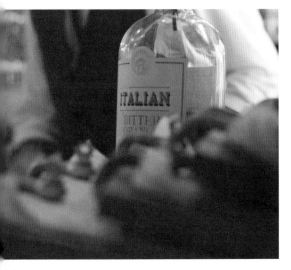

THINGS TO DO NEARBY

Pallet Home & Table
This hybrid cafe and contemporary homewares store in the township of Nairne is the perfect breakfast pit-stop, with menu items sourced from the verdant Adelaide Hills.
www.pallet-home.com.au

Bird in Hand Winery
Specialising in cool-climate wines, a haven for live music and containing a brilliant farm-to-table restaurant, this Adelaide Hills institution uses quality local produce.
www.birdinhand.com.au

Woodside Cheese Wrights
Swing by this delightful Woodside establishment to sample flavoursome artisan cheeses made from herd-specific buffalo, goat and sheep milk.
www.woodsidecheese. com.au

Kidman Flower Co
Set aside three hours for a masterclass on arranging Australian native plants and flowers combined with a scrumptious afternoon tea and farm tour (book ahead).
hkidmanhk.wixsite.com/ kidmanflowerco

Adelaide Hills Distillery is known for its ground-breaking Australian Green Ant Gin, using real insects in its distilling process. Green ants have long been foraged by Aboriginal Australian communities for medicinal benefits but it's their lime flavour that's key to this gin. The distillery sources the ants from a Northern Territory bush tucker farm and each bottle displays a permit number to reflect the sustainable harvest of the gin's namesake ingredient.

Native ingredients feature heavily in the distillery's other offerings, too. The quandong, or Australian wild peach, is critical to Adelaide Hills' award-winning Bitter Orange aperitif and strawberry gum is credited for providing the summery twist evident in the distillery's pink drink — the 78° Sunset Gin.

Set in the lush patchwork of farms, vineyards and bushland of the Adelaide Hills region, an extra bonus for visitors is that the distillery tasting room (set to open late 2018) sits in the same grounds as Mismatch Brewing Company and The Hills Cider Company. Expect tasting flights from the trio of businesses, as well as access to a large viewing platform so visitors can observe the still and brewhouse.

APPLEWOOD DISTILLERY

24 Victoria Street, Gumeracha, South Australia;
www.applewooddistillery.com.au; + 61 8 8389 1250

◆ Food ◆ Tours ◆ Bar
◆ Distillery ◆ Shop

Housed in an unassuming brick-and-corrugated-iron former apple store, arriving at Applewood you could mistakenly believe you've rolled up to a friend's farm in the Adelaide Hills. Inside you'll find a simple black-topped wooden bar, hosting an espresso machine and maybe a bunch of indigenous flowers, with Applewood's unique gins (plus sister wine label Unico Zelo) on sale along with some branded swag.

Each of the distillery's uniquely Australian gins is named after one of the seven deadly sins and infused with indigenous ingredients such as peppermint gum leaf, saltbush and desert limes. Tasting flights are delivered on a wooden board with a slim sake bottle of tonic to soften and develop the incredible botanicals and spices in each glass.

THINGS TO DO NEARBY

Driving tour of the Adelaide Hills
Rolling hills and historic villages lined with colourful European trees make Adelaide Hills perfect for motor touring. Pick-your-own fruit and cellar doors break up the journey.

Lost in a Forest
In a historic stone church, this restaurant–bar is the perfect spot to end your day in the hills. The soundtrack is as good as the wood-fired thin-crust pizzas.
www.lostinaforest.com.au

AMBLESIDE DISTILLERY

Cnr Ambleside & Mount Barker Rd, Hahndorf, South Australia; www.amblesidedistillers.com; +61 408 834 010

◆ Food ◆ Tours ◆ Bar
◆ Distillery ◆ Shop

With restorative views of the South Australian bush from its door, the simple-looking hangar that houses Ambleside Distillers has a far more rural vibe than one might expect, given its location in the touristy town of Hahndorf. Its tasting bar is the perfect escape from the throngs of crowds milling up and down the town's main street.

The distillery makes just three spirits, and its gin flight includes all of them: the No 8 Botanical Gin, laden with crisp citrus notes, and the fabulous Big Dry Gin, which explodes with pepper and fire thanks to its infusion of jalapenos, are particularly noteworthy. The tasting is best accompanied by a platter of delicious cheeses from local Adelaide Hills producers. Polish proceedings off with a Big Dry martini on the distillery's outdoor deck.

THINGS TO DO NEARBY

Beerenberg Farm
This Hills institution offers strawberry-picking for eight months of the year (late October to early May). The farm shop sells 80-plus goodies including jams, relishes and honey.
www.beerenberg.com.au

The Cedars
Set on beautiful acreage, the historic home of Sir Hans Heysen – one of Australia's most renowned landscape artists – displays some 200 of Heysen's works. ***www. hansheysen.com.au***

KANGAROO ISLAND SPIRITS

856 Playford Hwy, Cygnet River, South Australia;
www.kispirits.com.au; +61 8 8553 9211

◆ Food ◆ Shop
◆ Distillery ◆ Bar

THINGS TO DO NEARBY

Admirals Arch
Waves have gouged out
a ragged archway at the
island's southwesterly
tip. Pause to admire
this natural marvel,
beneath which seals
sunbathe, unbothered by
the furious currents.

Remarkable Rocks
The 500 million-year-
old granite boulders of
Kangaroo Island's Flinders
Chase National Park evoke
a Dalí painting: spattered
with orange lichen, these
gigantic globes have a
backdrop of churning ocean.

Island Beehive
Explore the opposite end of
the flavour spectrum to gin
by trying light Sugar Gum
and smoky Stringy Bark
honeys, or sipping a pollen-
flecked latte, at this apiary
cafe with tours. **www.
island-beehive.com.au**

Seal Bay Conservation Park
Get thrillingly close to
wild sea lions as they
honk, bicker and gallop
across the sand in this
protected reserve on
Kangaroo Island's south
coast. **www.sealbay.
sa.gov.au**

Though only a 45-minute ferry ride from mainland
Australia, Kangaroo Island's windblown isolation
is immediately apparent. This haven for fur seals,
sea lions and, yes, kangaroos is also home to Australia's first
dedicated gin distillery, which somehow succeeds in bottling
island aromas such as coastal plants and brisk sea breezes.

Founders Sarah and Jon Lark were inspired by a trip to a
London distillery, vowed to create their own operation back
home, and followed their noses to Kangaroo Island for the
isolated setting and emerging food and wine scene. The
island's flora infuses all they create, from Wild Gin with juniper
plucked from the coast, to O'Gin, scented with olearia, a

coastal daisy. 'Australia has the most amazing array [of native
plants]. We've only just scratched the surface,' says Sarah.

Settle beneath an outdoor marquee to sample zesty,
award-winning gins, flavoured with plant-life you can
practically see from your chair. Order an O'Gin and tonic for
a drink that tastes quintessentially Kangaroo Island. 'It's the
olearia, the smell of walking through sand dunes to the beach,'
enthuses Sarah. 'A lovely aroma to remember the island by.'

LARK DISTILLERY

14 Davey St, Hobart, Tasmana; www.larkdistillery.com;
+61 3 6231 9088

◆ Food　　◆ Tours　　◆ Bar
◆ Distillery　◆ Shop　　◆ Transport

All aboard the 'Drambulance'! Dedicated whisky fans won't need to be told twice; tours starting from Lark Distillery's cellar door in downtown Hobart involve boarding a white minivan that takes punters out to the distillery itself in Cambridge, which doubled in size in 2017.

While you won't find founder Bill Lark – considered the godfather of Australian whisky – driving the bus, he still remains a proud ambassador ('We can't keep him away,' is the affectionate response from distillers). Reverence for Bill is justified: 150 years after the last licensed distillery in

Tasmania closed, he campaigned to overturn the law banning whisky-making and single-handedly resurrected Australia's craft distillery industry, opening Lark in 1992. Toast him on the 90-minute tour, departing daily.

THINGS TO DO NEARBY

Institut Polaire
So cool. This Antarctic-meets-Tasmania-themed bar has classy cocktails, a chic interior, and food and drink experiences including speciality G&T flights. *www.institutpolaire.com.au*

Templo
Don't be fooled by the tiny, understated, neighbourhood restaurant facade. Templo seduces with sublime food, and an excellent value eight-course chef's menu. *www.templo.com.au*

HELLYERS ROAD DISTILLERY

153 Old Surrey Rd, Burnie, Tasmania;
www.hellyersroaddistillery.com.au; +61 3 6433 0439

◆ Food　　◆ Tours　　◆ Bar
◆ Distillery　◆ Shop　　◆ Transport

Named after Henry Hellyer, an irrepressible pioneer who blazed the original Old Surrey Rd through the Burnie hillsides in 1827, Hellyers Road is one of the more progressive and commercially astute distillers in Tasmania. The marketing is slick, but it isn't disguising any shortcomings in quality. Golden single malts – both American oak (bourbon) and French oak (Pinot Noir) barrel-matured – vie for your attention in the stylish tasting room, along with a clean-spirited local barley vodka and a slippery malt-coconut cream liqueur. Get in quick: the

distillery attracts 40,000 whisky fans annually, and many of Hellyers' original single malts from the early 2000s have sold out. If you're lucky you might get to sip some 12-year-old original product.

THINGS TO DO NEARBY

Makers' Workshop
Check the pulse of Burnie's creative heart at this dramatic structure – part museum, part arts centre – which rises above the western end of Burnie's main beach. *www.discoverburnie.net*

Burnie Regional Museum
The centrepiece of this absorbing Tasmanian museum is a lovingly crafted re-creation of a 1900 Burnie streetscape – including a blacksmith's shop and a bootmaker. *www.burnieregionalmuseum.net*

HARTSHORN DISTILLERY

Birchs Bay, Tasmania; www.grandvewe.com.au/
hartshorn-distillery; +61 3 6267 4099

◆ Food   ◆ Shop
◆ Distillery

THINGS TO DO NEARBY

Grandvewe
On the same site as the distillery, Grandvewe is the place to see the entire sheep product process, which includes tasting organic, award-winning cheese. **www.grandvewe. com.au**

Art Farm
Experience the annual Sculpture Trail (it runs April to June, but the trail is open year round) or just enjoy the cafe and gallery on this idyllic coastal farm. **www.artfarmbirchsbay. org.au**

Bruny Island
Take the car ferry across D'Entrecasteaux Channel to Bruny Island for windswept coastal scenery, hiking in South Bruny National Park, swimming and seafood. **www. brunyisland.org.au**

Peppermint Bay Hotel
Overlooking the D'Entrecasteaux Channel and Bruny Island, this hotel restaurant offers the best view for dining, fresh garden produce and a seasonal menu. **www.peppermintbay. com.au/restaurant**

After figuring out the difficult process of making vodka from unfiltered sheep whey (the only person in the world to do so), Ryan Hartshorn was awarded World's Best Vodka in 2018 at age 33. Incredibly, he started distilling via a still he purchased from eBay and many nights trawling internet forums, just a few years ago.

The source of the sheep whey is Grandvewe Cheese – the family business that Ryan runs with his mum Diane and sister Nicole (see Things To Do Nearby). When Ryan first started experimenting with distilling, the family thought it was a hobby. Now Ryan is fielding consultancy offers from as far as Iceland, leaving little time to hand-paint every bottle.

Ryan's personal touch and creativity is obvious, from the thought behind his sprayed black bottle design ('If I can create a young, edgy-looking bottle, what's inside it will be kickass too') to prioritising the World's Best batch (just 90 bottles) for subscribers. All this success means visitors will soon be able to enjoy a brand new distillery area. There's sheep whey gin on offer too, but best to see what all the fuss is about: taste the Sheep Whey Vodka neat, like a whisky.

MCHENRY DISTILLERY

Port Arthur, Tasmania; www.mchenrydistillery.com.au;
+61 3 6250 2533

◆ Food　　◆ Tours　　◆ Bar
◆ Distillery　◆ Shop

THINGS TO DO NEARBY

Port Arthur Historic Site
One of Australia's most significant sites, Port Arthur is a compelling 40 hectares of living history. Ghost tours, ruins, prisons and convict tales await the curious. ***www.port arthur.org.au***

Bangor Wine & Oyster Shed
Bangor is a paddock-to-plate restaurant and farm door next to a vineyard, with magnificent views and so much more than just (amazing) wine and oysters. ***www.bangorshed. com.au***

Three Capes Track
This four-day, three-night 46km hiking trail with eco-cabins en route is deservedly popular, taking in spectacular Cape Raoul, Cape Pillar and Cape Hauy. ***www.threecapestrack. com.au***

Sorell Fruit Farm
This pick-your-own fruit farm carries up to 11 different varieties. Try to time your visit with the cherry blossom festival (September to mid-October) for idyllic scenery. ***www. sorellfruitfarm.com***

'My wife really loves gin. And dad would always have a G&T, and these days I'm addicted to it. Have you seen our wombat?' Bill McHenry, master distiller, crouches at his natural spring on the slope of Mount Arthur as he points out McHenry Distillery's unofficial pet's hideaway. It's a far cry from his former career as the general manager of a start-up biotech company in Sydney. But when stressing so much he ran a red light, he realised it was time for a career change. A friend joked that with a name like William McHenry, he should be making whisky. And the challenge was set.

Bill's wife gave him a two-year deadline ('Ali, this is whisky, you've got no idea') and the family of five moved to Tasmania to set up Australia's southern-most whisky distillery in 2010. While waiting for the whisky to mature, it's McHenry's gin that has really captured attention. With help from Kim Dudson at local tour company Bespoke Tasmania, Bill set up gin workshops with a difference: visitors select the botanicals for and distil their own gin, then enjoy the end result with gin-themed food, such as a ceviche of ocean trout cured in gin, or oysters with a gin and saffron drizzle.

OLD KEMPTON DISTILLERY

Dysart House, Kempton, Tasmania;
www.oldkemptondistillery.com.au; +61 3 6259 3058

- ◆ Food
- ◆ Tours
- ◆ Bar
- ◆ Distillery
- ◆ Shop
- ◆ Transport

Like little agricultural Kempton itself, Old Kempton Distillery has a chequered history. Its stills started bubbling in 2012 at photogenic Derwent Valley hop farm Redlands Estate, established by George Read, purportedly the illegitimate son of King George IV, in 1818. Then in 2015 the distillery relocated to a noble 19th-century house in Kempton in Tasmania's Midlands. The town is named after Anthony Fenn Kemp, aka the 'Father of Tasmania'. Politician, pastoralist, bankrupt, booze-hound: Kemp fathered more than 12 children in Tasmania's early days. Given this heritage, it's no surprise Old Kempton's product is masculine and roguish: small-batch single malts using 100% Tasmanian barley, matured in sherry, port, Pinot Noir and bourbon barrels. Its 'Redlands Paddock to Bottle' single malt is a must-try dram.

THINGS TO DO NEARBY

CALLINGTON MILL

Spinning above the rooftops of nearby Oatlands, the once-derelict Callington Mill (1837) has been fully restored. It's the only working Lincolnshire-style flour windmill in Australia.
www.callingtonmill.com.au

ROSS BRIDGE

A half-hour north of Kempton, convict-built Ross Bridge (1836) is Australia's third-oldest bridge. Its stone carvings shimmer with spooky shadows when illuminated at night.
www.visitross.com.au

SULLIVANS COVE DISTILLERY

1/10 Lamb Place, Cambridge, Tasmania;
www.sullivanscove.com; +61 3 6248 5399

◆ Distillery ◆ Shop
◆ Tours

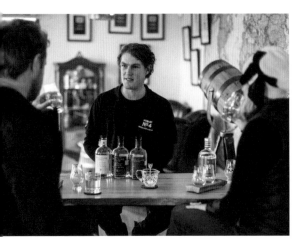

THINGS TO DO NEARBY

Seven Mile Beach
This safe swimming
beach fringed by pine
trees has picnic
and camping facilities
at the eastern end.
Surfers can occasionally
catch decent waves
along the point.

Frogmore Creek
At the heart of the Coal
Valley, Tasmania's fastest-
growing wine region, go
for Frogmore's Rieslings,
Chardonnays and Pinot
Noirs, stay for roast wallaby
or yuzu salmon. *www.*
frogmorecreek.com.au

Barilla Bay Oysters
Dine on a dozen freshly
shucked beauties or take
a one-hour tour that
includes the oyster farm,
abalone processing, and
its ginger beer brewery.
www.barillabay.com.au

Peter Rabbit Garden
This enchanting garden is
full of Beatrix Potter/Peter
Rabbit nostalgia. Take high
tea in the Riversdale Estate
Orangery or stay in the
cottages. *www.thepeter*
rabbitgarden.com.au

Follow the 'Whisky Fanatic Parking this way' sign
to Tasmania's second oldest whisky distillery after
Lark (p224). The distillery got its name from its
original location in 1994 at the old brickworks in Sullivans
Cove, but moved in 2004 to Cambridge where head distiller
Patrick Maguire took over the distillation, and still hand-
selects every cask today.

Visitors will be charmed by the creative, barrel-themed
decor on arrival (shredded barrels masquerading as
curtains, barrel-shaped spotlights) before exploring the vast
distillery beyond. 'Sullivans Cove has always matured its
whisky in big barrels,' says cellar door manager Tom Ambroz.
'This is where you'll find some of Australia's oldest whisky.'
There are whiskies ranging in age from eight to 18 years,
as well as Australia's most-awarded whisky, including the
World's Best Single Cask Single Malt (2018 World Whiskies
Awards): the American Oak.

So popular are Sullivans Cove's whiskies on the world
stage that demand can outpace production and some labels
can sell out. Distillery tours and tastings of its single malts
are popular and held daily on the hour from 10am until 4pm.
They can be done separately but best value is the combined
one-hour tour and tasting.

SHENE ESTATE & DISTILLERY

Pontville, Tasmania; www.shene.com.au;
+61 432 480 250

◆ Distillery ◆ Shop
◆ Tours ◆ Bar

A knock-out location for fans of heritage and history, Shene is a 19th-century estate built from convict labour for colonialist Gamaliel Butler. Since 2009 the sandstone 'living museum' has been lovingly restored by Anne and David Kernke. On a pre-booked tour you'll spy various artefacts, such as old gin bottles from the era, along with intriguing symbols etched into the walls to ward off evil spirits.

Their award-winning Poltergeist Gin (crafted with 12 Tasmanian botanicals) was named by daughter Myfanwy as a nod to the family's 'spirit' of conservation but also the detection of a 'presence' in their adjacent home. An adorably quaint bottle shop, which the owners call their 'roadside stall', is open every Sunday in the grounds of the estate – but do also book ahead for the gin tasting and tour.

THINGS TO DO NEARBY

Agrarian Kitchen
A 25-minute drive southwest of Shene, this restaurant (an adjunct to a famed cooking school further south) is repeatedly voted one of Tasmania's best. *www. theagrariankitchen.com*

Epsom House
This grand venue, one of Australia's 100 oldest houses, holds quality classical and jazz concerts in its ballroom, accompanied by food prepared by chef Ceinwen Macbeth. *www.epsomhouse.com*

THE WHISKERY

Cnr Scotchmans and Portarlington Rds, Drysdale, Victoria;
www.bellarinedistillery.com.au; +61 4 6892 6282

◆ Food ◆ Tours ◆ Bar
◆ Distillery ◆ Shop ◆ Transport

In a region famous for its wineries, there is now another reason to visit the beachy and bucolic Bellarine Peninsula – its first distillery. This small-batch, hands-on business is run by passionate owners Lorelle Warren and Russell Watson, who create the fresh and flavourful Teddy & the Fox gin. Infused with five botanicals, including orange, coriander and lemon myrtle, the gin has quickly taken off and there are plans to add to the range with a pink gin made from local Pinot Noir grapes. But the long game here is whisky and there is a much-anticipated single malt ageing in barrels for release in the next couple of years. Snuggle up in front of the fire in winter or catch some rays on the terrace in summer at the relaxed cellar door, housed in a converted chicken shed.

THINGS TO DO NEARBY

Scotchmans Hill
A little further along the road from The Whiskery is the region's oldest winery, a top-class operation with tastings and great food platters. *www.scotchmans.com.au*

Little Mussel Café
Stop by this tin shed cafe in Portarlington to chow down on local seafood, from mussel chowder to oysters and scallop pies. *www.advancemussel.com. au/shop*

TIMBOON RAILWAY SHED

The Railway Yard, 1 Bailey St, Timboon, Victoria;
www.timboondistillery.com.au; +61 3 5598 3555

◆ Food   ◆ Tours   ◆ Bar
◆ Distillery   ◆ Shop

Timboon is a town steeped in whisky history, known for its 19th-century bootleg whisky trade, and the legacy continues today thanks to distiller Josh Walker – a Timboon local who learnt his trade in Kentucky. Housed in the restored historic railway shed, the cellar door is decked out with Chesterfield sofas, a tasting bar, open fire and terrace deck for dining on excellent local produce.

The distillery produces two permanent lines – an easy-drinking signature port expression (42% ABV) aged in American oak, and a much punchier Christie's Cut (60% ABV) aged in French oak, along with special experimental releases a few times a year. Guided tours are held in the nearby bond store barrel room, where visitors can learn about the history, the distilling process and partake in tastings.

THINGS TO DO NEARBY

Timboon Fine Ice Cream
Cool your tongue on a couple of scoops of delicious ice cream (including a whisky cream flavour) made with local produce around Timboon.
www.timboonfineicecream.com.au

Twelve Apostles
Timboon is tantalisingly close to the Great Ocean Road, one of the world's best scenic drives. Just a 30-minute drive from town, these impressive rock stacks are a highlight of the journey.

STARWARD WHISKY DISTILLERY

50 Bertie St, Port Melbourne, Victoria;
www.starward.com.au; +61 3 9005 4420

◆ Food   ◆ Tours   ◆ Bar
◆ Distillery   ◆ Shop   ◆ Transport

'We wanted to take a deliberate step away from the traditional image of whisky,' says flat-cap-wearing brand ambassador Paul Slater, twisting orange peel over an Old Fashioned. This very modern distillery, in an industrial part of Port Melbourne, feels a little like a party-fuelled beer garden meets whisky warehouse.

Founder David Vitale, who worked at the Lark Distillery for three years, was keen to harness Melbourne's four-seasons-in-one-day climate into a unique whisky matured in Australian wine barrels. Starward is now Australia's fastest-growing whisky producer. Pop in for the one-hour tour, try a two-hour masterclass, or visit for the Thursday whisky flight nights. Stick around for the Melbourne-themed 'Hook Turn' cocktail – named after the city's notorious tram-influenced road rule.

THINGS TO DO NEARBY

South Melbourne Market
This market, trading since 1864, is the quintessential Melbourne multicultural food experience. There are 145-plus stalls; don't miss the famous dim sims.
www.southmelbournemarket.com.au

Lûmé
Multisensory fine dining in a South Melbourne terrace house, Lûmé offers ambitious tasting menus of the dry-aged emu and freeze-dried meringue ilk, plus excellent cocktails.
www.restaurantlume.com

HURDLE CREEK STILL

216 Whorouly-Bobinawarrah Rd, Bobinawarrah, Victoria; www.hurdlecreekstill.com.au; +61 4 1115 6773

◆ Distillery ◆ Tastings
◆ Shop

In a rusted tin shed at the end of a dirt road surrounded by paddocks is where you'll find Hurdle Creek Still. This excellent small-batch gin distillery is as authentically rustic and as laidback Aussie as it gets: it produces its own grain spirit using barley and oats, and uses a traditional mashing process. The alcohol is then distilled a minimum of three times and botanicals are vapour-infused in a conical Carterhead. Visitors can taste the range of gins made on-site while watching the distilling process or the still at work – and though there are no official tours, the owner is happy to talk visitors through what's going on. Don't leave without a bottle of Hurdle Creek's signature Yardarm Distilled gin, made with juniper from Montenegro and infused with a blend of traditional, native and locally grown botanicals.

THINGS TO DO NEARBY

Brown Brothers winery
Taste top-notch wines at this family-run winery around since 1889, then lunch at one of the region's best restaurants, the on-site Patricia's Table. *www.brownbrothers.com.au*

Milawa Cheese Company
A 10-minute drive from Hurdle Creek you can taste a range of indulgent cheeses here at the old Milawa Butter Factory. *www.milawacheese.com.au*

BASS & FLINDERS

3/40 Collins Rd, Dromana, Victoria;
www.bassandflindersdistillery.com; +61 3 5989 3154

◆ Distillery ◆ Bar
◆ Shop

THINGS TO DO NEARBY

Port Phillip Estate
This slick, dramatic modern building, which overlooks scenic vineyards, houses a gastronomic restaurant and fine wines for tasting at the cellar door. *www.portphillipestate.com.au*

Ten Minutes By Tractor
Taste some of the Mornington Peninsula's renowned wines and dine at the highly regarded restaurant. It's a 10-minute drive from the distillery. *www.tenminutesbytractor.com.au*

Arthurs Seat Eagle
Fly high above a scenic nature reserve on the Arthurs Seat chairlift and take in the views that reach across to Melbourne's skyline. *www.aseagle.com.au*

Peninsula Hot Springs
Soak your body in mineral-rich steaming hot-spring pools at this vast complex set amid rolling hills, 20 minutes from Bass & Flinders. *www.peninsulahotsprings.com*

For local Melburnians, Victoria's Mornington Peninsula had long been synonymous with wine. Then along came boutique distillery Bass & Flinders, offering something with a bit more punch, producing an excellent range of unusual gins, vodka, limoncello, grappa and five-year-aged ochre (aged brandy).

This being wine country, the distillery makes its own smooth base spirit using shiraz grapes. But that's just one way in which Bass & Flinders sets itself apart – if you ask head distiller Holly Klintworth, she'll say the distillery's diminutive size also helps, because it allows the team to 'be creative and produce products relevant to the current season'. This translates into unique flavours such as Truffle Gin, and the truly creative Angry Ant – a nod to the flora and fauna of Australia's outback, using indigenous botanicals sourced from outback Western Australia and infused with ant pheromone.

Book in for one of the popular gin masterclasses (A\$140) to create your own bespoke gin to take home or, if you prefer to leave it to the masters, stop by for tastings at Bass & Flinders' rustic-chic cellar door. Be sure to pick up a bottle of its bestselling Gin 10 – a deliciously spicy number using a blend of 10 botanicals with hints of cardamom, native pepper berry and orange.

FOUR PILLARS

2a Lilydale Road, Healesville, Victoria;
www.fourpillarsgin.com.au; +61 3 5962 2791

◆ Food   ◆ Tours   ◆ Bar
◆ Distillery   ◆ Shop   ◆ Transport

'It was like when a new iPhone is released – people started queuing outside the distillery hours before we opened.' Four Pillars Gin's operations manager Scott Gauld still marvels at the frenzied devotion to its limited-release Bloody Shiraz Gin. But anyone who visits the distillery, located in Victoria's Yarra Valley wine region, will appreciate this as a gin purists' paradise. Open to the public since 2015, Four Pillars' success lies in its unique Australian botanicals, pure Yarra Valley water and German stills.

The purchase in 2018 of a new 1800L still is tripling production to meet demand, both at home and abroad. Overseas, Four Pillars has rapidly been cultivating a global following and its collaboration with Sweden's Hernö distillery on the Dry Island Gin has only helped to cement its position as Australia's best-known gin internationally.

Visitors to the distillery are in for a treat, with an excellent cocktail list and tasting plates including Moonshine Cheese (made from the leftover gin distillery water), but also look out for various gin events around Australia. The barrel-aged gins offer exceptional drinking, but your best introduction is via the gin-tasting paddle: three gins, tonics, ice and garnishes.

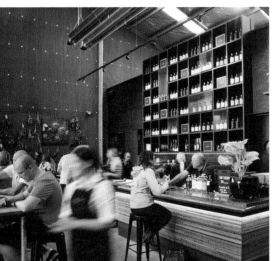

THINGS TO DO NEARBY

Tarrawarra Estate
This winery and restaurant, set on a sprawling estate surrounded by native bushland, is often visited in conjunction with the adjacent Tarrawarra Museum of Art. *www.tarrawarra.com.au*

Giant Steps
An excellent combination of a cellar door showcasing Yarra Valley cool-climate wines and a luxurious, chandelier-strewn, Thai-Euro restaurant. *www.giantstepswine.com.au*

Healesville Sanctuary
Visit this wildlife park for close encounters with Australia's animals, including wombats, kangaroos, platypuses, Tasmanian devils, koalas and dingoes. *www.zoo.org.au/healesville*

Healesville Hotel
Much applauded as a provincial dining destination in the past decade, Healesville Hotel offers accommodation, food and an excellent wine list. *www.yarravalleyharvest.com.au*

7 WEIRD & WONDERFUL SPIRITS

FROM AROUND THE WORLD

If ever there was an excuse to mix your drinks, it's these unusual intoxicants.
Some will delight you with their unexpected ingredients,
while others are a feat of endurance for your taste buds. Sip wisely...

Jeppson's Malört, USA

What? With daredevil slogans like 'the champagne of pain', Jeppson's Malört built its infamy on being almost undrinkable. Chicago immigrant Carl Jeppson distilled and popularised this wormwood-infused liqueur, a traditional beverage in his native Sweden. Malört escaped Prohibition because of its purported medicinal qualities and continues to be fondly described with tasting notes like 'petrol' and 'burning'.

Try it: In Chicago bars such as the award-winning Violet Hour (www.theviolethour.com), where it is served in artisanal cocktails.

Kava, Pacific Islands

What? Take the rumours with a grain of salt – or in this case, a pinch of pepper. This pepper plant–derived intoxicant won't send you on a hallucinogenic odyssey, but it does have sedative properties (expect your tongue to become comfortably numb). Fijian kava ceremonies are semi-formal affairs where drinkers gulp from a coconut shell, clapping in turn until everyone has sipped enough to feel thoroughly adjusted to 'Fiji time'.

Try it: Many Fijian resorts welcome guests with a kava ceremony attended by local villagers.

Feni, India

What? Goa is the only place on Earth where brandy is made from cashew apples. These sweet, tart fruits are crushed in a *bhatti* (an earthenware boiling pot) and the liquor double- or sometimes triple-distilled. For centuries feni was sipped by Goan labourers to ease the pains of a day in the fields. Today feni is catching the attention of mixologists from London

to NYC, who use it to add a splash of island flavour to their cocktails.
Try it: Swing by the Bay bar (www.swingbythebay.com) on Goa's Bogmalo Beach uses more than 25 local spirits in its cocktails, including plenty of feni.

Pulque, Mexico

What? Libation of the Aztec gods and enjoyed for more than a millennium, tequila's stickier ancestor is derived from fermented agave sap. Pulque is used as an aphrodisiac – try not to dwell on its creamy colour and texture – and is said to be rich in probiotics. If the sour-ish flavour is too overpowering, taste it *curado* – sweetened with guava or oatmeal.
Try it: Seek out pulquerias in Mexico City – these dedicated pulque bars first sprouted as a form of counter-culture under Spanish colonial rule.

Moss schnapps, Iceland

What? Brennivín is Iceland's more famous firewater, but the country's bitterly cold, surf-slapped coast is best evoked by Fjallagrasa moss schnapps. Lichens and mosses have a long history in traditional Icelandic medicine, though it's only recently that scientists have confirmed their immune system-stimulating properties – news that has vindicated Icelanders in the habit of glugging moss schnapps to cure a cough.
Try it: At Slippbarinn (www.slippbarinn.is) in Reykjavik,

where there's a broad menu of spirits on offer, from traditional cough remedies to classy cocktails.

Punsch, Sweden

What? Swedish punsch was originally named for its five ingredients (from the Sanskrit *pansch*) rather than its ability to pack a punch. It began as a social ritual where hot water and arrack (coconut sap liquor) were poured onto a sugarloaf to create an enticing warm drink. When pre-mixed punsch first went on sale, a craze was born – modern Swedes remain partial to punsch, whether hot, cold or topped up with sparkling wine.

Try it: Learn the finer points of Swedish punsch – and other spirits besides – at the Spritmuseum (p172) in Stockholm before testing your knowledge at the on-site bar.

Poire Williams, France & Switzerland

What? Enlivening dinner party conversations across France and Switzerland, bottles of Poire Williams *eau de vie* (clear brandy) often contain a full-sized pear, and the idea has now even spread to countries such as the US and Canada. It's no optical illusion: bottles are tied in place over budding fruit, which then grow within the bottle. The brandy slips down easy, but the real trick is getting the brandy-soaked pear out at the end...
Try it: You can learn how Canada has started to grow its own pear-in-a-bottle brandy (and pick up a bottle) at Ironworks Distillery (p34) in Nova Scotia.

NEW ZEALAND

How do you ask for a spirit without mixers? 'Hey bro, give it to me neat. Sweet mate.' In te reo Māori, the other official language of New Zealand, you could ask for 'waipiro inu'; direct translation 'dirty water'

Signature spirit? Traditionally, New Zealanders like to distil anything that's free. Kiwi or Fejoa fruit liqueurs are a 1970s classic

What to order with your spirits? Mode Srn Kiwi spirit drinkers are purists, but can often be tempted with a grazing board of local cheeses and meats.

Don't drink and drive. Public transport has barely been invented in New Zealand, and many watering holes are off the beaten track

Like many other Kiwi pastimes, distilling arrived with gold prospectors and early European settlers in the 1830s. Thrust into this wild and distant land, the frontier folk found comfort in their home-made moonshine until the 1880s, when the temperance movement gained traction. By the 1890s several areas of New Zealand fell under local prohibition laws, while bureaucracy elsewhere made the legal production and sale of alcohol largely untenable. During this time the McRae family shot to fame with their Hokonui moonshine: Scotch-style whisky made in copper pot stills hidden around the Hokonui Hills and delivered to high-end clients in unmarked billy cans.

A post-WWII relaxation of alcohol laws to aid the set-up of the RSA (Returning Serviceman's Association) ushered in new interest in home brewing and distilling. Although still technically illegal, many an old soldier living the quarter-acre dream passed on to their children the skill of turning fallen fruit into a passable liquor. By the late 1970s, sneaking some of grandpop's bootleg at family gatherings was considered a rite of passage, as was helping him scoop up all the ripe feijoas, kiwi fruits and damsons in the autumn. But a decade later many home stills had gone quiet, and the commercial stills mostly followed suit. New Zealand had gone mad for wine, and grandad was now more likely to be brewing – which was legal – than distilling in the garden shed.

In 1996, the New Zealand government did something unprecedented. It became the first and only Western country to make home distilling for personal use 100% legal. The uptake was slow at first, but by the mid-noughties many a backyard distiller was back in business. The global financial crisis drove more worshippers to the 'home crafting' alter, and can certainly take some of the credit for the incredible boom in craft beer. By 2010, many of those people who enjoyed diddling around in their lean-to were turning their eye to business, which gave birth to the boutique spirits industry.

Whisky was in the driving seat originally, probably because of the large number of expats returning from extended 'OEs' (overseas experiences) in the UK, US and Canada. The Kiwi passion for turning the abundance of free local fruit into a drinkable spirit was also given new life by New Zealand's many German migrants, with schnapps finding its way into both common parlance and high street bottle shops. But the global gin renaissance has now firmly caught hold and it is fair to say that there is a bevy of very sophisticated gins coming from these provincial shores, many of which place emphasis on their use of pure New Zealand water.

The new-wave spirits industry in Aotearoa is still quite young. Even its biggest commercial distilleries look like hobby houses compared with the European giants, and many aren't offering the same sort of public access as small-batch distilleries in countries such as Australia, the UK and US. But the goal has never been world domination of the Pernod Ricard variety. New Zealand's distillers are true artisans, making something special for the educated minority. Welcome to the fold.

> *"NZ distilling is still quite niche. People want to be artisans, to play around, spurred on by the craft brewing movement. It's a perfect storm, a convergence to reinvent an industry that had been missing for a long time"*
>
> **—JAMES MACKENZIE, THE NEW ZEALAND WHISKY COLLECTION**

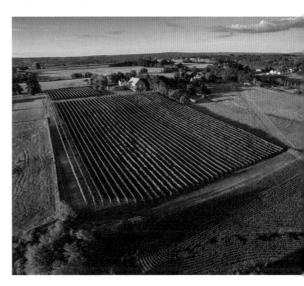

TOP 5 SPIRITS

- **Pink Gin** Cardrona Distillery, Wanaka
- **Dunedin DoubleWood Whisky** Willowbank, Oamaru
- **Kiwi blue agave** Kiwi Spirits, Golden Bay
- **Barrel Aged Gin** Dancing Sands, Golden Bay
- **Starka vodka** Puhoi Organic Distillery, Auckland

PUHOI ORGANIC DISTILLERY

9 Saleyards Rd, Puhoi, Auckland; www.spirits.net.nz;
+64 21 678 013

◆ Distillery ◆ Shop
◆ Tours

If you're after a genuinely boutique experience, this distillery should top your list. You'd be in good company – Prince William has visited – but tastings are strictly by appointment. There's no tour as such, but this facility is so tiny you see it all by default. 'We are one of the smallest distilleries in the world,' says proprietor Alex Kirichuck. 'And perhaps the only one with a medical doctor on staff.' He is referring to wife Iryna, who began distilling medicinal tonics after Alex – a Ukrainian nuclear engineer – had to visit Chernobyl. They moved to New Zealand in 2002, branching out into spirits.

The distillery is fed by water from an 8000-year-old aquifer, 221 metres deep, and uses organic ingredients; Alex even grows botanicals and keeps bees. Puhoi also claims to be the first distillery in New Zealand to use 100% solar energy and gravity-flow technology. The couple claim their unique 'adaptogenic' distilling method produces a beverage that will not leave you drunk or hung over.

Home to a beautiful double wood whisky and vodka made from Sauvignon Blanc, you must try Puhoi's oak-rested vodka, Starka, and hear Alex explain the traditional Polish origins.

THINGS TO DO NEARBY

Puhoi River Canoes
Take in the 8km stretch from Puhoi to beautiful Wenderholm Regional Park on a canoe. The park is perfect for a picnic, and it has a safe swimming beach.
www.puhoirivercanoes. co.nz

Puhoi Valley Cafe & Cheese Shop
Just up the road, Puhoi Valley artisan cheeses has an on-site cafe. It offers platters of hand-made produce and local wine in its garden.
www.puhoivalley.co.nz

Puhoi Pub
Established in 1879, Puhoi Pub is one of the oldest watering holes in the Southern Hemisphere. It's a good place to try Puhoi's spirits, and you can stay the night.
www.puhoipub.com

Puhoi Heritage Museum
Visit this quirky little time capsule to find out about the area's Māori history and the village's bohemian settler roots. Great for kids.
www.puhoiheritage museum.co.nz

PRENZEL

15 Sheffield Street, Riverlands Estate, Blenheim;
www.prenzel.com; +64 3 520 8215

◆ Distillery
◆ Shop

After World War II, French authorities banned traditional home distilling in the small region of Alsace, eastern France, and many small artisanal stills were hidden to avoid destruction. One such still, Allouette, made its way to New Zealand and was acquired by Robert Wuest, whose family were originally from Alsace. He began making fruit brandy in a shed at the back of a friend's cherry orchard in Blenheim in 1989.

From these fugitive beginnings, Prenzel was born and, just like many European distilleries, it offers a range of interesting fruit products such as dessert toppings and vinaigrettes, as well as its flagship range of schnapps, liqueurs and spirits. Make sure you try the distillery's seasonal, limited-edition brandy made from local fruit.

THINGS TO DO NEARBY

Omaka Classic Cars
This museum is home to more than 100 vehicles from the 1950s to the 1980s, all with a story and in original working condition. *www.omaka classiccars.co.nz*

Pick strawberries
Pick your own strawberries at one of the numerous local fruit farms, or eat fresh strawberry ice cream at family business Hedgerows. *www. hedgerows.co.nz*

LIQUID ALCHEMY

660 Main Road, Stoke, Nelson;
www.liquidalchemy.co.nz; +64 3 547 5357

◆ Food   ◆ Shop   ◆ Transport
◆ Distillery ◆ Bar

When Jürgen Voigtländer moved to Nelson from Germany 14 years ago, he found there was an abundance of fruit available for free. 'I'm a forager, and I hate waste,' says Jurgen, who is a cooper (barrel maker) with strong links to the wine industry, and found himself with plenty of grapes as well as feijoas, lemons and mandarins from local lifestyle blocks. 'I began making schnapps at home, playing around with ingredients, including wormwood which grows in my garden.'

Jürgen found sweet-toothed Kiwis love a good fruit liqueur, and the business took off. Now based at McCashin's Brewery with a 400-litre still, he also makes a hopped gin using Nelson's famous local hops and the botanicals he grows in his own backyard. Don't leave without trying his cherry liqueur.

THINGS TO DO NEARBY

Sea kayaking
Head up the coast to Motueka and hire kayaks for a guided tour of the beautiful bays around Abel Tasman national park. *www.seakayaknz.co.nz*

Pic's peanut butter factory
Pic Picot's nut butters are a NZ treasure, and here you can go on a free factory tour and make your own version of it. *www.picspeanutbutter.com*

CARDRONA DISTILLERY

2125 Cardrona Valley Rd, Cardrona;
www.cardronadistillery.com; +64 3 443 1393

◆ Food ◆ Tours ◆ Bar
◆ Distillery ◆ Shop

What does it take to start an award-winning distillery? Ash and Desiree Whittaker will tell you it takes a lot of hard work, but their secret ingredient is passion. The couple sold everything to build their dream and within a year had laid down their first whisky and won gold at the New York World Wine & Spirits Competition 2016 for their gin, The Source. Their products include a seasonal release of pink gin aged in Pinot Noir barrels to raise money for breast cancer awareness, and a vodka, The Reid, made from malted barley.

Currently, Cardrona Distillery offers the only behind-the-scenes distillery tour in New Zealand. It costs $25 per person, including a complimentary tasting, and you can view the whole process in 75 minutes, from the malted barley going in to the clear spirit that comes out. Afterwards, stick around and order one of their platters to soak up the booze.

THINGS TO DO NEARBY

Ski or bike Cardrona
The distillery is pretty much opposite this ski field, with its challenging, world-class terrain and some of New Zealand's best downhill mountain biking in summer.
www.cardrona.com

Cardrona Hotel
This iconic frontier hotel is worth a visit, whether you're staying the night or just fancy a beer. Built in 1863 to support the gold rush, it now houses an award-winning restaurant.
www.cardronahotel.co.nz

Horse trekking
Next door to the distillery is The Cardrona, offering horse trekking experiences through the mountains (no experience necessary). Petrol heads can jump on a quad bike instead.
www.thecardrona.co.nz

Roaring Meg Pack Track
The Pisa conservation area offers several walks, including this 20km hike, complete with beautiful views across the Roaring Meg dam.
www.doc.govt.nz

The clear mountain water around Wanaka underpins the unique products produced by Cardrona, but its gin takes the distillery's intrinsic link to the land a step further by including rosehips harvested from behind the distillery as one of its botanicals. Planted by Chinese gold miners more than 100 years ago, rosehips are part of the rich history of the area and give The Source a unique flavour profile – don't miss it.

NEW ZEALAND WHISKY COLLECTION

14-16 Harbour Street, Oamaru;
www.thenzwhisky.com; +64 3 434 8842
◆ Shop
◆ Transport

THINGS TO DO NEARBY

Blue Penguins
The world's smallest penguin can be seen in its natural habitat along Oamaru's harbour front, where a colony of the adorable seabirds live. *www.penguins.co.nz*

Whitestone City
Inside an original grain barn you'll find Oamaru's Victorian heritage uniquely preserved at this museum and gallery of well-curated history exhibits. *www.whitestonecity.com*

Steampunk HQ
Oamaru is an unlikely hub for steampunk, and a centre of weird and wonderful contraptions lies within this heritage building. *www.steampunkoamaru.co.nz*

Moeraki Boulders
Also known as 'God's marbles', these unique rock formations are 30 minutes north of Oamaru on Koekohe beach. *www.moerakiboulders.com*

Willowbank, New Zealand's last commercial whisky distillery, was shut down in 1997 by owners who felt whisky had had its day. Luckily Greg Ramsay, lover of a wee dram and possessor of incredible foresight, purchased the remaining 443 barrels of mothballed spirit in 2009. From these barrels, his team has created unique products such as the award-winning Dunedin DoubleWood and the cask-bottled Oamaruvian.

'The DoubleWood was born from necessity,' says James Mackenzie, blender and distiller. 'Our predecessors, the Preston family, found they had a limited number of American oak casks, but plenty of red wine casks. They took a calculated risk and the results were sensational.' So popular have these limited-edition spirits become, the team began distilling itself in 2016 and is working on a state-of-the-art distillery that will offer tastings, tours and more. The aim is to create different styles of whisky that are uniquely of New Zealand. 'It's a good time to be a distiller in New Zealand,' says James, who is excited about the challenge ahead.

In the meantime, take a whisky flight at the current cellar door to experience styles and flavours that will never be made again. It's home to New Zealand's oldest whisky at 30 years, and a good place to shop. Try the High Wheeler, made from un-malted barley and aged for 21 years in American oak.

DANCING SANDS

46A Commercial St, Takaka;
www.dancingsands.com; +64 3 525 9899

◆ Distillery ◆ Shop
◆ Tours

Many a distiller will tell you that a good spirit starts with great water. Dancing Sands distillery in Golden Bay, near Abel Tasman National Park, sits directly above an aquifer drawing water from Te Waikoropupu Springs – the clearest fresh water in the world.

'Pupu springs is *tapu* (sacred), according to Māori legend, and is not allowed to be touched by humans,' says Ben Bonoma, one half of the Dancing Sands team, along with wife Sarah. 'It has visibility of up to 63m. The only place with clearer water is the Weddell Sea in Antarctica. Our aquifer feeds the spring; it's the same water.'

Sarah and Ben use a 150-litre Jacob Karl still to handcraft small batches of their award-winning Sacred Spring gin, which comes in dry and barrel-aged varieties, as well as wasabi, saffron and chocolate flavour. They also produce a Dancing Sands vodka, and a white and dark rum sold under the label Murderer's Bay – the original name given to Golden Bay by Captain Cook.

Don't leave the tasting room without trying the unusual barrel-aged gin. Perfect for a Dirty Martini, you'll notice the locally sourced manuka honey botanical is enhanced by the vanilla of the French oak casks used to age it.

THINGS TO DO NEARBY

Mussel Inn
A short drive north to Onekaka, this spit-and-sawdust cafe serves mussel chowder, bowls of sausages and locally brewed beer; there's live music in summer.
www.musselinn.co.nz

Cape Farewell
Close to Wharariki Beach, you can visit the lighthouse or take a tour on the 26km sand spit, also a conservation area.
www.farewellspit.com

Wharariki Beach
See seal pups in the rock pools, view the beautiful archway rocks and perhaps take a horse trek up this remote beach, flung at the top of the South Island's most northerly tip.
www.horsetreksnz.co.nz

Te Waikoropupū Springs
Just a few minutes outside of Takaka, take a short walk and visit the sacred springs from which the distillery draws its pure waters.
www.doc.govt.nz

KIWI SPIRIT DISTILLERY

430 Abel Tasman Drive, Takaka;
www.kiwispiritdistillery.co.nz; +64 3 525 8575

◆ Distillery
◆ Shop

 A short drive from Takaka, Kiwi Spirits is run by Terry Knight and partner Rachel Raine. They're known for tequila-style spirit TeKiwi; the first of its kind in New Zealand, and it got Terry in trouble with the Mexican mafia. 'Tequila is like Champagne – you can only use the name if it's been made in the region,' explains head distiller Sue Bensemann. 'A local paper wrongly reported we were calling it tequila and Terry had some angry Mexicans on the phone!'

The spirit is on limited release of 300 bottles a year, and

Terry and Rachel have just seeded their own organic agave plantation on-site. They offer tastings, but check the website for times. Terry's Waitui honey single malt whisky, made with New Zealand's acclaimed manuka honey, is a must-try.

THINGS TO DO NEARBY

Rawhiti Cave
An incredible large limestone cave an hour's walk along Dry Creek Valley, offering the most extensive and diverse twilight zone cave flora in New Zealand.

Scenic flights
Adventure Flights Golden Bay offers scenic flights in small fixed-wing aircraft. Choose from four flight plans or pick your own path. *www.adventure flightsgoldenbay.co.nz*

LIGHTHOUSE GIN

89 Martins Rd, Martinborough;
www.lighthousegin.co.nz; +64 6 306 9122

◆ Distillery
◆ Shop

Flanked by the rolling vines of the Martinborough wine region, Lighthouse Gin distillery takes its name from nearby Cape Palliser Lighthouse, at the southernmost tip of the North Island. Founding distiller Neil Catherall spent several years experimenting with local botanicals and designed his own 200-litre still. His apprentice, Rachel Hall, took over in 2014. At the time of writing the distillery wasn't open to the public, but tastings are offered in a 130-year-old cottage at Te Kairanga Wines down the road.

This double-distilled gin uses a sugar cane base, water

from the nearby Remutaka ranges, and nine botanicals including navel oranges and Yen Ben lemons, resulting in a unique, citrus character. Try its Hawthorn Edition, which is perfect for classic cocktails like a Tom Collins.

THINGS TO DO NEARBY

Cape Palliser Lighthouse
Made of cast iron and established in 1897, this lighthouse stands above a local fur seal colony at the southernmost tip of the North Island. *www.wairarapanz.com/ cape-palliser*

Patuna Farm Adventures
Walk through a stunning limestone chasm, try your hand at clay-bird shooting and stay in a renovated sheep shearer's hut on this North Island farm. *www.patunafarm.co.nz*

COCKTAILS

WORLD'S TOP 10 COCKTAILS

1. NEGRONI

The story goes that while drinking in Florence's Casoni Bar in 1919, Italy's Count Camillo Negroni wanted something with a bit more oomph than his usual Americano (Campari, red vermouth and soda). A savvy bartender switched out the soda for gin and the rest is history. The cocktail's (pictured) popularity has rocketed in recent years thanks to the craft gin movement and a resurgence of love for bitter flavours. But it's also thanks to Italian bar staff dominating the world's cocktail scene. After all, if this deep-red, bitter orange, boozy and refreshing drink is their choice of tipple after a long, hard shift, why wouldn't it be your go-to as well?

2. OLD FASHIONED

Nothing screams vintage drinking like ordering an Old Fashioned. This cocktail dates back to long before the Prohibition era, but also conjures up images of stylish sipping once America was well and truly off the wagon. When it was dreamed up at the start of the 19th century, this combination of whisky with bitters, sugar and water was simply referred to as the 'Whisky Cocktail' and was imbibed in the mornings – quite the reversal to its nightcap status these days. For best results, stir vigorously over ice and drink slowly. This cocktail deserves considered sipping.

3. MARTINI

If you heard that Sinatra was a Jack Daniel's guy, you heard wrong. He was known to prop up the Savoy's American bar with a Martini (pictured below) in hand, too. And James Bond famously drank his shaken, not stirred. It can be gin- or vodka-based, and you'll likely find dozens of neo-martinis on the menus of modern cocktail bars, but the classic gin Martini can be loosely traced back to the mid to late 19th century, when it was made to the formula of six-parts gin, one part dry vermouth. Expect it in an extra-chilled martini glass with a twist of lemon or a green olive. And that shaken or stirred argument? We'll lap it up, either way.

4. MARGARITA

Ordering a Margarita (pictured above) is like saying 'hola' to party time. It's a bold, citrusy drink with serious cojones thanks to a good slug of blanco tequila and a sour lime kick – triple sec adds a sweetness that takes the edge off, as does a customary salt rim on the glass. This Mexican staple became popular with Americans in the age of travel, and although many question whether an American or a Mexican invented the drink, nobody disputes that it was created firmly on Mexican soil. It's now a global phenomenon with its own international day of celebration. Try a Tommy's Margarita, which swaps out triple sec for agave syrup, the choice of hardcore tequila drinkers.

5. MANHATTAN

Many bartenders pick the Manhattan as their favourite cocktail when it comes to their turn to order a drink for themselves. The New York classic is a strong, smooth drink with plenty going on – with a rye or bourbon base, a lick of sweet red vermouth, a dash of bitters and a maraschino cherry in its depths for a final reward when you reach the bottom (and go inevitably weak at the knees). Many contest The Manhattan Club's claim to have created this epiphany of a drink in 1874.

6. DAIQUIRI

This refreshing rum tipple (pictured below) was created at the turn of the 20th century when Cuban-American relations were far more harmonious than they are today. The original blend of white rum with sugar and lime was invented by an American engineer in the iron-ore mines of a small Cuban town called Daiquirí. Jennings Stockton Cox's creation spread in popularity both in Cuba (partly thanks to Hemingway) and back in the US, and has since morphed into fruity and frozen versions on cocktail menus around the world. But keep it as a straight-up classic and be rewarded with a refreshing, sour drink that shows off rum at its best and rightfully made the miners giddy.

7. APEROL SPRITZ

Look back five years and Aperol was such a forgotten aperitif, you wouldn't have even found it at the back of mum and dad's booze cupboard. It's now the toast of towns around the world thanks to its summer readiness when served in a Spritz. The Spritz cocktail is an Italian invention, based on an Austrian Spritzer, and interpretations of the drink include three key elements: wine, bitter flavour and bubbles. The Aperol Spritz (pictured above) looks as orange as the sun on steroids and that tartness is mellowed out with enough sweet notes to make this cocktail the perfect sparkling antidote to any heatwave.

8. PISCO SOUR

This South American superstar (and the delight of many a gap year student; pictured above) only reached a global audience in recent years once exports of Peru's national spirit, pisco, took off. Pisco is made from grapes and is a perfect bedfellow to lime, sugar syrup and egg whites, frothed up in a shaker to form a fluffy-topped tipple. A few dashes of bitters are added at the end to complete the formula. The Pisco Sour was created in Lima, but is the national drink of both Peru and Chile, and hugely popular across South America as a whole. World domination is surely in the offing.

9. MOJITO

In the 1990s you couldn't move for Mojitos, and although they're still a popular order at the bar, you may just get an eye roll from a bartender scarred by those Mojito-mad days. The obsession is obvious – white rum, sugar, mint and soda make the ultimate summer refresher. Its origins are in Cuba, that much is for sure. But although Havana bar-restaurant La Bodeguita del Medio lays claim to its creation, it's more likely it was concocted by slaves on the sugar cane fields or based on a drink popularised on Sir Francis Drake's ship when passing through Havana. He was meant to sack them of their treasures, but instead he gave them liquid gold.

10. ESPRESSO MARTINI

There are few cocktails that draw such levels of fanaticism as the Espresso Martini (pictured below) – and that's probably because its combination of caffeine and alcohol makes it the ultimate stimulant. In fact, that was practically its name for a stint, called the 'Pharmaceutical Stimulant' when first invented in London in the 1980s by the late Dick Bradsell. It was fabled that a supermodel – some guess at Naomi Campbell – requested a drink that would wake her up and then get her buzzing. Bradsell added a hot shot of espresso to vodka, coffee liqueur and sugar. It's gained global cult status in a relatively short amount of time, and from just one sip, it's easy to see why.

THE 5 BEST
GIN COCKTAILS

1. NEGRONI

One part gin, one part red vermouth, one part Campari: all parts amazing. This red-hued cocktail hailing from Italy is served in a rocks glass over ice, with an orange peel or wedge for garnish. It's a potent, refreshingly bitter tipple best enjoyed as an aperitif on a hot summer's day.

2. MARTINI

One of the few drinks to have its own emoji, the Martini is pretty iconic. You'll find it served every which way around the world, but the classic formula sees six parts gin and one part vermouth shaken or stirred with ice and garnished with a lemon peel or olive. Liquid perfection.

3. SINGAPORE SLING

Invented at Singapore's world-famous Raffles hotel around the turn of the 20th century, this pink drink is the fruitiest, booziest blend of gin, cherry liqueur, Benedictine and Cointreau with lime juice, pineapple juice, grenadine and bitters. Whether today's recipe rings true to the original is up for debate, but either way it tantalises the taste buds and Raffles' bar has become a pilgrimage for its fans.

4. CLOVER CLUB

A marshmallowy pink drink created in Philadelphia before America was hit by Prohibition, the Clover Club has stood the test of time. Indeed, post-Prohibition, New York has a bar dedicated to it. It's a combo of gin, lemon juice and raspberry syrup, with egg white giving the drink its frothy head.

5. AVIATION

A pre-Prohibiton classic (pictured) that's essentially a gin sour, this cocktail was born in a time when air travel was the ultimate luxury – like the crème de violette that gives the drink its bright and dreamy violet colour; a rare ingredient when the drink was first conceived. It's mixed with gin, lemon juice and maraschino to form a floral and sour novelty.

THE 5 BEST
WHISKY COCKTAILS

1. OLD FASHIONED

Make like Don Draper and order an Old Fashioned (pictured), a drink that's sophisticated as hell. Made using either bourbon or rye, muddled with sugar and stirred with ice, it's served in a tumbler with a twist of orange. Its origins date back to the 1800s, making it one of the stone-cold classics.

2. MANHATTAN

Whisky, sweet vermouth and bitters collide in one of five cocktails named after the boroughs of New York City – this one is without a doubt the most famous of the quintet. It's served in a cocktail or coupe glass and dressed with a boozy maraschino cherry bobbing in its depths.

3. WHISKY SOUR

Sours – like many drinks – were invented on the high seas, with citrus and sugar used to make spirits more palatable. And boy, were the Americans on to a winner when they made a whisky version. These days, find it with egg white for texture and a cherry and a wedge of orange for a decorative whiff of frivolous garnish.

4. SAZERAC

The naughty cousin to the Old Fashioned, the Sazerac is based on cognac, rye or bourbon, blended with sugar, a dash of absinthe and Peychaud's Bitters – the creator of Peychaud's came up with this cocktail as well as a formula for bitters. It's one of the oldest cocktails on record and the official drink of New Orleans.

5. MINT JULEP

Almost 120,000 Mint Juleps are served each year at the Kentucky Derby since the tradition began in 1938, although this herbaceous drink was first made in Virginia for medicinal purposes. It's a refreshing mix of bourbon, mint leaves and sugar, best served in a pewter cup.

THE 5 BEST
VODKA COCKTAILS

1. ESPRESSO MARTINI

A cocktail adored all over the world, the Espresso Martini is a modern tipple and the ultimate party drink thanks to a winning combination of booze and caffeine. Vodka and coffee liqueur are shaken over ice with fresh espresso. Some present-day interpretations use cold brew coffee instead of a hot shot.

2. BLOODY MARY

The Bloody Mary can be enjoyed any time of day, but is best known as the ultimate hair of the dog and breakfast of champions. Debate rages over whether it belongs to Paris or New York, but it has evolved to include the likes of tomato juice, Worcestershire sauce, Tabasco, lemon, black pepper and celery salt.

3. MOSCOW MULE

You'll recognise a Moscow Mule (pictured) from the copper vessel in which it's commonly served. The vodka, ginger beer and lime concoction was created at Hollywood's Cock 'n' Bull restaurant in 1948 – apparently, the team were trying to shift 'a lot of dead stock' from the cellar. No complaints here; it worked like magic.

4. COSMOPOLITAN

Carrie Bradshaw and co didn't just boost sales of the Rampant Rabbit. Bar orders for Cosmopolitans rocketed on the back of *Sex And The City*'s TV success. It's a suitably pink drink made from vodka, triple sec, cranberry juice and lime, which suited Carrie and her fashionista New York crowd to a tee.

5. WHITE RUSSIAN

More pop culture, with the White Russian popularised in the Coen Brothers' movie *The Big Lebowski*, being the drink of choice of 'The Dude'. But you don't have to wear a dressing gown to enjoy this mix of vodka and coffee liqueur poured over ice and given a calorific cream float.

THE 5 BEST
RUM COCKTAILS

1. DAIQUIRI

Frozen or fruity riffs of this classic litter the menus of bars around the world, especially ones looking to turn up the heat. But the original version – invented by an American in Cuba's mining town Daiquirí – is a refreshing mix of white rum, sugar syrup and lime juice served straight up.

2. MOJITO

The exact origins of this Havana concoction are hazy, but the results are as crisp and refreshing as drinking gets. White rum, lime juice, sugar syrup and mint leaves are topped with soda to create one of the world's biggest selling and best known mixed drinks.

3. MAI TAI

A true Tiki recipe, the Mai Tai's combination of aged rum with orange curaçao, lime, orgeat (almond) syrup and sugar syrup is island life in a glass. Most credit it to Trader Vic's, a Polynesian restaurant in California where a Tahitian guest exclaimed 'mai tai roa aé' after one sip, which loosely translates as 'out of this world!'

4. PIÑA COLADA

How many drinks have a song named after them? That's how iconic this sweet summer blend (pictured) is, a retro Puerto Rican concoction that sees pineapple, rum and cream of coconut meet. If you're not drinking it from a pineapple on a beach (or at least with a cocktail umbrella), you're probably doing it wrong.

5. DARK AND STORMY

If legend is to be believed, an old sailor compared this drink's colour to the storm clouds. The 'dark' is dark rum and the 'stormy' is ginger beer, and it's served in a highball with a squeeze of lime. It's the unofficial drink of Bermuda and has been trademarked by Bermuda rum brand Gosling's in most parts of the world.

AND LET'S NOT FORGET...
TEQUILA, PISCO ET AL

1. MARGARITA

Mid-20th century and the popularity of Mexico's Margarita began to spread, although nobody truly knows where it came from. One thing's for sure, it's a fiesta in a glass, made from tequila, orange liqueur and lime, and often served with a salt rim around the glass. *¡Ay caramba!*

2. APEROL SPRITZ

Venice's ultimate cooler-downer, the Aperol Spritz has become synonymous with summer. It's made from bright orange and bitter aperitif Aperol, which is mixed to the formula 'three-two-one': three parts white wine (prosecco is most popular), two parts Aperol, one part soda. Garnish with orange for a heatwave-ready, luminous tipple.

3. PISCO SOUR

Peru and Chile's national drink, the Pisco Sour began life in Lima. It's much like the whisky sour before it, but sees Peruvian spirit pisco (a local grape brandy made around the town of Pisco) used as the base, with lime, sugar and egg white shaken in. Three drops of bitters are added to a frothy head to give its signature look.

4. CAIPIRINHA

Lime and sugar are muddled together before adding ice and cachaça – a Brazilian spirit made from fresh sugar cane – to this tall, refreshing cocktail that originated in São Paulo. The drink soared in popularity around the world in 2016, thanks to Rio's Olympic Games.

5. PALOMA

While the Margarita has a global audience, it's the Paloma (which means 'dove' in Spanish; pictured) that the Mexicans drink more avidly. Tequila, lime and fresh grapefruit juice served in an icy tumbler quenches the thirst in a recipe straight from the town of Tequila. It was first made at tequila pilgrimage bar La Capilla (p257).

WORLD'S TOP 10 COCKTAIL BARS

1. SMUGGLER'S COVE, SAN FRANCISCO

'No pastime makes the stars so bright, as greeting dusk with rum's delight,' says a sign at Smuggler's Cove (pictured left). Staff are known as 'crew', fishing nets suspend sea debris and Hawaiian shirts abound. It may look like Captain Jack Sparrow's holiday home, but it's far from naff, with the largest collection of rum in North America (over 700 expressions) and a cocktail list that reads like a history of the sugar cane spirit. This could be the finest modern take on the Tiki bar trend.

2. EL FLORIDITA, HAVANA

From its flamingo-pink exterior to its ubiquitous salsa rhythms, El Floridita is unmistakably Cuban. It's been around for 200 years, yet has a feel of the 1950s, a golden age when Constante Ribalaigua ran the show – known as 'the cocktail king' and inventor of the frozen Daiquiri. This was also the era that Ernest 'Papa' Hemingway could regularly be found propping up the bar with a Daiquiri in hand. Today's *cantineros* (bartenders) in red blazers make around 3000 daiquiris a day for well-dressed locals as well as tourists. Take yours at the bar beside the life-size bronze statue of Hemingway.

3. THE AMERICAN BAR AT THE SAVOY, LONDON

The Savoy hotel's iconic white-walled, retro-carpeted bar has stayed fairly faithful to its art deco origins, despite a mega-dollar hotel refurb in 2010. It has a mini museum at the foot of its entrance dedicated to the bar's rich history – and

its very rich drinkers – and its cocktail menu reads like a who's who of Hollywood, with glitzy drinks dedicated to stars who have propped up the bar for 125 years. Staff (pictured above) in white suits have become celebrities in their own right, including Harry Craddock, the author of *The Savoy Cocktail Book* – bartenders reference his 1930 tome to this day.

4. HIGH FIVE, TOKYO

There's no menu at High Five, so it stands out from hundreds of fellow Ginza bars. Grab one of 12 seats at the bar and chat to Hidetsugo Ueno (described as 'the godfather of bartending' by famous US restaurateur and documentary maker David Chang), who whips up bespoke cocktails according to personal tastes. The bar stocks more than 200 whiskies, yet it's ice that's treated with reverence – carved into cubes for considered cocktail shaking (a 'hard shake' that moves ice more dynamically) or into 'ice diamonds', which dazzle in drinks.

5. BAR HEMINGWAY, PARIS

This cosseted space within Paris' Ritz Hotel attracts a sharp crowd often lured back by charming, white-suited bartender Colin Field (pictured below). He's been here for 24 years, revived the French 75 cocktail and created the revolutionary Clean Dirty Martini – a dry martini with a Mediterranean flavour thanks to a mystifyingly clear ice cube made from olive juice. Yet despite his cocktailing prowess, Colin claims his love of English literature got him the gig. The bar (like many!) was a Hemingway haunt, and walls are decorated with hand-written letters from the legend. Decadent drinks cost €30 each.

6. CLOVER CLUB, NEW YORK

Look to Clover Club for the definition of a neighbourhood bar, a Brooklyn hangout in its 10th year of twisting the classics. It's a narrow, buzzy room that has a cosy nook at the back with its own fireplace. It's a modern reimagining of Philadelphia's Clover Club, where lawyers and journalists would toast with the eponymous pink cocktail (pictured above). Owner Julie Reiner's iconic version adds a splash of dry vermouth. Fellow pre-Prohibition classics on the menu include cobblers and punches.

7. NATIVE, SINGAPORE

Plenty of column inches have been dedicated to Antz, a cocktail on Native's menu that includes creepy crawlies. It exemplifies the bar's approach to using locally foraged ingredients – less shocking are curry leaf and turmeric – and local spirits, in a bar that cares just as much about terroir as the world's top wineries. Founder Vijay Mudaliar also looks to the latest technologies, using a rotavap to distil subtle aromas such as pink jasmine into his creations.

8. BLACK PEARL, MELBOURNE

It's a family affair at Black Pearl; when Tash Conte founded the Fitzroy bar, she worked with her sister in the bar, her mother and brother were in the kitchen and her father kept the books. Fifteen years on, Conte still refers to the team as family, even though it's evolved to include world-class mixologists. Mum Mariane's sausage rolls are still on the menu and banter at the bar is ever-present, which makes the bare-brick space feel homely.

9. LA CAPILLA, TEQUILA

On a dusty road in a town called Tequila is La Capilla ('The Chapel'), a sacred ground for agave lovers. It's rustic, with adobe walls, plastic chairs and nothing in the way of signage. Focus is on hospitality – owner Don Javier Delgado Corona, now in his nineties, serves distillery owners and farm workers, who are all welcomed to write in a visitors' guestbook. Here, Don Javier invented the Paloma cocktail (tequila, grapefruit, lime), but the bar's signature creation is La Batanga (tequila, lime and cola), which he characteristically stirs with a butcher's knife.

10. NOTTINGHAM FOREST, MILAN

For cocktail pomp and ceremony there's Nottingham Forest. Despite the name, this bar in Milan looks every bit the wood-clad Brit pub (albeit with plants, animal prints and Buddha statues). Drinks are just as original, many requiring audience participation. Sip on test-tube Negronis or knock back pills, powders, potions, airs and emulsions. It's molecular mixology at its best, with owner Dario Comini considered on a par with Italy's best chefs.

INDEX

INDEX

INDEX

Woodstock Gin Company,
 Cape Town 18
Wyand Fockink, Amsterdam 158
Yamazaki Distillery, Osaka 102
Yoichi, Hokkaiso 99
Young Henrys, Sydney 218
Zuisen, Okinawa 106
Zwack Unicum Heritage Visitors'
 Centre, Budapest 141

E
eau de vie, *see also* brandy
 116–117, 122, 125, 126, 157, 237

F
France 114–135

G
genièvre 110–111
Germany 136–139
gin, *see also* genièvre, jenever
 15–16, 18–20, 25, 28–37, 49,
 60, 65–66, 69, 77, 79, 82,
 85–86, 92–93, 95, 97, 110,
 114, 132, 136–138, 146, 148,
 173, 175, 177–178, 180–195,
 201–202, 205, 207, 209,
 215–216, 218, 220–225, 228,
 231, 233–235, 237, 239, 242,
 244–245, 247–248, 251
ginja 162, 164–165
grappa 148–149, 152–153, 234

H
Hungary 140–141

I
Indonesia 93
Ireland 142–147
Irish whiskey 142–146, 196
Italy 148–153

J
Jamaica 43
Japan 96–107
jenever 154, 156–161

K
kava 236
kirsch 114, 117, 122

L
Lebanon 10–13
limoncello 148, 191, 234
liqueurs, *see also* amaro, Aperol,
 Bénédictine, Campari,
 Chartreuse, Cointreau, crème
 de cassis, crème de menthe,
 ginja, limoncello, Unicum
 33, 36, 62, 65, 85, 98,
 103–104, 117, 119, 129, 137, 142,
 158, 168–169, 182, 193, 236,
 238, 241, 251, 255

M
Malaysia 94
Martinique 44
Mekhong 92
Mexico 46–55
mezcal 46, 48–51
moonshine 60, 84, 86, 88–89

N
Netherlands 154–161
New Zealand 238–245
Nicaragua 56–57

P
pálinka 140
pastis 119
Peru 58–59
pisco 58–59, 250, 255
Portugal 162–165
pulque 237

R
rakija 166–167
rum 33, 38–45, 56–57, 60, 62, 65–66,
 92–95, 110, 184, 189, 220,
 244, 249, 250, 254
Russia 168–169
rye whiskey 29, 69, 71, 80, 83, 248, 252

S
sake 97–98, 101, 103–104
Sambuca 148
schnapps 136–137, 139, 174, 237, 239,
 241
Scotch whisky 178, 197–200, 202–204,
 206–208
shōchū 35, 97–98, 103, 106
singani 25–27
South Africa 14–21
Sweden 170–173
Switzerland 174–177

T
TeKiwi 245
tequila 46, 52–54, 248, 255
Thailand 95
Trinidad 45
tuak 94

U
Unicum 140–141
United Kingdom 178–211
USA 60–87

V
vodka 16, 27–37, 62–64, 66, 68, 74, 77,
 82–83, 85–87, 92, 114, 137,
 155, 161, 168–170, 182, 184,
 191, 215, 222, 227, 234, 240,
 244, 250, 253

W
whiskey 60, 62, 64, 66, 67, 69, 71, 75,
 77–87, 142
whisky, *see also* bourbon, Irish whiskey, moonshine, rye whiskey,
 Scotch whisky, whiskey
 15, 21, 25, 28–29, 31, 35–36,
 96, 99, 100, 102, 105, 107, 110,
 112, 115–116, 119, 132, 137, 184,
 188, 191, 193, 210–211, 214, 217,
 222, 226, 228–232, 238, 240,
 242–243, 245, 247, 252

Y
Yenoh 86

QUESOS

MEXICO

MEXICO

From the Source

*Authentic recipes from the
people who know them best*

Written by Kate Armstrong, Kristin Diaz de Sandi, Scarlett Lindeman, John Hecht and Michele Peterson
Photographed by Lindsay Lauckner Gundlock

CONTENTS

INTRODUCTION

A vibrant melting pot of striking flavours and pungent aromas, Mexican food is known the world over for its ingredients with a kick. Tangy chiles, sour lime and floral coriander characterise many of its recipes. Yet one of its best-kept secrets is that its dishes are also innately wholesome and satisfying. This a cuisine made to feed a community; comfort food at its best.

Mexico's local staples are steeped in history, shaped by the land and the sociology of its people. Many originate from a vegetarian Aztec diet; maize was cultivated by indigenous farmers thousands of years back. In Yucatán, ancient Maya flavours live on in the oft-used ingredients of sharp lime, oranges and the notorious habanero chilli. And with arrival of the Spanish in the 16th century came domesticated animals and other ingredients, giving the nation new twists to old methods.

Today Mexico is home to one of the world's most renowned street food cultures. In Mexico City, *antojitos* (street-food bites) bestow the streets with scents of homemade salsa, rich onion and beef-topped *chalupas* and woody, blackened corn. Head to Oaxaca for a colourful street food scene with snacks like *garnachas*, originally served as

party food at *velas* (festivals). Venture to Puebla and you'll experience the city that gave birth to the chocolate and chilli *mole poblano*.

But street food can be found away from the markets too, in diners and gourmet restaurants throughout the country, where the only palpable difference is presentation. In Baja California, for example, upmarket seafood, trendy craft breweries and vineyards stretch along one of the world's largest peninsulas. Here, young chefs combine local delicacies such as lobster and fish tacos with contemporary Asian flavours. The Pacific Coast is another slice of gourmet heaven: eat on sun-soaked terraces alongside shrimp markets, sampling local fruit, herbs and edible flowers that complement exotic dishes such as fish and coconut ceviche.

Despite its regional varieties, a common element unites this cuisine across the country: a collective resourcefulness. Communities pull together preparing for fiestas, at which food is created both to feed the masses and deliver a celebratory punch. Dishes come alive in the *pueblos*, with festivities marking patron saint celebrations, weddings and birthdays – especially *quinceañeras* (15th birthday celebrations) – think warming *chiles en nogada*, pork tacos and pots of *pozole* stew.

This is a culture in which local food, full of heart and prepared with an unlikely combination of humility and pride, is king. The Mexican food experience has earned the right to its status as one of the most exciting and authentic in the world.

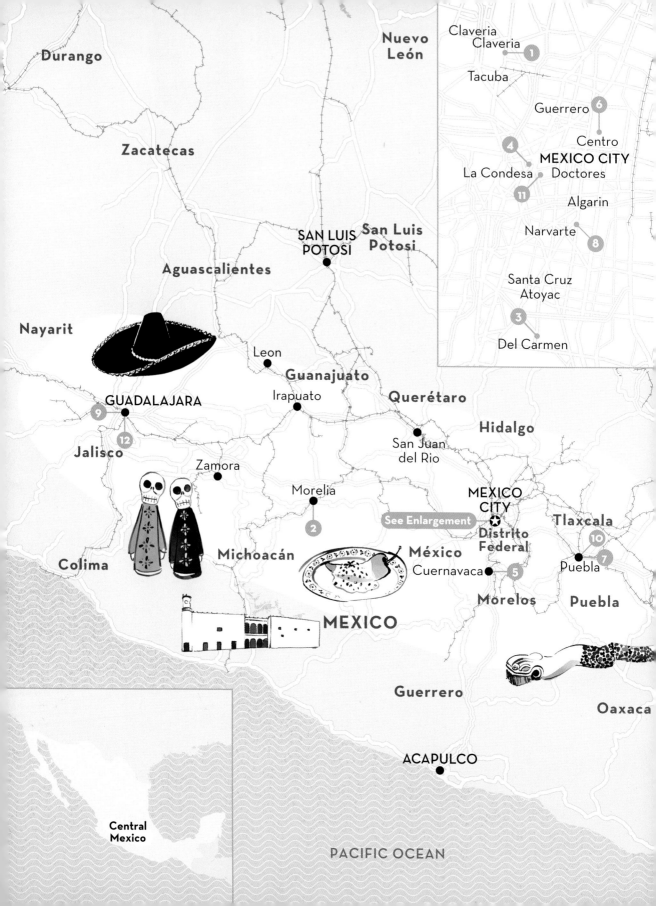

Durango

Nuevo León

Claveria
Claveria ———— 1

Tacuba

Guerrero — 6

Zacatecas

Centro

4

MEXICO CITY

La Condesa   Doctores

11

Algarin

Narvarte

8

San Luis Potosí
SAN LUIS POTOSÍ
San Luis Potosi

Santa Cruz
Atoyac

3

Del Carmen

Aguascalientes

Nayarit

Leon

Guanajuato

Irapuato

Querétaro

Hidalgo

GUADALAJARA

9

San Juan
del Rio

12

Jalisco

Zamora

**MEXICO
CITY**

Morelia

See Enlargement

Tlaxcala

2

10

**Distrito
Federal**

Colima

Michoacán

México

Cuernavaca   5

Puebla

7

Morelos

Puebla

MEXICO

Guerrero

Oaxaca

ACAPULCO

**Central
Mexico**

PACIFIC OCEAN

MEXICO CITY & CENTRAL MEXICO

The great melting pot of Mexican culture, Mexico City combines a vibrant street-food scene with the country's most celebrated haute-cuisine. Around the capital, several towns such as Guadalajara and Puebla have developed their own proudly distinctive local flavours

SOPA SECA DE NATAS
Crepes in creamy tomato sauce
page 12

SOPA TARASCA
Michoacán-style tortilla soup
page 16

TACOS DE JAMAICA
Hibiscus tacos
page 22

TOSTADAS DE ATÚN
Tuna tostadas
page 26

TACOS AL PASTOR
Marinated pork tacos
page 30

CHILAQUILES EN SALSA DE FRIJOL
Fried tortillas in bean sauce
page 34

CHALUPAS DE CAMARÓN CONFITADO
Shrimp confit chalupas
page 40

ESQUITES CON TUÉTANO
Fried corn kernels with bone marrow
page 44

CARNE EN SU JUGO
Meat in its juices
page 48

CHILE EN NOGADA
Stuffed poblano pepper in walnut sauce
page 52

LECHÓN CONFITADO CON SALSA TATEMADA
Suckling pig confit with tatemada sauce
page 56

JERICALLA
Guadalajara-style custard
page 60

SOPA SECA DE NATAS

Crepes in creamy tomato sauce

Nicos chef Gerardo Vazquez is passionate about preserving Mexico's culinary traditions and it shows in his sopa seca de natas, an exceedingly rare lasagne-like crepe dish, an intriguing marriage of Mexican and French flavours.

If it weren't for Mexico City restaurant Nicos, an old French-Mexican entrée known as sopa seca de natas could well find itself in danger of extinction. Chef Gerardo Vazquez, a pioneer of Mexico's slow-food movement, simply wants to give the dish the exposure it deserves.

'I am the only one who has put sopa seca de natas in a restaurant. It's important because many Mexican recipes have faded into obscurity, they go out of style and get lost along the way.'

The recipe comes from French nuns working in the kitchen at Guadalajara's Capuchinas Convent in the mid-19th century, around the time of the French intervention in Mexico. Fast forward about six decades, as the Mexican Revolution is winding down, and Vazquez's grandmother is hired as kitchen staff, and it's there where she learns the recipe for sopa seca de natas, which she would pass along to Vazquez's mother, Nicos' founder Maria Elena Lugo.

Sopa seca de natas is essentially a tropicalised, savoury version of French-inspired crepe cakes. Poblano chile pepper slices and shredded chicken are sandwiched between layers of paper-thin crepes, then the dish is oven-baked in a creamy tomato sauce. Natas refers to the cream obtained from boiling raw milk, but mascarpone cream works as an acceptable substitute.

Architect-turned-chef Vazquez has deep respect for Mexico's culinary traditions. Thanks in part to his advocacy efforts, in 2010 Mexico became the first country ever to have its cuisine recognised by Unesco as an intangible cultural heritage of humanity. Sopa seca de natas is just one of many important culinary traditions being kept alive at Nicos. Menu items also include seasonal *escamoles* (ant larva) and edible flowers, both of which have pre-Hispanic roots, and the restaurant buys some of its produce from *chinampas* (raised gardens along canals), a farming practice that dates back to the Aztec era.

Chef //
Gerardo Vazquez
Location //
Nicos, Mexico City

SOPA SECA DE NATAS
Crepes in creamy tomato sauce

Serves 8

Preparation & cooking time 2hr 50min

For the crepes
240ml (8½fl oz) milk
5 eggs
230g (8oz) flour
butter, as needed

For the sauce
1kg (2¼lb) tomatoes
240ml (8½fl oz) cream from boiled raw
    milk (or mascarpone cream)
salt, to taste

For the filling
½ chicken breast
¼ white onion
3 coriander (cilantro) sprigs
salt, to taste
4 poblano chile peppers

For baking
115g (4oz) butter, cut in small cubes

1   Preheat the oven to 200°C/390°F.

2   To make the crepes, mix the milk, eggs and flour in a bowl, then let rest for 30 minutes.

3   Heat a small pan with butter and pour a thin layer of batter into the pan. Cook over medium heat for one or two minutes, then flip the crepe. Repeat this process until you have no more batter. Set aside crepes in a container covered with a damp cloth.

4   For the sauce, boil the tomatoes until they are soft, then drain the water, blitz the tomatoes with a blender/liquidiser and strain the sauce into a pot. Over medium heat, reduce the sauce to a puree.

5   Blend two ladles of the tomato puree with the cream then add the rest of the puree, salt to taste and blend again. Set aside the sauce.

6   For the filling, boil the chicken breast for 45 minutes with the onion, coriander and salt to taste. Remove the chicken from the stock, let it cool, then shred it.

7   Char the poblano chiles directly over a stovetop flame then place them in a plastic bag and let rest for 10 minutes. Remove the chiles from the bag and peel the skin, remove the seeds and stems and cut the chiles into thin slices.

8   Coat a 25cm (10in)-long baking pan with butter. Spread some sauce on the bottom of the pan and cover with one layer of crepes.

9   Spread some sauce on the first crepe and top with chicken and poblano chile slices and add another layer. Continue the same process with each layer, then pour over the remaining sauce and evenly distribute the butter cubes over the top.

10   Bake for 1 hour or until browned on top. Cut into eight portions and serve.

SOPA TARASCA
Michoacán-style tortilla soup

This hearty tortilla soup from the central western state of Michoacán is a nod, even in name alone, to the rich heritage of a vast region once known as the Tarascan State.

Michoacán's lovely lakeside town of Pátzcuaro is known first and foremost for its colourful Day of the Dead festivities, but it's also the birthplace of sopa tarasca (tarascan soup in gringo-speak). The story begins with Rafael Garcia Correa, aka 'don Rafa', a cook working in Pátzcuaro's Gran Hotel in the 1960s.

Don Rafa wanted to create a dish with affordable and accessible ingredients, so he came up with a tomato-based tortilla soup. Little did he know that his concoction would become downright legendary. Nowadays sopa tarasca is a quintessential menu item at markets, diners and even up-market restaurants throughout Michoacán.

Lu Cocina Michoacana, 58km (36 miles) northeast of Pátzcuaro in downtown Morelia, does one of the finest tarascan soups around. More specifically it's a 'conde-style' soup, meaning it's made with a tomato and pureed bean base to go along with the tortilla strips, pasilla chile pepper, avocado and sour cream. The hot soup base is poured into the bowl right at your table, allowing the fried tortilla to keep its crispy texture.

Don Rafa would have been proud to know that the ingredients that go into the sopa tarasca here have remained the same for more than a decade. 'What we've been doing is modifying the dish with new techniques,' says Morelia-born head chef Lucero Soto, 'but always doing so with respect for the original elements that go into a sopa tarasca. The recipe has evolved, but the only thing that has really changed over the years is the presentation.'

In addition to its exquisite soup, Lu Cocina Michoacana's privileged location makes the experience even more memorable. Housed in Hotel Casino, an 18th-century neoclassical building that was once, in fact, home to a swanky casino, the restaurant lies in the middle of a historic centre so well preserved that it was declared a Unesco World Heritage site.

Chef //
Lucero Soto
Location //
Lu Cocina Michoacana,
Morelia

SOPA TARASCA
Michoacán-style tortilla soup

Serves 4

Preparation & cooking time 2hr 20min, not including overnight soaking

200g (7oz) pinto beans, soaked overnight
710ml (24fl oz) water, to cook the beans
2 cloves garlic
30g (1oz) onion, whole
20ml (⅔fl oz) vegetable oil, for oiling the pot
1 chicken breast with skin
100g (3½oz) onion, for the chicken broth, chopped
50g (1¾oz) celery, chopped
50g (1¾oz) carrot, chopped
pinch of thyme
pinch of marjoram
1 sprig coriander (cilantro), for chicken broth
1L (1¾pt) water, for the chicken broth
3 large pasilla chile peppers
¼ white onion, chopped
1 Roma tomato, whole
120ml (4fl oz) water, for boiling tomato
10ml (⅓fl oz) vegetable oil, for sautéeing
    beans & broth
salt, to taste
1 sprig coriander, whole, for beans & broth
1 sprig epazote, whole (optional)
200ml (6¾fl oz) vegetable oil, for frying tortillas
3 corn tortillas, cut into strips
30g (1oz) avocado, sliced, to serve
90ml (3fl oz) sour cream, to serve
90g (3¼oz) Cotija cheese (or feta)

1 Cover the beans with water and soak overnight. Drain and reserve.

2 Cook beans in a pressure cooker with 710ml of water, one of the whole garlic cloves and 30g of onion for 40 minutes or until tender. (If using a covered saucepan, it will take approx. 2 hours.) Remove the garlic and onion when the beans are done.

3 For the broth, add oil to a large pot then sear the chicken breast, 100g of onion, celery, carrot, thyme, marjoram and a sprig of coriander for 10 minutes, then add the litre of water, cover the pot and cook for 30 minutes. Strain the broth and set aside. (Rather than discard the chicken breast, you can shred it and serve separately atop tostadas or in tacos.)

4 Take one of the pasilla peppers and remove the stem and devein, then chop the ¼ onion and the remaining garlic clove. Cut the remaining two peppers lengthwise, giving you four half peppers. Set them aside.

5 Fry chopped onion until translucent, then add garlic and the one deveined pepper and sauté over medium heat, being careful not to burn.

6 Boil the whole tomato in 120ml of water for five minutes or until soft.

7   In a liquidiser/blender, blitz the tomato and its broth with 240ml (8fl oz) chicken broth from step 3, the one pasilla pepper, the onion and garlic mixture from step 5, and the cooked beans.

8   Pour this mixture along with 10ml vegetable oil into a pot and sauté for three minutes, then add the remaining chicken broth. Salt to taste and add a sprig of coriander and a sprig of epazote. Boil for 30 minutes then remove the coriander and epazote sprigs.

9   Preheat a pan with 200ml vegetable oil to medium heat, fry the tortilla strips until crispy then remove from the pan to a paper towel.

10 To serve, pour soup base into a bowl and add tortilla strips, a half pasilla pepper, several avocado slices, and top with a dollop of sour cream and 1 tbsp of crumbled cheese.

TACOS DE JAMAICA
Hibiscus tacos

Tacos de jamaica, a crunchy sweet appetizer made from repurposed hibiscus flowers, have long been popular in rural Mexico – but it's Alejandro Piñon who really put his rolled tacos on the culinary map.

If you've ever tried really good tacos de jamaica, like those at Corazón de Maguey in southern Mexico City, it's hard to understand why anyone would ever discard hibiscus sepals (the blossom's outermost leaves) after making agua de jamaica, a refreshing hibiscus-flavoured water. And yet that's exactly what happens in many places, especially in Mexico's large urban areas. The crimson-coloured sepals are boiled, strained from the water and tossed away.

In provincial Mexico, however, nothing goes to waste. If you make hibiscus water, a beverage rich in antioxidants and vitamin C, you'll probably be eating hibiscus tacos later, or at the very least a delectable jelly or sauce made from the remains.

Alejandro Piñon, former head chef at Corazón de Maguey, calls it *cocina de reciclaje* (repurposed food) and says it's a common practice in low-income Mexican households to reuse ingredients for more than one dish. In recent years it has become increasingly common to take dishes of rural origins, such as tacos de jamaica (hibiscus is known as Jamaican sorrel), and adopt them for an urban culinary scene.

Piñon's unique version of the tacos includes hydrated hibiscus, shredded jicama and carrot, which are rolled into a corn tortilla and fried. They are then topped with sour cream and a spicy green salsa, which provide just the right contrast with the sweet filling.

The idea was to create a dish that pairs well with mezcal, a distilled alcoholic agave drink served at Corazón de Maguey and sister restaurant Los Danzantes. So Piñon came up with a trifecta of ingredients from the central western state of Michoacán, where the best hibiscus grows.

'In Michoacán, you have the hibiscus, agave and native corn (used for tortillas) all growing in the same soil and there's an intangible synergy going on between the three. You notice it especially in the mezcal, which is a very spiritual drink.'

Chef //
Alejandro Piñon
Location //
Corazón de Maguey, Mexico City
(current chef Israel Gonzalez)

TACOS DE JAMAICA
Hibiscus tacos

Serves 12 as an appetizer

Preparation & cooking time 1 hour

50g (1¾oz) hydrated hibiscus
1½L (2½pt) water
vegetable oil, for frying
10g (⅓oz) white onion, finely chopped
1 clove garlic, chopped
20g (¾oz) carrot, shredded
20g (¾oz) jicama, shredded
pinch of thyme
1 whole allspice, ground
30ml (1fl oz) white vinegar
½tsp brown sugar
salt, to taste
6 corn tortillas

For the topping
4 leaves romaine lettuce, shredded
2 tbsp sour cream
½ avocado, thinly sliced
½ tomato, chopped

For the salsa verde
16 green tomatoes
6 jalapeño peppers
¼ white onion
½ garlic clove

1 Boil the hibiscus in a pan with 1½L of water for 10 minutes or until the water turns dark red, then drain.

2 In a pan, preheat the oil and sauté the onion for several minutes, then add the garlic.

3 Add the carrot and jicama to the pan and cook for three minutes over high heat.

4 Add the hibiscus and stir in the thyme, allspice, vinegar and cook for eight minutes, adding the sugar last, then salt to taste.

5 Roll each of the corn tortillas with about 15g (½oz) of filling and insert toothpicks on both ends to hold the rolled tacos together while frying.

6 Fry the rolled tacos in oil until golden brown, then cut in half and remove the toothpicks.

7 Puree all the salsa verde ingredients in a blender.

8 Top the tacos with lettuce, sour cream, avocado slices, tomato and serve with the salsa verde.

TOSTADAS DE ATÚN

Tuna tostadas

Gabriela Cámara's tostadas de atún, a citrus-cured tuna appetizer made famous at her buzzy Mexico City restaurant Contramar, have revolutionised the culinary scene, sparking an unprecedented raw fish craze in Mexico's landlocked capital.

Chef //
Gabriela Cámara
Location //
Contramar, Mexico City

Contramar's revered tuna tostadas bring together Mexican and Japanese influences and the balance is sublime. Crunchy corn tostadas are spread with a chipotle-mayo sauce and topped with sashimi-grade marinated tuna, avocado slices and crispy leeks.

When Gabriela Cámara launched Contramar in the up-and-coming Roma neighbourhood in 1998, the only places serving raw tuna at the time were Japanese restaurants and one up-market seafood establishment offering a version of the fish on a rice cracker.

Cámara recalls the tuna tostada lightbulb moment very well. She was eating at a thatched-roof seafood restaurant on the Pacific Coast when she thought, 'Why not make a remixed Mexican interpretation of a raw fish dish?' And the rest is history.

Much like her longtime mentor, Mexico cookbook guru Diana Kennedy, Cámara has an affinity for simple recipes. And yet, in all its simplicity, the tuna tostada dish has changed the way many people eat fish in Mexico City. Before Contramar, Cámara recalls, many people would trek out to the beach or pull up a stool at a market stall for the raw fish experience, but now pretty much any mid-range seafood joint worth its salt has some form of a sashimi or ceviche tostada. Contramar's is still the best, though, and the restaurant's soothing maritime decor transports you to the Pacific Coast, where the idea for the dish was conceived.

The type of tuna at Contramar changes from time to time, depending on what the fishmongers are offering (i.e. albacore or yellowfin), but product quality remains the one constant. And therein lies the secret. Says Cámara, 'It has everything that a good recipe should have, which is contrast in texture and consistency with the crispy leeks and avocado, it's unctuous on the mouth, there's acidity but it's comforting. But the main thing is that it's consistently good-quality fish.'

TOSTADAS DE ATÚN
Tuna tostadas

Serves 4 tostadas

Preparation & cooking time 25min

200g (7oz) sashimi-grade tuna
94ml (3¼fl oz) soy sauce
32ml (1fl oz) orange juice
25g (1oz) leeks
250ml (8½fl oz) vegetable oil
37g (1⅓oz) mayonnaise
8g (⅓oz) chipotle chile, chopped
½ tbsp chives, chopped
1 package of store-bought tostadas
40g (1½oz) avocado, sliced, to serve

1   Thinly slice the tuna, then mix the soy sauce and orange juice and marinate the tuna in it for no more than 10 minutes.

2   Cut leeks lengthwise into thin 5cm (2in)-long strips using the pale part of the leek. Discard the dark green parts and the root end of the leeks.

3   Fry the leeks in vegetable oil in a pan over medium heat until crispy and golden brown. Remove from the pan and place on a plate lined with absorbent paper towel.

4   Blend mayonnaise, chipotle and chives for a creamy sauce.

5   Spread mayo-chipotle sauce on corn tostadas and top each with two or three slices of the tuna.

6   Top with fried leeks and avocado slices.

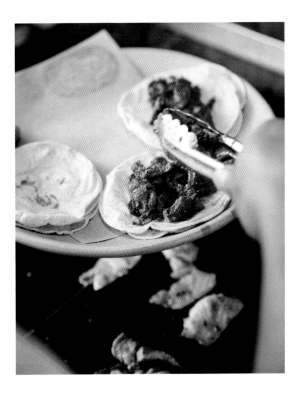

TACOS AL PASTOR
Marinated pork tacos

Spit-grilled marinated pork tacos have been popular in Central Mexico since the 1950s, and now Daniel Ovadía and Salvador Orozco have upped the stakes with a savoury take on the fast food staple at their Cuernavaca restaurant.

Al pastor (marinated pork) tacos, quite possibly Central Mexico's favourite snack food, owe their success to Lebanese immigrants who brought the concept of the shawarma (doner kebab) to Mexico in the 1930s. Much like the shawarma, layered meat is grilled on a vertical rotisserie (called a *trompo*), but Mexicans use pork rather than lamb or chicken.

It's pretty clear that today's al pastor looks more like a taco than a shawarma, with corn tortillas replacing pita bread, and spicy chile-based salsas taking the place of, say, tahini sauce. Even the marinade, usually made with achiote and chile, is very Mexican and has little to do with recipes introduced by Lebanese immigrants back in the day.

Open-air Paragüero stands out as probably the first restaurant to invent spit-roasted poc chuc, also a marinated pork taco but seasoned with a Yucatán-style *recado* (spice mixture, see p252) and topped with pickled onions.

Paragüero's chefs Ovadía and Orozco, partners in 10 Mexico restaurants, including Mexico City's trendy Nudo Negro, have taken al pastor to another level. The tacos are prepared on handmade tortillas and a high-quality pork is marinated overnight, allowing the meat to retain its moistness while it's rotated on the spit. Once the al pastor is grilled, the taquero slices down the meat onto a warmed tortilla. Then you top the fragrant pork with chopped coriander, diced onion, refreshingly sweet pineapple chunks and salsa taquera for a zesty kick. Good tacos al pastor should never be dry.

So what's the secret behind making great tacos al pastor? 'We make the marinade more aromatic than what you find at taquerias,' Ovadía says. 'We use cinnamon, oregano, fresh orange and pineapple juice, and the pork should always be marinated overnight to tenderise the meat. We basically do a taqueria-style presentation but it's our own interpretation.'

Chef //
Daniel Ovadía &
Salvador Orozco
Location //
Paragüero, Morelos

TACOS AL PASTOR
Marinated pork tacos

Makes 18–20 small tacos

Preparation & cooking time 1hr, not including overnight marinating

For the marinade

100ml (3½fl oz) fresh orange juice
100ml (3½fl oz) fresh pineapple juice
15g (½oz) Guajillo chile
100g (3½oz) achiote powder
5g (¼oz) garlic, chopped
100g (3½ oz) white onion, chopped
3 whole peppercorns
1 cinnamon stick
pinch of oregano
10ml (⅓fl oz) white vinegar
30g (1oz) lard
1kg (2¼lb) pork leg, preferably with fat,
    cut to ½cm fillets

For the salsa taquera

100g (3½oz) jalapeño chile
40g (1½ oz) white onion
5g (¼oz) garlic
150ml (5¼fl oz) vegetable oil
150ml (5¼fl oz) water
salt, to taste
pepper, to taste
100g (3½oz) avocado

For the tacos

¼ pineapple, chopped
½ onion, diced
1 bunch of coriander (cilantro), chopped
20 small 'taquero-style' corn tortillas

1 Devein the chile, removing the seeds. Bring a saucepan of water to a boil and add the chile, boiling for 10 minutes.

2 Remove the chile from the saucepan and blend with all the marinade ingredients, except the lard and pork.

3 In a pot, combine the lard and marinade mixture and cook over a medium heat for 20 minutes, stirring constantly. Strain when done and set aside.

4 Submerge ½cm (¼in)-thick pork fillets in the marinade and let sit overnight.

5 For the salsa, boil the chile, onion, garlic and ¼ of the oil in water for 10 minutes and let cool. Then blend the mixture with salt, pepper, remaining oil and avocado until smooth.

6 In a griddle or a grill over medium heat, cook the pork until the meat is well done and slightly charred on both sides.

7 Chop the pineapple into small chunks, dice the onion and chop the coriander.

8 Lay thinly sliced cuts of the pork onto warmed tortillas and top with onion, coriander, pineapple, and serve with salsa.

Tip

Assuming you don't have a spit at home, chef Ovadía recommends cooking the marinated meat over a grill or griddle. Be aware, though, that the marinade can burn quickly, so cook over a medium heat.

CHILAQUILES EN SALSA DE FRIJOL

Fried tortillas in bean sauce

Chef and cookbook author Ricardo Muñoz's exquisite recipe for this working-class favourite consists of fried tortillas bathed in salsa: a living legacy of ancient Mexican cooking, and quintessential comfort food.

Mexico's love affair with chilaquiles goes way back, long before the Spanish conquistadors set foot in the Americas. The word has its origins in the Aztec language Náhuatl and it essentially means *chilli* (chile), *atl* (water) and *quilitl* (green herb). The Aztecs would break hardened corn tortilla wedges into a spicy sauce loaded with fresh greens or herbs, and presto: there you have the genesis of chilaquiles.

'The Aztecs had primarily a vegetarian diet. The tortillas were stored and they became hard like tostadas, however, the concept of frying something didn't exist in Mexico back then. Part of what went into the salsa was *epazote* (Mexican tea), which we know has been around since ancient times,' says chef Muñoz, author of the *Larousse Encyclopedic Dictionary of Mexican Gastronomy*.

Of course, what you get at most places nowadays is a far cry from the Aztecs' recipe. Fried tortillas have replaced greens as the dish's main ingredient, and toppings usually include cream, crumbled cheese, sliced onion, and egg or chicken, making it a more protein-heavy rendition.

Chilaquiles remain highly valued in Mexican society, mostly because the dish makes use of leftover tortillas, so it's both practical and affordable.

Muñoz's Azul Histórico, a downtown Mexico City restaurant occupying a lovely 17th-century colonial palace, provides a glorious backdrop to get your chilaquiles on. Several versions are available: the chilaquiles in black bean sauce or *mole* are sublime, or you can order them prepared in traditional red and green salsas. Chilaquiles made in southern and southeastern Mexico usually get the red salsa treatment, whereas folks in central and northern Mexico prefer green sauce.

If you're visiting Mexico you'll note that diehard chilaquiles aficionados swear by the piquant salsas as the ultimate hangover cure, making it a favourite breakfast or brunch item, either as a side or main dish.

Chef //
Ricardo Muñoz
Location //
Azul Histórico, Mexico City

CHILAQUILES EN SALSA DE FRIJOL
Fried tortillas in bean sauce

Serves 6

Preparation & cooking time 2hr 15min, not including overnight soaking and drying time

300g (10½oz) black beans (soaked overnight)
12 corn tortillas
1½L (3¼pt) hot water
½ white onion, cut in quarters
2 garlic cloves, slightly crushed
3 dry avocado leaves (or 6 sprigs fresh
    coriander/cilantro)
2 tsp salt
12 sprigs coriander (cilantro), for blending
    with cooked beans
350ml water (12fl oz), for blending with cooked beans
570ml (1pt) vegetable oil, for frying
12 eggs
12 tbsp Cotija cheese, to serve
6 tbsp sour cream, to serve
18 thin slices of white onion, to serve
6 coriander (cilantro) sprigs, to garnish

1 Cover the black beans with water and leave to soak overnight. Drain and set aside.

2 Cut 12 corn tortillas into 12 wedges each, giving you 144 wedges. Place tortillas on a flat surface and let dry for several hours.

3 Bring water to a boil in a pressure cooker and add the black beans, onion, garlic, avocado leaves, then cover and cook for 1 to 1½ hours (if using a covered saucepan, it's 2¼–3 hours) or until beans are tender. Carefully remove the pressure cooker lid, then add salt and boil for an additional 10 minutes. Strain the bean mixture and reserve the liquid.

4 In a blender, mix the beans with the coriander, 355ml (2½fl oz) of bean broth, and 355ml (2½fl oz) of water and blend until you get a liquid consistency that's light enough to pass through a strainer. Strain the sauce and set aside.

5 Place the bean sauce in a pot over medium heat. When it begins to boil, remove from the stove, add salt and keep warm.

Tip
The key to making chilaquiles is not to drown the tortilla in salsa, otherwise it can become a mushy mess if the fried tortilla wedges lose their crispy texture.

6   Preheat 480ml (17fl oz) of the vegetable oil in a pan for 10 minutes and fry one portion of the tortilla wedges (50g/1¾oz) at a time for four minutes or until golden brown on both sides. Remove tortilla wedges from the pan and place on a plate lined with absorbent paper towel.

7   Fry or scramble the eggs in a pan coated with the remaining vegetable oil over high heat.

8   In a large pan, bring the bean sauce to a boil and dip the fried tortillas wedges into the sauce for no more than two seconds, then quickly remove and plate the six portions. Lightly distribute the leftover sauce over each dish and top with the eggs, 2 tbsp of crumbled Cotija cheese, 1 tbsp of sour cream and three thinly sliced onions. Garnish with a coriander sprig.

CHALUPAS DE CAMARÓN CONFITADO

Shrimp confit chalupas

Chalupas are a beloved street food in culinary capital Puebla and they've been reinvented to perfection at Moyuelo, where up-and-coming chef Fernando Hernandez wows diners with a shrimp confit topping.

C halupas have all the makings of a Mexican street food hit: they're fast, cheap and full of greasy goodness. A chalupa is a tortilla fried in lard, then spread with salsa and usually topped with shredded chicken or beef, and diced onion.

The size and even the shape of the chalupa, which literally means 'canoe', varies from one place to another, and no one knows for certain how the snack got its name. The most plausible theory is that the elongated form of chalupas resemble the canoes that once plied through Central Mexico's ubiquitous canals (this particular canoe just happens to be floating in grease). In the city of Puebla, however, today's chalupas are usually made on round corn tortillas.

Chef Fernando Hernandez honed his craft working at restaurants in Spain for three years but he always dreamed of returning to his native Puebla to open his own place. So, at age 26, he launched Moyuelo, near Puebla's historic centre, which specialises in gourmet-style local faves, such as chalupas and *cemitas* (sandwiches).

He calls the chalupa a convent dish: colonial-era fare made by nuns. Corn tortilla existed long before colonial times but frying them in lard comes from the Spaniards.

'Puebla is a city with a history of many convents and with that came the convents' culinary culture, for example chalupas and chile en nogada (stuffed poblano peppers) are convent cuisine,' he says. 'Chalupas are a relatively simple dish, so we decided to reinvent them as a main dish.'

Moyuelo's chalupas come prepared on blue corn tortillas fried in grease rendered from a mixture of duck, pork and beef, making it a highly concentrated flavour. The tortilla then gets a layer of red sauce made from chipotle chile pepper and dehydrated shrimp, which pairs flawlessly with the shrimp confit and a gremolata condiment.

Chef //
Fernando Hernandez
Location //
Moyuelo, Puebla

CHALUPAS DE CAMARÓN CONFITADO
Shrimp confit chalupas

Serves 8 chalupas

Preparation & cooking time 2hr 45min

For the dried shrimp sauce

1kg (2¼lb) tomatoes
130g (4½oz) store-bought dried shrimp
150g (5¼ oz) white onion, chopped
2 tsp dried chipotle chile powder
pepper, to taste

For the pickled carrot

2 large carrots, peeled into strips
250ml (8¾fl oz) water
500ml (17fl oz) white vinegar
salt, to taste
pepper, to taste
1 tbsp thyme
1 tbsp oregano

For the gremolata

6 garlic cloves, finely chopped
15g (½oz) parsley, finely chopped
20ml (¾fl oz) extra virgin olive oil
3 lemons, zested & juiced
salt, to taste

For the shrimp

8 large shrimp
1L (1¾pt) melted lard (or, ideally, 750ml/1⅓pt melted duck fat & 250ml/8¾fl oz melted lard)

To serve

8 corn tortillas (blue tortilla, if available)
100g (3½oz) coriander (cilantro), finely chopped
½ red onion, thinly sliced
olive oil, to taste
sea salt, to taste

1 For the shrimp sauce, cook the tomato, dried shrimp and onion in a pot over a low heat until the tomato is cooked, then blend the mixture in a liquidiser/blender and strain. Season with chipotle chile powder and ground pepper to taste, then set aside.

2 To make the pickled carrot, peel long slices of carrot. Put in a pot of water over low heat with vinegar, salt, pepper and the herbs. Let the water boil for several minutes to soften the carrots, then turn off and set aside.

3 For the gremolata, mix finely chopped garlic and parsley, olive oil, lemon juice and lemon zest in a bowl. Salt to taste.

4 Sauté the shrimp in lard and duck fat (if available) over low heat until cooked. Remove the shrimps from the pan.

5 Use the same pan to fry the tortilla until puffed up and crisp, adding additional lard as needed, then remove from the pan and spread the shrimp sauce (from step 1) onto the tortilla.

6 Place the sautéed shrimp on the tortillas and top with the gremolata and the pickled carrots. Add coriander, onion and finish with several drops of olive oil and a sprinkle of salt.

ESQUITES CON TUÉTANO

Fried corn kernels with bone marrow

Street stalls selling esquites (corn kernels) abound in Mexico's capital but few are as wildly popular as Esquites Don Josué, where locals brave a long line for a maize fix.

Josué Maya's street stand in the Mexico City neighbourhood of Álamos does a roaring trade in esquites – a line often swings around the corner and the wait can take up to an hour for a cup o' corn. After more than 40 years in the *esquites* business, 'don Josué' (as he's fondly known) and his wife Santa churn out up to 100kg (220lb) of corn on a good night.

Maize, aka corn, has been around in Mexico for some 10,000 years when it was domesticated by indigenous farmers. To refer to maize in Mexico as simply a grain or a staple would be a huge understatement – a mythical creationist tale of the ancient Maya speaks of humans moulded out of cornmeal, and to this day corn remains an essential part of Mexicans' historical, cultural and spiritual identity.

'For us maize is the food of our ancestors and there are still parts in Mexico where the only thing people eat is maize. Perhaps they have it with salt, or a little salsa, but in some humble households that's all they eat,' says Maya, whose thriving esquites business lifted his family out of poverty.

Esquites comes from the Náhuatl word *izquitl*, which means toasted corn, but most esquites prepared in Mexico City nowadays involve frying shaved corn kernels in oil or lard. The key to making good esquites or corn on the cob, another of don Josué's popular menu items, is finding tender corn and making sure the kernels do not get undercooked. His standard esquites come topped with mayonnaise, chile powder, lime juice and crumbled cheese, but regulars usually opt for the esquites prepared with *pollo* (chicken), *longaniza* (sausage), *huitlacoche* (corn smut), *hongos* (mushrooms), or the star attraction, *tuétano* (bone marrow). So, essentially, you get a two-course meal in a cup for less than US$2, and a mighty tasty one at that.

Chef //
Josué Maya & Santa Loreto
Location //
Esquites Don Josué, Mexico City

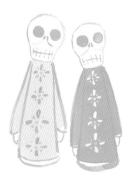

ESQUITES CON TUÉTANO
Fried corn kernels with bone marrow

Serves 4

Preparation & cooking time 55min

6 ears of corn, preferably of a native variety
4 tbsp epazote leaves, chopped (optional)
50ml (1½fl oz) vegetable oil
4 beef bones with marrow
2L (4¼pt) water
3 chile de árbol (tree chile), chopped (or cayenne
    pepper, if unavailable)
salt, to taste
4 tbsp mayonnaise
2 limes, juiced
50g (1¾oz) Cotija cheese, crumbled
2 tbsp chile powder, preferably Tajín brand

1 Shuck the corn, remove the silks and cut the corn kernels from the cob.

2 Preheat the oil in a pan and fry the corn kernels over medium heat for 15 minutes or until tender, stirring constantly.

3 Add the epazote when the corn is tender.

4 Boil beef bones for 15 minutes in 2L of water, reserve the beef broth.

5 Extract marrow by inserting a spoon into each bone's soft centre and pushing the marrow out. Add the marrow to the corn kernels along with 250ml (8½fl oz) of the beef broth.

6 Add chopped chile de árbol and salt to taste.

7 Spoon the kernels into large cups and top with mayonnaise, lime juice, crumbled cheese and a sprinkle of chile powder.

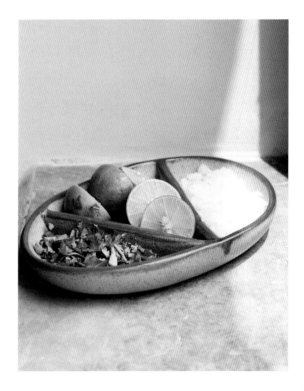

CARNE EN SU JUGO
Meat in its juices

From a small street stall in the 1970s, Karne Garibaldi has morphed into a giant on the local culinary scene, thanks to this highly coveted brothy beef dish and the family's lightning-quick service.

L
ike many successful Mexican restaurants, Karne Garibaldi's story begins on the street. Founder Nestor Flores recalls that first day when he had just four small tables on a footpath and simmered about 15kg (33lb) of beef to prepare what would become his classic carne en su jugo (chopped beef, whole beans and crispy bacon in broth). How times have changed – Garibaldi's six restaurant locations now churn out about 500kg (1100lb) of beef every day!

Since the early years, out of sheer necessity the family-run restaurant has relied on a service so quick that it puts fast food restaurants to shame. 'We built the first restaurant in the early 1970s but it was never big enough for the growing demand, and that's why the service has always been fast, so that the clients wouldn't have to wait long for a table,' says Flores.

We're talking really fast: in 1996 Karne Garibaldi landed a spot in the Guinness Book of World Records for the speediest service ever (13.5 seconds from kitchen to table). Has the record been exploited for marketing purposes? Absolutely, but, quite frankly, the food speaks for itself. The brothy carne en su jugo is served with a zesty salsa, Garibaldi's very own fiery refried beans and corn chips, making this one of the most definitive Guadalajara meals. The beans, made with lard, corn kernels, serrano chile pepper and sea salt, have won over so many customers that Karne Garibaldi now packages and sells the beans to supermarkets.

Karne Garibaldi unquestionably has played a leading role in Guadalajara's carne en su jugo boom, but it does not claim to have invented the dish. Credit for that (in Jalisco state) goes to Juan José Gálvez, aka 'el gallo' (the rooster), who created it in 1965. Flores says he can't even take full credit for Karne Garibaldi's version. 'To be honest, the recipe is my father's, he was a great chef, and that's how all this began.'

Chef //
Nestor Flores
Location //
Karne Garibaldi, Guadalajara

CARNE EN SU JUGO

Meat in its juices

Serves 4

Preparation & cooking time 40min (not including soaking time for beans, if required)

400g (14oz) whole pinto beans
6 slices bacon, chopped
1kg (2lb) beef sirloin, cut into 1cm x 1cm (½in x ½in) pieces
salt & pepper, to taste
2.7L (4¾pt) water
4 small green tomatoes
2 serrano chile peppers
1 garlic clove
2 chicken bouillon/stock cubes
½ white onion, diced, to serve
4 tsp coriander (cilantro), finely chopped, to serve
corn tortillas, to serve

1 If you don't have a pressure cooker, cover the beans with water and soak overnight.

2 Fry the bacon in a pan until crisp and place on a plate lined with an absorbent paper towel. Set aside. Use the same pan (slightly coated with bacon grease) to sear the beef until the meat is browned. Season with salt and pepper to taste.

3 In a pressure cooker, cook two cups of whole pinto beans in 2L of the water for 30 to 40 minutes, or until tender. (Alternatively you can cook in a saucepan, but it will take 2–2½ hours.) Set aside, keeping the broth.

4 Boil the tomatoes, serrano chile peppers and garlic in a pot with the remaining 700ml of water and 2 chicken bouillon/stock cubes for 10 minutes, then liquefy all ingredients in a blender.

5 Strain the mixture into the pressure cooker with the seared beef and its juice

6 Cook the beef in the pressure cooker over medium heat until it reaches operating pressure, then immediately reduce to low heat and cook for 30 minutes. (If using a covered saucepan, cook the meat for 60–75 minutes.)

7 To the beef and its juices, add the whole beans and their broth, chopped onion and coriander, and top with the crispy bacon pieces. Serve in a concave dish or bowl alongside corn tortillas.

CHILE EN NOGADA

Stuffed poblano pepper in walnut sauce

This dish's vibrant red, white and green presentation bears the colours of the Mexican flag; after all, it was chile en nogada that was ceremoniously served to celebrate Mexico's independence from Spain.

Hailing from culinary capital Puebla (also the birthplace of *mole*), the chile en nogada consists of a poblano chile pepper stuffed with ground meat, fruit and nuts, then bathed in a rich walnut sauce topped with pomegranate seeds. It requires a serious commitment in the kitchen but it's well worth the effort.

The most famous of all chiles en nogada, but probably not the first, was prepared by Augustinian nuns for Mexican General Agustín de Iturbide in 1821 to honour Mexico's independence from Spain – the same time that Mexico was flying its newly minted tricolour flag. The flag's colours ae represented by the green pepper, white walnut sauce and red pomegranate seeds.

After de Iturbide helped to defeat the Spanish, a lavish banquet was held in his honour at the Episcopal Palace of Puebla, an imposing complex that once encompassed an entire city block of the present-day historic centre. 'It's said that the chile was prepared as a dessert dish for a 13-course banquet on that occasion,' says Liz Galicia, chef at El Mural de los Poblanos, a chile en nogada institution. El Mural de los Poblanos sits pretty in a 17th-century colonial building on that same city block and it keeps the culinary tradition alive by serving seasonal chiles en nogada from mid-July until the end of September. Why seasonal? While you can find the dish year round, most places resort to freezing seasonal ingredients, such as the *nuez de Castilla* (the walnuts used for the sauce).

El Mural de los Poblanos works strictly with locally sourced ingredients and that's what makes Galicia's chiles so special. 'We get everything we need from a small but very fertile land run by independent producers. That includes seasonal fruits and nuts, chile peppers and pomegranates. You can substitute the ingredients for similar products available year-round, but it's not the same.'

Foodies will drive two hours from Mexico City to Puebla just to eat these chiles, they're that good.

Chef //
Liz Galicia
Location //
El Mural de los
Poblanos, Puebla

CHILE EN NOGADA
Stuffed poblano pepper in walnut sauce

Serves 5

Preparation & cooking time 2hr 50min

For the stuffing
vegetable oil, for frying
100g (3½oz) white onion, finely chopped
20g (¾oz) garlic, finely chopped
300g (10½oz) tomato, chopped
500g (1lb) eye of round steak, minced
500g (1lb) pork shoulder, minced
salt, to taste
1kg (2¼lb) Fuji apples, peeled & cubed
1kg (2¼lb) pears, peeled & cubed
1kg (2¼lb) hard peaches, peeled & cubed
200g (7oz) almonds, peeled & chopped
200g (7oz) raisins
10g (⅓oz) cinnamon sticks
250g (9oz) sugar
400g (14oz) plantain, chopped

For the walnut sauce
650ml (1⅓pt) whole milk
300g (10½oz) peeled almonds
250g (9oz) sugar
pinch of cinnamon powder
20g (¾oz) fresh goats cheese
50ml (1¾fl oz) sherry, preferably La Ina brand
crumbs of 1 small day-old bread roll
500g (1lb) peeled walnuts, nuez de Castilla, if available
100ml (3⅓fl oz) cream

To assemble
5 poblano chile peppers
100g (3½oz) flour, plus a pinch for batter
4 eggs
10g (⅓oz) salt
250ml (8½fl oz) vegetable oil
seeds of 2 pomegranates, to garnish
parsley, to garnish

1 In a large pan of vegetable oil, fry the onion, garlic, tomato and meat over medium heat for 15 minutes. Add salt to taste and set aside.

2 Using the same pan, sauté first the apple, then add the pear, then the peach. Once the fruit is cooked, add the meat to the pan once again with the almonds, raisins and cinnamon sticks. Cook for 20 minutes, stirring constantly, then stir in the sugar and plantain. Remove the cinnamon sticks and set aside.

3 In a blender/liquidiser, blitz all of the ingredients for the walnut sauce, except the walnuts and cream. When the mixture is blended, add the walnuts but only blitz briefly; the texture should still contain small walnut pieces. Mix in the cream.

4 Roast the peppers over an open flame and place in a plastic bag for several minutes, then remove the blackened outer skin.

5 Cut a slit in each chile and devein. Spoon the stuffing into the slit, close the slit and dredge the chile in 100g of the flour.

6 For the batter, separate the egg whites and whisk them until they have a foamy texture, then add half of the yolks, pinches of flour and salt, and mix.

7 To fry the chile, dunk in the batter and cook in oil at high heat until golden brown. Place on a paper towel to absorb excess oil, then spoon over the walnut sauce and top with pomegranate seeds and a few leaves of parsley on each chile to garnish.

LECHÓN CONFITADO CON SALSA TATEMADA

Suckling pig confit with tatemada sauce

Chef Eduardo Garcia's menu often changes daily, but the one constant is suckling pig confit with tatemada sauce – a fairly simple recipe, yet its unctuous texture and flavour is anything but simple.

If you like carnitas (deep-fried pork), and who among carnivores doesn't, you'll love Máximo Bistrot's street food-inspired suckling pig confit with tatemada sauce. Pork legs are roasted at a low temperature for eight hours in lard and served with guacamole and a charred tomato-chile sauce.

'It comes from the idea of Mexican carnitas but it uses a more tender pork and the French technique of slow-cooking meat in its own grease,' says chef Garcia. 'And you always see carnitas eaten with lime and salsa, and that's because you need the acidity of the tomato and spiciness of the chile to neutralise the grease in your mouth.'

After the suckling pig is cooked it's placed skin-side down in an oven pan for about 10 minutes to make it crispy on the outside, while it remains delightfully succulent on the inside.

Before opening his acclaimed French-Mexican restaurant, Garcia honed his cooking skills at one of Mexico's finest (and deemed one of the world's 50 best) contemporary restaurants, Pujol, under the tutelage of famed chef Enrique Olvera. Now with several restaurants in Mexico City, Garcia has joined the ranks of Mexico's top chefs.

It's been a long climb to the top for Garcia, who recalls working the fields in the US at the age of 14 with his parents, both migrant workers hailing from the northern central state of Guanajuato. Before joining Olvera at Pujol, Garcia worked at the Michelin-starred New York French restaurant, Le Bernardin.

What makes recipes like the suckling pig confit truly remarkable is Garcia's ability to combine his classic French training with everyday eating experiences in Mexico. At a young age he got his first taste of salsa *tatemada* in his rural hometown and the 'simple and delicious' flavour left such a lasting impression that it remains an essential component of one of his signature dishes.

Chef //
Eduardo Garcia
Location //
Máximo Bistrot Local,
Mexico City

LECHÓN CONFITADO CON SALSA TATEMADA

Suckling pig confit with tatemada sauce

Serves 4

Preparation & cooking time 8hr 35min

For the suckling pig confit

2 rear suckling pig legs, cut in halves
2kg (4½lb) lard, melted
½ white onion, cut in large pieces
2 carrots, whole
1 garlic clove, cut in large chunks
1 bouquet garni of thyme, parsley and laurel
2 cloves
4 whole peppercorns
1 whole allspice

For the salsa tatemada

4 Roma tomatoes
2 serrano chile peppers
salt, to taste

For the guacamole

2 avocados
½ serrano chile pepper, finely chopped
1 lime, juiced
1 tbsp ground sea salt
parsley, to garnish

1 Preheat oven to 90°C/195°F.

2 Place all the ingredients for the suckling pig confit in a large pan, making sure that the legs are completely submerged in the lard. Cook for eight hours, turning the heat down to 85°C/185°F then remove from the oven.

3 Preheat the oven to 180°C/350°F.

4 For the salsa *tatemada*, in a pan char four tomatoes and two serrano chile peppers over high heat for five to 10 minutes or until both sides are blackened. Grind the tomatoes and chiles in a mortar or alternatively use a blender. Add salt to taste.

5 For the guacamole, mash avocados in a glass bowl with chopped serrano pepper. Add lime juice and salt.

6 Place the previously cooked pig legs in an oven-safe pan and return them to the oven to cook skin-side down for 10 minutes or until skin is crisp. Do not cook with the lard.

7 Serve on a plate with the salsa *tatemada* and guacamole, and garnish with a few leaves of parsley.

JERICALLA
Guadalajara-style custard

Guadalajara may be the home of mariachi music but it's also the birthplace of jericalla. The go-to spot for this custard dessert is Kamilos 333, where the recipe has been handed down for three generations.

Jericalla is the accidental creation of a nun working in the kitchen of a Guadalajara orphanage in the 19th century. The story goes that she aimed to make a kid-friendly, high-protein dessert, something that would provide nutritional value for the ailing orphans. So she whipped up an egg-laden custard, but the distractions in a busy kitchen are many, and when she pulled out the custard cups from the oven she found them slightly burnt on top. Much to her delight, however, the hardened golden brown layer provided just the right texture and colour contrast with the creamy, tan custard base. Of course, never did she imagine that eventually this would become Guadalajara's most emblematic dessert dish.

The origin of the name jericalla remains unclear. Some say it comes from a nickname given to the nun (la jericallas). Others believe it's derived from the nun's birthplace, said to be Jérica, in the Castellón province of Spain.

Jericalla is similar to flan or crème brûlée, but there are notable differences, says Kamilos co-owner and jericalla guru Larissa Camarena. 'Jericalla isn't as sweet and it usually calls for more eggs, so flan has a more solid consistency. Also, for flan you caramelise the sugar but you don't do that with jericalla.' Camarena's recipe comes from her grandma. Her mother calls it a 'rustic' version, because unlike some jericallas, it's not overly sweet.

Kamilos has been in business for four decades and takes you back to the Guadalajara of yesteryear, with its simple furnishings and antique wall decorations, some older than jericalla itself. It's also known for its *carne en su jugo* (meat in its juices, see p48), another classic Guadalajara dish that should not be missed. You can't get a more *tapatío* (Guadalajaran) meal than a brothy carne en su jugo followed by a chilled jericalla.

Co-owner //
Larissa Camarena
Location //
Kamilos 333, Guadalajara

JERICALLA
Guadalajara-style custard

Serves 12

Preparation & cooking time 1hr 35min, not including cooling time

2L (4¼pt) milk
600g (1⅓lb) sugar
1 vanilla bean or 10ml (⅓fl oz) vanilla extract
8 eggs
water, for baking

1 Preheat the oven to 200°C/390°F.

2 In a saucepan, bring the milk, sugar and vanilla to a boil and cook over medium heat for three minutes.

3 Allow to cool for 25 minutes, then place in the refrigerator.

4 Once cool, mix with eggs, then spoon the mixture into glass custard cups.

5 Pour 2cm (¾in) of water into a large 5cm (2in)-high baking pan. Place the custard cups in the pan and bake in a water bath for 30 minutes or until golden brown on top.

6 Remove from the oven, allow to cool and refrigerate before serving.

Oaxaca

Jalatlaco

La Paz

3

11

5

1

Juárez

6

Morelos

García Vigil

Alcalá

OAXACA

Ubjo

Vasconcelos

Independencia

Morelos

4

Hidalgo

Independencia

Centro

10

Unidad
Modelo

Hidalgo

Post

12

Bustamante

Reforma

Etla

Oaxaca

MEXICO

San Lorenzo
Cacaotepec

Santa Maria
Atzompa

See Enlargement

7

8

Santa Lucía
del Camino

San Francisco Tutla

13

OAXACA

Santa Maria
del Tule

Teotitlán
del Valle

Huajuapan

Cuilápan

Zaachila

Coyotepec

Santa Cruz Papalutia

Tlacolula de
Matamoros

OAXACA

This southern state of Mexico is famed for its unique dishes. Greatest renown belongs to its many moles, along with its regional chile peppers, herbs, chocolate, and the potent liquor mezcal

SOPA DE TORTILLA
Tortilla soup
page 66

MOLOTES
Corn-based fritters stuffed with potato and meat
page 72

GARNACHAS
Mini tortillas with meat, salsa, cheese & pickled cabbage
page 78

EMPANADA DE FLOR DE CALABAZA
Pastry parcel with cheese & courgette/ zucchini flowers
page 84

TLAYUDA
Giant tortilla with topping
page 88

ENCHILADAS DE SAN PEDRO TOTOLAPAM
Meat-filled tortillas with chile sauce
page 94

CERDO DE RELLENO
Stuffed pork loin, potatoes & chayote
page 100

CHILEAJO MIXTECO
Chile-garlic mole (sauce) from Mixteca
page 104

PASTEL DE ELOTE
Corn cake
page 108

BUÑUELOS DE CHOCOLATE Y CHILE PASILLA
Chocolate- & chile-spiked buñuelos
page 112

NIEVES DE MEZCAL
Ice cream–sorbet
page 118

AGUA FRESCA: LIMÓN CON CHIA
Lime & chia seed cordial
page 122

CHOCOLATE OAXAQUEÑA
Oaxacan hot chocolate
page 126

SOPA DE TORTILLA

Tortilla soup

This tomato broth, with fried tortilla strips, chunks of avocado and cheese, is one of the most traditional Mexican soups, but at Los Danzantes chef Hugo Arnaud gives this old favourite a new twist.

One of Oaxaca's admired chefs, Hugo Arnaud of Los Danzantes, makes a mean sopa de tortilla. And while it's one of the most traditional soups of Mexico, Hugo loves including it on his menu. He explains the soup originated in Tlaxcala out of 'necessity' of the people using ingredients at hand – but it has been adapted in different ways in different places around Mexico.

'I knew it as something a little different, as I learnt it from my mother and grandmother in Michoacán. It's different there,' Hugo says. 'Here, we've added a local meat of Oaxaca, *tasajo* beef; it's a twist of the restaurant', he explains. 'Normally to the spiced tomato broth we add a lightly scorched tortilla for flavour, plus cheese and avocado and nothing more. Here, what we're trying to do is to play with ingredients and add the extra something different – Mexican cuisine with Oaxacan ingredients.'

He explains that sopa de tortilla is an everyday Mexican soup, not a celebratory soup. But he features it on the menu of Los Danzantes, 'to preserve our roots and identity of the kitchen, so that people keep knowing about it. Although it's a common soup, it's important to continue this tradition. It represents our own identity as Mexicans,' he says.

The colours are characteristic of Mexico: rich red, with white, green and yellow. To serve the sopa de tortilla, Hugo arranges tortillas, avocado and cheese in an attractive pile in the base of a bowl. From a small jug, he then pours the thick broth over the ingredients, which mingle together in the liquid. As for the taste? 'I love how it plays on the mouth – the richness of the broth, the crunch of the tortilla, the chew of the cheese, the creaminess of the avocado,' he says. And his secret for making one of the best sopa de tortillas? 'The love. The love for what I do. All the team that works here has this too. If you do it with love, it works out well.'

Chef //
Hugo Arnaud
Location //
Los Danzantes, Oaxaca

SOPA DE TORTILLA
Tortilla soup

Serves 12

Preparation & cooking time 1hr 45min

For the caldo de pollo (chicken stock)
(alternatively, use 3L/5¼pt ready-made
stock)
3½L (6pt) water
500g (17½oz) chicken pieces
125g (4½oz) onion, chopped
15g (½oz) garlic, chopped
½ courgette (zucchini), chopped
1 carrot, chopped
15g (½oz) celery, chopped (optional)
2 cloves
3 peppercorns

For the *caldo de pollo* (chicken stock)

1 In a pot boil 3½L of water and the chicken pieces. When the chicken meat begins to separate from the bones, with a slotted spoon skim off the froth, fat and the solids and discard. You may need to add another 500ml (17½fl oz) of water, depending on the quantity of liquid lost during this process.

2 Chop the onion, garlic, courgette, carrot and celery (if using) into small pieces and add to the broth with the cloves and peppercorns.

For the sopa de tortilla (to make 3L/5¼pt)

2L (3½pt) chicken stock

1½kg (3¼lb) red tomatoes

½ Guajillo chile, deseeded and roasted

½ onion

½ head of garlic

2 fried tortillas

oil, for frying

15g (½oz) coriander (cilantro; Mexicans use epazote)

rock salt, to taste

For each portion of soup

30g (1oz) fried tortilla strips (julienne style), or
 substitute tortilla chips

50g (1¾oz) avocado

10g (½oz) chicharrón (fried pork rinds)

250ml (8¾fl oz) sopa de tortilla

55g (2oz) queso fresco (or fresh, crumbly cheese)

20g (¾oz) cream

20g (¾oz) tasajo (thinly sliced, cured beef
 strips, optional)

For the _sopa de tortilla_

1 In a pot, boil together the chicken stock, red tomatoes, chile, onion, garlic and tortillas.

2 When the vegetables are tender, allow to cool slightly and place all the mixture in blender, then strain to ensure smooth consistency.

3 In a separate pot, heat some oil for around 30 seconds. Add the strained soup, along with the chopped coriander and simmer for several minutes. Season with salt.

To serve

1 In each bowl, arrange a handful of tortilla strips, avocado and chicharrón. Pour sopa de tortilla into each bowl (the ingredients will blend together).

2 Top with queso fresco and a dash of cream, and serve with _tasajo_ if desired.

MOLOTES

*Corn-based fritters
stuffed with potato & meat*

*These
quintessential
Mexican snacks,
often served on
special occasions,
are given a
flourish by this
local caterer, with
guacamole, queso
fresco and chile
salsa piled on the
traditional meat-
and-potato stuffed
corn-based fritters.*

Chef //
Raquel Patricia Garzón
Hernandez
Location //
Private caterer, Oaxaca

Señora Raquel Patricia Garzón Hernandez has come a long way since she tried to cook a meal for her husband. She failed miserably. That was in 1979. These days, she is an 'accidental caterer' – she started cooking for a relative's 10th wedding anniversary party and it was enjoyed so much they invited her to do another dinner. Then, through word-of-mouth, keen locals invited her to prepare their party feasts.

Among other things, Señora Raquel is renowned for preparing *molotes*, football-shaped, corn-based fritters that are stuffed with potato and meat pieces (such as chorizo). Señora Raquel serves hers on a lettuce leaf and covers the molote with guacamole, queso fresco (fresh cheese) and a chile or green tomato salsa.

Molotes are a popular *antojito* (street food snack; literally, 'little cravings') in Mexico and are so common that Señora Raquel is unaware of their history, although she knows they've been around for centuries. 'The Oaxacan women take advantage of things around them and use resources at their hand. It's probable that one woman didn't know what to cook and "invented" it using the ingredients she had available. My grandmother grew maize, harvested it, ground it in a *metate* (stone used for grinding corn), cooked it on a *comal* (hotplate) and made tortillas and *molotes*. Her grandmother did the same.'

These days she says that *molotes* are prepared and eaten for parties: birthdays, *fiestas patrominales* (Patron Saints Days) of the villages when you'll find *puestos molotes* (stalls selling *molotes*). While *molotes* are associated with special occasions, local women will often sell them outside their houses in the evenings. And it's easy to understand their popularity. These modest snack foods are a textural and taste sensation: the fried dough gives a crispy exterior, which gives way to a soft and juicy interior. The chorizo provides something to get your teeth into. Similarly, the spicy stuffing contrasts with the mild fritter – unless you like piling on the chile sauce – in which case you wait for a delayed kick.

MOLOTES

*Corn-based fritters stuffed
with potato & meat*

Serves 18 molotes

Preparation & cooking time 1 hr 30 min

For the tortillas
450g (1lb) masa harina *(see boxed text)*
salt, to taste
*360ml (12½fl oz) hot water (or enough as required
    to form a dough, as per* masa harina *packet
    instructions)*
flour, for dusting

For the filling
2 medium potatoes
water, for boiling
*200g (7oz) chorizo (or dried sausage of choice),
    chopped roughly*

For the guacamole
small green chile (jalapeño)
2 tbsp coriander (cilantro), chopped
1 small onion
1 small green tomato
1 ripe avocado
60ml (2fl oz) water
juice of ½ lime
salt, to taste

**For the salsa (picante) de cacahuate
    (spicy peanut & chile salsa)**
6 almonds
50g (1¾oz) dry unsalted peanuts
2 garlic cloves
½ dried chile (chile de árbol or bird's eye chilli)
olive oil, for frying

olive oil/vegetable oil, for frying
18 whole iceberg lettuce leaves
*queso fresco (or crumbly cheese such as Feta),
    to serve*

For the tortillas

1 In a large bowl combine the *masa harina* and salt. Slowly add water and mix with hands until the dough is malleable.

2 Knead the dough until springy and smooth and it forms a ball in your hand. (If too dry add 1 tbsp water; if too moist and sticky, sprinkle in 1 tbsp of *masa harina*).

3 Pinch off a golf-ball sized piece of dough and roll it in your hands. This will make a tortilla of approximately 10cm (4in).

4 Place the ball of dough between two sheets of plastic (something thicker than cling wrap is preferable). Then, use a flat-bottomed round ceramic bowl or equivalent to press down and create a flat disk shape. Use a rolling pin or the palms of your hand to work the edges of the dough outwards to spread (but maintain) the round shape approximately 4mm (⅛in) thick. Continue until you have 18 plastic-wrapped tortillas.

For the filling

1 Cut two potatoes into quarters, cover with water in a saucepan and bring to a boil. Cook for around 15 minutes or until tender (but not mushy).

2 Drain the potatoes and mash them roughly with a fork, then mix in the chorizo and set aside.

For the guacamole

1 Deseed the chile then wash your hands.

2 Finely chop the coriander, onion, tomato and small chile.

3 Mash the avocado with a fork.

4 Mix all ingredients together in a small bowl. Add water to desired consistency.

5 Add half a squeezed lime, and salt to taste, then set aside.

For the *salsa (picante) de cacahuate* (spicy peanut & chile salsa)

1 Chop all ingredients finely.

2 Heat a small amount of olive oil in a frying pan and fry the almonds and peanuts, then add the garlic, followed by the chile.

3 When fried, switch off the heat and allow the oil to cool in the pan.

4 When cool, pour entire contents of pan – oil and condiments – into a blender and blend thoroughly, then set aside.

To assemble

1 Remove the top layer of plastic from one of the tortilla dough discs and place 2 tsp of the potato filling into the middle. Spread a line of the filling across the disc.

2 Using the bottom plastic layer to assist, roll the circle of dough as though rolling a thick cigar (around 6cm/2½in in diameter).

3 Squeeze the ends together to seal in the filling. Roll and pat to create a fritter shape.

4 Heat oil in a frying pan. When warm, place two or three fritters in the pan at a time. Fry, turning frequently, for around two to three minutes or until golden brown.

5 Set the fritters/*molotes* aside with a slotted spoon and drain on absorbent paper.

6 When slightly cooled, place each *molote* on a lettuce leaf, spoon across the guacamole mixture and sprinkle *queso fresco* on top. Add the *salsa picante* to your taste.

7 Roll the lettuce leaf around the *molote* and eat with your hands.

Masa harina

Masa harina (or *masa de harina*) is not the same as cornmeal (which is gritty) nor cornstarch (US) nor even cornflour (UK). *Masa harina* comprises corn kernels that have been soaked in limewater (the lime, or calcium hydroxide, is known by Mexicans as *cal*). *Cal* is an alkaline solution that alters the corn structure, making it softer and 'freeing up' its nutritional content. The corn is then finely ground into flour. *Masa harina* is available at many supermarkets and Latin American shops, as well as online grocery stores.

GARNACHAS
Mini tortillas with meat, salsa, cheese & pickled cabbage

Once traditional party fare, these small meaty fried tortillas (with a pickled cabbage chile kick) are common street food in Oaxaca, but Doña Aurora's garnachera skills take them to another level.

Ever since she was a little girl, Doña Aurora Toledo Martínez recalls making garnachas in her home within Oaxaca's region of Istmo de Tehuantepec. She's carried over the tradition of what she calls 'the most representative dish' of her region to her restaurant, Zandunga, in Oaxaca City.

A garnacha is a very small fried tortilla cut in half into two whole circles. On top of each tortilla circle is a layer of meat, onion, salsa, dried cheese and a small wad of pickled cabbage. These days, garnachas are a common street food throughout Oaxaca. Traditionally, however, they were a 'party food' and are still an important part of the *velas* (a festival celebrating the harvest season, where locals follow a strict, and very colourful, dress code).

'My aunt was very renowned for being the best *garnachera* (garnacha maker) and I inherited this skill,' says Doña Aurora. 'One little bite holds an intense concentration of amazing flavours. The crispness of the tortilla and the flavour of the meat, cabbage and also the spiciness of the chile makes your mouth water.'

'The ingredients that make this dish are a mix of local products and other ingredients from other parts of the world. The intensity of the flavour is, in part, thanks to the many ethnic groups who arrived over the centuries with ingredients such as cabbage and spices. The vinegar of pickled cabbage is infused with thyme, oregano, clove, pepper, laurel leaf. But these flavours are not overwhelming! The grace of this dish is that all the flavours are uniform to give it equilibrium.'

Indeed, when you pick up a garnacha and bite into it, you see what she means: the crunch of the base gives way to a juicy, slightly sweet meat combination (surprisingly, not overly hot, despite the chile). A subtle hint of spices rolls over your tongue. The pickled cabbage cuts across the sweetness of the meat. But the most important thing? Love. 'I have passion and love for cooking. I want the flavours to be on my customers' tongues as an everlasting memory of my care and my region.'

Chef //
Doña Aurora Toledo Martínez
Location //
Zandunga Sabor
Istmeño, Oaxaca

GARNACHAS

*Mini tortillas with meat, salsa,
cheese & pickled cabbage*

Serves 30 garnachas

**Preparation & cooking time 2hr (excluding
pickling the cabbage)**

For the tortillas
500g (1lb) masa (or harina de maíz, *see*
    molotes p74)
240ml (8½fl oz) water

For the salsa
250g (8¾oz) red tomatoes
1 garlic clove
¼ small onion
120ml (4¼fl oz) water
oil, for frying
salt, to taste

For the meat
500g (1lb) beef
water, for boiling
2 cloves garlic, whole
½ onion, for the stock
pinch of salt
¼ onion, very finely chopped

For the tortillas

1 Follow the method as per *molotes* recipe (p74).

For the salsa

1 Put all the ingredients in a saucepan and bring to the boil. Simmer for a few minutes.

2 When the liquid has reduced, blend well and fry with a dash of oil. Add salt to taste.

For the meat

1 Cut the meat into pieces and add to a saucepan with the whole garlic cloves, the onion half and salt. Bring to the boil and simmer until the meat is cooked through.

2 Remove the beef from the water and drain, discarding the garlic and onion. Chop the beef finely (or grind).

3 Add the chopped onion to the meat.

For the pickled cabbage

¼ cabbage, roughly chopped

2 carrots, roughly chopped

2 jalapeño chiles, sliced

500ml (17½fl oz) pineapple vinegar (or a
    sweet/alternative fruit vinegar)

salt, to taste

pepper, to taste

1 clove

pinch oregano

queso seco, to serve (or a mild feta)

*'In this recipe we have
reduced the amount of fat in
the garnachas – less salt and
sugar in the mixture –
so people can have it and
don't feel guilty.'*

Doña Aurora

For the pickled cabbage

1 Combine the cabbage, carrots, sliced chiles and pineapple vinegar in a bowl and add the salt, pepper and spices.

2 Leave to rest for two hours to ensure the cabbage is infused with the flavours of the combined ingredients.

To serve

1 Cut the tortillas through the middle if possible, so you have two full circular halves (if not, leave the tortilla as one piece).

2 Top each tortilla half with meat.

3 In a frying pan, add a little oil and lightly fry the tortillas topped with meat.

4 Add with care 1 tbsp of tomato salsa on top of each tortilla and leave to fry a further 30 seconds.

5 Remove the *garnachas* from the pan and arrange on a plate. Sprinkle *queso seco* over and top with a generous 'pinch' of pickled cabbage.

Tip

*You can buy ready-made tortillas for this recipe, though beware,
they will be larger than this recipe calls for. Cut them to size.*

EMPANADA DE FLOR DE CALABAZA

Pastry parcel with cheese & courgette (zucchini) flowers

They may be common Oaxacan street snacks, but these warm pastries stuffed with quesillo cheese and courgette flowers at Señora Lucila's market stall, La Florecita, have been loved for almost half a century.

Over the past 44 years, at La Florecita, a modest *fonda* (food stall) in Oaxaca's Mercado El Merced, Señora Lucila has sold thousands, possibly millions of empanadas de flor de calabaza, one of the many common Oaxacan street or 'snack' foods. This empanada is a heated semi-circular parcel of pastry that's filled with *quesillo* (a type of stringy cheese and speciality of Oaxaca) and courgette flowers.

Hundreds of locals flock to La Florecita daily, especially on a Sunday. A market wall covered with hundreds of signatures of famous personalities attests to their love of everything, from *estofados* (stews) to enchiladas and, of course, empanadas.

Empanadas have always been so popular in Oaxaca that Señora Lucila can't explain their background. 'In Oaxaca we always eat empanadas. For traditional parties. Patron Saints' days. For many celebrations people make empanadas!' As with many recipes in Mexico, empanadas' ingredients are local and readily available, and making empanadas is half the fun. First, a golf-ball-sized piece of dough is placed between two plastic sheets and flattened in a tortilla press. The disc is removed, spread with a layer of pork lard (very important for flavour) before a generous handful of *quesillo* is sprinkled over the entire area. A courgette flower is placed on top of the cheese. Señora Lucila deftly folds the empanada and presses it around the edges to seal the semi-circular parcel. The empanada is briefly heated on the *comal* (a clay platter used over hot coals: 'this gives the dough a pleasant "burnt" taste plus crispiness on the outside,' she says), before being put into the coal oven.

Empanadas are not something to gobble down quickly. Pull the cooked pastry apart with both hands and wait for the steam to subside. As you first bite through the crispy outer layer into the soft inside, a smoky taste hits you, followed by a surprisingly mild-tasting cheese flavour. The slight tang of the flower helps cuts the cheese's fats. A spoonful of chile salsa (obligatory on any Mexican table) will add the requisite spice hit.

Chef //
Señora Lucila Flor Ruiz
Location //
La Florecita, Oaxaca

EMPANADA DE FLOR DE CALABAZA

Pastry parcel with cheese & courgette (zucchini) flowers

Serves 6

Preparation & cooking time 1hour 10min

1 kg (2¼lb) masa (a ready-made dough made from
   corn-maize flour; alternatively see molotes, p74,
   to make your own dough using masa harina)
6 tbsp pork lard
500g (17½oz) quesillo (stringy cheese;
   substitute with mozzarella)
500g (17½oz) courgette/zucchini flowers
   (squash blossoms)
25g (1oz) epazote (optional, could also
   substitute coriander)
salt, to taste

1 Preheat the oven to 190°C/375°F.

2 Roll out the masa to make tortillas to desired size – around the size of a plate is considered 'normal'.

3 Spread on a thin layer of pork lard with a knife.

4 Over half of the tortilla circle, sprinkle on a generous amount of *quesillo* cheese.

5 On top of the cheese, layer over two courgette flowers, epazote (if using) and sprinkle with a little salt.

6 Fold the tortilla into a semi-circle and pinch the edges to form a sealed parcel (empanada).

7 Fry the empanada briefly on a pan over hot coals (or heat on an oven tray on a hot plate/gas burner).

8 Place the empanada in the oven for 10 minutes or until the cheese is melted.

9 Remove from the oven and allow to cool slightly before serving.

TLAYUDA
Giant tortilla with topping

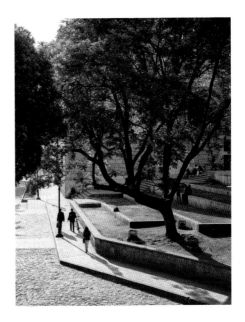

Popular with families on Sundays, the pizza-like tlayuda *is a quintessential Oaxacan meal, and a street-food favourite. But at Casa Oaxaca, chef Alejandro Ruiz's interpretation has a surprising addition.*

The fact that one of Mexico's top chefs serves a *tlayuda*, a staple Oaxacan street food, in his chic restaurant Casa Oaxaca, says a lot. Chef Alejandro Ruiz is adamant that it is featured on the menu. A *tlayuda* (pronounced tla-ooh-da) is a corn tortilla that is cooked, smeared with pork lard and bean paste, topped with *quesillo* (Oaxaca's famous stringy cheese), and cabbage and meat. They are sometimes folded.

'For me the *tlayuda* is the most novel dish of Oaxacan food. I feel it's important to include because it's part of our culture. It's what I'd ask for if I came here for the first time,' Alejandro says. 'Historically, it's one of the most representative meals in Oaxaca, as corn was discovered in the Central Valleys area 8000 years ago. *Tlayuda* is a way to preserve corn and tortillas. My parents were farmers. One of the first things I learned to grow was corn. One of the first things you eat as a kid is [a corn] tortilla.'

In a twist to the traditional *tlayuda* recipe, Alejandro substitutes the meat – usually *cecina* (cured meat), *tasajo* (dried beef) chorizo (or even *chapulínes*, grasshoppers) – with a massive chunk of rib-eye steak coated in a *chicatana* (ant) marinade.

'Just as São Paolo Brazil's Sunday meal is pizza; in Oaxaca it's a *tlayuda*. Families get together on a Sunday afternoon to have *tlayudas* – it unites them. Everyone sits around the *anafre* (grill) where they're being prepared.'

Tasting a *tlayuda* is a deliciously tactile experience. Bite into a slightly crunchy exterior and a hint of chargrilled flavour lingers on your tongue. The diverse ingredients are a palate-pleasing combination – think of a tang of chile, a salty overtone of pork lard and the mildness of chewy cheese. And the secret to the perfect *tlayuda*? According to Alejandro, it's 'good corn. Technique. Beans. Pork lard. Cheese. Salsa.' He laughs. 'In the end? Everything! You need good ingredients.'

Chef //
Alejandro Ruiz
Location //
Casa Oaxaca El
Restaurante, Oaxaca

TLAYUDA
Giant tortilla with topping

Serves 1 or 2

Preparation & cooking time 1 hr 30 mins

For the bean paste (excess bean paste can be stored in fridge for up to 24 hours)
85g (3oz) black beans
1½L (2½pt) water
⅓ white onion
5 garlic cloves, cut in half
1 sprig epazote (or coriander)
1 chile de árbol, deseeded, sliced and roasted
100g (3½oz) pork lard
50g (1¾oz) white onion, sliced
salt, to taste

For the rib-eye steak (minus the ant marinade)
370g (13oz) rib-eye steak
salt, to taste
pepper, to taste

For the bean paste

1   In a saucepan, cook the beans in the water with the white onion, garlic cloves and epazote for 45 minutes until soft. Drain the beans and reserve the stock.

2   Blitz the beans in a blender with the chile and the stock.

3   Melt the pork lard in a skillet and fry the sliced onion until slightly browned. Remove the onion and add in the blended bean mix. When warmed, return the onion to the pan and stir constantly until it forms a paste.

4   Season with salt.

For the rib-eye steak (minus the ant marinade)

1   Season the meat with salt and pepper.

2   Cooking over hot coals if possible (or a grill), seal the meat, then cook on each side for 3–4 minutes (for medium-rare).

3   Remove from the heat and allow the meat to rest for 10 minutes before serving.

For the salsa

1 clove garlic, roasted

1 jalapeño chile, roasted

2 tomatoes, roasted

30ml (1oz) water

1 tbsp coriander/cilantro, chopped

1 tbsp onion, chopped

salt, to taste

For the tlayuda

120g (4¼oz) masa (a ready-made dough
made from corn-maize flour, alternatively
see molotes, p74, to make your own
tlayuda *dough using masa harina)*

15g (½oz) pork lard

25g (1oz) of your prepared bean paste

25g (1oz) quesillo *(or mozzarella)*

15g (½oz) cabbage, chopped

¼ radish, to garnish

1 sprig parsley, to garnish

'A tlayuda is a complete
meal. It has protein,
minerals, and carbohydrates.
It's something you can have
for breakfast, lunch and
dinner and it's something
that almost every citizen of
Oaxaca can eat.'

Chef Alejandro Ruiz

For the salsa

1 In a mortar and pestle, crush the garlic with the jalapeño pepper. Then add the tomatoes and crush them gently and briefly to mix, but maintain a chunky texture.

2 Add water and stir. Add the coriander and onion and stir, then season with salt.

For the *tlayuda*

1 Roll out the masa to make the *tlayuda* to desired size – around the size of a plate is considered 'normal'.

2 Spread the pork lard over the *tlayuda*.

3 Spread a layer of bean paste on top of this, making sure the *tlayuda* is well covered with both the lard and the paste.

4 Crumble the *quesillo* and sprinkle it over the *tlayuda*.

5 Add the cabbage.

6 Fold the *tlayuda* in half. Grill over a hot coal fire, turning frequently until the *quesillo* melts and the *tlayuda* starts to partially 'burn' to give it the charcoal flavour.

7 Remove from the heat and cut in half or quarters. Serve alongside the rib-eye steak, with the salsa in a separate dish. Garnish with radish and parsley.

ENCHILADAS DE SAN PEDRO TOTOLAPAM

Meat-filled tortillas with chile sauce

This enchilada dish with succulent shredded chicken and a fiery, nutty, yet sweet and sour sauce is a bestseller in José Luis Diaz's restaurant Chilhuacle Rojo, renowned for its home-grown produce.

Chef //
José Luis Diaz
Location //
Restaurante Chilhuacle
Rojo, Oaxaca

C hef José Luis Diaz is passionate about enchiladas de San Pedro Totolapam, rolled tortillas filled with meat and served with a classic *mole coloradito* (Oaxacan sauce). Why? First, this version of the dish comes from his hometown, the small rural village of San Pedro Totolapam, in the Central Valleys region. And secondly, he has fond memories of the dish: 'It goes back to days when we were kids and we had this for special occasions – weddings, birthdays and *quinceañeras* (15th birthdays; these are important milestones in Mexico). Even today, when I go home my mum always makes them for us.'

And the enchilada dish is a bestseller in José's small restaurant, Chilhuacle Rojo, in the centre of Oaxaca city. 'People say after eating them, "I just want to lick the plate!" For the meat filling of his enchiladas José uses chickens from his ranch (he grows all his own produce), while his mother, Señora Guadalupe Robledo Nazariego, prepares the *mole*: a delicious blend of pecans, raisins, walnuts, herbs and spices.

When it comes to the history of enchiladas, their background is unclear, though it's generally accepted that somebody once decided to wrap a tortilla around fish or meat. 'They've always been there, always been around,' says Señora Guadalupe. 'All the [village] ladies made them. But they definitely represent a merging of cultures. The new spices that the Spanish introduce explains the sweet and bitter flavours.'

Even these days, women in San Pedro Totolapam get together – often starting at 2am – to help prepare enchiladas for fiestas or weddings. 'There's a lot of unity preparing for these fiestas. If there's no unity, you can't do this,' she says. There's harmony, too, in the flavours of this enchilada dish. Cut into one of the stuffed tortilla tubes, and you'll get the idea. The elasticity of the tortilla gives way to a pillow of shredded chicken. It's a satisfying experience: first chewing the meat, then distinguishing the flavours: a peppercorn bite, a fragrant raisin, a crunchy peanut... Meanwhile, the silky *mole* that coats your tongue, is sweet and sour and oh so gratifying.

ENCHILADAS DE SAN PEDRO TOTOLAPAM

Meat-filled tortillas with chile sauce

Serves 6

Preparation & cooking time 1 hr 30 min

For the mole coloradito
5 Chilhuacle Rojo chiles (or any mild – or mild
*   to hot – red chillis for all mentioned here)*
5 Ancho chiles
5 Guajillo chiles
5 tbsp corn or soybean oil
200g (7oz) traditional Oaxacan chocolate (can be
*   substituted with 80g/3oz of bitter chocolate and*
*   160g/5½oz sugar)*
30g (1oz) almonds
30g (1oz) unsalted peanuts
30g (1oz) sultanas
2 bay leaves
1kg (2¼lb) red tomatoes, roughly chopped
¼ banana
1 medium onion, roughly chopped
½ head of garlic, roughly chopped
2 cloves
2 tbsp sesame seeds
1 tbsp cinnamon
1 tbsp oregano
pinch of cumin
2 peppercorns
¼ tsp salt
480ml (17fl oz) chicken stock (or boiling water)
2 corn tortillas
oil/pork fat, for frying

For the *mole coloradito*

1   De-seed the chiles, cut into halves and fry gently in a deep saucepan until browned.

2   Add the rest of the *mole coloradito* ingredients, apart from the chicken stock, tortillas and oil/pork fat, to the pan of chiles one by one, taking care not to burn.

3   Reserve a few tbsp of the chicken stock and set aside for step 5, then add the remainder of the stock to the mixture, bring to the boil and simmer for several minutes. Allow to cool.

4   Once cooled, blend the liquid in a processor until it becomes a smooth paste. Add the tortillas in at this stage, which helps thicken the *mole*.

5   In a deep pan, heat a little oil (or pork fat). Lightly fry the mole paste, gradually adding the reserved chicken stock.

6   Reduce the heat until the *mole* reaches a consistency where it 'trickles' down a plate.

For the chicken filling

250g (9oz) finely chopped (or shredded)
boiled/cooked chicken
olive or corn oil, for frying
150g (5oz) finely chopped onion
2 tbsp finely chopped garlic
720ml (1¼pt) chicken stock
200g (7oz) finely chopped tomato
150g (5oz) finely chopped peanuts
150g (5oz) finely chopped raisins
25g (1oz) finely chopped parsley
1 tbsp dried oregano
1 tbsp powdered cinnamon
7 ground peppercorns
1 ground clove
salt, to taste
12 tortillas

queso fresco (or crumbled feta or goats
cheese) to serve (optional)
parsley, to serve (optional)

For the chicken filling

1 In a pan lightly fry the chicken, onion and garlic in a little oil for 5 minutes or until the ingredients turn lightly golden.

2 Add the remaining ingredients (apart from the tortillas), including the chicken stock.

3 Bring to the boil and allow it to reduce until the liquid has evaporated completely. Add salt to taste.

4 To assemble, place a spoonful of chicken on each tortilla and roll it like a cigar. Complete until finished.

5 Fry each chicken tortilla lightly in a pan of oil for about one minute and lay them on a plate, side by side.

6 Cover the tortillas generously in the *mole coloradito*, sprinkle with cheese and parsley, and serve.

'We grew up with fresh produce
– for us it's not a "movement"!'

Chef José Luis Diaz

CERDO DE RELLENO

Stuffed pork loin, potatoes & chayote

A hearty, filling and tasty dish of meat and vegetables, coated with a modicum of salsa is one of Doña Deyanira Aquino Pineda's best-selling dishes. The key is in the simplicity.

Cerdo de Relleno is a favourite dish of Doña Deyanira Aquino Pineda because it's from Istmo de Tehuantepec, the region of her birthplace. Owner and matriarch of La Teca Restaurante, Doña Deyanira believes it's one of her best-selling dishes because people from all around the world love its taste and simplicity.

'Locals eat this at weddings and parties in the pueblos (villages) of Istmo de Tehuantepec. The dish is prepared at home in a *cazuelas de barro* (a clay dish specific to Mexico). But when for a wedding or party, the cooks prepare it in a large traditional oven because of the huge quantities required,' explains Doña Deyanira.

She believes the dish originated with local women centuries ago, who used whatever they had at hand. 'Many nationalities – Arabs, Chinese, Japanese, Spanish, French – entered the Istmo region by sea and they introduced new ingredients and spices, including *mostaza* (mustard; used in this recipe). They roasted the pork (or whatever meat was available to them) with vegetables and potatoes. In former times, they cooked all the animal, including the heart and innards.'

Cerdo de relleno literally translates as 'stuffed pork loin', though this version is more liberal in its presentation. Much of the dish is white: chunks of pork, chayote strips, potato chunks (though the chile releases a reddish oil) – but the pleasant, mild taste with its subtle mustard overtones makes up for the lack of Kahlo-esque colour.

To tenderise the meat, Doña Deyanira submerges it in water mixed with vinegar, garlic and black pepper for one to two hours. She then roasts the meat in the oven, along with oil, chayote, and potato chunks. She says the secret is to roast the meat slowly so that it becomes tender or firm as you like (depending on the cut quality). She says, 'It doesn't matter too much because the outer is sealed, and in any case, the juice moistens it.'

The meal takes time to savour, but is worth lingering over, particularly in the welcoming atmosphere of La Teca, which may be the closest you'll feel to dining in a local's home.

Chef //
Doña Deyanira Aquino Pineda
Location //
La Teca Restaurante:
Gastronomia Istemeña, Oaxaca

CERDO DE RELLENO
Stuffed pork loin, potatoes & chayote

Serves 6

Preparation & cooking time 1 hr 15 min

1kg (2¼lb) pork loin (or leg)
500ml (17fl oz) white vinegar
2–3 Guajillo chiles (or any mild dried red chillies)
800ml (1½pt) water
1 large plantain banana (or regular banana,
*   if unavailable)*
½ tsp black pepper
1 tbsp French (Dijon) mustard
10 small cloves garlic, crushed
1 tbsp oregano
1 tsp cinnamon
salt, to taste
1 chayote (or any type of squash), diced
2 large potatoes, diced

Tip
While the traditional recipe calls for 'mustard'
(it's a generic brand in Mexico, but replicates
the milder French Dijon), you can use whatever
mustard you like to vary its 'bite'.

1 Pre-heat the oven to 250°C/480°F.

2 Cover and soak the pork with water and vinegar for 15 minutes.

3 Drain the pork and rinse it well to rid it of the aroma of vinegar.

4 Cut the chiles in half and remove their seeds. Boil them in a saucepan of 300ml (10½fl oz) of the water for about five minutes or until they are soft, then remove from the water.

5 In a bowl, blend the remaining 500ml (17½fl oz) of water with the soft chiles. Add the plantain, pepper, mustard, garlic, oregano and cinnamon. Add salt to taste. This mixture will serve as a salsa for the pork.

6 Put the rinsed pork in a large casserole pot, surrounded by the chayote and potatoes, and cover with the salsa. Cook in the oven for roughly 45 minutes to one hour, or until meat is done and tender.

Tip
You should not need to add extra oil when
cooking; the meat's own fat should be sufficient
(but if it's really lean meat, add a couple of
tablespoons of olive oil).

'I was born with the aroma of corn, fruit and flowers. I was born with the love of cooking. My maternal grandmother taught me this beautiful road of food and gastronomy.'

Doña Deyanira Aquino Pineda

CHILEAJO MIXTECO

Chile-garlic mole (sauce) from Mixteca

Tierra del Sol is the only restaurant in Oaxaca City that specialises in La Mixteca cuisine, and this chile-garlic mole (sauce) stewed with pork cuts is most emblematic of the region.

The Mixteca region of Mexico is renowned for its rich and vibrant culture. No-one appreciates this more than chef Olga Cabrera. One of a long line of female and Mixtec chefs, her restaurant Tierra del Sol is the only restaurant in Oaxaca City that specialises solely in cuisine of her region.

As is common in Mexico, so important is the *mole* – rather than its bulkier meat ingredients – it defines a dish. Why? 'For Mixtecos, *mole* means Chileajo Mixteco,' says Olga. 'Chileajo is in our blood: the power of cooking it. The power of eating it. It's a *mole* of much tradition. Over 300 years ago when people started to herd livestock from the Mixtec region to other regions [much of the stock had been introduced by the Spanish], they would travel with the animals from the coastal regions to Districto Federal [Mexico City]. Back then, there wasn't money so the Mixteca and people from the coast exchanged products.'

'In the Mixteca region they grew garlic. On the coast they grew chile. So when those from the coast passed through the Mixteca, they traded their items. Chileajo simply means "chile and *ajo* (garlic)". The Mixtecos used the meat they had and made a *mole*. We eat it as an everyday plate, whatever the occasion.'

Olga places a dish on the table: it resembles more of a soup than a stew: oodles of bright red *mole* covers large pieces of meat. 'It's a hearty dish. It has protein, vegetables, and is hot and spicy,' she says proudly. Indeed, when you carve into a piece of meat – tender after being braised for around two hours – and raise it to your lips, the spicy kick of the sauce is immediate. The meat brings welcome relief to the palate, while the potato provides a milder balance to the chile. By sharing the recipe, Olga hopes to ensure the survival of this hearty dish. For another few centuries at least.

Chef //
Olga Cabrera
Location //
Restaurante Tierra
del Sol, Oaxaca

CHILEAJO MIXTECO

Chile-garlic mole (sauce) from Mixteca

Serves 6

Preparation & cooking time 2 hr 30 min

For the meat
3L (5¼pt) water
2 cloves peeled garlic, whole
½ small onion
1kg (2¼lb) pork ribs or pork loin

For the mole
250g (8¾oz) Costeño chile or Guajillo chile (or any
*   hot dried red chilli)*
water, for soaking chiles
2 cloves
pinch oregano
pinch cumin
5 cloves garlic, whole
oil, to fry the meat
250g (8¾oz) red or green tomatoes
salt, to taste
3 small potatoes

1 Boil the water in a large saucepan with the two cloves of garlic, onion, salt and pork until cooked (approximately one hour).

2 Meanwhile, to make the *mole*, clean and deseed the chile and cover in a little water to soften for a few minutes.

3 Blend the drained chile with the cloves, oregano, cumin and the five cloves of garlic and put aside.

4 Remove meat from the saucepan, conserving the liquid in the saucepan, then lightly fry the meat in a little oil until sealed.

5 Add the liquefied chile mix to the meat and fry well.

6 Liquefy the tomatoes in a food processor or blender, and add to the *mole* in the pan. Fry for around 10 minutes and add a little salt.

7 Cut potatoes into small pieces and add to the *mole*.

8 Add a little of the reserved meat broth until it just covers the meat. Leave until the potatoes are cooked through. The chileajo will thicken (and that's the consistency you're after).

'Yes, [there's] competition in families as to the best recipe: Whose is the tastiest? My aunt's? No, my sister-in-law's? In my family the best is that of my 88-year-old grandmother. This is her recipe.'

Olga Cabrera

PASTEL DE ELOTE

Corn cake

Considered 'staple cakes' in Mexican homes, these semi-sweet corn cakes have many different variations in texture and colour, and are a tribute to the sheer diversity of native corn in the Oaxaca region.

In Mexico, there are more ways to prepare corn than kernels on a cob. This isn't surprising, given that the country is the birthplace of maize; it's believed to have been domesticated in Meso-America thousands of years ago. In Mayan mythology, people were created from corn. And today, the region of Oaxaca still has one of the highest diversities of native corn species in the world. Maize forms the base of much of the Mexican diet, especially in the form of tortillas. But it's used in other ways, too, such as the *pastel de elote*, a semi-sweet corn cake.

Doña Lourdes Escobedo Banda has made many a pastel de elote for her large and extended family, and for many years when she ran a *cocina económica* (economical homemade food that people could buy to take home). She says that the *pastel de elote* has an interesting role in history: it's an example of the historic merging of the Spanish colonial and indigenous cuisines.

'Corn was – and is – so plentiful. In the past, village locals would take gifts when they visited the Dominican monks and nuns (who were renowned for enjoying desserts, many of which were adapted from Spanish recipes). These tokens included *elote* (corn cob).'

She says it makes sense that someone – probably a nun – 'invented' the *pastel de elote*, given that the ingredients were readily available: 'Villagers cut sugarcane to make sugar. They raised chickens for the eggs. And the nuns then made the condensed milk themselves.'

This cake has different versions – milk, sugar, egg and flour quantities can differ, as can the corn (especially if fresh, instead of canned, corn is used). This can affect the density and flavour – from a moister and heavier, slightly stickier example, to a bread-like texture, with a fluffier consistency. Its colour can vary according to the corn type. And that's the gift: like the Dominican nuns before you, you can perfect it to your taste.

Chef //
Doña Lourdes Escobedo Banda
Location //
Home cook, Oaxaca City

PASTEL DE ELOTE
Corn cake

Serves 10

Preparation & cooking time 1 hr

5 eggs
500g (17½oz) corn kernels (approx. 8 natural
*   cobs, or 2 large tins of corn, drained)*
400g (14oz) condensed milk
1 tsp vanilla extract (or cinnamon, if preferred)
130g (4½oz) plain flour
1 tbsp baking powder
1 tbsp butter, for greasing

'I think I've been blessed:
God gave me "flavour
drops"; I cook with love.
I think that makes my
cooking taste better.'

Doña Lourdes Escobedo Banda

1   Preheat oven to 180°C/350°F.

2   Beat eggs in a bowl until fluffy.

3   If using fresh corn, cover the cobs with water in a large saucepan and bring to the boil. Cook for approx 20 minutes until tender, then remove the kernels by slicing them off with a knife.

4   In a blender, combine the corn kernels, condensed milk and vanilla extract. Puree until smooth.

5   In a separate bowl, combine the flour and baking powder and sift into the eggs. Mix well, but don't overbeat. Fold the corn puree into the mixture.

6   Grease a 20cm (8in) cake tin with butter and pour in the mixture.

7   Bake in the oven for around 45 minutes or until golden brown on top.

8   Serve either cooled or warm.

BUÑUELOS DE CHOCOLATE Y CHILE PASILLA

Chocolate- & chile-spiked buñuelos

One of Mexico's top chefs, Rodolfo Castellanos likes to experiment at his restaurant Origen, giving these traditional deep-fried pastries a decadent twist with a chocolate and chile truffle surprise.

P laying around with traditional ingredients and dishes is what chef Rodolfo Castellanos is renowned for. His renditions of Mexican and international cuisine earned him the title of Mexico's Top Chef (2016), an accolade from the Top Chef reality TV show, and foodies flock to his restaurant Origen for the unexpected.

Buñuelos are a classic South American pastry and, though different variations appear around the continent, they generally resemble fritters: round balls that are deep fried. A traditional Oaxacan *buñuelo*, however, consists of a thin flour tortilla that is deep fried, sprinkled with sugar or cinnamon or star anise and dipped into syrup. Then there is the '*buñuelo*' of Rodolfo Castellanos – it's more like the South American version, but with an important twist. 'I stuff it with a chocolate and a chile pasilla truffle.' He says. 'It's dipped in batter and deep fried. Locals first said: "Ok, but they are not *buñuelos*, those are truffles." But they love them.'

It's easy to see why. Think crunchy doughnut-flavoured outer that, when you cut it with a spoon, oozes a silky and molten chile-infused chocolate. Chef Rodolfo's *buñuelos* are then topped with a seasonal fruit compote – guava or sometimes pineapple or berries. 'The fruit adds a nice acidity and this balances both the sweetness and the creaminess of the chocolate.'

He serves the *buñuelos* with ice cream flavoured with verbena (a common plant, often infused with mezcal, or imbibed as a tisane). 'It's a very nice combination because one is refreshing and the other is spicy at the very end,' he says.

Buñuelos are generally consumed at Christmas. According to Rodolfo, this habit was introduced to Mexico from Spain by the Franciscan and Dominican monks and nuns, who also brought sugar and spices, including cinnamon, and combined these with readily available products in their cooking. Fortunately for us, truffles, one of Origen's signature dishes, are on the menu year-round.

Chef //
Rodolfo Castellanos
Location //
Origen, Oaxaca

BUÑUELOS DE CHOCOLATE Y CHILE PASILLA

Chocolate- & chile-spiked buñuelos

Serves 15 portions

*Preparation & cooking time 1hr
(not including 12hr for freezing ice
cream, 8hr freezing of truffles)*

For the lemon verbena ice-cream

500ml (17½fl oz) milk
500ml (17½fl oz) cream
*50g (1¾oz) fresh lemon verbena leaves
(or substitute with lemon tea)*
12 egg yolks
190g (6¾oz) sugar

For the chocolate oaxaqueño truffles

*10g (⅓oz) pasilla chile (or any mild-medium
dry chilli)*
500ml (17½fl oz) unthickened cream
*500g (17½oz) chocolate oaxaqueño
(or good quality 70% chocolate with ½ tsp
ground cinnamon)*
100g (3½oz) powered cocoa

For the guava & mint compote

*500g (17½oz) guava (or any red fruits/berries,
if unavailable)*
150g (5¼oz) sugar
100g (3½oz) mint leaves

For the lemon verbena ice-cream

1 Bring the milk to a boil with half the cream and the lemon verbena in a saucepan.

2 In a bowl, mix the egg yolks and sugar, adding a little of the boiling milk while constantly stirring.

3 Return the blended egg mixture to the saucepan and continue cooking on a medium flame for six to eight minutes.

4 Remove from the heat, add the remaining cold cream and strain into a dish, discarding the lemon verbena leaves/zest.

5 Freeze for 12 hours.

For the chocolate *oaxaqueño* truffles

1 Deseed and finely chop the pasilla chile.

2 In a saucepan, bring the cream to a boil with the pasilla chile.

3 Break the chocolate into small pieces and gradually fold it into the cream and chile mixture.

4 Pour the warm chocolate mixture into a bowl and refrigerate overnight (or at least several hours) until firm.

5 When the chocolate mixture has set, remove it from the fridge and scoop out spoonfuls to roll into small balls (around 20g/¾oz for each)..

6 Roll each ball on a plate dusted with the powdered cocoa, then freeze for at least eight hours before frying.

For the fritter batter

200g (7oz) all-purpose flour

30g (1oz) cocoa

45g (1½oz) sugar

¼ tsp baking powder

¼ tsp salt

110ml (4fl oz) milk

2 eggs

30g (1oz) melted butter

100ml (3½fl oz) water (or more milk,
*   if preferred)*

500ml (17½fl oz) vegetable oil (for frying)

icing sugar, to serve

For the guava & mint compote

1 Cut the guava in half and remove the seeds. Cut into small cubes.

2 Put the chopped guava and the sugar in a saucepan with the mint leaves and let the mixture cook on a low heat for 10 minutes until soft. Set aside.

For the fritter batter

1 Mix the flour, cocoa, sugar, baking powder, salt, milk, eggs and melted butter to make a smooth batter. Add water (or more milk) for consistency.

2 Heat the vegetable oil in a deep frying pan until the oil is bubbling.

3 Using a metal skewer, pick up a chocolate truffle, dip it in the fritter batter, then ease the skewer into the hot oil. Repeat with each truffle and fry them until light brown.

4 Drain these fried *buñuelos* on some absorbent kitchen paper, allow to cool slightly before removing the skewers, then serve while still warm with a scoop of lemon verbena ice cream and the guava compote. Sprinkle the *buñuelos* with icing sugar.

'A dessert is just as important as
the savoury part so why not
give it the same emphasis?'

Rodolfo Castellanos

NIEVES DE MEZCAL

Mezcal flavoured ice cream-sorbet

Numerous Mexican presidents have enjoyed the nieves of Manolo Nieves, such is its fame. A mix between ice cream and sorbet, the nieves *here are handmade the traditional way.*

Manolo Nieves' fifth generation ice-cream maker and current Director General, Francisco Velasco, make *nieves* (an icy Mexican treat) the traditional way – this means many of his flavours comprise organic fruit, unrefined sugar and unpasteurised (natural) milk.

The history of Manolo Nieves began in 1857 when Francisco's great-great grandmother, María, learned how to make ice cream from her Spanish employers before making her own *nieves* to sell. It soon became a full-time pursuit. She would collect ice from Cerro de la Nevería (Ice Mountain) near her home village, conserving it in a hole covered with layers of soil, cacao bean shells, and petates (fibre mats). Back in Oaxaca, she used this to make her vanilla- and lime-flavoured ice creams and sold them. Family legend goes that one day she accidentally burned the milk while making a batch of vanilla *nieves*, 'inventing' the popular flavour of *leche quemado* ('burnt' milk).

Subsequent family generations continued to make and sell ice creams in the town's plazas, but in the 1950s, Manolo, Francisco's father, peddled his wares from a bicycle stall. These days, Manola Nieves has several shops and an ice cream truck.

The company makes around 300 flavours (with 35 or so available at any one time), from zingy fruity concoctions to those with a chile bite. And natural fruits mean beautiful colours. Vibrant reds. Luscious yellows. Jungle-like greens. But they're not only feasts for the eyes – as the miniature icicles melt on your tongue the sensation is curious: it's neither creamy, nor like a frozen 'slushy', but a quirky mix of the two. ('Beware: the creamier the ice cream the more preservatives,' explains Francisco).

Making *nieves* is a laborious process. After a steel tub full of the liquid is immersed into a bucket of ice cubes, the tub must be turned. And turned. As small icicles start to appear on the sides of the tub, you scrape these off gently. But the rewards? Getting your mouth around the tastes of Mexico: coconut, pear and chile, chocolate, mezcal. Delicious.

Ice cream maker//
Francisco Velasco
Location //
Manolo Nieves, Oaxaca

NIEVES DE MEZCAL
Mezcal flavoured ice cream-sorbet

Serves 20

Preparation & cooking time 1 hr 30 min

*Requires an ice-cream maker or a large
    barrel or container*

2 eggs
400g (14oz) sugar
4L (7pt) unpasteurised milk
*140ml (5fl oz) mezcal (of the type made with espadín
    agave, if possible)*
8 trays of ice cubes
salt

1 Separate egg whites and yolks and set aside.

2 Dissolve half of the sugar with milk in a saucepan. Add the egg whites and bring to the boil.

3 Beat the yolks with the remaining sugar and fold into the milk mixture over a reduced heat.

4 Cool the mixture until it's at room temperature and then mix in the mezcal. Pour into a steel pot. (If using an ice-cream maker, omit steps 5 and 6 and follow your usual instruction manual.)

5 Put ice cubes with salt into the bottom of a wooden barrel (or large receptacle) and insert the steel bowl to rest within the barrel, ensuring that ice covers the outsides of the steel bowl.

6 Spin the steel bowl continuously within the barrel, ensuring that the outsides are well covered with ice. After about 45 minutes the liquid will start to freeze and harden. Gently scrape the sides occasionally with a spatula to mix in. Continue to turn until the entire contents have an icy texture, then you're ready to scoop the *nieves* and serve.

Tip
*Much of the country's mezcal is made in
Oaxaca. This smoky, artisanal spirit is made
of the agave plant (warning: mezcal has a high
alcoholic content).*

AGUA FRESCA:
LIMÓN CON CHIA

Lime & chia seed cordial

This pale yellow agua fresca packs a zesty punch, and the chia seeds provide the perfect post-sip 'micro-nibble'. It captures in a cup the perfect fruity flavour of Mexico.

Aguas frescas are cold, non-alcoholic drinks consisting of water flavoured with fruits, flowers, grains and sugar. While these colourful refreshments are served all over Mexico, they are particularly popular in Oaxaca, due to the seasonal heat and prevalence of fruits. Of the many flavours, one of the most refreshing is *limón con chia* (lime and chia seed) and Señora Irinea Valera's stall, Aguas Frescas Casilda, sells gallons of it weekly.

Señora Irinea's family has been running the stall since 1926, after her grandmother, Casilda, started it as a 16-year-old. 'Because there was no ice, they used to keep the *aguas* (water) cool in *ollas* (large clay jugs) that were immersed into damp sand in a wooden pan. They started with three flavours only, one was *limón con chia*. My aunt and grandmother added flavours: *jamaica* (hibiscus flower), *tamarindo* (tamarind), *sandía* (watermelon), *ciruela* (plum) and *zapote* (fruit native to Mexico),' says Señora Irinea. Today, Aguas Frescas Casilda serves around 20 flavours or 30 to 35 with combinations.

Some believe flavoured water originated back with the Aztecs, who used to sustain themselves on long journeys with a water and mashed fruit combination. Irinea says that for years fruit drinks have been important to religious occasions, particularly Easter. 'It's a tradition here during Semana Santa (Easter Holy Week) to gift the church with water.' (This is based on the Biblical story of a young woman who tried to give Jesus a drink of water on the way to the cross.)

'But people also drink *aguas frescas* at any time because they like it. It's very popular in the afternoons when they're in the market to eat. And of course, in the hot weather – March, April, May. And Saturdays is busy with the people who come from the pueblos (surrounding villages),' says Señora Irinea. The *limón con chia* may not be as colourful as the other the *aguas frescas* flavours, but it's guaranteed to quench a thirst.

Chef //
Irinea Valera Abella
Location //
Aguas Frescas Casilda, Oaxaca

AGUA FRESCA:
LIMÓN CON CHIA
Lime & chia seed cordial

Serves 10

Preparation & cooking time 30min (not including 3hr soaking of limes)

15 limes
960ml (1½pt) water, for soaking limes
2L (4pt) water, for the drink
100g (3½ oz) of chia seeds
120ml (4¼fl oz) water, for soaking chia seeds
sugar, to taste
ice, to serve

1   Wash the limes, put in a large dish and cover them in water. Leave to soak for around three hours (this makes it easier to grate them). Discard this water.

2   Grate the limes over a bowl, ensuring you don't get too much of the pith, and capture the small amount of juice that might escape as you do this. (In Mexico this is done in a *chirmolera* – a special pottery grinding bowl – but a normal grater is fine). Put the zested whole limes to one side, we won't be juicing them, per se.

3   Strain the lime zest through a muslin (or fine linen) fabric. (You may have to squeeze it a little at this point to extract juice). Discard the lime zest and keep the small amount of juice.

4   Pour 2L water into a jug. Add the lime juice and sugar to taste.

5   Prepare the chia seeds by soaking them for about five minutes in a little water to soften them.

6   Drain the chia seeds and stir them into the lime and water mixture.

7   Add ice as desired, and serve.

CHOCOLATE OAXAQUEÑA
Oaxacan hot chocolate

Hot chocolate is enjoyed daily in the village of Teotitlán del Valle, and Reyna Mendoza prepares it from scratch at her cooking school using a traditional Oaxacan method, roasting and crushing cacao beans.

Reyna Mendoza is a chocolate 'specialist'. Not only because she is from Teotitlán del Valle, a village 28km (17½ miles) southeast of Oaxaca, where hot chocolate is imbibed daily, but because she teaches her students the art of preparing it the traditional way at her cooking school, El Sabor Zapoteco, in the same village.

Traces of chocolate found in archaeological sites in the Central Valles date back thousands of years. Mayan art shows people with cacao-based drinks. In Meso-American times, cacao beans were so valuable, they were used as currency. One special pre-Hispanic, cacao-based 'power drink' is the *tejate* (which Mendoza also makes according to a long and complicated traditional process).

And then there's chocolate Oaxaqueña, a drink that is integral to daily life and traditions. Mendoza says, 'In our village, we serve chocolate at the *Dia de la Contendada*. This is when a boyfriend goes to the family of the girlfriend to *contentar* (to make them happy again) after he has 'stolen' his intended bride from her family. At this important gathering, the marriage date is set.'

Oaxacan hot chocolate consists of a blend of cacao beans that are toasted and ground and mixed with sugar and cinnamon. The chocolate blocks are sold throughout Oaxaca. But it is possible (albeit with modifications) to prepare both the chocolate blocks and drink from scratch, as Mendoza does, following a traditional process that is as time consuming as it is delicious.

Mendoza soaks cacao beans in water before roasting them deftly over a *comal* (a clay platter warmed by hot coals). Once roasted, she removes the shells, before crushing the cacao beans with a metate, a grinding tool and stone slab. Once ground to an oily paste, it is mixed with sugar and cinnamon (which has also been crushed by the metate) and patted into blocks. Then, finally, to prepare the hot chocolate drink, Mendoza melts a block with water and mixes it with a *molinillo*, an elaborately carved wooden tool, which she rubs between her hands to create a froth. The result? An ever-so-sweet, ancient taste of Mexico.

Chef //
Reyna Mendoza
Location //
El Sabor Zapoteco,
Teotitlán del Valle

CHOCOLATE OAXAQUEÑA

Oaxacan hot chocolate

Serves 4

Preparation & cooking time 3 hr (traditional method); 10 min (modern method)

For the traditional method

125g (4½oz) cacao beans
30ml (1fl oz) water
8g (¼oz) cinnamon sticks
250g (8¾oz) sugar
960ml (1¾pt) hot water, to serve

1 Put the cacao beans in a bowl and cover with water for 10 minutes.

2 Drain the beans and arrange on a *comal* (or clay plate) to toast over hot coals for 15 minutes or until dark and the outer shell starts to crack.

3 Allow to cool for several minutes then remove and discard the shell (do not leave any parts of the shell; this will ruin the drink).

4 If you are using a metate to crush the ingredients, heat it on low coals for around 20 minutes. (Before using, it must be well heated.)

5 Start to crush the products: first the cinnamon sticks, then the cacao beans until they release their fats. Mix in the sugar – briefly 'knead' it in using the stone tool.

6 Make a small pile of the mixture and use your hands to press the chocolate substance together. Cut into cubes about 4cm x 4cm (1½in x 1½in). Spread pieces in a tray and leave to cool.

7 Each cube makes four serves of hot chocolate when mixed with 960ml hot water (1¾pt).

*'Xoco latl means 'bitter water' [in the Aztec Nahuatl
language]. We drink chocolate daily here but always with
water, not milk. Milk was brought to Mexico by the Spanish.'*

Reyna Mendoza

For the modern method
480ml (17fl oz) water
480ml (17fl oz) milk
*150g (5¼oz) quality dark chocolate
(75% cacao or more)*
*½ tsp cinnamon powder (or 4 cinnamon
sticks, to serve)*
sugar, to taste

1   Pour the milk and water into a saucepan and bring to the boil.

2   When the milk and water mixture is boiling, take it off the heat and add the chocolate, mixing vigorously with an egg whisk.

3   Add cinnamon powder and stir, or you could serve each hot chocolate with a cinnamon stick (to stir each cup).

4   Add sugar to taste.

Tip
*These days, many Mexicans will take the cacao beans
to a mill where they are ground in a machine. Do not try
to grind cacao beans in a coffee grinder; the oil will clog up
the internal mechanism.*

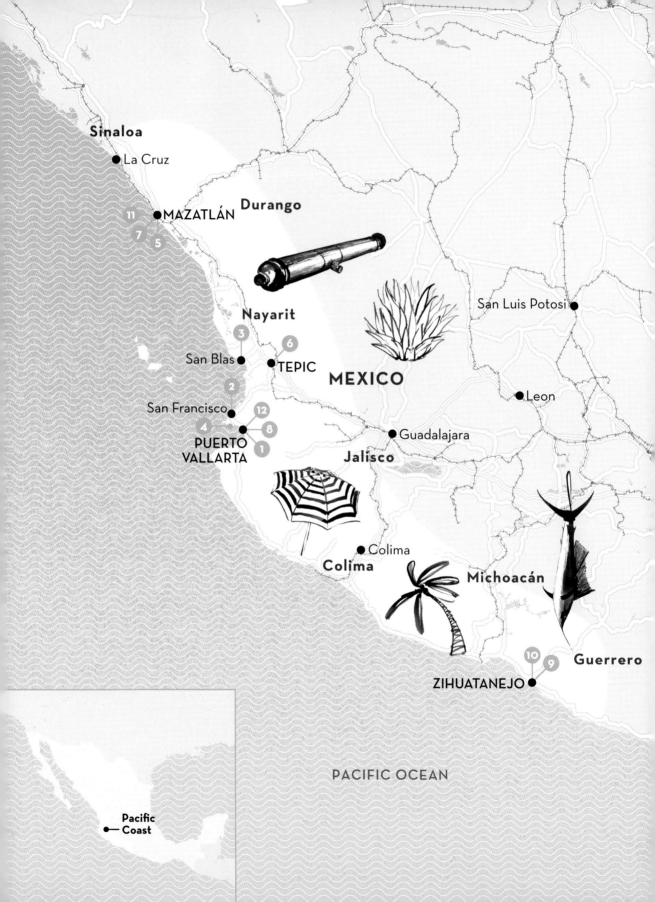

Sinaloa

● La Cruz

Durango

11
● MAZATLÁN
7
5

Nayarit

3
San Blas ●
6
● TEPIC

MEXICO

San Luis Potosi ●

2

San Francisco ●
12
4
8
1

PUERTO
VALLARTA

Jalisco

Guadalajara ●

Leon ●

● Colima

Colima

Michoacán

Guerrero

10
9

ZIHUATANEJO ●

PACIFIC OCEAN

Pacific
● Coast

PACIFIC COAST

Alongside the sandy coves, coconut plantations and rugged headlands of the Pacific Coast are some of Mexico's freshest fish and seafood dishes. It also produces much of the country's staple grains, cheeses and chiles

CALDO DE MARISCOS
Seafood soup
page 134

AGUACHILE
Shrimp marinated in lime-chile water
page 138

OYSTER SOPES
Tiny tortillas topped with oysters
page 142

CEVICHE PUNTA MITA
Coconut, green apple & grapefruit ceviche
page 148

ENCHILADAS DE CAMARÓN Y PULPO
Rolled tortillas stuffed with shrimp & octopus
page 152

BIRRIA DE RES DE TEPIC
Spicy beef stew Tepic style
page 156

MACHACA CON HUEVO
Shredded beef with scrambled egg
page 160

PESCADO ZARANDEADO
Grilled Fish Zarandeado
page 164

POZOLE GUERRERENSE
Hominy & pork pozole stew, Guerrero-style
page 168

PULPO A LA PARRILLA
Grilled octopus
page 174

PASTEL MEMINA
Contemporary twist on classic chocolate cake
page 178

CUALA DE COCO VALLARTA
Coconut custard
page 184

CALDO DE MARISCOS
Seafood bisque

Elizabeth Taylor and Richard Burton fell in love on its tropical shores, and Puerto Vallarta continues to lure couples and food fans. This elegant seafood soup captures the spirit and flavour of this idyllic coastline.

Although Puerto Vallarta has grown from a small fishing village to become one of the Pacific Coast's largest resort cities, its mix of golden sand beaches, red-tiled roofs and cobblestone streets make its Zona Romantica one of the world's most enduring destinations for romance. And the easy availability of seafood – reputed for its powers as both a hangover cure and as an aphrodisiac – makes caldo de mariscos an especially popular weekend dish.

Seafood soup as an expression of romance is even more notable when prepared by executive chef Tony Martinez, who took up cooking at the age of 16 for the sheer love of food. His father and grandfather were both chefs in hotels in Puerto Vallarta, specialising in Spanish cuisine, but Martinez was less interested in following in their footsteps than he was inspired by his passion for the kitchen.

Now helming the three restaurants within Villa Premiere, a boutique adults-only hotel at the edge of the *malecón* (breakwater) in Old Town Vallarta, he elevates traditional flavours and presentation through molecular gastronomy, creative herb garnishes and decadent flourishes, such as gold leaf. There's no better way to see his artistry in action than in this sophisticated seafood soup. 'A consommé base is the key to a great soup,' says Martinez, who draws on the bounty of the Bahía de Banderas, a deep body of water rich with marine life, yielding fresh caught yellowfin tuna, red snapper and shrimp. Manta rays, humpback and gray whales also come here to mate in the bay's warm fertile waters.

Seafood soup, created most often by simmering seafood within a tomato-based broth, is a fixture on menus throughout Puerto Vallarta. At La Corona, it's deconstructed in order to emphasise the flavour of the ingredients and create drama. The robust, warming, red chile broth is poured over a mix of fresh grilled fish, shrimp, octopus and scallops, which add a meaty sweetness. Enjoyed al fresco overlooking the sparkling Bahía de Banderas, with its fishing skiffs, sailboats and legends of *sirenas* (mermaids), it's a sure recipe for romance.

Chef //
Tony Martinez
Location //
La Corona, Puerto
Vallarta, Jalisco

CALDO DE MARISCOS
Seafood bisque

Serves 4

Preparation & cooking time 1 hr

1kg (2¼lb) shrimp shells
water, to cover shrimp shells
150g (5¼oz) red peppers
100g (3½oz) onion
150g (5¼oz) tomatoes
15g (½oz) garlic, peeled
150g (5¼oz) butter
500g (1lb) red snapper, cubed
1L (1¾pt) water
1L (1¾pt) double (heavy) cream
50g (1¾oz) cream cheese
shrimp bouillon (such as Knorr), to taste
pepper, to taste
salt, to taste
5g (⅛oz) Cajun spice
5g (⅛oz) paprika
10g (⅓oz) coriander (cilantro) leaves
100g (3½oz) leek (white part only)
150g (5¼oz) scallops
150g (5¼oz) clams
150g (5¼oz) shrimp
120g (4oz) mussels
150g (5¼oz) octopus tentacles

1   Preheat the oven to 200°C/400°F.

2   Put the shrimp shells in the oven to brown for 30 minutes.

3   Meanwhile, cut the red peppers, onions, and tomatoes into small pieces and cook in a saucepan with the whole garlic, half the butter and the red snapper cubes.

4   Add the baked shrimp shells to a pot and cover with water. Add half the heavy cream and all of the cream cheese, the shrimp bouillon, pepper, salt, Cajun spice and paprika to the shrimp shell water. Simmer on a low heat until ingredients are well cooked and soft.

5   Pass the shrimp shell mixture and the veg-red snapper mixture through a medium sieve, pressing the shells to pass as much liquid through as possible. Discard the shells.

6   Liquefy this sieved mixture, along with coriander and leeks, adding remaining butter and cream directly to a blender. Adjust seasonings.

7   Press the mixture through a fine sieve and reserve consommé.

8   Grill the scallops, clams, shrimp, mussels and octopus separately, place on a presentation plate and pour the reserved consommé on top.

AGUACHILE

Shrimp marinated in lime-chile water

Aguachile *is a lively mix of raw shrimp marinated in lime juice infused with serrano chile peppers. At Las Palmas, chef Sergio Romo serves four riffs on this classic seafood snack.*

Fast-developing Riviera Nayarit is home to a string of upscale beach destinations, such as Punta de Mita and boho-chic Sayulita. In still-under-the-radar San Francisco, beside a leafy square where a statue of St Francis de Assisi gazes over the village of 2000 people, lies Restaurant Las Palmas, where three generations of the Contreras family have been serving seafood since 1974. Although it has grown from a simple eatery, Las Palmas has stayed true to its roots. Mother Angelica Contreras still bustles about chatting with patrons, but son Sergio Romo, who studied at culinary school in Guadalajara, now helms the kitchen.

He enjoys adding new twists on classic dishes and one specialty is *aguachile*, a snack often prepared by marinating fresh shrimp in lime juice and serrano chile. 'It's traditionally enjoyed after a late night out or on weekends,' he says. Unlike ceviche, which can include fish, scallops or any mix of raw seafood, *aguachile* is always made with shrimp. And, it's sliced thinly and not necessarily 'cooked' in lime. 'Mexicans prefer to eat the shrimp before it changes colour, while tourists like it pink,' he explains.

Romo's variations include an *aguachile negro*, an Asian-inspired dish featuring charred Habanero; *aguachile rojo*, which gets extra heat from red chile morita – a fiery cousin to chipotle; and *aguachile naranjado*, an orange-hued version topped with a chiffonade of carrots. But it's his traditional green *aguachile* that is the perfect marriage of ultra-fresh shrimp, sea salt from Colima, slivers of red onion, and chunks of crunchy cucumber topped with slices of ripe avocado.

At Las Palmas, sink your toes into the sand beneath one of the tables while you wait for your order to be prepared. Your *aguachile* will arrive served in a stone molcajete (a traditional Mexican mortar and pestle). Topped with a squirt of Salsa Huichol and scooped over saltines, it delivers a rush of heat that's quickly balanced by the coolness of the cucumbers. Unlike its cooked counterpart, raw shrimp is so tender it's like taking a bite of the sea itself. A Pacífico beer rounds out the beachside experience.

Chef //
Sergio Romo
Location //
Las Palmas Restaurant, San Francisco, Nayarit

AGUACHILE
Shrimp marinated in lime-chile water

Serves 2

Preparation & cooking time 15 min

12 fresh large-sized shrimp
2 pepino criollo (if not available, choose
*   cucumbers with few seeds)*
½ red onion
juice of 1 lime
2 hot chile peppers (1 jalapeño, 1 serrano),
*   seeds removed (wear gloves for deseeding)*
3 leafy stalks coriander (cilantro)
2 tbsp water
1 clove garlic, peeled
salt, to taste
pepper, to taste
1 avocado, sliced thinly
sea salt, to serve (ideally from Colima but
*   any white sea salt will do)*
tostadas/saltines, to serve

1   Peel, devein and remove the heads of the shrimp. Cut the shrimp in half lengthwise and set aside.

2   Cut the pepino criollo and red onions into half-moons and thinly slice.

3   Blend the lime juice, chiles, coriander, water and garlic in a blender until smooth. Place in a large bowl and season with salt and pepper.

4   Add shrimp to the lime-chile mixture and fold in the pepino criollo and red onion.

5   Serve immediately (or let stand for a few minutes to 'cook' the shrimp), topped with thin slices of avocado and a sprinkle of sea salt.

6   Enjoy spooned over crispy tostadas or saltines.

Tip
The key to delicious aguachile is ultra-fresh shrimp.
How can a person tell if shrimp is fresh? 'It should be
firm and smell like the sea, with no fishy odour,' says
chef Romo, who gets shrimp delivered daily by fishers
in San Blas or La Cruz de Huanacaxtle.

OYSTER SOPES

Tiny tortillas topped with oysters

On weekends, local families head to San Blas to sunbathe, and feast on freshly shucked oysters. This appetizer by MasterChef Mexico judge Betty Vázquez combines sweet briny oysters with earthy maize.

n his 1882 poem *The Bells of San Blas*, Henry Wadsworth Longfellow portrays San Blas, located 65km (40 miles) west of Nayarit's state capital of Tepic, as a link between past and present. It's also a link between ocean and land, and there's no better dish to showcase the two than oyster sopes.

'For us, corn is part of our history and tradition,' says Betty Vázquez, MasterChef Mexico judge and executive chef at El Delfín Restaurant. 'We can't imagine a meal without tortillas.' Oyster sopes, tiny tortillas with pinched edges, are enjoyed as afternoon snacks or on weekends after a day at El Borrego Beach.

The estuaries and lagoons surrounding San Blas are an ideal incubator for shrimp, oysters and other marine life. Although it's possible to purchase oysters from vendors who 'cultivate' them within boxes set in local rivers, Vázquez relies on those sold by master oyster divers.

It's fascinating to watch oysters being harvested. Divers head to the San Cristobal River, where the salty Pacific and 'sweet' freshwaters meet before the water is filtered through the roots of mangroves. A diver will swim to an oyster bed towing an inner tube filled with a net and then dive beneath the murky surface to pry oysters off the rocks with a chiseled piece of rebar. The oysters are then shucked on shore.

Vázquez believes this proximity to nature and a traditional way of life keeps her grounded. After completing training at Le Cordon Bleu School in Paris, she returned to El Delfín, located within her family's Hotel Garza Canela. Here she decompresses from the hectic pace of life as a celebrity chef, enjoys the produce from the hotel's orchards and explores San Blas' culinary heritage, a legacy drawn from the influences of early traders from Asia, Germany, France and Spain.

High in protein, low in fat and immensely satisfying, oyster sopes are the perfect snack. The oysters' briny, delicate flavour shines atop the nuttiness of the tortilla, topped with *curtido* (pickled vegetables) and salty cheese. A true marriage of ocean and land.

Chef //
Betty Vázquez
Location //
Restaurant El Delfín, San Blas, Nayarit

OYSTER SOPES
Tiny tortillas topped with oysters

Serves 4

*Preparation & cooking time 30min (not
including overnight marinating of
vegetables)*

For the pickled vegetables
250g (8¾oz) carrots, julienned
½ medium white onion, sliced
serrano chile, to taste
½ tsp salt
1 garlic clove, minced
pinch oregano
250ml (8¾fl oz) water
250ml (8¾fl oz) white vinegar

For the sopes
1kg (2¼lb) masa harina (see boxed text, pxxx)
650ml (23fl oz) water or oyster water
1 tsp salt
vegetable oil, for deep frying

For the enchilada sauce
5 Guajillos chiles, deseeded, roughly chopped
⅓ white onion, roughly chopped
1 garlic clove, peeled
2 tomatoes, roughly chopped
¼ tsp cumin
½ tbsp oregano

For the pickled vegetables

1   Mix all the ingredients together and rest in the refrigerator for 24 hours.

For the sopes

1   Mix all ingredients together apart from the oil.

2   Knead the mixture on a floured surface for a few minutes until it forms a dough, then let it rest for 10 minutes.

3   To make the sopes, use a tortilla press, or use a plate to make the press. Pinch off a ping-pong ball sized piece of dough and place in the press.

4   Pinch the edges of the sope and then deep fry them in oil until slightly browned (approx. one minute). Then drain on a plate lined with absorbent paper towel.

For the enchilada sauce

1   In a saucepan bring the chile, onion, garlic and tomatoes to the boil. Simmer for around 30 minutes until soft.

2   Press the mixture through a sieve to remove the seeds, then stir through the cumin and oregano.

For the tomato sauce

5 tomatoes, roughly chopped
½ white onion, roughly chopped
water, for boiling
1 garlic clove, minced
salt, to taste
pinch of oregano

oil, for griddling
Cotija cheese, to serve (or feta)
Miramontes tequila (or other small-batch tequila), to serve

For the tomato sauce

1. Put the tomatoes and onions in a saucepan and cover with water (or use oyster water). Bring to the boil and simmer for 15 minutes.

2. Blend the mixture with the raw garlic and add salt and a pinch of oregano.

To assemble

1. Dip the *sopes* in the enchilada sauce and let each one cook for two minutes each side on a hot griddle in oil.

2. Remove from griddle and place oyster on top of each *sopes*.

3. Spoon tomato sauce over the oyster.

4. Top with pickled vegetables and Cotija cheese.

5. Serve with a shot of Miramontes tequila.

Salsa Huichol

Mexico's second most popular salsa, Salsa Huichol is produced within a modern factory in Tepic, Nayarit according to a secret family recipe developed more than 25 years ago. It's different to other Mexican hot sauces because it contains only Cascabel chile, a dark red pepper that gives the salsa a sultry, smoky flavour.

CEVICHE PUNTA MITA

*Coconut, green apple &
grapefruit ceviche*

*W Hotel's take
on standard ceviche
– traditionally a
mix of raw fish or
seafood marinated
in lime juice,
tomato, onion
and coriander –
is creative and
stylish. This
signature version
is made with
coconut milk.*

In Mexico, ceviche is as ubiquitous as the beach vendors who ply serapes up and down the Pacific Coast. In its most stripped down form, it's basically raw fish, usually a flaky white fish like robalo (snook) 'cooked' in fresh-squeezed lime juice and then mixed with chile, coriander and onion.

'We decided to switch things up a bit,' says Manuel Alejandro Jimenez Magallon, ceviche master at the W Hotel Punta de Mita, a sleek new resort in Riviera Nayarit. He presides over the action at the Chevicheria, a ceviche bar beneath a palapa-topped Chevrolet 3800 pick-up truck, set on the sand facing the crashing Pacific surf. The decor also features tiles patterned on the peyote-inspired beadwork of the Huichol people, and original art by Revolución Del Sueño, a local design studio.

When developing the ceviche menu, Jimenez drew on his experiences in Puerto Rico and Sinaloa for inspiration. Then, in collaboration with sous chef Marco Aquinas, he spent two weeks experimenting with taste combinations to create an inventory of 25 ceviches. Even the lime juice is customised and could include the house-made 'green juice': a concoction of green apple, celery, orange juice and serrano pepper or hibiscus flower syrup.

'We customise each ceviche based on the guest's mood and personality,' he says. His workstation contains a painter's palate of ingredients, such as mezcal, wasabi, fish sauce, tortilla ashes and pea shoots. Presentation is as important as the taste. Unlike traditional ceviche mounded in a bowl, these are works of art, with tendrils of pea shoots, cucumber, jicama, tortilla strips and dried Ancho chiles serving as sculptural elements.

Biting into a spoonful of the pearl-hued Punta Mita ceviche is a mouthful of freshness. Bright hits of Habanero chile and red onion are balanced by the creamy subtle sweetness of coconut, crunchy green apple and red grapefruit.

'Sometimes we cooks are behind the scenes in the kitchen, so it's a privilege to be outdoors in nature,' says Jimenez. Judging by the number of patrons seated beneath the shade of the Chevicheria, it's evident he's not alone.

Chef //
Manuel Alejandro
Jimenez Magallon (left),
pictured with mixologist
Gerardo Giron
Location //
W Hotel, Punta de Mita, Nayarit

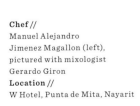

CEVICHE PUNTA MITA
Coconut, green apple & grapefruit ceviche

Serves 2

Preparation & cooking time 10 min

200g (7oz) Pacific Robalo (or any semi-firm white fish)
juice of 10 limes

For the coconut sauce
100ml (3½fl oz) coconut milk
½ clove garlic, minced
¼ white onion, finely diced
celery salt, to taste
pepper, to taste

For the avocado accompaniment
½ avocado, mashed
¼ white onion
½ clove garlic
50g (1¾oz) coriander (cilantro)
¼ serrano chile, deseeded
salt, to taste
1 lime, juiced
pepper, to taste

To serve
50g (1¾oz) green apple, diced
30g (1oz) red onion, minced
1 Habanero chile, minced & deseeded
3 red grapefruit segments, to serve
10 stalks of fresh mint/coriander (cilantro)
   leaves, to serve

1 Cut the fish into cubes to desired size.

2 Squeeze the juice of the 10 limes over the fish and let it stand for 10 minutes.

3 For the sauce, mix coconut milk, garlic, white onion, celery salt and pepper to taste. Liquefy in a blender, then add to the fish 'cooked' in the lime juice.

4 Mash avocado, onion, garlic, coriander, serrano chile, salt, lime juice and pepper to taste and liquefy in a blender. Dab drops, preferably using a piping bag, of the chile mixture over the top of the ceviche.

5 Garnish with diced green apple, minced red onion and Habanero chile, to taste.

6 Arrange red grapefruit sections and mint or coriander leaves over the top, to serve.

ENCHILADAS DE CAMARÓN Y PULPO

Rolled tortillas stuffed with shrimp & octopus

In Mazatlán, shrimp is more than an ingredient; it's an economic powerhouse. At La Mazatleca, chef Alan Zamudio brings his international influences to create a fusion experience in this lively resort city.

From September to March, up to 550 trawlers – the largest fleet in Mexico – head out from Mazatlán on three-week expeditions, returning with holds brimming with yellowleg, whiteleg, blue, and crystal shrimp. The best place to purchase these beauties is Las Changueras market where, under curbside awnings, vendors such as Ana y Claudia Mariscos weigh and sell shrimp graded by size. Across the street, other shrimpers' families sort and bag the tiny coral-hued, sun-dried shrimp popular for *botanas* (snacks) or soup.

Shrimp in many forms feature prominently in the menus of Mazatlán restaurants, most often butterflied and breaded or grilled. Executive chef Alan Zamudio of La Mazatleca wanted to shake things up a bit when he returned from culinary school in Monterrey to launch La Mazatleca, an upscale beachfront sports-bar located in the Zona Dorada (Golden Zone), the north Mazatlán neighbourhood filled with hotels, nightclubs and restaurants. Given the mix of patrons, the bar's menu needed to appeal to tourists as well as locals.

'I was influenced by my travels to Italy, Thailand and Argentina,' says Zamudio, 'And wanted to bring a fusion of global and Mexican flavours to a beach setting.'

It took him six months to perfect his shrimp and octopus enchilada dish called La Tambora. 'Everyone typically eats *mole* sauce with chicken so we decided to substitute shrimp and octopus,' he explains. 'At first glance people think "Um, I don't think so" but once they try it they love it.'

To make it, tender shrimp and octopus are tucked with white rice inside three rolled corn tortillas bathed in *mole*. The *mole's* velvety richness with its hints of cacao and spice complement the buttery sweetness of the seafood. A topping of red onion and radish escabeche and shredded lettuce is a welcome twist on the heavy melted cheese typically seen on most traditional enchiladas. Served with a chilled local Pacífico beer, it's best enjoyed with a view of Las Gaviotas beach.

Chef //
Alan Zamudio
Location //
La Mazatleca, Mazatlán

ENCHILADAS DE CAMARÓN Y PULPO
Rolled tortillas stuffed with shrimp & octopus

Serves 2

Preparation & cooking time 25 min

110g (4oz) white rice
½ red onion
2 limes, juiced
1 tsp salt
100g (3½oz) radish
100g (3½oz) romaine lettuce
100g (3½fl oz) Mole 'Dona Maria' or other
    prepared mole sauce
1 tbsp chicken stock/water
20g (¾oz) butter
60g (2oz) raw shrimp
60g (2oz) cooked octopus
salt, to taste
pepper, to taste
3 corn tortillas
oil, for frying
100g (3½oz) white sesame seeds, to serve

1. Slice radish thinly and cover with water for 30 minutes.

2. Prepare the rice as per packet instructions.

3. Slice the onion finely and marinate in the lime juice and salt.

4. Julienne the lettuce and set aside.

5. Dilute the mole with 1 tbsp of chicken stock or water and bring to a boil.

6. Meanwhile, place the butter in a frying pan and fry the shrimp until pink, then add the cooked octopus. Season with salt and pepper, to taste.

7. Fry the three tortillas in a little oil. Fill with the shrimp and octopus stew and the rice to make an enchilada.

8. Place the rolled enchilada on a plate, pour over the *mole* then sprinkle with sesame seeds, lettuce and radish.

Tip
You can use smaller, less expensive shrimp in this dish.

BIRRIA DE RES DE TEPIC

Spicy beef stew Tepic style

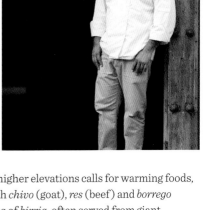

Served at special occasions, birria is a spicy stew made of goat, mutton or beef that's popular in the coastal highlands of Jalisco and Nayarit. At Emiliano, it's a power lunch for the city's elite.

The cooler temperatures at the Sierra's higher elevations calls for warming foods, such as the meaty dish *birria* made with *chivo* (goat), *res* (beef) and *borrego* (lamb). There's many different versions of *birria*, often served from giant clay pots at the side of the road. Also popular as a hangover or fortifying cure, signs announcing its availability begin appearing in the mornings.

'Every family has their own recipe for *birria*,' says Marco Valdivia, executive chef at Emiliano, an elegant restaurant set within an 18th-century historic building in the heart of Tepic, the state capital. Born in the pueblo of El Tambor, Valdivia began his career chopping onions at a hotel restaurant in Puerto Vallarta, but within a year had mastered enough skills to return to Tepic and helm his own kitchen. He is now considered one of the Pacific Coast's most talented young chefs.

His culinary philosophy is based on sourcing ingredients locally. A walk through Tepic's central market offers the opportunity to see the region's vast range of meats, and products such as wild mushrooms and fresh farm cheeses from Santiago Ixcuintla. Valdivia's innovative use of traditional ingredients places him in high demand, which means he can be found preparing dessert for the governor one day and catering for a wedding the next. Many dishes are accompanied by *raspadas*, a tostada created by toasting a tortilla on a *comal* (a ceramic dish/metal hotplate) separating it into layers and then deep frying it to crispy perfection.

At Emiliano, diners enjoy a deep mahogany-hued *birria* redolent with chile, cumin and faint notes of cinnamon. A spoonful of broth is an infusion of warmth that pairs nicely with Nance liqueur, made from the tart yellow fruit that grows wild regionally. Seated within the courtyard, when the ceiling rolls back to reveal the night stars, there is a natural connection through food and centuries of tradition to the time of Emiliano Zapata, himself a champion of agrarian land reform.

Chef //
Marco Valdivia
Location //
Emiliano Restaurant, Tepic

BIRRIA DE RES DE TEPIC
Spicy beef stew Tepic style

Serves 6

Preparation & cooking time 6 hr (not including overnight marinading of meat)

15 pieces dried Ancho chiles, soaked in water
4 cloves garlic, whole
500g (17½oz) white onion
2 tbsp oregano
1 pinch cumin
20 black peppercorns
5 cloves
240ml (8½fl oz) cane vinegar (or substitute rice vinegar)
1 pinch thyme
800g (28oz) cooked tomato with juices
salt and pepper, to taste
3kg (6½lb) beef shank with bone and marrow
coriander (cilantro), chopped, to serve
onion, cut into slivers, to serve
lime wedges, to serve
corn tortillas, to serve

1 Blend the chiles with all ingredients, except the beef, lime, onion, coriander and corn tortillas. Pour the chile mixture over the meat and marinate in the fridge overnight.

2 Put the meat and its marinade in a covered pot and bake in a 160°C/320°F oven for five hours.

3 Remove the pot from the oven and skim any fat from the surface with a spoon. Remove the meat from the pot, then let the broth simmer uncovered on the stovetop for the remaining hour to reduce the liquid. Let the meat cool a little, shred, then set aside.

4 Ladle the broth into a bowl and top with the shredded meat. Sprinkle the *birria* with chopped coriander and slivered onions. Serve with lime wedges and tortillas.

Tip
In Nayarit and Jalisco, the broth is prepared by slow-cooking it over a wood-fire in a clay pot but an oven works just as well, as long as you ensure the meat remains fully covered by liquid at all times.

MACHACA CON HUEVO

Shredded beef with scrambled egg

Bring your appetite for this hearty dish, originally eaten by ranchers who relied on beef jerky for sustenance during cattle drives and long days on the arid terrain of the Sierra Madre Mountains.

With its shrimp markets, tuna processing factory and one of the world's longest oceanfront promenades, it would be tempting to think of Mazatlán as being all about the sea. But Sinaloa is bordered by the states of Durango, Chihuahua and Sonora, prime cattle ranching territory renowned for high quality beef. This meat-loving side of Mazatlán's identity is captured in machaca, a dish featuring a dried, salted and shredded beef that's similar to jerky.

'Machaca is always made the same way and is well-known in every family,' says Jose Feliciano 'Pepe' Martinez Rodriguez, executive chef at Lucila's in Viejo Mazatlán (Historic Mazatlán). He developed his cooking skills while taking care of seven siblings as he grew up, and his menu offers two classic versions of machaca, one plain and another with scrambled eggs. Lucila's is an ideal spot to try them both. It's set beneath the 20ft ceilings of a restored 19th-century mansion that had fallen into disrepair until rescued and restored into an eight-room luxury boutique hotel by owner, Mazatlán native Conchita Valades de Boccard, who named the restaurant for her mother.

'In Sonora, the machaca is drier and saltier than it is here,' explains chef Pepe. 'In Mazatlán, it's moister and has vegetables.' He recommends purchasing machaca prepackaged at José Maria Pino Suarez Mercado, the city's central market. With its soaring atrium of glass and wrought iron, it's a hive of activity, where you can see strolling mariachis, meat cleavers flashing in *carnicerías* (butchers' shops), pyramids of fruit, and rows of plastic bags filled with shredded cured beef.

At Lucila's breakfast is enjoyed on the terrace, where each plate of machaca con huevo comes served with a dollop of refried beans and a *tamale de elote* (sweet corn) or a *tamale de colocha* (a spicy courgette/zucchini developed by esteemed chef Patricia Quintana). Similar to corned beef hash, machaca is comfort food. The oversized portions and savoury spiced beef evoke the sweeping landscapes of Northern Mexico, providing plenty of fuel for a day of adventure.

Chef //
Jose Feliciano 'Pepe'
Martinez Rodriguez
Location //
Lucila's Restaurant, Historic
Mazatlàn

MACHACA CON HUEVO
Shredded beef with scrambled egg

Serves 4

Preparation & cooking time 15min

10g (⅓oz) fresh poblano chile (or any mild green chilli)
10g (⅓oz) white onion
1 medium tomato
2 tbsp vegetable oil
80g (2¾oz) machaca (dried beef jerky)
2 eggs
refried beans, to serve
tortillas, to serve

Tip
If you can't find machaca in your local Latin store, make it at home by braising a skirt steak or pot roast in water with garlic, oregano, pepper and onion for two hours and then shredding it. You'll then need to add salt to this recipe.

1 Wearing gloves and using a knife, remove all the membranes and seeds from the chile. You may wish to use less chile than specified, depending on heat preference.

2 Mince the onion, tomato and chile into small pieces. Set the tomatoes aside.

3 Pour vegetable oil into a large skillet. Sauté onions and chile over medium-high heat for two to three minutes until brown and caramelised.

4 Add machaca to the onions and chile and keep stirring and mixing until the machaca begins to get crispy.

5 Add the tomatoes and continue frying the mixture until tomatoes are softened.

6 Beat two eggs in a separate bowl until thick and creamy. Add eggs to the mixture in the skillet, stirring until scrambled and fully cooked.

7 Serve with refried beans and handmade tortillas.

PESCADO ZARANDEADO

Zarandeado grilled fish

This dish's origins are hotly contested; both Nayarit and Sinaloa claim to be its birthplace. Marinated and grilled, the fish is served whole, with diners filling their tortillas with fish and toppings to taste.

The actual definition of the Spanish verb *zarandear* is to turn something from one side to the other in a rapid movement,' says Mavi Graf, a chef who was born in Sinaloa but moved to Puerto Vallarta over thirty years ago. 'The turning of the fish on both sides is what makes this fish *zarandeado.*'

For Graf, cooking is a family affair. One of nine children, she learned her craft and gained an appreciation food, ritual and tradition from her mother and grandmother. She now leads cooking classes that include tours of Puerto Vallarta's fruit markets, *carnicerías* (butchers' shops) and Mercado del Mar, a busy fish market in the 5 de Diciembre neighbourhood where you can hear fishmongers shouting out the day's offerings, gawk at gigantic lobsters and ogle local fish, octopus and shrimp on ice.

Zarandeado grilled fish is both easy to prepare and delicious. It's ideal for family get-togethers where extra side dishes can be added if more guests arrive. Traditionally grilled over hot coals of mesquite wood, it can also be grilled over charcoal or on a gas barbecue. The spices are basted onto the fish prior to grilling, which gives the finished dish a beautiful ochre colour.

At Arte Culinario, dinner is enjoyed on the terrace, an oasis filled with patio containers spilling with herbs and edible flowers. Although the views of the marina and mountains are stellar, it's the Pescado Zarandeado that's the centrepiece. Charred with a smoky flavour, it's tender and juicy enough to slip within a warm tortilla and top to taste with refried beans, avocado, red onion, rice and salsa. Served with a chilled beer or glass of Jamaica water and enjoyed with family at the beach or poolside, it's an idyllic melding of food, geography and heritage.

Chef //
Mavi Graf
Location //
Arte Culinario Cooking School,
Puerto Vallarta

PESCADO ZARANDEADO
Zarandeado grilled fish

Serves 6

Preparation & cooking time 30min (not including 1hr for marinating fish)

1.5kg (3⅓lb) whole sea bass (or mahimahi, sole or
   red snapper), cleaned, scaled and butterflied by a
   fishmonger, with backbone removed
5 garlic cloves
2 tbsp mayonnaise
1 tbsp mustard
1 tbsp Worcestershire sauce
1 tbsp Maggi seasoning sauce
1 tbsp soy sauce
3 tbsp Huichol salsa
juice of 1 lime
salt, to taste
pepper, to taste
50g (1¾oz) butter
salsa, to serve
refried beans, to serve
guacamole, to serve
warm tortillas, to serve

Tip
*The secret to grilling fish zarandeado style
is turning the fish over once rather than
repeatedly. Allow the fish to brown on the
first side before turning it over to finish it
on the foil side and don't overcook it.*

1 Wash the fish and pat it dry.

2 Mince three of the garlic cloves into a
small bowl then add mayonnaise, mustard,
Worcestershire sauce, Maggi seasoning sauce,
soy sauce and Huichol salsa. Mix together until
completely blended.

3 Squeeze the lime juice over the whole fish,
season with salt and pepper and spread the
sauce mixture inside and outside of the fish.
Let it marinate for one hour.

4 Mince the two remaining garlic cloves and put
them together with the butter in a small frying
pan over low heat so the butter melts and the
garlic cooks without burning. Let it cool.

5 Open your fish rack for grilling and cover one
side of the rack with tin foil. Place the fish with
the skin side facing the tin foil, close the fish
grilling rack. Brush some of the garlic butter
on the fish and cook the exposed side of the fish
first for about five to seven minutes. Then turn
it over and cook it for 10 minutes longer on the
skin side.

6 Serve the fish at the centre of the table. Spoon
salsa into a bowl to serve alongside it, as well
as some refried beans, guacamole and warm
tortillas.

POZOLE GUERRERENSE

*Hominy & pork pozole stew,
Guerrero-style*

*If it's Thursday
in Zihuatanejo,
it's Pozole Day.
Although beloved
across Mexico, at
Restaurant Any,
this hominy and
pork stew is an art,
a tradition, and the
spirit of Guerrero
conviviality all in
one steaming bowl.*

P ozole's popularity – in a beach town where summer temperatures can be scorching – is a mystery. 'I really can't explain it,' says Jose Munoz Gutierrez of Restaurant Any, a pozoleria near Zihuatanejo's central market. 'Some people think eating hot food in a hot climate cools you down, but I think we love it because we associate it with family and good times.'

At Restaurant Any, the pozole love affair began around 20 years ago with Gutierrez's wife Any, his father-in-law and mother-in-law. The menu features pozole daily, unlike other restaurants and *cenadurías* (pop-up restaurants in people's homes) where it's only available Thursdays. 'In other regions of Mexico, pozole can be red, white or green and made with either chicken or pork, but here it's always pork,' says Gutierrez who is quick to point out he is not a chef but instead mastered his recipe at home.

Making pozole is labour-intensive. It begins by soaking hominy corn in an alkaline solution to remove the hull and germ. The plump kernels are then simmered in a broth made of a pig's head, trotters and shank. Since most customers request green pozole instead of the traditional white version, seasonings such as oregano, coriander, tomatillos, jalapeño, garlic and *pepitoria* (shelled pumpkin seeds) are blended, added to the broth and then thickened with shredded pork.

With its colourful murals, piñatas rustling in the breeze and ranchera music spilling through open archways, dining at Restaurant Any is like joining an instant party. Pozole arrives brimming in a bowl surrounded by toppings of *chicharrón* (fried pork shin), red onion, radishes, avocado, peppers, taco chips, a chalupa (boat-shaped tortilla) with Cotija cheese, as well as two clay *jarritos* (small clay jars) of mezcal.

Eating pozole follows a time-honoured ritual. Choose the toppings you like, sprinkle them over the stew and squeeze fresh lime over it. Then, take a spoonful of pozole, a bite of chalupa with salty cheese, and a sip of sweet, vanilla-noted mezcal. For the next spoon, opt for a crumble of crispy *chicharrónes* or crunchy radish. It's an addictive rhythm of tantalising tastes that will have you wishing every city celebrated Pozole Thursday.

Chef //
Jose Munoz Gutierrez
Location //
Restaurant Any, also known
as La Casa del Pozole,
Zihuatanejo

POZOLE GUERRERENSE
Hominy & pork pozole stew, Guerrero-style

Serves 10–12

Preparation & cooking time 7 hrs

For the meat
10L (8¾qt) water
3 tsp salt
1 head of garlic, mashed
½ pork head
1kg (2¼lb) pork shank
3 medium pork trotters
1kg (2¼lb) dry white hominy, nixtamalized by
    cooking in water with calcium hydroxide to
    soften the corn kernel (or 4 x 375g/13¼oz cans
    of drained and rinsed white hominy)

For the green sauce
100g (3½oz) pepitas (pumpkin seeds)
2 jalapeño peppers
500g (1lb) tomatillos, husks removed
2 pieces of epazote (just the leaves)
3 stalks coriander/cilantro
2 tsp oregano

1 Measure 10 litres of water (or enough to fully cover meat) into a large pot. Add garlic and pork. Bring to a boil, skim off any grey foam and simmer at medium heat for three or more hours, until meat is tender. In Mexico, this might take place all morning.

2 Once the meat is tender, strain, remove and discard bones and reserve the meat.

3 Skim any fat from the broth and add the soaked, prepared hominy to the pot. Return to a boil and simmer for another two hours. If using canned hominy, skip this step.

4 Toast the pumpkin seeds in a dry skillet until they pop and are golden brown. Add, along with the rest of the sauce ingredients, to a blender or food processor. Process until smooth.

5 Add the green sauce to the broth and hominy mixture. If you're using canned hominy, this is the time to add it. Simmer for one hour. Add the shredded meat and allow to warm thoroughly.

½ piece poblano chile (or any mild-
    medium green chilli)
6 cloves of garlic
1 onion
475ml (16¾fl oz) pork broth or water
handful radish leaves

**For the toppings (amounts as per
    personal preference)**
radishes, sliced
red onion, diced
chalupa or tortilla with white Cotija
    cheese
chicharrónes
avocado, sliced
lime wedges
tostadas or tacos chips
salt, to taste
pepper, to taste

mezcal (preferably Tobala), to serve

6   Ladle pozole into individual bowls set on round plates.
Either circle each bowl with toppings or place toppings in
the centre of the table so each person can add their own.

7   Serve with shots of mezcal, preferably Tobala.

PULPO A LA PARRILLA

Grilled octopus

Pulpo *(octopus), a popular dish along Guerrero's central coast, is eaten weekly by locals as an economical alternative to meat or shrimp. At La Marea it's rubbed with spices and grilled to showcase its delicate flavour.*

Chef //
Eduardo Avila Zarraga
Location //
La Marea Restaurant,
Zihuatanejo

Chef Eduardo Avila has cooked his way around the finest restaurants in the Caribbean and Mexico, but his latest role, as executive chef at the Viceroy Zihuatanejo, an upscale resort set on the beachfront at Playa La Ropa, has him convinced that the seafood on Mexico's Pacific Coast is something special. Although the ocean's bounty includes red snapper, yellowfin tuna and mahimahi, the star of the day is octopus.

'Octopus practically jumps out of the sea here,' he says. 'The flavour is so superior it's even able to stand alone in dishes.' Much like wine that has a special terroir, the cool water of the Pacific Ocean gives octopus a sweetness that it lacks in other locations. Grilling it and serving it with smoked paprika and potatoes is a tribute to the classic Galician dish from northern Spain that highlights its lobster-like flavour.

'When shopping for fresh octopus, look for ones that are pale in colour and tender to the touch,' says Avila. 'And remember it's going to shrink by around 30% when it's cooked, so plan ahead.' He should know a thing or two about shopping. The youngest in a family of nine, he helped his mother shop seasonally and source ingredients. Although he earned his Certified Chef de Cuisine (CCC) from the American Culinary Federation, and mastered his craft at exclusive clubs in the Bahamas, as well as at luxury hotels, such as the St Regis and The Four Seasons, his culinary philosophy is to keep it simple.

His version of grilled *pulpo* is a thing of beauty – its shape echoing the organic curves of La Marea Restaurant itself, a spiral adobe structure designed by influential Zihuatanejo architect Enrique Zozaya. The seared octopus is caramelised, yet the tentacles shine with deep purple tones and are tender, the taste of the sea balanced by the smokiness of the paprika and the grill. The addition of potatoes and asparagus makes it a light yet satisfying meal.

PULPO A LA PARRILLA
Grilled octopus

Serves 4

Preparation & cooking time 2 hrs

1 Spanish onion
water, to cover octopus
175ml (6fl oz) white wine
2 tbsp garlic, chopped
2 tsp rock sea salt
bouquet garni
1½kg (3⅓lb) fresh, cleaned octopus
2¼kg (5lb) Idaho potatoes (or any baking potatoes)
2 tbsp olive oil
8 stalks fresh asparagus
1 tsp salt
1 tsp crushed black pepper
2 tbsp smoked paprika
225g (8oz) coriander (cilantro), chopped

'Be sure to use sea salt when boiling octopus; it makes a real difference in the flavour.'

Eduardo Avila Zarraga

1 Preheat the oven to 150°C/300°F.

2 Chop just one-third of the onion (the remainder will be sliced).

3 Fill a medium-sized pot with water, add white wine, garlic, the chopped onion, salt and bouquet garni. Place over medium heat, bring to a boil, add octopus and simmer for 1 to 1½ hours.

4 While octopus is cooking, slice the remaining onion. Peel potatoes and cut into ⅓cm (⅛in) slices.

5 In a skillet over medium high heat, add olive oil and sauté potatoes and onion until golden brown. Finish cooking them in the oven until tender.

6 Once octopus is fully cooked, remove it from the stock, dry on a paper towel and season octopus and asparagus with salt, pepper and paprika. Let the octopus rest for at least one hour.

7 Grill asparagus for a few minutes until cooked.

8 Grill the octopus until just caramelised. Depending on size, cut into pieces, preserving tentacles intact for presentation and place on top of a bed of potatoes.

9 Top with grilled asparagus and sprinkle with coriander.

PASTEL MEMINA
Contemporary twist on
classic chocolate cake

This elegant interpretation of classic chocolate cake created by chef Marino Maganda, ambassador for Mazatlán's new culinary movement, showcases the city's heritage, as well as Mexican ingredients of cacao, agave and local fruit.

Porfirio Díaz, who served seven terms as president beginning in the 1800s, was apparently so enamoured of everything French that Mexico became known as 'Paris of the Americas' during his regime. The period's legacy of neoclassical architecture is especially evident in Mazatlán's historic centre, where the stately buildings reflect the wealth and commercial power of the city's early entrepreneurs. Casa 46, housed in a restored mansion featuring a 2nd-storey terrace overlooking the wrought iron gazebo and palm trees of Plaza Machado, is an ideal place to soak up the nostalgia of this formative era, including its cuisine.

'In order for the new generation to understand the evolution of gastronomy they must understand its roots,' says Marino Maganda, executive chef of Pueblo Bonito Resorts and Casa 46, two of Mazatlán's most privileged addresses. At Casa 46, the decor in each dining room represents a facet of Mazatlecan high society. From the Carnaval Room lined with sequined masquerade masks to the Mariners Room displaying vintage black-and-white photos of yachts and fishing tournaments, the cosy atmosphere of faded opulence feels like dining at the home of a wealthy aunt. The restaurant's special occasion chocolate cake – known as Pastel Memina – is based on a favourite recipe of the owner's mother. A sophisticated interpretation of a classic, it features many local ingredients, such as blue agave distillate by Los Osuna, founded in 1876.

'We take ingredients such as cacao, lime and berries that are representative of the region and transform them, elevating the dish to another level,' says chef Maganda, who also heads up Raíces Culinarias, a new gastronomy festival in Mazatlán that showcases the city as well as its cuisine.

Topped with a wafer of glossy chocolate, this cake is as pretty as an elegantly wrapped gift. The sweet ice cream offers a mouthful of strawberry ripeness against the bitter chocolate, then there's the richness of the layers of milky chocolate and an explosion of freshness from the lime and tequila foam. It's a decadent slice celebrating the good life and its milestones.

Chef //
Marino Maganda Pacheco
Location //
Casa 46, Mazatlán

PASTEL MEMINA

Contemporary twist on classic chocolate cake

Serves 8

Preparation & cooking time 1 hr 25 min

For the classic cake
113g (4oz) butter
150g (5¼oz) sugar
3 eggs
200g (7oz) flour
13g (½oz) baking powder
35g (1¼oz) cocoa
250ml (8¾fl oz) warm milk

For the chocolate bath
200g (7fl oz) water
20g (¾oz) sugar
30g (1oz) cocoa

For the dark chocolate icing
125ml (4fl oz) milk
125g (4fl oz) cream
45g (1½oz) sugar
50g (1¾oz) yolks
125g (4½oz) dark 70% chocolate
2 leaves of gelatin

For the cocoa streusel
115g (4oz) cold butter, cubed
100g (3½oz) sugar
175g (6oz) flour
50g (1¾oz) cocoa
1 tsp salt

For the classic cake

1   Preheat the oven to 170°C/340°F.

2   Beat butter and sugar in a bowl, adding eggs one at a time.

3   Then add the sifted flour, baking powder and cocoa, followed by warm milk.

4   Pour into 20cm x 20cm (8in x 8in) pan and bake for 30 minutes. Cut in 2½cm x 10cm (1in x 4in) portions.

For the chocolate bath

1   Mix together all the ingredients in a saucepan and bring to a low boil. Simmer for a few minutes, then set aside.

For the cocoa streusel

1   Preheat oven to 160°C/320°F.

2   Mix ingredients in a blender until crumbly.

3   Cool in the refrigerator for approx one hour and then bake in the oven for 15 minutes.

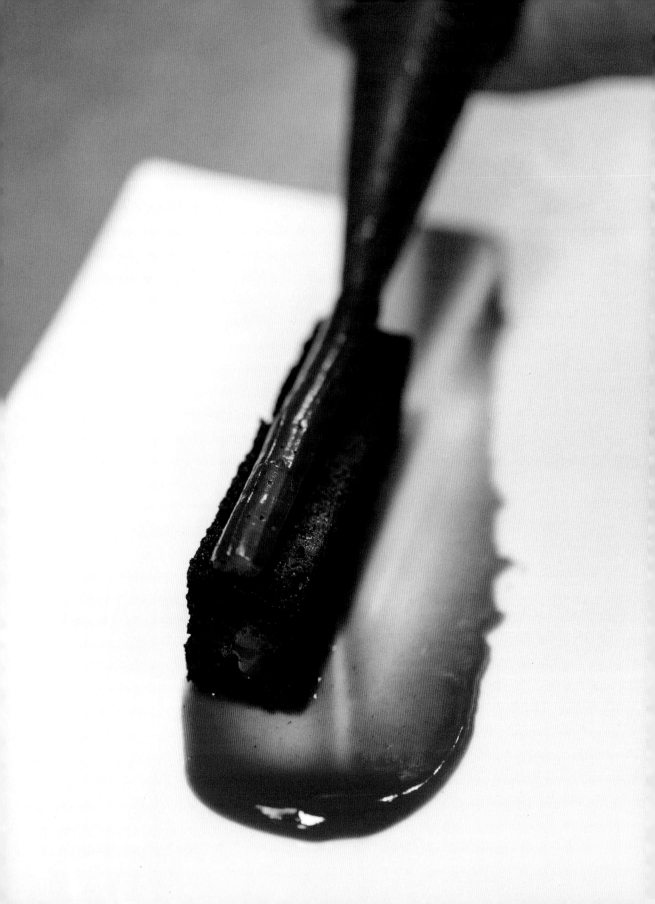

For the strawberry jam

500g (17½oz) strawberries, mashed
200g (7oz) sugar
20g (¾oz) pectin

For the strawberry butter ice cream

100g (3½oz) butter
350g (12¼oz) mashed strawberry pulp
60g (2oz) sugar
20g (¾oz) dextrose
50g (1¾oz) ice cream stabiliser, such
*   as Procrema*
25g (¾oz) glycerine
tsp salt

For the lime tequila foam

40g (1½oz) syrup (comprising half
*   water and half sugar)*
1½ leaves of gelatin
pinch of xanthan gum
150g (5¼fl oz) egg whites
130g (4½fl oz) lime juice
60g (2fl oz) distilled agave Los Osuna or tequila

10cm x 2½cm (4in x 1in) pre-purchased
*   chocolate icing sheet*

For the strawberry jam

1. Heat the strawberry pulp with half of the sugar, then add the remaining sugar mixed with pectin.

2. Boil for five minutes, stirring constantly.

3. Remove from the heat, cover and refrigerate.

For the strawberry butter ice cream

1. Heat the butter, strawberry pulp and sugar until blended.

2. Cool the strawberry mixture then blitz with the remaining ingredients in the blender. Freeze.

For the lime tequila foam

1. Heat syrup in a saucepan and dissolve in the gelatin.

2. Refrigerate the syrup then, once cool, incorporate the xanthan and mix in a blender.

3. Beat egg whites, combine with the lime juice and the syrup gelatine mixture. Add the agave tequila and mix in a blender.

4. Pour the mixture into a cold whipping siphon, shake and foam.

To assemble

1. Smear about a quarter of the strawberry jam on a plate with a spatula. Place the cake in the centre of the plate.

2. Top the chocolate cake with the remaining strawberry jam. Brush with chocolate bath. Top the cake with the pre-purchased sheet of chocolate.

3. Sprinkle some streusel at the base of the cake. Place ice cream on streusel.

4. Finally, using the siphon, add lime tequila foam on side.

CUALA
DE COCO
VALLARTA
Coconut custard

*Peddled by street
vendors on the
cobblestone
streets of Puerto
Vallarta's historic
Zona Romantica,
this traditional
Vallartense treat
is a delicious blend
of coconut oil, corn
masa, cinnamon
and milk.*

I f you listen carefully during the ringing of the midday bells of Nuestra Señora
de Guadalupe Church in Puerto Vallarta's historic zone, you can hear the voices
of street vendors calling 'cuala de coco'. 'The dish isn't known outside of Puerto
Vallarta,' says Chef Julio César Castillón of Gaby's Restaurant, a family-run
establishment located two blocks from the iconic church. 'But here it's something every
local craves on a hot afternoon.'

Ordinarily, the dessert is made in vendors' homes and its main ingredients
consist of the crushed seed of a *coco de aceite* (coconut oil palm), cinnamon and
condensed or evaporated milk. The mixture is heated and then chilled until it takes
on the consistency of gelatin and is sold in plastic cups. 'At Gaby's, we've elevated
the presentation to make it a more formal dessert,' says César of his version, which
includes a coulis of chipotle and hibiscus flower. 'We wanted to pay tribute to the
traditional home recipe but also showcase it visually.'

This evolution of a traditional local dessert parallels the transformation of Gaby's
Restaurant itself. From humble beginnings in 1989 when grandparents Cristina
Pérez and César Castillón created a *lonchería* (snack bar) using a plank of wood for a
counter, it expanded over decades to serve *comida corrida* (fast food) for workers in the
downtown area. Now helmed by grandson, chef Julio César, who studied gastronomy at
the Higher Technological Institute of Puerto Vallarta, and his sister Gabby César who
handles the business side of the enterprise, it has expanded to become a multistorey
restaurant with garden terraces. The menu has also grown, and now features a wide
range of Mexican specialties, such as chile rellenos (stuffed peppers) and *raicilla*, a
potent agave distillate similar to mezcal.

Tasting coconut cuala at Gaby's is a treat. The ruby red coulis adds a sweet tartness
to the rich, earthy flavour of the masa coconut base, which itself is like *atole* (hot
cornmeal drink), flan and custard, all mixed into one. Listening to the church bells
ringing, it's tempting to pretend you're a local, and this is your midday treat.

Chef //
Julio César Castillón
Location //
Gaby's Restaurant,
Puerto Vallarta

CUALA DE COCO VALLARTA
Coconut custard

Serves 6

Preparation & cooking time 1 hr 25 min

For the cuala
500ml (17½fl oz) whole milk
60g (2oz) masa (ready-made dough made
from corn-maize flour)
1 stick whole cinnamon
15g (½oz) sugar
150ml (5¼fl oz) evaporated milk
200ml (7fl oz) condensed milk
120ml (4¼oz) coquito de aceite (crushed seed
of coco palm; or use shredded unsweetened
coconut with 1 tbsp vegetable oil)

For the coulis
250ml (8¾fl oz) Jamaica concentrate
(or pomegranate or cranberry concentrate)
100g (3½oz) sugar
250ml (8¾oz) water
2 tbsp honey
50g (1¾oz) chile chipotle adobado (smoke-dried
chipotles in adobo sauce)

sprinkles of dessicated/finely shredded
coconut, to serve

1 Bring half the milk to a boil in a saucepan.

2 Dissolve the masa in the remaining milk.

3 In a blender, blitz the cinnamon with the sugar, evaporated milk and the condensed milk.

4 Smash the coconut seed in a dishtowel (or use shredded coconut) and then blitz in a blender until fine.

5 Combine all the milks with the coconut and heat in a saucepan over medium-low heat until it begins to thicken. Continue to cook for 25 minutes.

6 Pour into a 20cm x 20cm (8in x 8in) cake pan or six individual cups, allow to cool and then slice or dispense into individual serving cups.

7 Prepare the coulis by mixing Jamaica concentrate, sugar, water and honey then boil in a saucepan until reduced to a thick syrup.

8 Liquefy the chipotles in a blender until smooth, then add to the syrup.

9 Garnish the cuala with the cooled coulis and sprinkles of coconut.

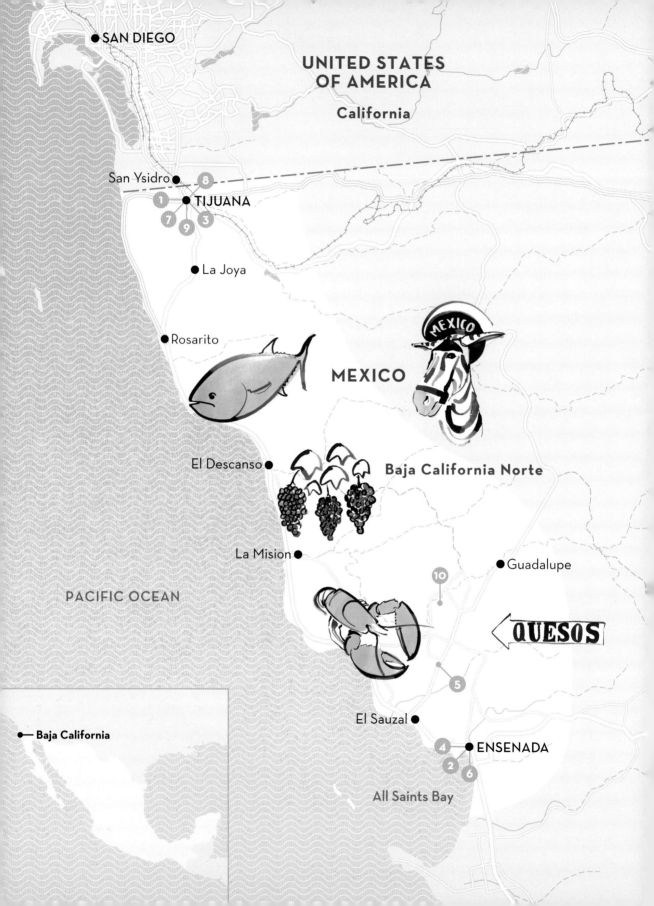

BAJA CALIFORNIA

The northernmost tip of Mexico plays host to some of the top restaurants in Latin America. Its Mediterranean climate and coastal air is prime for the vineyards of Valle de Guadalupe, which produce most of Mexico's wine

ENSALADA CESAR
Caesar Salad
page 190

ALMEJA PISMO PREPARADA
Prepared Pismo clam
page 194

TACOS DE LANGOSTA
Lobster tacos
page 198

TACOS DE PESCADO
Fish tacos
page 204

CRÈME BRÛLÉE DE TUETANO CON ERIZO
Beef bone marrow with sea urchin crème brûlée
page 208

EL GATO DE CODORNIZ
Cat's game of quail (tic-tac-toe)
page 212

CERDO ADOBADO Y ARROZ FRITO CON KIMCHI
Adobada pork with kimchi fried rice
page 216

PESCADO AHUMADO EN HUESO EN SALSA DE OSTION CON PURE DE BETABEL
Smoked fish with oyster sauce & beetroot puree
page 220

CAMOTE AHUMADO CON NÉCTAR DE CAFE
Smoked sweet potato with coffee nectar
page 224

BETABELES ROSTIZADOS CON AJO
Roasted beetroot with garlic
page 228

ENSALADA CESAR
Caesar Salad

Tijuana's gift to the world, this version of the original Caesar salad recipe calls for the romaine leaves being left long, as this dish was originally eaten with the hands.

D id you know that the Caesar salad was invented in Tijuana? Legend has it that Italian-American Caesar Cardini opened up Caesar's Restaurant in Tijuana during the 1920s. It was at the time of Prohibition in the US, and Cardini's restaurant became extremely popular in Mexico as frustration built up across the border. It is said that on a busy night in the restaurant, these ingredients were thrown together as a 'salad concoction', preparing it tableside for the diners to see. It was there and then that this internationally renowned salad was born.

In the Prohibition era, the US government was also closing the border entry at 6pm, so Cardini figured it was a great time to open up Caesar's hotel, which remains in the same location where the legendary restaurant stands today. Though it wasn't all good times for Caesar's – after Cardini left Tijuana to open restaurants in San Diego, a few generations of his family carried on the business. Then, due to low tourism, this living part of Tijuana history on Revolution St was forced to close its doors in 2009. It was in 2010 that the Plascencia family of restaurateurs brought new life to Caesar's, with a grand re-opening, and Caesar salad's birthplace continues to thrive today.

Armando Villegas is one of the *ensaladeros* (the salad preparers who assembles this dish for diners at their table) and has been serving this salad for 31 years. He says that from the very fxirst time he saw the Caesar salad prepared, it was the croutons that were added to finish the dish that sticks in his mind. They were made daily at the restaurant and, in this recipe, it's important that the croutons are slices cut from a baguette and toasted to perfection. They add a nice crunch to the pleasantly acidic and creamy dressing that covers the crisp green leaves of romaine. Once you make this version, you will never look at bottled Caesar salad dressing the same way again.

Chef //
Nadya Fernandez (pictured
left is Armando Villegas,
ensaladeros)
Location //
Caesar's Restaurante, Tijuana

ENSALADA CESAR

Caesar Salad

Serves 2

Preparation time 5–7 min

1 head romaine lettuce (cos lettuce)
180ml (6fl oz) extra virgin olive oil
¼ tbsp mustard powder (ground mustard)
6 anchovy fillets, chopped
1 clove garlic, crushed
1 lime, juiced
1 tsp Worcestershire sauce
60g (2oz) grated Parmesan cheese
1 egg
240ml (8fl oz) water
4 slices cut from a baguette
freshly ground black pepper, to taste
salt, to taste

1   Clean lettuce thoroughly and refrigerate until crisp, at least 1 hour or more.

2   Preheat the oven to 180°C/350°F.

3   In a wooden bowl, combine olive oil, ground mustard, anchovies, garlic, lime juice, Worcestershire sauce and half of the Parmesan cheese. Whisk until well combined.

4   Toast the baguette slices on a baking sheet in the oven for 10 to 12 minutes, turning them over halfway through.

5   To coddle the egg, bring a pan of 240ml (8fl oz) water to a boil. Submerge the egg for exactly one minute. Use a slotted spoon to remove the egg into a small bowl with water and ice cubes.

6   Once cooled, crack the egg and separate the yolk. Whisk the yolk into the dressing until thoroughly blended. Add the whole romaine lettuce leaves, gently rolling them into the dressing.

7   Serve on a platter and add the rest of the grated Parmesan cheese, the baguette/croutons, freshly ground black pepper, and salt to taste.

ALMEJA PISMO PREPARADA

Pismo clams

Sabina Bandera's street food cart La Guerrerense serves up mariscos that are so fresh and delicious, very few ingredients are needed, apart from her famous home-made salsa: the seafood speaks for itself.

Chef //
Sabina Bandera
Location //
La Guerrerense, Ensenada

W hen Anthony Bourdain, renowned chef and TV personality, made a pilgrimage to Sabina Bandera's street food cart for the Baja episode of his show *No Reservations*, he proclaimed her as 'a genius' and the food 'shockingly good'. There can be no higher acclaim. Sabrina is more than thankful for his visit, along with those she receives from other international stars who have made their way to Baja for her seafood-studded tostadas.

Originally from the state of Guerrero, Sabina Bandera grew up around livestock, making fresh *requesón* (a ricotta-like cheese) and *crema* (cream), and enjoying such dishes as *pozole* and *cochinita pibil* (see p254). She had little to no knowledge about mariscos, until she moved to the port city of Ensenada. It wasn't until her in-laws, who founded this curbside cart, showed her their seafood ways that she became a maestro in cooking with these ingredients.

This internationally known cart has been set up since 1960, and the lines are not slowing down anytime soon. As soon as La Guerrerense came to life, so did Sabina's passion for creating her own salsas. She began to prepare them from the ingredients in her garden, experimenting with different chiles. Now, these incredible sauces can be purchased from her cart, and are more than worth the trip to her little corner of Baja California. A fond favourite is the chile de árbol with peanuts.

La Guerrerense is renowned for its ceviche and tostadas piled high with mariscos, such as sea snail, octopus, and sea urchin. For this recipe, the large Pismo clam, and its tenderly sweet meat is topped with local ingredients: pico de gallo, plenty of freshly squeezed lime juice, creamy slices of avocado, and just a few drops of hot sauce.

ALMEJA PISMO PREPARADA
Pismo clams

Serves 4–6

Preparation time 10 min

For the pico de gallo
1 tomato, diced
1 white onion, diced
1 bunch coriander (cilantro), roughly chopped
salt, to taste

To serve
4–6 Pismo clams
4–6 limes, juiced
ketchup, to taste
hot sauce, to taste
2 avocados, thinly sliced

1 In a small bowl, mix all of the pico de gallo ingredients together.

2 Shuck open a clam, and cut the meat of the clam away from the shell, then cut the meat into slices. Place the slices of clam meat back into the shell. Repeat for each clam.

3 Add approx 1 tbsp of the pico de gallo on top of each serve of clam meat.

4 Squeeze the juice of one lime over the pico de gallo and each serving of clam meat. Drizzle with ketchup, and hot sauce to taste. Top with slices of fresh avocado.

TACOS DE LANGOSTA
Lobster tacos

Chef Oso Campos' passion for seafood inspires innovative dishes, such as this lobster taco: an ode to Puerto Nuevo (also known as 'lobster village) in the seaside town of Rosarito.

Oso Campos is one of the incredible young chefs who are coming straight out of culinary school and taking over the food scene in Baja. He started with Tacos Kokopelli in 2012, a new venture on wheels with two close friends, grilling up seafood tacos curbside on the streets of Tijuana. Fast forward a few years and there's been a name change – Tras/Horizonte – and a new bricks-and-mortar location, featuring an eclectically coloured interior with pieces from local artists. The dishes coming out of the kitchen are just as vivacious.

Oso is a master of salsas, and in Mexico, salsas are more than just a sauce used to top off your taco. Salsas can be anything from simple produce roasted and blended together, to a range of exotic spices from different regions, which result in gorgeous flavours and colours.

This lobster taco is Oso's homage to Puerto Nuevo, a 50-minute drive south from Tijuana. Puerto Nuevo is famous for serving up giant lobsters drenched in butter, with all of the trimmings. These include fluffy arroz rojo (red rice), refried beans, and homemade flour tortillas. While corn tortillas are definitely the common staple in this region, there is more than a soft spot for the flour version, which is the vessel called for in this recipe. The tortilla is filled to the brim with melted cheese, roasted poblano chile, lobster covered in rich blackened butter, and topped with mango chiltepin salsa, and a sprinkling of fresh pomegranate seeds. A bite into this beauty and your taste buds are in for an explosion of sensations. There's a subtle sweetness from the plump lobster, but the blackened butter swathes through with an extra dimension. The addition of the extra 'pop' from the pomegranate seeds is playful, while the heat from the chiltepin penetrates the juicy pieces of mango.

Chef //
Guillermo 'Oso' Campos
Location //
Tras/Horizonte, Tijuana

TACOS DE LANGOSTA
Lobster tacos

Serves 2

Preparation & cooking time 1hr 45min

For the lobster stock
2 fresh lobster tails
2L water (or enough to cover lobster)

For the blackened butter
200g (7oz) butter
1 clove garlic, finely minced
200ml (7fl oz) lobster stock
100g (3½oz) chimole (see below)
½ tsp oregano
¼ tsp cumin
2 tsp salt
2 tbsp red wine vinegar

For the chimole
1 whole white or yellow onion
10 garlic cloves
1 small carrot
2 tsp olive oil, for drizzling over the veg,
*   + 1 tsp for blending*
1 tsp vinegar
salt & pepper, to taste

For the lobster stock & blackened butter

1. Fill a large pot with enough water to fully submerge the lobster tails. Bring to a boil. Once the water comes to a boil, place the lobster tails in the water for 30 seconds. Remove the tails (keeping the hot water/stock) and immediately put the lobster tails in a cold water bath. This will remove the meat from the shell, while the meat is still raw.

2. Place the shells from the lobster tails back into the broth, and bring the water to a low boil to create the lobster stock. Simmer for about one hour. Meanwhile, prepare the *chimole* (see below).

3. To a pan, add the lobster stock together with the blackened butter ingredients, and let it reduce by 50%. Place the meat of the lobster tails into the pan and cook for a maximum of three to four minutes.

For the chimole

1. Preheat oven to 220°C/425°F.

2. Put the onion, garlic cloves, and carrot on parchment paper or a foil-lined baking sheet and drizzle with olive oil. Roast in the oven until the vegetables are cooked evenly, rotating halfway through.

3. Let the vegetables cool slightly for about five minutes, then place in a blender or food processor, with the additional 1 tsp of olive oil and vinegar. Season to taste. Blend and pour into a bowl to serve.

For the poblano chiles

2 large poblano chiles (or fresh serrano peppers)
480g (1lb) white onion, thinly sliced
1 tsp salt
2 tbsp canola oil
150g (5¼oz) sour cream
pinch of ground cumin

For the mango salsa

500g (1lb) mango pulp
100 ml (3½fl oz) water
60ml (2fl oz) grape vinegar
1 sprig mint leaves
8 pieces chiltepin chile (or bird's eye chillis)

To serve

2 small flour tortillas
60g (2oz) Monterey Jack cheese
    (or Gouda), grated
2 tbsp fresh pomegranate seeds

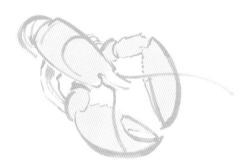

For the poblano chiles

1. Char the poblano chiles over a gas flame, or under a grill/broiler until blackened. Place in a ziplock bag until slightly cooled. When cool to touch, peel off the outer skin, deseed the chiles, and slice them into strips.

2. In a hot pan, sauté the onion with the salt in the canola oil and cover for about seven minutes.

3. Add the poblano chiles to the onion mixture, and sauté together for two more minutes. Add in the sour cream and cumin, until all ingredients are well incorporated. Cover and set aside.

For the mango salsa

1. Put all of the ingredients into a blender, and blitz until smooth.

To assemble

1. Place your tortillas on a hot dry skillet or *comal* (ceramic dish/metal hotplate) and add an even amount of cheese to each, to make a quesadilla.

2. Place your poblano chile mixture on top of the melted cheese.

3. Place the lobster in blackened butter on top of the poblano chiles.

4. Drizzle with the mango salsa.

5. Garnish with fresh pomegranate seeds.

TACOS DE PESCADO

Fish tacos

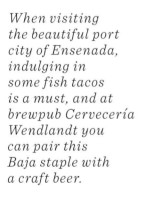

When visiting the beautiful port city of Ensenada, indulging in some fish tacos is a must, and at brewpub Cervecería Wendlandt you can pair this Baja staple with a craft beer.

The natives of Ensenada are extremely proud of their beloved regional fish taco. It's said that the influx of migrant Japanese fishers who worked and lived in the region greatly influenced this creation. You will notice with the way that it is fried, it is very much inspired by the Japanese tempura technique. Traditionally, a sturdy piece of shark or white fish is dipped in the batter, and then fried until it achieves its gorgeous crunchy exterior, and tender flaky interior.

Each Ensenada street food stand or restaurant will have its own variations of salsas and condiments to pile high on top of your tacos. But at Cervecería Wendlandt, one of Baja's top craft breweries, chef Krista Velasco keeps it classic with a cool *crema* (sour cream), fresh pico de gallo, shredded cabbage, and a squeeze of fresh lime juice, but then adds in just the right amount of heat with the topping of pickled onion and Habanero chile.

The dimly lit Wendlandt brewpub has warm wood tables, and industrial touches, like the exposed metal light fixtures, and high stools. The beer taps span the wall, pouring some of the top craft beers in the region. That's the added bonus here: as well as experiencing outstanding tacos, there's the Baja California craft beer scene to enjoy, which is increasingly keeping apace with the culinary movement. Nothing pairs quite like an icy cold brew and plate full of tacos.

Fill your glass with brews ranging from Amber ale, Saison and Imperial Pale Ale, to American wheat, and stout. Rosarito born chef Krista Velasco serves up both American fare, and Baja classics. 'The fish taco takes me back to my childhood. It was something we used to eat a lot. With my recipe, I'm trying to highlight all the great ingredients that we have in Baja.'

Chef //
Krista Velasco
Location //
Cervecería Wendlandt,
Ensenada

TACOS DE PESCADO

Fish tacos

Serves 6

Preparation & cooking time 1 hr

For the pickled onions with Habanero chile
1 white onion, finely sliced
2 fresh Habanero chiles, finely diced
juice of 3 limes
2 tbsp white vinegar
1 tbsp dried oregano
½ tbsp salt

For the beer batter
130g (4½oz) flour
1 tbsp salt
1 tsp black pepper
350ml (12fl oz) light beer
3 tbsp sriracha sauce

For the dressing
115g (4oz) mayonnaise
60g (2oz) sour cream
juice of 2 limes
½ clove of garlic, grated
salt & pepper, to taste

For the pico de gallo
6 tomatoes, deseeded & diced
1 white onion, finely diced
3 serrano chiles, deseeded & diced
1 bunch coriander (cilantro), roughly chopped
juice of 2 limes
½ tbsp salt

For the fish
vegetable oil (or grapeseed oil), for frying
500g (1lb) mako shark or white fish, cut into 18 strips

To serve
18 corn tortillas
½ head of cabbage, finely shredded
5 avocados, thinly sliced
lime juice, to taste

1 In a small bowl, mix all of the ingredients for the pickled onions and Habanero chile, and refrigerate.

2 In a large bowl, whisk all the beer batter ingredients together, and let sit at room temperature.

3 In a small bowl, mix all of the ingredients for the dressing and refrigerate.

4 In a small bowl, mix all of the ingredients for the pico de gallo and refrigerate.

5 Heat oil in a deep fryer or a pot that can hold 2½cm to 4cm (1in to 1½in) of oil, to prepare to fry the fish pieces.

6 Take the fish strips and dip them in the beer batter. Shake off excess batter. Gently drop fish strips into the hot oil. Once the fish is golden brown, use a scoop to take them out of the oil and leave to dry on absorbent kitchen towel.

7 Heat your corn tortillas on a *comal* (or dry skillet).

8 To serve, take a corn tortilla, top it with a piece of fish, then the dressing, some cabbage, a dollop of pico de gallo, some of the pickled onion with Habanero chile, a slice of avocado and a squeeze of fresh lime juice.

CRÈME BRÛLÉE DE TUETANO CON ERIZO

Beef bone marrow with sea urchin crème brûlée

Chef Roberto Alcocer brings the land and sea together for this sinfully satisfying rendition of crème brûlée, uniting the rich and savoury flavours of beef bone marrow with creamy sea urchin.

After over a decade working in top kitchens throughout the world, chef Roberto Alcocer took it upon himself to open up Malva, an open-air restaurant perched among the trees in Mexico's famed wine country (it shares the property with the Mina Penélope vineyards). His dishes are inspired not just by the love for his home country of Mexico or the region of Baja California but his own life experiences.

The property has its own livestock and grows its own produce, including such herbs as the restaurant's namesake, malva leaf (a nutritious edible green). You will also find most of the cheeses are made on-site as well. The beauty of Valle de Guadalupe is that it's not only possible to enjoy the wonderful wines and culinary creations that come out of the region, but also to see the detail that goes into preserving the lush surrounding areas. Chefs, cooks, vignerons and locals alike take pride in their land, and do all that is possible to keep it thriving.

This dish is a prime example of using both the land and sea that surrounds Baja California, maximising the use of fresh local ingredients. 'The surf and turf idea brings non common ingredients together,' says Roberto Alcocer, 'but both are so delicious, and the cooking process transforms the marrow into a texture very similar to traditional crème brûlée.'

As soon as your spoon cracks into the thin layer of lightly brûléed crust, the salty bits of cheese, briny slivers of sea urchin (a local delicacy), and tender pieces of bone marrow combine, which tempers the traditionally rich flavour of the bone marrow, elevating this dish to a whole new level. A glass of Mina Penélope's Julio Syrah pairs swimmingly with this dish. It's sophisticated, yet classic, and a beautiful homage to the region.

Chef //
Roberto Alcocer
Location //
Malva, Valle de Guadalupe

CRÈME BRÛLÉE DE TUETANO CON ERIZO

Beef bone marrow with sea urchin crème brûlée

Serves 2

Preparation & cooking time 1 hr

570g (1¼lb) beef bone marrow
360 ml (12½fl oz) heavy cream
2 egg yolks
1 whole egg
5 tbsp sugar
1 tsp aged cheese, grated
2 slivers of sea urchin
purslane sprouts (or watercress), to serve
1 tbsp gremolata, to serve
salt & pepper, to taste

1 Preheat the oven to 160°C/320°F.

2 Remove the marrow from each bone until you have 60g (2oz).

3 In a pot of boiling water, put a bowl of the marrow and melt it down, rather like chocolate, constantly whisking. It should take approximately 10 minutes.

4 Place the cream in a saucepan over medium-high heat and bring to a boil. Fold the bone marrow into the cream.

5 In a bowl, whisk the whole egg together with the two egg yolks. Slowly pour the cream into the eggs while constantly stirring. Then strain this mixture through a fine mesh sieve.

6 Pour the mixture evenly into ramekins. Place the ramekins into a cake tin. Pour enough hot water into the tin so the water comes halfway up the sides of the ramekins. Place the cake tin into the hot oven for about 45 minutes. Remove ramekins and leave to set at room temperature.

7 Sprinkle sugar and cheese on top of each ramekin. Then put the pieces of sea urchin on the top and pass a blowtorch over slightly. (Alternatively, put under a grill or use the top rack under a broiler for five to 10 minutes on high heat until caramelised.) Garnish with purslane sprouts and gremolata, and season with salt and pepper.

EL GATO DE CODORNIZ

Cat's game of quail (tic-tac-toe)

The waterside eatery Manzanilla is run by husband-and-wife star chef duo Benito Molina and Solange Muris. This playful dish of quail is among the famous dishes for which the restaurant is renowned

Known for its coastal views, and Mediterranean-like climate, Ensenada, otherwise known as 'The Cinderella of the Pacific' is resplendent with open-air fish markets and *carretas de mariscos* (seafood carts). While street food is very apparent in this region, it's restaurants like Manzanilla that have grabbed the attention of gourmands worldwide.

Benito Molina hails from Mexico City and his wife Solange Muris comes from Cuernavaca Morelos. They decided to make Ensenada their home and were among the first Mexican chefs to open their own restaurant here in 2000. The location of the seaside port city is what drew them to the cuisine; the fresh seafood market is just blocks away, and while their menu is abundant with seafood, it's this whimsical tic-tac-toe (noughts and crosses) game of quail that has become celebrated by many. The dish is presented on a tic-tac-toe board, with calamari ink used for drawing on the symbols.

While the dish is a tribute to local flavours – the quail (as well as the olive oil, and wines served in the restaurant) is sourced from the Valle de Guadalupe, a mere 15 minutes away – there is also an Asian influence. As you take a bite into the crisp skin and tender quail interior, you'll note bits of tangy kimchi coming in to round out the richness of the meaty chile-spiced mushrooms. Make sure to grab a bit of every ingredient on your fork and don't forget to drag it through the calamari ink too, because that, along with the capers, make for the saltiness that cuts through the quail juice and tasty pig's foot sauce.

Chef //
Benito Molina & Solange Muris
Location //
Manzanilla, Ensenada

EL GATO DE CODORNIZ

Cat's game of quail (tic-tac-toe)

Serves 2

Preparation & cooking time 40 min

For the pig's foot sauce
1 piece of pig's foot
½ tsp pork or chicken broth

For the quail
3 small sage leaves
1 tbsp vegetable oil
3 quail breasts
1 tbsp butter

For the mushrooms
1 tbsp olive oil
1 mushroom, sliced
½ tbsp onion, finely diced
½ tbsp garlic, finely minced
½ tbsp capers
2 tbsp Guajillo salsa
½ tbsp quail cooking juices

calamari ink, to serve
kimchi, to serve

1 In a blender place the pig's foot and broth, blitz until well combined.

2 Place the sage leaves underneath the skin of the quail breasts.

3 In a hot frying pan, add the vegetable oil, and brown the quail breasts on each side. Melt the butter in the same pan and spoon it over the quail. Reserve ½ tbsp of the quail cooking juices.

4 Heat olive oil in a pan on a medium-high heat and add the mushroom, browning on each side. Remove from the pan and set aside.

5 To the same pan, add the onion and sauté until translucent, then add in the garlic and capers. Return the cooked mushrooms to the pan, along with the Guajillo salsa, and quail stock.

6 On a plate, sketch out a tic-tac-toe board with the calamari ink, forming a total of nine spaces (squares). Place the quail breasts on the board in a diagonal fashion. The kimchi is then placed on top of the mushrooms in two of the squares. The pig's foot sauce is spooned into another square. Eat by grabbing a piece of each ingredient and running it through the sauce.

CERDO ADOBADO Y ARROZ FRITO CON KIMCHI

Adobada pork with kimchi fried rice

Chef Adria Montaño is standing at the forefront of the younger generation of Baja California's chefs. This dish is the perfect example of Asian Mexican fusion, using both local and traditional ingredients.

Chef //
Adria Montaño
Location //
Don Ramen, Tijuana

The Baja capital of Mexicali has a very prominent migration of Asian cultures, and throughout this region you will find many dishes where chefs have added their own touches and a fusion of Asian flavours. The food carts have been doing a roaring trade on the street corners of Tijuana for decades, but only recently was there a transformation in the traditional offerings, with a wider variety of ingredients and increasingly elaborate cooking techniques.

Besides the quintessential tacos, burritos, tortas and tostadas that head the majority of the carts' menus, you can find truly unique dishes that highlight the local cuisine, while adding touches of flair. Telefónica Gastro Park is one of many food cart 'hubs' in the city, with such varied offerings as local cheeses, duck quesadillas, brioche french toast, house made sausages, and coffee with desserts. It's here you'll find Don Ramen: the first mobile food truck to serve ramen in Tijuana.

'As I started creating my own dishes, I knew I had to use Korean ingredients,' says Adria. 'Yet, I also knew these weren't as popular with the local public as they were with myself, and although I knew it was something that could be promoted at a more gourmet, upscale level, that wasn't my intention. I wanted it to be something that could be eaten as comfort food, because that was what it meant to me.'

All of Don Ramen's Asian style dishes are inspired by the street food scene in Tijuana. Adobada (achiote rubbed) pork is found on spits all over the city, and is usually being sliced off into piping hot tortillas for tacos. In this case, the slightly smoky and fiery pork, is placed on a bed of crisped up fried rice, studded with tangy kimchi. The ponzu sauce adds a delightful acidity, and as soon as you cut into the fried egg, out comes the oozing rich yellow yolk to round out the dish.

CERDO ADOBADO Y ARROZ FRITO CON KIMCHI

Adobada pork with kimchi fried rice

Serves 4

Preparation & cooking time 30 min

900g (2lb) rice (preferably short grain)
3 tbsp butter
1 tsp extra virgin olive oil
200g (7oz) daikon (or red radish) kimchi,
*   roughly chopped*
2 tbsp kimchi juice
100g (3½oz) cooked pork shoulder
*   (adobada style; see tip)*
30ml (1fl oz) ponzu sauce
salsa macha, to taste, plus extra to serve (see tip)
4 tbsp coriander (cilantro), chopped
½ small spring onion/green onion + 1 tsp
*   minced, for garnish*
1 tsp fresh lime juice
1 tbsp vegetable oil
4 eggs
salt, to taste
1 tsp roasted peanuts, to garnish

1   Cook the rice according to packet instructions, then let cool.

2   In a nonstick pan, melt butter over a medium-low heat, add olive oil and the cooked rice. Stir-fry until the rice starts to get crispy, about two minutes.

3   Add kimchi and the kimchi juice to the pan. Stir until it comes to the boil. Add adobada pork, and cook until sauce is nearly completely absorbed. Add the ponzu sauce.

4   Cook, stirring, until the rice has absorbed the sauce and is very hot – this should take about five minutes. Add salsa macha, coriander, spring onion and lime juice, to taste.

5   Place a small nonstick pan over medium heat and add the vegetable oil. When it is hot, add eggs, season with salt, and fry.

6   Serve rice topped with fried eggs, peanuts, a sprinkle of green onions and salsa macha.

Adobada rub

To make the pork adobada style, rub with Guajillo chile, garlic, salt, white vinegar, onion and achiote.

Salsa macha

Salsa macha can be made by frying garlic, dried chiles and peanuts in a generous amount of oil. Remove the chiles, peanuts and garlic from the oil, and blend them in a mortar and pestle or food processor, to create a paste. Then add in the oil from the pan to create a delicious spicy salsa.

PESCADO AHUMADO EN HUESO EN SALSA DE OSTION CON PURE DE BETABEL

Smoked fish with oyster sauce
& beetroot puree

Baja oysters transform into a silky sauce, bringing out both the savoury and wood-fired essence of this smoked fish delicacy by chef Humberto Aviles of Malinche in Tijuana.

Chef //
Humberto Aviles
Location //
Malinche, Tijuana

When asked what three ingredients chef Humberto always has on hand in his Tijuana kitchen, he replied, 'Wood, seafood, and locally grown vegetables.' Like most chefs of this region, he finds it a pleasure to have the bounty of the Pacific Ocean and fully stocked gardens within arm's reach.

Having gained experience through his time spent in kitchens in Playa del Carmen, Puerto Vallarta and Spain, he decided to further his knowledge and study at the Culinary Art School in Tijuana. His latest restaurant, Malinche, has bright, yellow-hued interiors with gorgeous tile accents, and rustic furniture. The whole feel is of wide open spaces, making it difficult to remember you're situated in the middle of the bustling streets of Tijuana.

Humberto pays close attention to naturally plating his food, letting the flavours and textures tell the story. The beauty of impeccably fresh ingredients can seem so simple, yet it's just what makes dining in Baja so unforgettable. 'I'm in search of the top regional ingredients, so that I am able to express both the essence of the Californias, and its distinct cultures through my food,' he says. This smoked fish combines the essence of the ocean with a briny oyster sauce, which greets the mineral-rich beetroot with texture and a pop of colour. The pineapple dressing sets a subtle tone of sweet acidity in the background while letting the natural flavours shine through.

PESCADO AHUMADO EN HUESO EN SALSA DE OSTION CON PURE DE BETABEL

Smoked fish with oyster sauce & beetroot puree

Serves 2

Preparation & cooking time 20 min

230g (½lb) whole fish (such as mackerel)

2 medium beetroots

240ml (8½fl oz) chicken broth

6 oysters

1 tbsp oyster sauce

2–3 pieces chicken skin (to produce 1 tbsp chicken skin crumbs)

2 tbsp olive oil

200g (7oz) onion, sliced

1 tsp pineapple vinegar

1   Preheat the oven to 190°C/375°F.

2   Smoke fish on a perforated pan over a hot charcoal grill for 12 minutes (six minutes on each side).

3   Place the beetroots on a sheet of foil and drizzle with olive oil. Fold up the sides to enclose the beetroots and place on a baking sheet in the oven for 45 minutes to one hour, until tender. Set aside.

4   Heat chicken broth, oysters and oyster sauce in a saucepan over a low heat. Reduce mixture until it thickens.

5   Dry the chicken skin, then bake for about an hour, until the skin crisps up and turns brown. Once cooled, crumble it into tiny pieces and set aside.

6   Place one of the beetroots in a blender with 1 tbsp of the olive oil, and blend until smooth. Slice the other beetroot for garnish.

7   Place the onion in a dry skillet over medium-high heat on the stovetop and char for about three minutes each. Set aside.

8   In a bowl, whisk together the pineapple vinegar and the remaining 1 tbsp olive oil.

9   To serve, spread the beetroot puree on a plate, top with smoked fish, sprinkle with chicken skin, and drizzle pineapple vinegar mixture over the top. Garnish with the sliced beetroot and the onion.

CAMOTE AHUMADO CON NÉCTAR DE CAFE

Smoked sweet potato
with coffee nectar

Inspired by the rising coffee scene in Tijuana, chef Javier Plascencia created this dish of smoked sweet potato with coffee nectar. It represents his distinct style at Misión 19, while using sustainable and local ingredients.

If you roam the streets of Tijuana, the scent of charcoal-grilled carne asada (grilled beef) tacos wafts through the air. It is a very distinct aroma, and to chef Javier Plascencia, it's both a fond memory and an inspiration for his kitchen at Misión 19.

Javier was born into a family of restaurateurs and has been raised in the kitchens of Baja California since childhood. He set out to develop his own style using the best products that this cross-border region has to offer. The city of Tijuana is extremely close to his heart, and showing the world what this vivacious city has to offer on the gastronomic front has been no small feat. Javier has travelled throughout Mexico and the rest of the world, but it's his hometown roots that stand out in every single meal he creates. All of the ingredients and wine that are served at Misión 19, come from within a 193km (120-mile) radius of the restaurant in Tijuana. This encompasses not only the bustling markets in Tijuana, but also the Valle de Guadalupe, and even San Diego across the Californian border.

Javier's inspired use of cold brew coffee nectar in this dish, stems from the burgeoning coffee scene in Tijuana. An increasing number of small craft coffee spots are popping up, and cooks and coffee enthusiasts alike are showing their love for this liquid gold. Before even taking a bite into this dish, the smoky aromatics flow up to your nose: this is regional cuisine at its finest. The tender cuts of beef with bits of flaky salt create that little bit of crunch, next to the perfectly cooked rounds of sweet potato. The caramelised pieces of onion bring out just the right amount of sweetness, tying in perfectly with the hints of mesquite and cold brew coffee nectar sauce.

Chef //
Javier Plascencia
Location //
Misión 19, Tijuana

CAMOTE AHUMADO CON NÉCTAR DE CAFE

Smoked sweet potato with coffee nectar

Serves 4

Preparation & cooking time 1 hr 15 min

3 small sweet japanese sweet potatoes (or
*   any sweet potatoes)*
115g (4oz) beef tenderloin, cubed
salt, to taste
pepper, to taste
85g (3oz) large dates, pitted
30g (1oz) ginger, finely chopped
60ml (2fl oz) grapeseed oil
30g (1oz) morita chipotle powder
15ml (½fl oz) balsamic vinegar
1 small Spanish onion
4 small tomatillos, to serve
60g (2oz) okra leaves, to serve
30g (1oz) regaliz (liquorice root), grated, to serve
115ml (4fl oz) Mexican cold brew coffee nectar (or
*   any cold brew concentrate)*

1 Preheat oven to 180°C/360°F. Place whole sweet potatoes on a baking dish and roast until cooked through, about 15–20 minutes. Let cool.

2 Cut the beef into small cubes and smoke them on a perforated pan over hot wood for 10 minutes, season with salt and pepper. Let cool slightly, about seven minutes.

3 Take the pits out of the dates and place them on a perforated pan directly over hot wood or charcoal and char them completely. Let cool, about four minutes, and chop finely.

4 Add the dates to the beef mixture. Add in ginger, grapeseed oil, and morita chipotle powder, mix well. Add the balsamic vinegar and place in the fridge.

5 Cut the cooled sweet potato into 5cm (2in) rounds and set them on a perforated pan over the hot wood/charcoal. Smoke them for 10 minutes. Set aside.

6 Cut onion in half, place on a small skillet on a stovetop until it caramelises and chars. Repeat on the other side of the onion. Let cool and cut into quarters.

To assemble

1 Set out four medium-sized bowls and place 1 tbsp of the beef mixture in each.

2 Add four sweet potato rounds to encircle each serve of beef.

3 Garnish each bowl with two tomatillo halves, okra leaves, the charred onion, grated liquorice root, and sprinkle with salt. Pour cold coffee nectar over each bowl and serve.

4 Serve with shots of mezcal, preferably Tobala.

BETABELES ROSTIZADOS CON AJO

Roasted beetroot with garlic

A simple dish but true to its terroir, this roasted beetroot with garlic is a wonderful starter. The vibrant colours and unique blend of flavours exemplifies Diego Hernandez's farm-to-fork philosophy.

Chef //
Diego Hernandez
Location //
Corazon de Tierra, Valle de Guadalupe

Wind your way through the paved dirt roads and sprawling vineyards into the heart of Mexico's wine country and to Corazon de Tierra, where chef Diego Hernandez and his team carefully curate plates of seasonal fare. Renowned for its farm-to-fork menu, the restaurant's six courses change daily, depending on what's available in the garden or from local artisans in the region.

An Ensenada native, Diego maintains that 'love of the land' aspect this region is famous for. Floor-to-ceiling windows lead out to the stunning garden, lined with a variety of flowers, vegetables, fruit trees, and even the corn to make their own masa for tortillas and tamales. Olive oil is pressed on-site and they also harvest their own honey.

Chef Diego Hernandez has fond memories of walking the markets with his grandma in Toluca, Mexico. It was from these moments that he knew he would turn into a chef one day. After graduating from the Culinary Art School in Tijuana, he trained under some of the most renowned chefs in Mexico, including the region's own Benito Molina of Manzanilla, Enrique Olvera of Pujol in Mexico City, and Guillermo Gonzalez of Pangea in Monterrey. It was under the inspiration of the chefs in these kitchens that he was able to come into his own style.

For this dish of roasted beetroot with garlic, the simplicity relies on ingredients so fresh that each brings its own characteristic and burst of flavour to the overall experience. Earthy beetroot combined with bites of the slightly sweet roasted garlic, acidity from the fresh lime juice, and the ever-so-slightly-tart hibiscus meld harmoniously together. Corazon de Tierra shares the property with Vena Cava winery, which is rather convenient; a glass of its extra brut rosé is pleasantly crisp and pairs perfectly with this dish.

BETABELES ROSTIZADOS CON AJO

Roasted beetroot with garlic

Serves 2

Preparation & cooking time 35min

200g (7oz) dried hibiscus
3 heads of garlic
200g (7fl oz) crème fraiche (or sour cream)
salt, to taste
pepper, to taste
2 limes, juiced
3 medium-sized beetroots
30g (1oz) aged Ramonetti cheese (or other aged cheese)
hollyhock flower (or other edible flower), to garnish

Tip
Ramonetti cheese is local to Baja California. Use your favourite aged cheese that you have available for this recipe.

1   Preheat the oven to 200°C/390°F.

2   Toast hibiscus in a dry pan, let cool slightly and blitz in a blender or food processor until a powder is formed. Set aside.

3   Wrap the garlic heads in aluminum foil and roast in the oven for 30 minutes. Remove the garlic cloves from the foil, let cool slightly, for about four to five minutes, then mix in a bowl with the crème fraiche. Season with salt and pepper, and the juice of the limes.

4   Roast the beetroot wrapped in foil on a baking sheet in a 220°C/440°F oven for 12 minutes. The beetroot should still have a little crunch to it for this dish.

5   To serve, cut each beetroot into quarters (or more pieces, depending on their size). Arrange on a plate with slices of the cheese and tiny spoonfuls of the garlic puree. Garnish with the hollyhock flower and sprinkle with a dusting of the hibiscus powder.

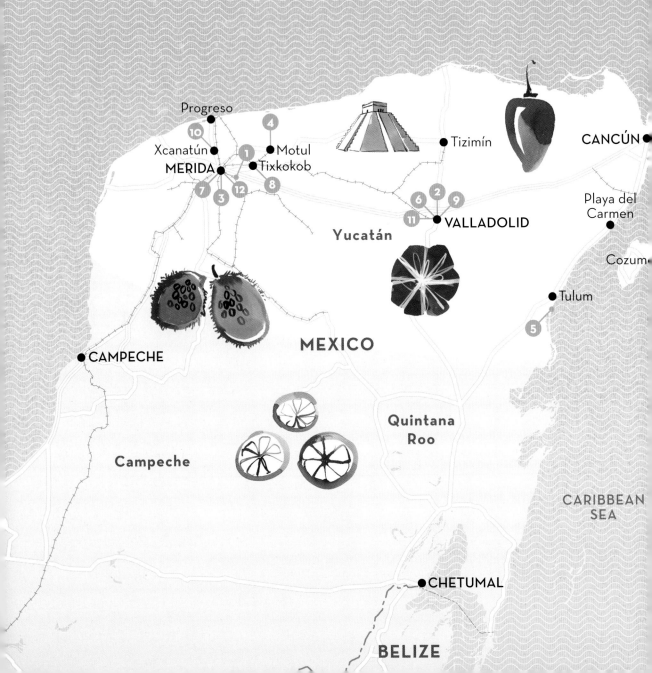

Yucatán
Peninsula

GULF OF MEXICO

Progreso

10

Xcanatún

MERIDA

7   3   12

1   Motul

Tixkokob

4

8

Tizimín

CANCÚN

6   2   9

11   VALLADOLID

Yucatán

Playa del
Carmen

Cozum

Tulum

5

MEXICO

CAMPECHE

Quintana
Roo

Campeche

CARIBBEAN
SEA

CHETUMAL

BELIZE

YUCATÁN

Caribbean flavours and indigenous Maya recipes influence the cuisine of this southeast corner of Mexico. Tropical fruits such as tamarind and bitter oranges are often used in the Yucatán Peninsula's distinctive salsas

SOPA DE LIMA
Lime soup
page 234

PANUCHOS
Bean-filled, fried tortilla snacks
page 238

PAPADZULES
Chopped egg enchiladas
page 242

HUEVOS MOTULEÑOS
Fried eggs in tomato sauce with bean-spread tostadas, ham & peas
page 246

POLLO CON RECADO ROJO
Chicken legs with red chile spices
page 250

COCHINITA PIBIL
Slow-roasted pork with achiote & orange
page 254

LÉCHON
Slow-roasted pork with crackling
page 258

RELLENO NEGRO
Blackened-chile turkey soup with sausage balls
page 262

JAACH PA'AP HABANERO SALSA
Habanero salsa
page 268

SIKIL PAK
Ground pumpkinseed dip
page 272

DULCE DE COCO
Candied coconut
page 276

DULCE DE PAPAYA
Papaya preserves
page 280

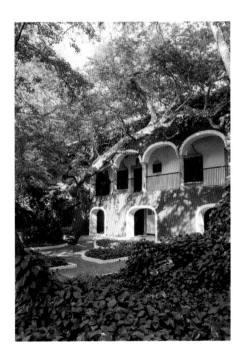

SOPA DE LIMA
Lime soup

Showcasing the distinctive limes of the Yucatán peninsula, this simple chicken-broth based soup uses both the juice and the rind of the limes, resulting in a refreshing, yet calming potage.

Chef //
Cárdenas family (pictured: Bernardo Fernández-Cárdenas)
Location //
Hacienda Teya, Mérida

In 1974 Jorje Cárdenas traded his car for a piece of land just outside of Mérida. The plot was home to Hacienda de San Ildefonso Teya, a working farm founded in 1683 that later switched to henequen production, a spiny plant in the agave family that is used to make a natural cording. But what Jorje Cárdenas and his family acquired was a crumbling old mansion, roof caved in, columns toppled, the jungle creeping in on all sides. Today, it is hard to imagine Hacienda Teya in disarray – it is stunningly beautiful, the main house and its surroundings restored, with antique wooden furniture, citron trees, and two peacocks that roam the grounds.

Beyond the beauty of the estate, the Cárdenas family kitchen has been a culinary force for over 40 years, drawing in travellers leaving or going to Mérida. On the ground floor of the main building, clusters of families dine on classic renditions of Yucatecan cuisine, like queso relleno, poc chuc (citrus marinated grilled pork), and léchon (see p258). Children sip *agua de chaya* (a spinach-like vegetable that is often turned into a green coloured juice) while their parents hold snifters of brandy and debate whether to order the *dulce de papaya* (see also p280) or the flan. The answer is: both.

Sopa de lima, made from citrus limetta (sweet limes), is one of the jewels of the menu. The soup looks like your regular, run-of-the-mill chicken soup, a golden stock with shredded meat, a handful of tortilla strips, and a couple of wheels of lime, but you can smell it from across the room. The limes must be crushed against the bowl with a spoon, releasing a heady aroma as complex and fragrant as a Thai curry.

The soup has an arresting flavour and perfume; there's tartness from the lime, restorative properties from the chicken broth, and crunch from the freshly fried tortilla strips. While there is no substitute for the limes of the region, a mix of lime, lemon, and orange juices, come closest to their unique characteristics.

SOPA DE LIMA
Lime soup

Serves 4

Preparation & cooking time 1hr 50min

300g (10½oz) chicken breast
1 clove of garlic
1 pinch of dried oregano
1 small bunch of coriander (cilantro)
salt, to taste
2L (3½pt) water
500g (1lb) white onions
400g (14oz) green peppers
200g (7oz) tomatoes
2fl oz (60ml) vegetable oil
6 sweet limes, plus 1 more thinly sliced, to garnish
(if you don't have sweet limes, drop the lime
count to 4 and include the juice of 1 lemon and
½ orange)
2 stock cubes chicken consommé
4 corn tortillas, thinly sliced into strips and
fried until golden

1   Make chicken stock by simmering the chicken breasts, the clove of garlic, the oregano, the coriander, and salt in 2L water. Once the stock has simmered for an hour, remove the chicken breasts, strain the stock and reserve.

2   Once the chicken breasts have cooled to the touch, shred the meat and reserve.

3   Chop the onions, green peppers and tomatoes and fry in oil in a large pot until onions have softened and are transparent.

4   Return the chicken broth to the pot, add in the juice of the six limes (or its substitute), the chicken stock cubes, and bring to a simmer for 10 minutes. Add in the shredded chicken.

5   Serve the soup with the fried strips of tortilla on top and a slice or two of fresh lime.

'The lime isn't just for garnish. Make sure you take your spoon and express the lime, to release the juice and aromatic oils into the soup. It adds an extra burst of flavour.'

Bernardo Fernandez

PANUCHCOS

Bean-filled, fried tortilla snacks

This corn masa snack is popular in the Yucatán, and Valladolid is often recognised as the place to eat it, with Doña Maria's restaurant, La Selva, at the top of the list.

La Selva opened its doors in 1985 as a family business and today remains that way. There aren't actually any doors to open – it's an open-walled palapa structure, shading a handful of tables and chairs. La Selva is open only during the evenings, and owner Dulce Maria Pat Xuluc carries the culinary torch (and lives just next door) while various extended family members work the floor; her 95-year-old grandfather still operates the till some evenings. 'I guess I have my mother's *sazón*,' says Doña Maria, or the 'indefinable flavour' that buoys the kitchen at La Selva.

The adroit dishes at La Selva are not just due to Doña Maria's culinary skill but her affinity to focus on the details: she prefers a specific type of wood to heat her kitchen stove; she cooks the beans, daily, from scratch. 'Many places use canned beans and you can really tell the difference,' she says. She offers her famous *panuchos* (fried tortillas filled with those refried beans) on a sliding scale of crunchy – *bien dorados* (really crunchy), *media* (somewhere in the middle) or *suave* (just given a quick dip in the fryer).

For such an everyday snack, panuchos require a lengthy, multistepped preparation. In order to get the beans inside of the tortillas, they have to be made fresh that day and they have to inflate, meaning the tortillas magically rise and puff as they are toasted on the *comal*. Inside this pocket, a tablespoon or so of bean paste is slipped. They are then fried for a few minutes in hot pork fat. The tortillas are ladled with various toppings, like *cochinita pibil* (p254) or shredded chicken; with shredded lettuce or cabbage, tomato, onion, and avocado; or with just a sprinkle of pickled red onion.

Always amenable, Doña Maria will serve this *ahogados* (drenched), if requested – *panuchos* on a plate with a bowl of hot consommé on the side, which people spoon on, to moisten, as they like. Others prefer them 'natural': the *panuchos* fried and left unadorned, which allows the earthy flavors of the beans and corn to come through.

Chef //
Dulce Maria Pat Xuluc
Location //
La Selva, Valladolid

PANUCHCOS
Bean-filled, fried tortilla snacks

Serves 8

Preparation & cooking time 9 hr

500g (1lb) black beans
water, to boil beans
1 sprig epazote (or coriander/cilantro, if unavailable)
salt, to taste
500g (1lb) ready-made masa (or see p74 to make
    your own)
350g (12oz) lard (or vegetable oil)
shredded cabbage, to serve, optional
pickled red onion, to serve, optional
poached, shredded chicken breast, to serve, optional
sliced tomato, to serve, optional
sliced avocado, to serve, optional

*'The consistency of the
bean puree is important.
Not too dry or it won't
spread well throughout the
tortilla, and not too wet
either because it will leak
out when fried. Swipe your
hand to the edges of the
tortilla to spread the beans
all the way to the edges.'*

Dulce Maria Pat Xuluc

Note

*La Selva should not be confused with Hacienda
La Selva, also in Valladolid. Look for the palm
frond-covered palapa on a corner of the Santa
Lucía neighbourhood.*

1 Wash the beans and pick through, discarding any pebbles. Cover well with water and add the epazote. Bring the beans to a boil, then reduce the heat and simmer until they are really cooked well, about six hours over a medium-low heat. Occasionally check to see if more water is needed.

2 When the beans are cooked, transfer them in batches with their cooking liquid to a blender and puree until smooth. Often their skins will get stuck and compacted at the bottom of the blender; discard as many as you can when transferring the puree to a pot.

3 Cook the bean puree down until it is a thick paste, stirring constantly over a medium-low heat, for about an hour and a half. Season with salt. Cool to room temperature or refrigerate if you aren't going to assemble the *panuchos* today.

4 To assemble the *panuchos*, form tortillas (about the size of a drink coaster) with the masa and toast them over a medium-high heat on a *comal* (or hot plate) about two minutes per side. They should inflate naturally.

5 Once all the tortillas are formed, with a knife, cut open each tortilla and fill it with a tablespoon or so of bean puree, spreading the beans to the edges with your fingers. Continue until all tortillas are filled. You may have a little bean puree left, which will keep for a week in the refrigerator.

6 Fry the *panuchos* in the lard in batches in a skillet, over medium-high heat, three to five minutes each, transferring them with a slotted spoon to a paper-towel lined plate, to drain.

7 Load the *panuchos* with your choice of topping/s (shredded cabbage, pickled red onion, shredded chicken, tomato and/or avocado) and serve.

PAPADZULES
Chopped egg enchiladas

Papadzules *are essentially a type of enchilada – here, the tortillas are filled with chopped hard-boiled egg and drenched in a rich, creamy sauce made from ground pepitas, the prized green pumpkinseeds of the Yucatán.*

Papadzules, at least by etymology, are Mayan, and can be written papatzul, papasul, papak-tsul, or papak-sul. The dish is one of the champions of Yucatecan gastronomy, and while it is a unique variation in the enchilada canon, it's a commonplace dish served at almost every sit-down restaurant in Mérida. The sauce is made with pepitas, the green hearts of the white, fibrous pumpkinseed, mined from the centres of the local variety of pumpkin, *xka'al*. When ground and pressed, the seeds generate rivulets of jade-like oil that is often drizzled over top of the dish.

Cocina Mary, an open-air *puesto* (street stand) in the Santa Ana Square of Mérida, has been in operation for over 30 years and turns out a superlative version of *papadzules*. It is among the dozen or so small, casual restaurants that serve similar dishes in the shadow of a sunflower-yellow chapel flanked by palm trees. In a shoebox of a space, a collective of women work together – chef Mariana Huchin Ake tends the kitchen, chatting with manager Madeline El Kal about the day's orders. Most of the employees have been with Cocina Mary for over a decade. In the early morning, light already fierce, waiters flap their menus at passersby, trying to lure them with their offerings. Families in plastic red chairs at oil-cloth covered tables settle in for *caldos* (broth) and plates of eggs, as waiters ferry over goblets of *agua de chaya* (a spinach-like green juice) and fruit *licuados* (juices).

Egg-stuffed *papadzules* makes an excellent breakfast. It's possible that the dish was made in pre-Hispanic times, with the eggs from quails, ducks, or even iguanas, but chicken eggs – ubiquitous, cheap sources of protein, are the basis for most *papadzules* throughout the region. The pastel green sauce, creamy without cream, nutty and mild, is a balm for the nerves when they've been rubbed raw by too much sun or prickling chiles. But note – you can always dial up the heat with a splash of the roasted Habanero and sour orange condiment, which sits on every table. It's as loose as juice and one hundred times spicier.

Chef //
Mariana Huchin Ake
Location //
Cocina Mary, Mérida

PAPADZULES
Chopped egg enchiladas

Serves 4

Preparation & cooking time 40 min

8 eggs
4 medium tomatoes, chopped
½ small white onion, peeled & chopped
1 tbsp water (or chicken stock), for blending
salt, to taste
1 Habanero chile, whole
300g (10½oz) pepitas (shelled green
  pumpkinseeds)
1L (1¾ pint) chicken stock (or water)
1 sprig epazote (or coriander/cilantro, if
  unavailable)
16 corn tortillas

1 Put the eggs in a saucepan and cover with water. Bring to the boil on a medium-high heat and cook for eight to 10 minutes, until hard-boiled. When cool, crack, peel, and chop the eggs. Set aside until ready to use.

2 Make the tomato sauce by blending the tomatoes, onion, and a splash of water or stock in a blender until smooth.

3 Strain the tomato sauce into a pot and bring to a simmer. Season with salt.

4 Slip the Habanero chile into the tomato sauce and let simmer for 10 minutes, stirring occasionally. Reserve and keep warm until ready to use.

5 Make the pumpkinseed sauce by bringing the pepitas to a boil with the stock (or water) and sprig of epazote. Simmer for 10 minutes and then puree the sauce in a blender with salt to season. The sauce should be thickish and creamy; if it is too loose, reduce it a bit on the stovetop over medium heat, stirring constantly. If too thick, loosen with a bit of water.

6 Warm the tortillas on the stovetop or in a microwave.

7 Fill each tortilla with a tablespoon or two of the chopped egg, and roll up. Serve four tortillas to a plate with the pumpkinseed sauce poured over the top, a bit of the tomato sauce and a little hardboiled egg.

Tip
'Make sure the Habanero simmers in the sauce gently. You just want its essence.'

Mariana Huchin Ake

HUEVOS MOTULEÑOS

Fried eggs in tomato sauce with bean-spread tostadas, ham & peas

This breakfast dish, originating from the tiny town of Motul, is an intriguing mix of cubed ham and peas cooked in a tomato sauce, poured over eggs and bean-spread tortillas, showcasing Mayan, European, and Cuban influences.

At 8am on the second floor of the municipal market of Motul (45km/28 miles northeast of Mérida), Doña Evelia is presiding over three aluminium cauldrons of refried black beans, which pop and sputter with steam. Everyone sitting in the plastic chairs at Doña Evelia's Cafeteria Soberanis Arce is eating the same dish: *huevos motuleños*, which features those refried black beans, spread over expertly fried tostadas, fried eggs, and a sauce made from miniscule cubes of ham, peas cooked to army green, and tomatoes. There's only this dish on the menu (and pork and frijoles on certain days) so the only decision you'll have to make is if you want two or three eggs.

The plate arrives, heavy with sauce and a pile of eggs and tostadas taller than a short stack of pancakes. One Habanero chile, complete with its stem, sits like a cherry on top. Doña Evelia recounts the origins of the dish: 'It was created in the early 1920s by Felipe Carrillo Puerto, well...,' she pauses, 'It was dubbed by him. He was a socialist revolutionary born in Motul, who later became the governor of the Yucatán. Story has it that [philosopher and politician] José Vasconcelos was visiting Motul and they ate eggs with tomato sauce and bits of Jamón Serrano brought over by the Europeans, and peas. Why peas? No-one really knows. Vasconcelos asked Carillo, "What is this dish?" and Carillo Puerto answered, "The eggs of Motul, *huevos motuleños*." The name stuck.'

On Sundays at Doña Evelia's, you will probably have to wait for a table. If the thought of eating hot, saucy eggs seems counter-intuitive to combat Motul's high temperatures, she might give you a paper fan, printed with the hours of the cafeteria. But it's worth the virtual sauna. The dish is a riot of textures and flavours, the tostadas deliciously crisp, the rich egg yolk countering the tart tomato sauce with Habanero aromatics, with the occasional pop of a pea. A few fried planks of plantain lay to the side, which mesh well with the savoury spiciness of the dish: 'a little bit of sweet to go with the sour'.

Chef //
Doña Evelia
Location //
Cafeteria Soberanis Arce, Motul

HUEVOS MOTULEÑOS
Fried eggs in tomato sauce with bean-spread tostadas, ham & peas

Serves 4

Preparation & cooking time 1 hr

2 plantains (or green bananas, if unavailable)
8 tbsp vegetable oil
350g (12¼oz) refried black beans
6 tomatoes, finely chopped
1 white onion, diced
200g (7oz) ham, diced
200g (7oz) cooked peas
4 Habanero chiles
salt, to taste
8 eggs
8 tostadas (fried corn tortillas)
8 cooked Habanero chiles (whole), to garnish

1 Cut the plantains into segments and fry until golden in half of the vegetable oil. Set aside and reserve.

2 Warm refried beans in a small pot, set aside.

3 Heat the remaining oil in a saucepan over medium heat. Add the tomatoes, onions, ham, and peas, the whole Habanero chiles, and cook for 30 to 40 minutes, stirring occasionally until the tomatoes lose their shape and melt into a loose sauce. Season with salt.

4 Fry the eggs in a little oil, until cooked to desired preference.

5 To serve, spread warm beans onto one tostada, top with a fried egg, top the egg with another tostada and another egg. Pour the warm sauce all over the stack, and place a cooked Habanero chile on top. Serve with the fried plantain on the side of the plate.

Note
Many versions of this dish will have a mild, white cheese, like Cotija, crumbled overtop but not Doña Evelia's, which also deviates from the norm by including cooked Habanero chiles on top. The chiles do not add much spice to the dish, just their perfume.

POLLO CON RECADO ROJO

Chicken legs with red chile spices

Recados are the base seasoning of many dishes from the Yucatán and Quintana Roo. While most restaurants in the region rely on recado *producers, at Hartwood restaurant they relish in making their own.*

If one had to capture the aroma of the Yucatán, a number of fragrances come to mind: the salty wind that blows off the ocean, the heady fragrance of Habanero chiles, and the ubiquitous, appetite-generating smell of flame-roasted chicken. In the region, there are simple rotisserie restaurants (and lots of backyard grills with a dozen or so chickens to sell) on almost every corner, spinning poultry dyed orange from the marinades and blistered with char. It's region-wide comfort food.

Simple grilled chicken may not be what you expect at Hartwood, a restaurant opened by Eric Werner and his wife Mya in 2010, nestled in between the beach and the jungle in Tulum. As rustic and freewheeling as the restaurant's atmosphere feels – it's got a real Swiss Family Robinson vibe – the food is always thoughtful, elegant and more complex than the menu would indicate. It's a stopping point for celebrity chefs, such as René Redzepi, when visiting the area, a foodie destination (notably, it's made the World's Top 50 restaurant list), and emblematic of new kinds of restaurants carving out their niche in the region.

Werner and his kitchen staff have the utmost respect for traditional techniques and local ingredients while creating something entirely new, and such is their approach to this dish. Traditionally, *recado* is made from a laundry list of spices (cumin, coriander, black pepper, allspice), aromatic vegetables, (onions, garlic, and chiles), and often achiote, the dusky seeds of the achiote tree. Werner says you can buy *recado* in pre-packaged block form but likes to make his own. 'The key ingredient is achiote seeds (also called annatto seeds), which give the paste an amazing garnet colour and add a peppery, nutmeggy flavour that pulls off the trick of tasting zingy and earthy at the same time.'

Werner grills the chicken legs first then finishes them in the oven, where they're kept moist by the *recado*, which is thinned with orange juice and used as the braising liquid. Pulling the pan from the oven and releasing the plumes of steam is the equivalent of being transported to an aromatic street corner in Quintana Roo.

Chef //
Eric Werner
Location //
Hartwood, Tulum

POLLO CON RECADO ROJO

Chicken legs with red chile spices

Serves 8

Preparation & cooking time 1 hr 30 min

For the recado rojo

1 tbsp achiote seeds
80ml (2¾fl oz) orange juice
1 tbsp coriander seeds
1 tbsp cumin seeds
1 tbsp cloves
1 tbsp allspice berries
1 tbsp black peppercorns
1 tbsp ground cinnamon
1 tbsp dried oregano
1 dried avocado leaves (or 1 tbsp fennel seeds,
  if unavailable)
2 large garlic cloves
1 tbsp salt

For the chicken

8 whole chicken legs
1 tbsp kosher salt
2 tbsp freshly ground black pepper
470ml (16fl oz) water
2 tbsp apple cider vinegar
1 lime, halved, for garnish

1 Preheat the oven to 200°C/400°F.

2 To make the *recado rojo*, soak the achiote seeds in the orange juice in a small bowl until softened, about 15 minutes.

3 Toast the coriander, cumin, cloves, allspice, and black peppercorns in a cast-iron skillet over medium heat until fragrant, which takes two to four minutes. Let cool, then pulse in a spice grinder until finely ground. Mix with the cinnamon and set aside.

4 Pulse the oregano and avocado leaves in the spice grinder until fine, then sift through a fine-mesh sieve (to catch any fibres that weren't chopped up by the grinder) and set aside. Crush the garlic with the salt in a mortar and pestle until a rough paste forms.

5 Combine the achiote seeds with the orange juice, the spices, and garlic paste in a blender and blend until smooth, about 1 minute.

6 Prepare a grill for medium-high heat. Season the chicken legs with the salt and pepper. Oil the grill grate. Grill the chicken skin-side down until the skin colours and clear grill marks form, about eight minutes. Do not flip – you want colour on one side. Remove from the grill.

7 Rub the *recado rojo* all over the chicken.

8 Place the chicken legs (with the grill marks facing up) in a shallow baking pan. Pour the vinegar mixture into the pan and cover tightly with aluminum foil. Put the chicken in the oven and cook for 45 minutes, or until cooked through. Uncover and return to the oven for 10 to 15 minutes to let the skin crisp up. Serve with the braising liquid and lime.

Tip

*The recado rojo can be made in advance.
Consider made double or triple the
quantity to use in other dishes. It can be
stored in the extra in the refrigerator
for up to two weeks.*

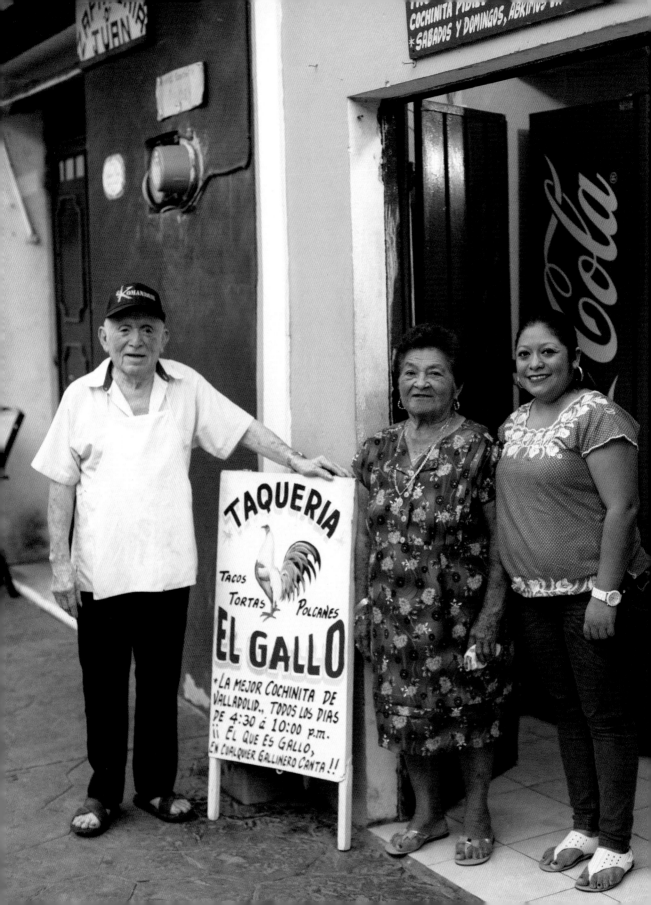

CONCHINITA PIBIL
Slow-roasted pork

The crowning jewel of the Yucatán peninsula's gastronomy, cochinita *is pork rubbed with* recado rojo, *a paste given its characteristic lurid orange from achiote, a pebbly seed from the spiny pod of the achiote tree.*

If you've followed the peregrinations of *cochinita pibil* in Valladolid over the past 50 years you've no doubt kept tabs on El Gallo. For 28 years it operated out of a cart parked in the city centre plaza. In 2010 it relocated to another street corner then, relatively recently, the cart found a new home in a small room off Calle 46, in downtown Valladolid. And where were they even before the city centre? The Silva family, Marcello Silva, 82 years old, his wife Aida Santoyo Fernandez, and their progeny, pause to think. 'Before that, we were off to the side of the main plaza. The city has moved us around a bit throughout the years,' recalls Aida.

It's a long history filled with exceptional *cochinita pibil*. The *cochinita* is cooked off-site, in two *pib* pits (Mayan wood-fired ground ovens) on the grounds of their house. The pork goes in early, cooks for six hours, is pulled out, shredded, and brought to the restaurant. Their *cochinita* is redder than most of what is served in Mérida and more heavily spiced and robustly seasoned. The meat is so tender it seems to fall apart with a mere glance. Marcello Silva shreds it all, carefully, by hand. Veronica, his daughter, laughs, 'We like to say that the flavour is in his hands.'

For tacos, tortillas are filled and rolled into slim cylinders. Also on the menu are *volcanes* (finger-length corn masa fritters stuffed with beans), topped with the *cochinita*. The Silvas bake their own bread for their tortas, called *pan frances*: the loaves are toasty brown and squared off on the ends. They're baked in a wood oven and have a crunchy exterior and squishy insides, perfect to saturate with *cochinita* drippings. 'The bread is .... artisanal?' says Veronica. 'Or that's what people say.'

Chef //
Marcello Silva & Aida Santoyo Fernandez
Location //
El Gallo, Valladolid

CONCHINITA PIBIL
Slow-roasted pork

Serves 10

Preparation & cooking time 3½ hrs

2kg (4½lb) boneless pork meat, loin, leg, or
    shoulder, cut into large pieces
200g (7oz) recado rojo (see p252)
2 tbsp salt
350ml (12fl oz) hot water
470ml (16fl oz) water
tacos/tortas, to serve (optional)

<u>Tip</u>
*The Silvas use pork that is butchered
daily and never refrigerated from a
local butcher, which they attribute
to some of their cochinita's success.
They buy their recado rojo from
a local market, but it can also be
bought online, or made as per p252.*

1 Preheat the oven to 215°C/420°F. Place pork in a large roasting pan.

2 Mix the *recado rojo* with the salt and hot water, then rub the mixture all over the pork with your hands, making sure to really coat and cover all of the pieces. If the *recado* is too firm to work by hand, place in a blender with a splash of water to loosen it a bit. Puree and then proceed with marinating the pork.

3 Add 470ml of water to the bottom of the pan. This will prevent any burning. Cover the pan with aluminum foil and let roast for two hours.

4 After the pork has been cooking for two hours, check and make sure the pork is moist and not burning. Add a splash of water to the pan if it looks dry. Continue to cook for another hour, then remove from the oven and let sit until cool enough to be shredded by hand.

5 Serve the pork in tacos, tortas, or on its own on a large plate.

LÉCHON

Slow-roasted pork with crackling

Léchon may have Spanish lineage, but this slow-roasted pork dish is pure Yucatán. Traditionally cooked in a 'pib' (Mayan wood-fired ground oven), this recipe has been converted so you can make it in a regular oven.

If *cochinita pibil* (p254) tends to hog the gastronomic limelight, *lechón* is her younger, quietly confident sister and often the true favourite. Both are marinated pork, cooked in the same manner in the traditional *pib* oven, but while *cochinita* preens with orange achiote and citrus, *lechón* tends to allow the clean flavours of pork, smoke and salt shine through. One of the most outstanding versions of *lechón* is served in the Mercado de Santiago in Mérida by Pedro Medina and his team.

The place is called La Lupita, a corner *puesto* next to other early-morning outposts, and Medina's *lechón* sells out quickly, often by noon. The employees ladle out *aguas frescas* (p122) and ferry plates of food to the folding metal tables. The *lechón* – soft, mild, almost milky, with subtle currents of smoke and salt – is set on tacos or on crunchy rolls, as tortas. A *torta de lechón* is the perfect canvas for diced, pickled red onions, and sliced Habanero chiles marinating in sour orange juice; a piece of *chicharrón* (rendered, fried pork skin) is set on top, crunching like a rippled potato chip slipped into a sandwich.

'Our *chicharrón* is quite special, in my opinion,' says Medina. 'People come through and ask for a half-kilo to go but we have to decline. We can't give it to them because we only have what we have.' They treat it carefully, pulling it off the pigskin in sheets, scraping it clean, and passing it through boiling lard, creating a puffy, pork-flavoured crackling. Some places buy extra *chicharrón* to put on their tortas, but La Lupita only uses what comes from the pigs they cook, so it's a scarce commodity.

La Lupita has been in operation for over 50 years; and before that, Medina's father had a locale in the same market, too. The recipes have been handed down and perfected over the generations. 'I don't consider myself a chef,' says Medina, 'I'm a cook. And while this may be a commercial business, it's really about the love of good food and trying to share it with people. It's about the love!'

Chef //
Pedro Medina Casanova
(pictured with his wife
Guadalupe Solis Romero, who
also works in the restaurant
kitchen)
Location //
La Lupita, Mérida

LÉCHON
Slow-roasted pork with crackling

Serves10

Preparation & cooking time 6 hr

2kg pork leg or shoulder with fat, boneless,
  cut into large pieces
2 tbsp salt
6 garlic cloves
2 tsp black pepper
¼ tsp allspice
½ stick of cinnamon
2 tsp oregano
4 bay leaves
250ml (8¾oz) sour orange juice (half lime,
  half orange juice mixed together)
470ml (16fl oz) water

1 Preheat your oven to 210°C/420°F. Place pork in a large roasting pan and season with salt.

2 Combine the garlic, black pepper, allspice, cinnamon, oregano, bay leaves, and 25ml (1fl oz) of the sour orange juice in a blender. Blend to a paste.

3 Rub the paste all over the pork with your hands, making sure to really coat and cover all of the pieces. Make sure the pieces sit skin-side up.

4 Splash the remaining sour orange juice over the pork and add 470ml of water to the bottom of the pan. This will prevent any burning. Cover the pan with aluminum foil and let roast for two hours.

5 After the pork has been cooking for two hours, remove the aluminum foil and let roast another 30 minutes or until the pork is golden and the skin is crispy. Serve the pork in tacos, tortas, or on its own on a large plate.

Note

Léchon is an essentially mestizo *dish melding Spanish and Mayan cooking. Medina explains,
'The Spanish brought over pigs and they have a dish called* cochinillo *made from roasted suckling pigs. We took it and put a Yucatán spin on it. We had to adapt it to our surroundings. Cochinillo is served with a vinegar escabeche condiment so we thought "What do we have that's similar?" We didn't have vinegar, so we swapped in sour orange juice for acid.'*

RELLENO NEGRO

Blackened-chile turkey soup with sausage balls

This dish uses recado negro and recados as seasoning for broth in which turkeys and pork sausage are cooked. The meat is sliced, set into tacos, tortas, or served in their cooking liquid as a soupy stew.

Chef //
Silvio Campos
Location //
Plato Limpio Taquitos,
Tixkokob

Tixkokob is a petite town nestled into the deep jungle 25km (15½ miles) east of Mérida, and it's where you'll find Silvio Campos' *puesto* (street stand), Plato Limpio Taquitos. Campos is known for his *relleno negro* but people also line up for his *léchon* (see also p258) and *cochinita pibil* (see also p254) served on different days of the week. You might say he is a mastermind of the holy trinity of meat-intensive Yucatán specialties.

Silvio and his family work in an outdoor kitchen attached to their home. Cooking predominantly over a wood fire, they then carry in the wares in large pots to their *puesto* in the main municipal market of Tixkokob. They dole out their home-cooked food starting when the sun clears the tops of the dense foliage surrounding the town.

Sundays are reserved for *relleno*, both black and white versions, which are essentially the same dish with different coloured *recados* as their base. The black version, *relleno negro*, is, according to Silvio, the most popular. Entire turkeys are simmered in a broth spiked black with *recado*, along with large, softball-sized orbs of pork sausage called *but* that harbour hard-boiled eggs at their centres. Originally, the pork sausage was stuffed into the cavity of the turkey, but as all Thanksgiving-cooks know, the turkey-to-sausage ratio is off, which is why the sausage is often rolled and cooked separately.

The family form a production line, slicing the *but* into eighths, shredding the turkey, and filling plastic bags with *relleno negro*, to go. The *relleno negro* can be used several ways: to fill tacos, doused in its cooking liquid and made into tortas, or served on its own with the broth. The soup hums with the flavours of the *recado negro* (charred *chile de árbol*, onion, cumin, oregano, thyme, cinnamon and garlic) and the meat rounds out the spicy, rich broth.

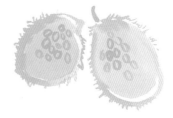

RELLENO NEGRO

Blackened-chile turkey soup with sausage balls

Serves 8

Preparation & cooking time 2 hours

½ turkey breast or 1 full chicken breast, on-the-bone
3 tomatoes, chopped
3 xcatic chiles, chopped (or 3 banana chile
*   peppers plus one Habanero)*
1 white onion, chopped
50g (1¾oz) lard
350g (12¼oz) recado negro (see tip on p267)
10g (⅓oz) achiote paste

For the sausage balls
500g (1lb) minced/ground pork (leg or shoulder)
1 raw egg
salt, to taste
3 hardboiled eggs, peeled
1 small bunch of epazote (or coriander/cilantro)
pinch of oregano

Note
Xcatic chile is a long yellowish green
pepper with the same floral aroma
of Habanero but not quite the same
level of heat.

1 Place the turkey (or chicken) in a large pot, barely cover with water, and bring to a simmer.

2 Liquefy the tomatoes, chiles, and onion in a blender with a splash of water, if needed, to get it moving.

3 In a frying pan (skillet), heat the lard over medium-high heat and add the blended tomato sauce to the pan. Fry the sauce, stirring frequently until much of the water has evaporated and the sauce becomes a thick paste. Set aside.

4 Whisk the *recado negro* and the achiote paste in a little water to dissolve. Reserve 120ml (4fl oz) of this mixture, then strain the remaining mixture into the pot with the turkey.

5 Add three quarters of the tomato sauce from step 3 to the turkey pot, setting the rest aside. Simmer the turkey for 40 minutes, then remove to rest at room temperature. Reserve this broth to simmer the sausage balls.

6 To make the sausage, mix together the ground pork, the raw egg, the reserved *recado negro* from step 4 and the remaining reserved tomato sauce from step 3. Season well with salt and mix everything together with clean hands until well incorporated.

7 Take a handful of the pork, flatten it in your palm. Press a hardboiled egg into the centre and wrap the pork around the egg to fully cover. Pack the pork around the egg into a tennis ball-sized ball. Continue forming balls until all the hardboiled eggs are used.

8 Add the epazote to the turkey pot along with a pinch of oregano, and slip the pork sausages into the simmering broth. Simmer the balls for 40 minutes, then remove.

9 To serve, cut slices of turkey breast. Cut the sausages in half and each half into eight wedges. Serve a bowl of the broth with slices of turkey and wedges of the sausage.

JAACH PA'AP
HABANERO SALSA
Habanero salsa

Less of a sauce and more of a super-concentrated chile oil, the heat of this salsa does not overwhelm the floral, tropical notes of fresh Habanero chiles, one of the spiciest of the territory.

The municipal market of Valladolid is not too big, like some mega cities with football-field sized markets. It's not too small, so you're left wanting. It's just the right size. Farmers from the countryside bring in their homegrown wares, such as electric-pink radishes; sprightly green, shell beans; wild mushrooms; and every manner of herb. One side of the market is reserved for meats, with fresh cuts of protein. There are stands specialising in sweets, and a handful of *puestos* (street stands) serving cooked food if you should need a snack while perusing.

Though its listed name is La Bendición de Dios, Francisco Silva and his mother Marciala Silva's *puesto* is often referred to as 'La Mudita' – the little mute. Doña Silva doesn't speak but she has little trouble communicating and her food speaks volumes. The main dish served is *lomitos*, a spicy pork stew from Valladolid, made with tomato, onion, achiote, and meltingly tender chunks of pork. The saucy number is served on top of tacos, tortas, and *polcanes*, little torpedo-shaped fried masa fritters stuffed with beans and *pibihua*, the same bean-stuffed masa snacks, not fried but cooked directly on wood fires underground. Each item on the menu is enhanced with the house-made salsa, which sits in little plastic bowls on the counter and in plastic bottles, for sale, to take home.

At first glance, it may look like they are skimping on the sauce. There's only a tablespoon or so in the plastic bowls to go around. It's a reddish-orange slurry, with a neon oil floating on top, and a heat so fierce it will take your breath away. Habanero chile is the distinctive pepper that adds intense spice to many of the classic dishes in the peninsula and comes in a kaleidoscope of colours, ranging from red, green, yellow, and various shades of orange. The Silvias use only red Habaneros for this salsa. They fry the peppers low and slow, encapsulating their essence and the inimitable flavour of the region, in a simple condiment.

Chef //
Marciala Silva
Location //
La Bendición de Dios, Valladolid

JAACH PA'AP HABANERO SALSA
Habanero salsa

Serves many, as a condiment

Preparation & cooking time 1 hr

250ml (8¾fl oz) vegetable oil
250g (9oz) red Habanero chiles, de-stemmed
salt, to taste

1 In a shallow pot, heat the oil and the Habanero chiles over a low heat. Let the chiles fry for 30 minutes. Remove the pot from the heat and let cool slightly.

2 Transfer the oil and the chiles to a blender. Season the mixture with a bit of salt and blend for a full minute.

3 Return the mixture to a saucepan and continue to fry the sauce, cooking some of the water out and reducing it for another 30 minutes, stirring frequently. Serve as an extremely spicy condiment to add to any savoury dish.

SIKIL PAK
Ground pumpkinseed dip

An easy comparison to this dish would be hummus, but this Mayan dip outshines any chickpea puree. Made from ground pumpkinseeds, it's nutty and rich, with a citrus tang and a slow burn from roasted chiles.

A 15-minute drive north of Mérida's city centre, Hermana República is a straight shot towards El Progreso, the closest beach for when the blinding summer heat becomes a little bit too much. Hermana República is a mixed-use space: a microbrewery, a beer garden, and a restaurant, featuring half a dozen Patito brand beers, made on-site and served in stylish cans or on tap, and food that pairs well with it.

There's a big sign that marks the spot, which you will inevitably read too late and have to turn around to re-catch the turnoff, but once you get there it's an oasis of great food and cold beer on the edge of the Yucatán jungle.

Alex Mendez, the restaurant's young chef, is Mérida born and bred. He ran kitchens in Mexico City before returning to open Hermana República with his business partners. Sikil pak is just one of his signature dishes that rounds out a menu of creative takes on local cuisine. Of the pumpkinseed dip Mendez says, 'It's a classic *botana* (snack) of the Yucatán, served in cantinas to accompany you while drinking. *Botanas* are free, but they keep you drinking.'

That same sense of par-excellence Yucatán hospitality can be witnessed at Hermana República. To encourage clientele to hop in their cars and head just out of the city for a drink and a snack, there's a stage for live bands, food-trucks pulling into the yard, prime soccer games on the wide-screen at the comfortable bar, and growlers of your choice of beer, to-go.

While the olive-green paste may not be the prettiest dish on the menu, it carries leagues of flavour. Mendez adds a substantial amount of *naranja agria* (sour orange juice) to his sikil pak, which lends a tart fruitiness, along with the creeping heat of charred Habanero chiles and garlic. Naturally, it's the perfect accompaniment to corn chips and a round, or three, of cold beers. Mendez smiles while pulling a pint, 'It's ideal drinking food.'

Chef //
Alex Mendez
Location //
Hermana República, Mérida

SIKIL PAK

Ground pumpkinseed dip

Serves 8

Preparation & cooking time 30 min

7 plum or small tomatoes, whole
5 cloves garlic, peeled
1 small red onion, peeled and roughly chopped
375g (13¼oz) pepitas (green pumpkinseeds)
150ml (3½fl oz) sour orange juice (or half
    lime juice with half orange juice)
1–2 tbsp of Habanero salsa
small bunch of coriander (cilantro), leaves
    chopped, stems discarded
salt, to taste
pepper, to taste

1   Grill/broil the tomatoes with the onion and the garlic cloves until well-charred, turning occasionally.

2   Blend onion, garlic and tomatoes together in a food processor. Add the pepitas and pulse until a loose paste is formed.

3   Add in the citrus juice, the Habanero salsa and the coriander. Season well with salt and pepper and pulse to combine. The dip should be pureed well and creamy but still retain a bit of texture. Add a little water as need to achieve the desired consistency.

'One of the tenets of our business model is that all employees are allowed to have any beer they like, after their shift. Everyone deserves a beer after they work, no?'

Alex Mendez

DULCE DE COCO
Candied coconut

This Yucatecan sweet contains fresh coconut meat, harvested by hand. Expectedly, it's a difficult task. But it's worth the work for the tropical flavour they lend to the caramelised base.

Pedro Kauil Castillo and his wife Maria Rosaura Och Cob, better known as Rosi, started their business over 20 years ago, operating out of their house with just a pot, a wood-fire, a few recipes, and a lot of hard work. Rosi, the business' namesake, is the candy-making machine in residence. She makes beautiful, handmade sweets that they sell in the market in Valladolid, everything from the wheels of amber pepitas cast in sugar and the marzipan skulls inscribed with colourful icing, to the little sugary chess pawns called *zapotitos*, dusted in cinnamon. Many of the recipes she learned from her mother, starting with meringues.

'It's funny,' says Rosi, 'I love making sweets but I don't eat much of them. I didn't like them much as a child either.' The family prides themselves on both their ingredients and their technique. With meringues, for example, they eschew industrial powdered sugar for a more unrefined sugar, flavouring the whipped egg whites with a bit of lime zest, strawberry puree, or guava. Their wood-fired oven can be tricky for consistent heat but it is the classic way to cook here and gives a faint smoky flavor to many of their treats.

Rosi recalls that when she started, she received her fair share of burns. 'You have to be secure in your movements,' she said, 'because boiling sugar is dangerous'. These days her practised hand results in an impressive roster of fruits preserved in syrup, special sweets for holidays, and seasonal desserts that you have to catch when they appear, for just a week or so. Rosi's dulce de coco is a pitch-perfect version of a common sweet of the Yucatán. As wide and round as a drink coaster, it's the colour of café con leche and stippled with chunks of coconut. It only contains three ingredients but its simplicity belies the layers of flavour it contains. Fortunately, this is one of Rosi's specialties that's available year round.

Chef //
Pedro Kauil Castillo & Maria Rosaura Och Cob
Location //
Dulcería Rosi, Valladolid

DULCE DE COCO
Candied coconut

Serves 8

Preparation & cooking time 2hr 15min

meat from two coconuts
500g (1lb) sugar
1L (1¾pt) water

1 Trim off any brown skin from the meat of the coconut. Cut into strips and then cut into 1cm (½in) squares. Rinse the coconut meat in three changes of water.

2 Put the coconut in a pot, add the sugar and water and bring to a boil, then reduce to a low simmer. Simmer the mixture, stirring frequently. After an hour or so, the sugar will start to turn golden. Let it go a little longer. Depending on the humidity, temperature, and the water content of your coconuts, it can take up to two hours for the mixture to turn a golden brown colour. Test the mixture by pouring a spoonful onto a white plate; once it's the colour of dark honey, remove the pot from the heat.

3 Make sure you have a clean working surface ready; clean baking trays work well (though at Dulcería Rosi they pour the mixture directly onto a wooden table). Carefully ladle out tablespoons of the mixture. They will spread into 5cm to 7cm (2in to 2¾in) rounds. Let the sweets cool for ten minutes then use a spatula to remove sweets from the surface.

DULCE DE PAPAYA

Papaya preserves

This classic sweet of the Yucatán uses a simple, albeit unusual, preparation. The flesh of unripe papayas are soaked in an alkaline solution (water mixed with cal or calcium-oxide), which softens the fruit and creates its unique texture.

The plate hits the table with little fanfare, almost an afterthought. A small white oval holding what looks like some kind of alien fruit – geometric wedges of matte scarlet, leaking golden syrup. Is that cheese on top? This is dulce de papaya, not an unearthly dessert but an ancient tradition of preserving fruit in sugar syrup; and, because we're in the Yucatán, that means papaya.

It is the ideal dessert after a lengthy meal of Yucatán classics at La Tradición, in Mérida. Here, third-generation restaurateur, chef David Cetina has taken large strides from the restaurant's origins as a *lonchería* (snack bar) on the side of the road where he cooked next to his mother and grandmother. There is crisp, white linen on the tables and good wine stocked on the shelves, but the recipes have remained consistent. Cetina is a stickler for tradition and relishes in the tedium associated with some dishes, like his *queso relleno*. This involves taking a 2kg (4½lb) ball of cheese and painstakingly hollowing out the inside with a spoon to fill with raisin-studded picadillo, which is then slowly steamed in a bain-marie until the insides are almost liquid and the exterior retains its shape.

That same cheese, Edam to English speakers, and known locally as *queso de bolla*, *queso hollandesa* or *queso gallo* was brought over by Europeans and has been incorporated into some of the Yucatán's most iconic dishes. The mild, salty cheese is shaved over the top of the dulce de papaya, which amplifies the treacle-esque sweetness of the fruit while providing a savoury counter.

As one of Mexico's culinary ambassadors, Cetina takes his reverence for culinary traditions with him on his travels. Literally. To cook a special dinner of *cochinita pibil* (see p254) in China for 6000 people, Cetina carted kilos of local Yucatán water with him across the sea. 'I always pack my own herbs when I go abroad. Little vials of cal, jars of oregano.' He laughs, 'The custom officers always freak when they open my bags. They must think I'm a drug dealer or something.'

Chef //
David Cetina
Location //
La Tradición, Mérida

DULCE DE PAPAYA
Papaya preserves

Serves 8

Preparation & cooking time 2 hr 30 min

1 large green (unripe) papaya (approx 3kg/6½lb)
50g (1¾oz) calcium oxide
2 kg (4½lb) sugar
1 cinnamon stick
100g (3½oz) Edam cheese

'Water is very important. It's the most basic ingredient but it does actually have a flavour. I'm a little bit eccentric, I know.'

David Cetina

Tip

This dish is created by soaking the papaya in an alkaline water-cal bath. 'The cal is what creates cicatriz, the scar, of the papaya,' says Cetina, referring to the pleasantly firm exterior of the fruit and its jelly-like insides. The high alkalinity of cal when applied to foods is called nixtimalization, a process that is most well known for turning corn into masa for tortillas.

1 Trim off all of the skin of the papaya. Cut it in half, scoop out the seeds and discard.

2 Slice the papaya into strips. Put the papaya in a big pot with water to cover and sprinkle in the calcium oxide, stirring with a spoon to combine. Let the papaya sit in the water for 30 minutes, then drain and rinse well.

3 Rinse out the pot and place the papaya back into that pot and barely cover the fruit with fresh water. Bring to a simmer over medium heat.

4 In a large skillet over medium heat, cook the sugar, undisturbed, until it starts to melt. Watch the sugar carefully until it turns golden brown, like the colour of honey. Remove the pan from the heat.

5 Add a couple of cups of the simmering papaya water to the pan to release the sugar then pour it into the papaya pot along with the stick of cinnamon.

6 Simmer the papaya for two hours on medium-low heat until the papaya is soft inside with a thick-ish, ridged skin. Let cool in its syrup.

7 Serve slices of papaya cold with the Edam cheese grated over the top.

RECIPE SOURCES

MEXICO CITY & CENTRAL MEXICO

1 Gerardo Vazquez, Nicos, Av Cuitláhuac 3102, Colonia Azcapotzalco, Mexico City (pp12–15)

2 Lucero Soto, Lu Cocina Michoacana, Portal Hidalgo 229, Centro, Morelia, Michoacán (pp16–21)

3 Alejandro Piñon (at the time of writing), Corazón de Maguey, Jardín del Centenario 9A, Colonia Coyoacán, Mexico City (pp22–5)

4 Gabriela Cámara, Contramar, Durango 200, Colonia Roma, Mexico City (pp26–9)

5 Daniel Ovadía & Salvador Orozco, Paragüero, Rio Balsas 102, Plaza Bugambilias, Colonia Vista Hermosa, Cuernavaca, Morelos (pp30–33)

6 Ricardo Muñoz, Azul Histórico, Isabel la Católica 30, Colonia Centro, Mexico City (pp34–9)

7 Fernando Hernandez, Moyuelo, Avenida Juárez 1918, Zona Esmeralda, Puebla (pp40–43)

8 Josué Maya & Santa Loreto, Esquites Don Josué (street stall), cnr Avenida Xola & Eje Central Lázaro Cárdenas, Colonia Álamos, Mexico City (pp44–7)

9 Nestor Flores, Karne Garibaldi, Calle Garibaldi 1306, Barrio Santa Teresita, Guadalajara, Jalisco (pp48–51)

10 Liz Galicia, El Mural de los Poblanos, 16 de Septiembre 506, Colonia Centro, Puebla (pp52–5)

11 Eduardo Garcia, Máximo Bistrot Local, Tonalá 133, Colonia Roma, Mexico City (pp56–9)

12 Larissa Camarena, Kamilos 333, Jose Clemente Orozco 333, Barrio Santa Teresita, Guadalajara, Jalisco (pp60–63)

OAXACA

1 Hugo Arnaud, Los Danzantes, Macedonio Alacalá 403, Oaxaca (pp66–71)

2 Raquel Patricia Garzón Hernandez, caterer, Oaxaca (pp72–7)

3 Aurora Toledo Martínez, Zandunga Sabor Istmeño, Calle de Manuel García Vigil 512E, Oaxaca (pp78–83)

4 Lucila Flor Ruiz, La Florecita, Locale 37, Mercado El Merced, Oaxaca (pp84–7)

5 Alejandro Ruiz, Casa Oaxaca El Restaurante, Constitución 104A, Oaxaca (pp88–93)

6 José Luis Diaz, Restaurante Chilhuacle Rojo, García Vigil 304, Oaxaca (pp94–9)

7 Deyanira Aquino Pineda, La Teca Restaurante: Gastronomia Istemeña, Violetas 200A, Colonia Reforma, Oaxaca (pp100–103)

8 Olga Cabrera, Restaurante Tierra del Sol, 2a Privada de Tabachines, 2 San Francisco Tutla, Oaxaca (pp104–107)

9 Lourdes Escobedo Banda, home cook, Oaxaca City (pp108–111)

10 Rodolfo Castellanos, Avenida Hidalgo 820, Oaxaca (pp112–7)

11 Francisco Velasco, Manolo Nieves, Calle Macedonio Alcalá 706, Oaxaca (pp118–121)

12 Irinea Valera Abella, Aguas Frescas Casilda, Mercado Benito Juarez, Oaxaca (pp122–5)

13 Reyna Mendoza, El Sabor Zapoteco, Teotitlán del Valle (pp126–131) DISH: Chocolate Oaxaqueña

PACIFIC COAST

1 Tony Martinez, La Corona, Puerto Vallarta, Jalisco (pp134–7)

2 Julio Romo, Las Palmas Restaurant, San Francisco, Nayarit (pp138–41)

3 Betty Vazquez, El Delfin Restaurant, San Blas, Nayarit (pp142–7)

4 Manuel Alejandro Jimenez Magallon, W Hotel, Punta de Mita, Nayarit (pp148–51)

5 Alan Zamudio, La Mazatleca, Golden Zone, Mazatlan, Sinaloa (pp152–5)

6 Marco Valdivia, Emiliano Restaurant, Tepic, Nayarit (pp156–9)

7 Jose Feliciano 'Pepe' Martinez Rodriguez, Lucila's Restaurant, Historic Mazatlan, Sinaloa (pp160–63)

8 Mavi Graf, Arte Culinario Cooking School, Puerto Vallarta, Jalisco (pp164–7)

9 Jose Munoz Gutierrez, Restaurant Any, also known as La Casa del Pozole, Zihuatanejo, Guerrero (pp168–173)

10 **Eduardo Avila Zarraga,** La Marea Restaurant, Zihuatanejo, Guerrero (pp174–7)

11 **Marino Maganda Pacheco,** Casa 46, Historico Centro Mazatlan, Sinaloa (pp178–83)

12 **Julio César Castillón,** Gaby's Restaurant, Puerto Vallarta, Jalisco (pp184–7)

BAJA CALIFORNIA
1 **Nadya Fernandez,** Caesar's Restaurante, Av. Revolución (between 4th St. and 5th St.), Tijuana, Baja California (pp190–3)

2 **Sabina Bandera,** La Guerrerense, 1st St. and Blvd. Alvarado, Ensenada, Baja California (pp194–7)

3 **Guillermo 'Oso' Campos,** Tras/ Horizonte, Rio Colorado, Tijuana, Baja California, 22015 (pp198–203)

4 **Krista Velasco,** Cerveceria Wendlandt, Blvd. Costero 248, Ensenada, Baja California (pp204–207)

5 **Roberto Alcocer,** Malva, Carretera Ensenada Tecate Km 96, San Antonio de las Minas, Ensenada, Baja California (pp208–11)

6 **Benito Molina & Solange Muris, Manzanilla,** Teniente Azueta, #139 Recinto Portuario, 22800, Ensenada, Baja California (pp212–15)

7 **Adria Montaño,** Don Ramen, Av. Ocampo #2036 (between 11th St. and Blvd. Agua Caliente), Tijuana, Baja California (pp216–19)

8 **Humberto Aviles,** Malinche, Between 6th St. and 7th St on Blvd. Sánchez Taboada, TIjuana, Baja California (pp220–23)

9 **Javier Plascencia,** Misión 19, Misión San Javier 10643, Zona Urbana Río, Tijuana, Baja California (pp224–7)

10 **Diego Hernandez,** Corazon de Tierra, Rancho San Marcos S/N, El Porvenir, 22750, Ensenada, Baja California (pp228–31)

YUCATÁN
1 **Cárdenes family,** Hacienda Teya, Carretera Mérida-Cancún, Km 12.5, Merida 01 (99) 9988 0800 (pp234– 237)

2 **Dulce Maria Pat Xuluc,** La Selva, Calle 42 #178, Colonia Santa Lucia, Valladolid (pp238–41)

3 **Mariana Huchin Ake & Madeline El Kal,** Cocina Mary, Local 31, Mercado de Santa Ana. Calle 47/58-60, Merida (pp242–245)

4 **Doña Evelia, Cafeteria Soberanis Arce,** Local 71, Planta Alta. Mercado 20 de Noviembre, Motul (pp246–9)

5 **Eric Werner, Hartwood,** Carretera Tulum Boca Paila 7.6Km, 77780 Tulum (pp250–3)

6 **Marcello Silva and Aida Santoyo Fernandez,** El Gallo, Calle 46 #200, between 39 and 41, Valladolid (pp254–7)

7 **Pedro Medina Casanova,** La Lupita, Mercado de Santiago, Calle 59/70-72, Merida (pp258–61)

8 **Silvio Campos,** Plato Limpio Taquitos, Calle 21 #99, Mercado 'Manuel Romero Ancona', Tixkokob (pp262–7)

9 **Marciala Silva,** La Bendicion de Dios, Calle 32, Mercado Municipal de Valladolid (pp268–71)

10 **Alex Mendez,** Hermana Republica, Predio Turistico No. 14714 Lote 9 Manzana 1, Xcanatún, Merida (pp272–5)

11 **Pedro Kauil Castillo & Maria Rosaura Och Cob,** Dulceria Rosi, Calle 32, Mercado Municipal de Valladolid (pp276–9)

12 **David Cetina,** La Tradición, Calle 60, 293, entre 25 y 27, Merida (pp280–3)

INDEX

ABOUT THE WRITERS

When hungry (frequently), **Kate Armstrong** has no pangs about heading to Mexico for her fill of great cuisine. She has contributed to over 40 Lonely Planet guides and publications and writes regularly for international newspapers and magazines (often about food). See more of her adventures at www.katearmstrongtravelwriter.com and @nomaditis.

Thanks to Jess Cole at LP for the opportunity to stimulate my taste buds and learn so much about this extraordinary country. A huge gracias, too, to Eric Mindling of Traditions Mexico, John Noble, Ellen and Hank, Rebecca Bailey, Maria Crespo, Chef Rafael of Los Danzantes, Adriana and Marina Guzman and Alejandro Valencia. Finally, I am indebted to all the chefs of Oaxaca – from professional to home cooks – who shared their love, secrets and the flavour of Mexico.

Kristin Diaz de Sandi is a freelance food and travel writer based in Southern California. Her blog Life & Food is a lifestyle journal that covers family travel and the vibrant culture and culinary scene that make up Baja California and Southern California. Along with fellow bloggers, she is also co-founder of Club Tengo Hambre, a roving supper club that features culinary outings in Baja California, Mexico City and LA.

A special thank you to the chefs, cooks, tastemakers, artisans, winemakers, and locals that all make Baja California the true gem that it is.

Scarlett Lindeman is a journalist based in Mexico City. Her work has been featured in Lucky Peach, T Mag, Gastronomica, and Saveur, among others. Follow her on IG at escarlatta.

With thanks to: • Gamma by Fiesta Inn Hotel. Calle 5 B No. 290 A x 20 A y 60. Merida. • Hacienda Teya. Carretera Mérida-Cancún, Km 12.5, 01. Merida. • Mesón del Marqués. Calle 39 #203 x 40 y 42. Valladolid. • Hotel Quinta Marciala. Calle 39 239. Valladolid. • Papaya Playa Project. Km 4.5 Carretera Tulum-Boca Paila. Tulum. • The Explorean Cozumel by Fiesta Americana. Carretera a Chankanaab km 7.5. Cozumel. • Petit Lafitte. Carretera Cancún - Chetumal km 296 + 2.1. Playa del Carmen.

John Hecht headed down Mexico way two decades ago and he's still livin' the dream, which usually comes in the form of a plastic plate full of tacos. He's collaborated on more than a dozen Lonely Planet titles, including *Mexico, Best in Travel, Cancún, Cozumel & the Yucatán* and *Puerto Vallarta & Pacific Mexico.*

A heartfelt thanks to all the good folks who shared their interesting stories and recipes with me. Mexico's rich culinary heritage never ceases to amaze me and I can say that's truer than ever now. Special gratitude also goes out to the fellow authors of this book, the editorial team, photographer Lindsay Lauckner Gundlock and as always, to Lau for all her support.

Michele Peterson is an award-winning culinary travel writer, editor and blogger who divides her time between Canada, Mexico and Guatemala. Her work has appeared in more than 100 magazines, literary travel anthologies, apps and guidebooks as well as her own food, drink and sun destination blog, A Taste for Travel at www.atastefortravel.ca.

Many thanks to the talented chefs, producers and food industry pros along Mexico's Pacific Coast who generously shared their time, insights, stories and recipes during this culinary adventure. Special thanks to Richard Zarkin, Gustavo Rivas, Julio Birrueta, Marian Gerlich, Mary van den Heuvel, Betty Vazquez (and family), Catie Mayer and Lesley Peterson for your invaluable assistance from start to finish. Mil gracias to my husband Javier Sanchez for being an enthusiastic eater and recipe tester.

ABOUT THE PHOTOGRAPHER

Lindsay Lauckner Gundlock, an editorial photographer from Toronto, Canada, earned a B.F.A. in Visual Arts from York University. Her favourite things to photograph are food, people and spaces. When she's not making pictures, she is likely reading a novel, visiting an art gallery or eating far too many pastries.

Many thanks to the wonderful people involved in this book who were all so dedicated, warm and welcoming! Thank you to my husband, Brett, for all of his love and support.

Published in August 2017 by Lonely Planet Global Ltd
CRN 554153
www.lonelyplanet.com
ISBN 978 1 7865 7893 8
© Lonely Planet 2017
Photographs © Lindsay Lauckner Gundlock 2016
Printed in China
10 9 8 7 6 5 4 3 2 1

Managing Director, Publishing Piers Pickard
Associate Publisher Robin Barton
Commissioning Editor Jessica Cole
Art Direction Daniel Di Paolo
Layout Designer Mariana Sameiro
Editors Karyn Noble, Claire Naylor, Christina Webb
Print production Larissa Frost, Nigel Longuet

Written by John Hecht (Central Mexico); Kate Armstrong (Oaxaca); Michele Peterson (Pacific Coast); Kristin Diaz de Sandi (Baja California); Scarlett Lindeman (Yucatán).

With thanks to the recipe testers Aaron London, Alex MacLeish, Amanda McCadams, Bob Bull, Christina Webb, David Gorvett, Dawn Waswick, Doug Rimington, Ellie Simpson, Emma Totney, Gabrielle Jaffe, Gwen Cotter, Jane Grisman, Jessica Cole, Joe Davis, Kathryn Rowan, Luisa Cosio, Lydia Smith, Matt Parish, Neil Robinson, Rebecca Law, Sarah Nicholson, Subodh Nijsure.

STAY IN TOUCH lonelyplanet.com/contact

AUSTRALIA The Malt Store, Level 3, 551 Swanston St, Carlton, Victoria 3053 T: 03 8379 8000

IRELAND Unit E, Digital Court, The Digital Hub, Rainsford St, Dublin 8

USA 124 Linden St, Oakland, CA 94607
T: 510 250 6400

UK 240 Blackfriars Rd, London SE1 8NW
T: 020 3771 5100

Although the authors and Lonely Planet have taken all reasonable care in preparing this book, we make no warranty about the accuracy or completeness of its content and, to the maximum extent permitted, disclaim all liability from its use.

QUESOS